MAGIC MUSIC FROM THE TELHARMONIUM

by
Reynold Weidenaar

THE SCARECROW PRESS, INC.
METUCHEN, N.J., & LONDON
1995

Based on the author's Ph.D. dissertation, "The Telharmonium: A History of the First Music Synthesizer, 1893–1918," New York University, 1988.

British Library Cataloguing-in-Publication data available

Library of Congress Cataloging-in-Publication Data

Weidenaar, Reynold, 1945–
    Magic music from the telharmonium / by Reynold Weidenaar.
    p.   cm.
    Includes bibliographical references and indexes.
    ISBN 0-8108-2692-5 (acid-free paper)
    1. Telharmonium—History.   I. Title.
ML1092.W42   1995
786.5'9—dc20   94-24901

To the Memory of a Great Dreamer,
Thaddeus Cahill

TABLE OF CONTENTS

LIST OF TABLES

LIST OF FIGURES

LIST OF ABBREVIATIONS

ac	alternating current
A.C.C.	Archives of the County Clerk of New York County
A.T.T.A.	A.T.&T. Corporate Archives
A.T.T.B.L.A.	A.T.&T. Bell Laboratories Archives
B.E.	Board of Estimate, Bureau of Franchises, City of New York
B.M.I.A.	Broadcast Music, Inc., Archives
C.R.L.C.	Center for Research Libraries, Chicago
dc	direct current
ed.	editor
eds.	editors
f.	facing page
F.E.M.	Foothill Electronics Museum
H.P.L.	Holyoke Public Library
H.U.	Harvard University Archives
J.E.P.	James Edward Pierce
J.S.	Jeanbett Schiott
L.C.M.D.	Library of Congress, Manuscript Division
M.C.S.	Margaret Cahill Schwartz
M.R.	Magyar Radio, Budapest
N.B.H.	National Baseball Hall of Fame and Museum
n.d.	no date
n.i.	no issue number
n.n.	no name
n.p.	no page number
n.v.	no volume number
N.Y.P.L.	New York Public Library
N.Y.P.L.T.	New York Public Library, Theatre Collection
O.C.A.	Oberlin College Archives
p.	page
P.C.M.M.L.	Picture Collection, Mid-Manhattan Library
pt.	part

P.T.O.	Patent and Trademark Office
R.O.H.C.	Register's Office of Hudson County, New Jersey
R.W.	Reynold Weidenaar
S.C.	Struniewski Collection
sec.	section
S.I.	Smithsonian Institution
S.L.	Stoddard Lincoln
S.S.	Secretary of State
S.S.N.J.	Secretary of State, New Jersey
S.S.N.Y.	Secretary of State, New York
supp.	supplement
tr.	translated by
vol.	volume
Y.U.	Yale University Library, Manuscripts and Archives

INTRODUCTION

The history of American invention is often told as glamorous tales of the inevitable. From the telegraph to the transistor, success is never in doubt. The inclination to write about winners is no different in other arenas: for example, how many more biographies do we have of Calvin Coolidge than of his 1924 presidential opponent, John W. Davis?

Yet the history of technology profitably records a few past failures—among them, Elisha Gray's telephone and Thomas Edison's kinetophone (motion pictures with synchronous sound). In some cases, inventors learned lessons from flops, which served at least to provide the seeds of future advances. Technological development is rarely stilled at detours and dead ends; instead, it is redirected and refocused. Such continuity to success, however, is exactly what we must *not* seek to impose on technological history, and that is why failures are studied. The view of progress as an autonomous and inevitable march to perfection is of limited use and very often mistaken.

The history of technology is more valuable for its illumination of an age, its revelation of sociocultural contexts, than it is for disclosure of successful inventions and processes. The story of a device that lacked ultimate victory can still shed much light on attitudes and values—often unexpected and unique—that held great sway, dramatically influencing people's lives. It may even have the advantage of holding a truer, less romanticized window on a vanished world: subjects are not glorified, failings are not minimized, stupid decisions are not ignored. Life then as now had many imperfections; a glimpse at those of the past enables us to see how life was really lived. Technology is not culturally neutral and it cannot be divorced from the context of its makers' society and values.

Furthermore, there is something undeniably enchanting about a glorious failure, a grandiose scheme that marshaled great resources of thought, design, fabrication, money, and commercial deployment, and yet tumbled through all these infrastructures—ultimately, to ruin. A worthwhile distinction can be made between the history of a failed device that is truly insignificant and the narrative of a sustained, sometimes heroic attempt to fulfill a great new technological promise—a promise whose eventual collapse was due as much to uncontrollable outside forces, and to one or two tragic mistakes, as to its own internal inadequacies. The latter form of history often reveals temporary periods of surprising and surpassing success.

In the very long run, the wildest successes ultimately become detritus. The player piano transformed the musical instrument industry; how many player pianos are manufactured today? The vacuum tube was one of the seminal inventions of the twentieth century; just try to buy a 12AX7 today. Even the Moog synthesizer is no longer made—its relatively brief life was not much longer than the Telharmonium's. All these have been reduced to cultural artifacts, and diverse technologies may profitably be studied as such. Their value is a good deal greater than simply being remembered as neutral tools of progress in some authorized corporate history.

In 1893 Thaddeus Cahill was a 26-year-old lawyer and inventor living in Washington, D.C. He had been inventing and patenting piano, organ, and typewriter mechanisms since the age of 18, yet the limitations of individual musical instruments were weighing heavily on his mind. And so that year he was forcibly struck by a grand new idea. Why not, he reasoned, build up complex tones such as musical instruments produced directly from electrical dynamos? Why not create a small electrical generating plant that could fashion an infinity of timbres from the ground up? It would have the powers of all instruments and the defects of none. It would replace the piano, organ, and violin as the preferred parlor instruments. Soon Cahill realized that such an instrument, of vastly greater size, would have the power to send music anywhere electricity could be transported. No longer would concert music be the province of the rich. Over a network of telephone lines, Cahill could transmit music from his central station to tens of thousands of places at once.

That idea became the Telharmonium and this is its story. It begins as the tale of the first U.S. patents for electric music, from an unsuccessful application in 1895 to the approval of a fifth patent in 1919. It is next the tale of three instruments actually completed: one prototype in 1900 and two commercial versions in 1906 and 1911. Arduously constructed of massive power dynamos because audio amplification was unknown, the latter were each said to weigh 200 tons (about right), comprise 30 carloads (fully packed, one or two modern railroad boxcars would be more like it), and cost $200,000 (all told, over a million dollars was spent to build and promote just the second instrument).[1] It continues as the tale of a whirlwind of success that swept New York early in 1907, when the opening season at Telharmonic Hall garnered daily plaudits in the city's newspapers. It goes on as the tale of a business marriage with the New York Telephone Co. that was roughly sundered when Telharmonic music proved to interfere with the telephone system, and when the difficulties of perfecting an instrument that would supplant musicians and make millions of dollars became apparent. It becomes the tale of Lee de Forest's early experimental broadcasts of the Telharmonium, struggling to transmit clear sound. (De Forest then had no idea of the two great capabilities of his newly invented vacuum tube—oscillation and amplification—which would be demonstrated by A.T.&T. engineers eight years later.) It is then the hopeful tale of a valiant second season in 1907 and 1908 that was mounted in the terrifying face of the Panic of 1907 and eventually deteriorated into a desperate musical freak show. The tale revives after the failure of the licensee companies in 1908, as Thaddeus Cahill arduously won back the rights to exploit his instrument himself. He signed a long-sought franchise contract with New York City in 1911 to run wires for Telharmonic service and erected a new central station there. Financing, however, dried up as World War I approached and the feasibility of radio broadcasting became apparent. The end came slowly for the Telharmonium. It was prolonged by a stubborn vision that had first seen a viable precursor of radio broadcasting some 25 years before it became reality, and the embodiment of the electric organ nearly 40 years before that instrument was developed using the vacuum tube.

Note

1. The claims of 200 tons and $200,000 appear repeatedly in published accounts contemporary with the Telharmonium. The claim of 30 carloads

first appeared in Benjamin F. Miessner (1890–1976), "Electronic Music and Instruments," *Proceedings of the Institute of Radio Engineers,* November 1936, 24:11, page 1442, and subsequently in many secondary accounts: "[Cahill's] apparatus was actually built in Holyoke, Massachusetts, and transported to New York City where it was set up and operated. It comprised more than thirty carloads of equipment." No doubt over 30 shipments were made as the instrument was disassembled in 1906; we cannot, however, infer that each shipment filled an entire railroad boxcar. The value of Miessner's connection to a reliable primary source is indicated by his publication (on page 1443) of two photographs of the Telharmonium never previously published.

ACKNOWLEDGMENTS

The author was fortunate indeed to secure the knowledgeable and supportive assistance and advice of Dr. John V. Gilbert, Dr. Philip N. Hosay, and Dr. Lawrence Ferrara, all of New York University. Their contributions are far greater than can possibly be enumerated, and to them the author expresses sincere appreciation.

The enthusiastic interest and good will shown by so many persons and institutions in supplying data were a source of substantial encouragement to the author. Their contributions are individually described in Appendix 2: Sources of Data. To all of them, the author expresses profound gratitude and no little admiration.

The author is also grateful to Barbara Blegen, who assisted with library research and typed the initial drafts of the manuscript. Finally, the author appreciates the helpful and insightful comments of Richard Kostelanetz, Dr. Robert A. Moog, Dr. Thomas L. Rhea, Marisella Veiga, and Gerald Warfield.

All copy photographs were taken by the author on Eastman Panatomic-X 35mm b&w negative film using a Canon FD 50mm macro lens.

CHAPTER I

THE FIRST TELHARMONIUM
AND ITS ORIGINS

EARLY TELEPHONE CONCERTS TO 1881

Astonishingly, music transmitted over wires is older than the telephone itself. As early as 1851 the mayor of Keene, N.H., Edward Farrar, began experimenting with a fledgling musical telegraph. He devised a reed melodeon for sending tones over telegraph lines to an electromagnetic receiver. The instrument was diminutive and its sonorities crude and simple. However, Farrar's goal was not the transmission of music but the invention of equipment capable of sending and receiving speech. To Farrar, generating pitched tones was the most fruitful path toward the speaking telephone. Upon reporting his contrivances to Professor Benjamin Silliman, teacher of general and applied chemistry at Yale University, the good professor lamentably discouraged Farrar from further efforts. Farrar abandoned the project, leaving the conversion of speech to electrical energy some 25 years in the future.[1]

Around 1860 Philip Reis of Friedrichsdorf, Germany, developed a similar form of quasi-telephonic transmitter and receiver. The transmitter could generate make-and-break musical pitches (through abrupt on/off switching—an electric buzzer), but it had no speech capability. The receiver was a wooden sounding box encasing an electromagnet with elongated pole pieces. Like Farrar, Reis was principally absorbed with musical tones as an assist to researching speech transmission. Both inventors may have realized that they had indeed brought forth receivers capable of electrically reproducing speech as well as music, but unluckily they were incapable of proving it. Neither their transmitters nor any other had speech capability. Interestingly enough, years later it was shown that their receivers could have performed passably as transmitters, but at too low a level for practical telephony.[2]

In the mid-1870s Elisha Gray took up wire transmission of musical tones, eventually for three different purposes. His earliest pursuit was multiplex telegraphy, meant to convey simultaneous messages over a single wire by employing signals of different frequencies. He set aside this goal to engage in the presentation of public musical concert entertainments by wire. Finally Gray resolved to invent the telephone. His transmitters were tuned reeds activated by electromagnets, interrupting the current at the vibrating frequency of the reed. One transmitter had a two-octave diatonic musical keyboard. Gray tinkered with many receivers. He attached electromagnets to a violin body, tin cans, small paper drums, a tin hoop with foil stretched over it, coins, and tissue paper. One of the most effective was a small metal dishpan. Gray first publicly exhibited the apparatus at a concert in Chicago in 1874 and continued such demonstrations at musical events for several years.[3]

Alexander Graham Bell also experimented with multiple-pitch or harmonic telegraphy, but spurned that for a careful study of vibrating reeds and membranes, which led to his invention of the speaking telephone in 1876. Later the same year in Canada, Bell transmitted the first experimental long-distance telephone concert from Paris, Ont., to Brantford, Ont., over telegraph wires. A triple mouthpiece was affixed to the speech transmitter so that several vocalists could sing into it together.[4]

The next year, on April 2, 1877, Elisha Gray staged a widely publicized so-called telephone concert at Steinway Hall on East 14th Street in New York. No telephone was in fact employed. A well-known pianist of the day, Frederick Boscovitz, performed on Gray's 16-key telegraphic reed transmitter in the Western Union office in Philadelphia. The audience in New York listened in rapt incredulity to the buzzer-tone music, nearly all of which was played with one hand. The receiver was built of 16 resonant hollow wooden tubes, ranging from six inches to two feet in length, joined by wooden bars. An electromagnet that received the telegraph signals was affixed to one bar. The receiving apparatus was mounted on an otherwise unused grand piano on the stage of Steinway Hall. The tones were said to be distinct, although the higher notes were very faint. The timbre somewhat resembled an organ. In the opinion of one reviewer, the music "as a novelty, was highly entertaining, though unless an almost incredible improvement be effected, it is difficult to see how the transmission of music over the new instrument can be of permanent practical value."[5] Gray provided more reed-transmitter concerts that week—three in Steinway Hall, one at the Brooklyn Academy of Music, and one at Lincoln Hall in Washington.[6]

In August 1877 a genuine telephone concert from the Western Union building in New York to Saratoga Springs, N.Y., using Thomas Edison's new carbon speech transmitter, was overheard on telegraph receivers—which could reproduce speech to a limited degree—in both Providence and Boston. There turned out to be a 16-mile section along which the New York–Albany telegraph line ran parallel to the New York–Boston line. The music had transferred by capacitance, induction, and conduction leakage, leading to considerable study of the latter two phenomena.[7]

Telephonic transmission, musical and otherwise, was much enhanced in power during the late 1870s by the invention of the carbon transmitter. Edison was among the numerous experimenters who independently devised and perfected it. One of his assistants was a Hungarian, Théodor Puskás, who had joined him in 1875. It was Puskás who conceived the idea of a central station to link all telephone subscribers, a year after the telephone was invented.[8]

In 1878 Puskás returned to Europe to establish a telephone network in Paris. Three years later he was involved in the startling stereophonic telephone concerts of Clément Ader at the Paris International Exhibition of Electricity. Ader had designed a carbon transmitter with a pinewood diaphragm. Twenty-four were strung along the footlights, half on either side of the prompter's box at the Paris Opéra. The lines were run underground two kilometers to the Palais d'Industrie of the Exhibition, where each transmitter was able to energize eight receivers. The listener was given two earpieces, one from a transmitter on each side of the prompter's box, and could thus detect movement and location of the singers onstage.[9]

This first demonstration of stereophonic sound was sponsored on a grand scale by the General Telephone Company of Paris—some 160,000 francs were expended in wiring the Opéra, the Opéra Comique, and the Théâtre Française. Transmissions from the latter two ran into technical troubles, including loud air currents from the flaming-jet gas footlights at the Théâtre Française. The telephone concerts, which attracted a great crowd each evening, were held in five rooms, with twenty pairs of earpieces to each room. Carpets were hung all about the rooms to deaden the rumble of machinery from other exhibits. To their great disappointment and annoyance, crowds were allowed to listen only briefly—no more than five minutes, sometimes only two. Transmitters at the extremes of the stage favored the large orchestral instruments, while those near the center conveyed the voice of the prompter. To ameliorate these difficulties, Ader paired the earpieces given to a listener, one from a transmitter at far stage left with one from center right, and so on, thus averaging out problems in balance. Understandably, the pair linking half-left and half-right yielded the most satisfying sound.[10]

Since the transmitters were right in the footlights and favored the singers, the delighted audience professed to hear the words of the performers even more clearly than if they actually had been present at the Opéra. Because of the close microphone positioning, the sonic perspective was even more pronounced than in the hall itself, with the closer singers far louder than those upstage. It was even possible to detect nearby singers' intake of air. The first opera presented in telephonic stereophony was Meyerbeer's *Robert le Diable.*[11]

Following the close of the exhibition, the Théâtrophone, as it became known, was installed at the Elysée Palace. It would become the basis for a commercial telephone broadcasting system in Paris ten years later.[12]

While in Paris, Puskás directed his brother François to begin preparations for a telephone network in Budapest. This system was inaugurated in 1881, several months before the Paris Exhibition opened. After the Exhibition closed that autumn, Théodor joined his brother in Budapest. He directed a stereo telephone concert of an opera at the National Theatre in January 1882. It was relayed to guests attending the Writers' Ball at the Vigado Building. Telephone concerts continued throughout the 1880s as the Puskás brothers developed the Budapest Telephone Service and other plans for distributing news and music by telephone.[13]

THADDEUS CAHILL'S YOUTH

Thaddeus Cahill was the eldest son of Dr. Timothy and Ellen Harrington Cahill, both immigrants from Ireland. The father was

Irish and the mother was of English extraction. Timothy, born in 1836, had emigrated to Nashua, N.H., around 1857, where the two were married the same year; their first child, Mary, was born in 1858. He worked as a tradesman and then began to study medicine in a local doctor's office. He entered Harvard Medical School in 1862. In August of that year he was induced to join the 10th New Hampshire Volunteers as an Assistant Surgeon. However, the position was afterwards given to another and Timothy became a hospital steward instead. Within two months he was suffering chronic severe swelling and inflammation of the mucous membranes of his eyelids and ulcerations of his corneas—pinkeye, a very contagious disease. Having to sleep on snow-covered ground made matters worse. Timothy was discharged from the Army for this disability in November and resumed his medical studies. He served in the New Hampshire House of Representatives in 1863 and 1864 as a Democrat from Nashua; there he was a member of the Insane Asylum Committee. He was graduated from Harvard with an M.D. in 1864. In 1865, Dr. Cahill practiced medicine in Providence, R.I., but within a year or so moved his wife and three daughters to Iowa. There Thaddeus was born on June 18, 1867, in Mt. Zion, near the family's home in Summit Station.[14]

Soon the father's eye condition began to worsen. Medicinal crayons of copper sulfate were often touched to the granulated lids of Dr. Cahill by his eldest daughter and his wife. In the Fall of 1871, he had violent eye paroxysms, almost as if they would burst from the tension. The excruciating pain was aggravated by a lack of medicine and then by applying a medication that was supposed to have been dissolved in water but which turned out to have been dissolved in acid. The pain drove him nearly mad. He lost sight in his right eye and retained only dim vision in the left. Light and cold exacerbated Dr. Cahill's condition, and he was unable to bear a temperature below 85 or 90 degrees Fahrenheit. He became confined to a darkened room that had to be provided with a fire even on warm summer nights. The Army granted him a pension of $31.25 per month in 1874. A month later, on May 24, 1874, at the age of 36, Ellen Cahill died, "in great peace" according to her tombstone. Thaddeus was nearly seven years old. The mother had given birth to five sons and three daughters; two of the sons did not survive infancy. Shortly after her death the family moved to the village of Oberlin, Ohio. After a few years, the doctor's pension was increased to a princely $72.00—any amount above $25.00 (which could be brought by the loss of a leg) was rare. To his sufferings had been added chronic diarrhea and bleeding hemorrhoids; he had come to require constant care and attention.[15] As his children cared for him, the invalided Dr. Cahill exercised a keen interest in their education. He taught them daily, cultivating their minds, and guided their reading, discussing and explaining things to them. Thaddeus proved to be an unusual child with little interest in childhood games or Mother Goose stories. Although the other children were sent to school, Thaddeus's father kept him home and took complete charge of his son's education, grooming him as a genius. Private tutors were engaged for studies in Latin and Greek.[16]

The boy exhibited a memory of crystal clarity and an effortless ability to correlate a wide range of facts and events, no matter how distant or seemingly unimportant. He developed an extraordinary quality of judgment, and his opinions were regarded with respect by persons many years his senior. He is said to have learned the multiplication table up to twelve times twelve in a single day.[17]

Thaddeus began inventing around the age of 13 or 14, after the Bell Company had refused to sell him telephone instruments to experiment with.[18] Many inventors and amateurs were attempting to transmit music, and Thaddeus also put it to the test. He found that musical sounds came through weak in amplitude and of rather poor tone quality. When he tried to send louder sounds through the apparatus, so that the receiver would not have to be held tightly to the ear, the timbre of the music became rough and distorted.[19]

At about the same time Thaddeus became the official stenographer of an Ohio court. He was beginning to evince an interest in the law, and several lawyers on the circuit invited him to join their offices and study law with them. He was also becoming familiar with the imperfections of the typewriters used in court and beginning to think of improvements he could invent.[20]

Later in his teens Thaddeus began to experiment with musical devices. Oberlin was a town with an excellent conservatory of music, and he became very appreciative of good music, although he did not master any instrument. Thaddeus soon developed a keen interest in the scientific side of music. As with the typewriter, he began to notice the inefficiencies and "defects" of various instruments. The piano, which was the main source of music in most homes, could not be kept in tune. Furthermore, the volume of a note or chord was soon lost. The organ was better in these respects, but had limited power of expression. The violin did not possess these problems, but it had little chord capacity. Thaddeus wondered if it would be possible to construct an instrument that would unite all the virtues of existing instruments and eliminate their defects. He experimented with various methods of producing music electrically, but got no satisfactory results. He had no thought then of distribution by wire, only the idea that a perfect musical instrument could be created for the home.[21]

Today we may smile at the notion of wanting or expecting one instrument to do everything. The inadequacy of one instrument can easily be overcome by using another, and access and distribution are not problems. However, in the days preceding sound recordings and broadcasting, it would have filled a great need to supply the home with an instrument possessing the rudimentary powers of a small orchestra or band—ensembles which were usually mediocre, if they could be heard at all, outside the large cities of the United States.

After the Christmas holidays in 1883, at the age of 16, Thaddeus finally went to school. He entered the graduating class of Oberlin High School. The following year he graduated, the youngest in his class and at the head of it. He recited an oration in Latin at commencement.[22]

In 1884 he undertook studies at Oberlin College. Archival records show him as having been enrolled in the Oberlin Conservatory of Music in 1884 and 1885, but academic records exist only for recitations in three 1885 preparatory department classes: Latin (2nd Virgil) in which he received a B, Greek a C, and algebra a D.[23] For whatever reason, he was not getting along at college, and he broke away that same year in order to have more time for inventive work. For the next three years he experimented with musical devices and typewriters, while he continued his college studies under private tutors.[24]

Thaddeus Cahill applied for his first patent in August 1885 at the age of 18; this was a wind-valve mechanism attached to an organ key for governing the loudness of the tone. The patent was granted the following year. Thaddeus assigned two-thirds to his father.[25] As his inventing career was thus inaugurated, news came of scientific developments in Germany which would direct its course in startling new ways.

HERMANN LUDWIG FERDINAND HELMHOLTZ

A colossal new study in the science of acoustics appeared in English in 1885. It was the result of many years of research by the great German scientist Hermann Helmholtz, who had begun his career as a young military doctor in 1843. By developing a cogent proof of the principle of conservation of energy, he attained the prestige necessary to secure his first academic position in 1848. He devoted his energies to research in physiology and anatomy until in 1856 he turned to psychoacoustics. He published numerous papers, which culminated in the appearance of the first edition of his magnum opus, *On the Sensations of Tone,* in 1862. Helmholtz then turned to a wide range of other scientific activity—optics, electrodynamics, and hydrodynamics—but continued his work in acoustics. The fourth and final edition of the book appeared in 1877 and was brilliantly translated into English by Alexander J. Ellis in 1885.[26]

This edition became widely circulated and well known. It disseminated several unique concepts that later influenced Thaddeus Cahill's design of the electric music machine known as the Telharmonium. The first was the harmonic series, a fundamental sound combined with a group of higher sounds that give each musical tone its quality or timbre. The fundamental, or lowest tone, as well as each upper partial, vibrate in the simple form known as a sine wave. These combine in an infinity of particular amplitudes to form the myriad compound vibrations that produce the sounds of musical instruments. It takes very little strain on the imagination to speculate on the possibilities of forming, or synthesizing, musical sounds by producing and governing the component harmonics.

Helmholtz constructed an electromechanical one-note synthesizer that was able to imitate the sounds of the vowels of the human voice. On a fundamental of $B^b = 120$ Hz, he assembled tuning forks on the first eight harmonics, later adding four more harmonics. Each fork was activated by an electromagnet and attached to a resonance chamber with a lid that could regulate volume; a variable aperture regulated tuning and phase. He reported on simulation of various vowel sounds at length, giving tables of dynamics for each fork-resonator needed to produce each German vowel.[27] An appendix furnished a schematic picture and detailed practical directions for constructing and operating the device.[28]

Helmholtz articulated another idea for which he is not much remembered today, but which resonated vividly with Thaddeus Cahill: the various "defects" of different musical instruments. The piano was held to lack real expression, the trombone had poor mobility, the flute could not alter its force of tone without altering pitch, chords on trumpets were endurable only in the open air, and so on. These observations formed part of an extensive explanation of the acoustic bases—principally the composition of harmonics and the mechanical resonances—of each instrument's sonic peculiarities. This first primer in synthesizing musical sounds included the suggestive observation that the organ had an advantage over other instruments, since the performer could alter and control vastly different mixtures of sound at will.[29]

THADDEUS CAHILL'S EARLY INVENTIONS

At the age of 20 Thaddeus Cahill received his second patent, for an improved piano action, in 1887. It featured a reduced hammer resistance to strengthen the tone.[30] His third patent arrived a week later. This was a very interesting assault on an alleged glaring defect in the state of the musical art—that loudness could not be expressed in a mathematically definite way. A great composer could easily specify pitches and durations using exact numerical relationships, so they could be perfectly recreated. However, he had no hope of conveying loudnesses in a similarly precise manner, since such terms as *pianissimo* and *forte* had no basis in any system. Cahill introduced a dynamic scale and invented an organ with a separate loudness manual (keyboard) on which to play this scale. It would enable the mediocre performer to acquire more knowledge of expression than heretofore possible. This new art of exact dynamics employed a scale with the same mathematical relations as those of the natural diatonic pitch scale (24, 27, 30, 32, 36, 40, 45, 48, and so on, through succeeding octaves). Cahill was sailing on uncharted waters, as it would be many years before the decibel would be defined as the method of expressing acoustic intensity. Even Helmholtz had very little to say about loudness, except for a few references to string amplitude. The great physicist used the standard imprecise terms common to musical parlance. Were Cahill somehow able to make his scale accurate, for the measuring equipment to do the job did not exist, his eighth note (octave) would be twice the intensity, or 3 decibels louder, than the first. This would give a change of about $^1/_2$ decibel for a whole step on the keyboard, allowing for very smooth volume changes. It would also require a dynamic manual 20 octaves long to control a dynamic range of 60 decibels. However, since a *perceived* doubling of intensity is usually closer to 10 decibels, Cahill's eighth note could be that much louder and only six octaves would then be needed to cover the 60-decibel range. The dynamic scale degrees were written using notes on a staff. Intermediate soft and loud degrees corresponding to flats and sharps could be interpolated between the diatonic "notes." Hence, a standard black-and-white keyboard manual could be used to play the loudness levels. Tenaciously carrying the implication to its absurd conclusion, Cahill proclaimed the birth of 24 "dynamic keys" corresponding to the 24 major and minor pitch keys. For the fullest expression in performance, a second musician was required (just as in the later Telharmonium) to play the dynamic manual. The instrument, promised Cahill, would produce effects which could previously be obtained only by orchestras with many performers, as well as many new musical effects hitherto impossible.[31]

At 22 Cahill obtained a clerkship with Congressman Amos J. Cummings and moved to Washington, D.C. After serving as Cummings's private secretary, he became clerk of the Committee on the Library of Congress and later the stationery clerk of the House of Representatives. In the evenings he studied law at Columbian (now George Washington) University.[32]

Cahill pursued his inventive work. His first laboratories were in his living quarters and an old basement. The work consisted partly of constructing models and experimenting but chiefly of making and remaking one elaborate set of drawings after another. He kept two draftsmen at work. He first experimented with sirens and then returned to musical and typewriting mechanisms.[33]

LOOKING BACKWARD

Edward Bellamy, born in 1850, was a lawyer and newspaperman who turned to writing short stories and romantic novels in the 1870s and

1880s. He electrified the popular imagination with *Looking Backward* (1887), a socialist utopian novel set in the year 2000. The protagonist, Julian West, awakens from a 113-year trance in an underground chamber and becomes acquainted with the ideal new order. Fresh in West's mind are the widespread industrial problems and social unrest of the 1880s, a world of unrelieved misery and widespread inequality. In the year 2000 the nation had emerged as one gigantic business corporation, with the proceeds shared equally by all. There could be no relationship between individual effort and return. There was no national debt, no military, no criminal class, and no taxes.[34]

Looking Backward was largely concerned with industrial economics and social organization. As in most utopian schemes, it left precious little room for the arts. Bellamy dealt with music at some length, but strictly as a commodity to be purchased and distributed. Everyone in the new society learned to sing as part of his or her general voice training. Professional musicians worked in the musical service. Music was distributed 24 hours a day to homes, which had music rooms filled with perfectly rendered performances. All were live concerts emanating from halls connected by telephone to any subscriber who would pay the fee. This cable service carried a choice of four musical programs. These were also on tap in the bedroom, each of which had a telephone attachment at the head of the bed, to provide balm for sleepless nights. Miraculously, if two persons lay side by side and one desired to sleep, the sound could be made audible only to the other. The two would be awakened next morning by "inspiring" alarm music. On Sunday mornings church services by wire were offered. One prominent minister was said to preach only by telephone to an audience of 150,000.[35]

Looking Backward had an immense circulation and set off a spate of imitations and responses. Many ignored music altogether but some took up the question. One was *Looking Beyond* by Ludwig A. Geissler, published in 1891. Geissler appropriated Bellamy's telephonic music apparatus but with much greater feeling for the role of music. Magical effects, stirrings of the blood, sublime joy, and spiritual intoxication were all ascribed to music, ranging from popular airs to twentieth-century symphonic masterpieces. In Geissler's utopia people attended concerts as social and cultural events. Orchestral concerts by telephone were presented in numerous halls simultaneously. The city had but one opera house with seating for 40,000 people.[36]

Bellamy expanded somewhat the technological accomplishments of the year 2000 in *Equality*, his sequel published in 1897. A response to his many critics, this leaden volume was far more prolix than its forerunner and achieved little popular or critical acclaim. The "electroscope," a sort of life-size television, now occupied the domestic music room. It was used primarily for receiving economics lectures and pictures of roving tours all over the planet. Any point of particular interest could be specially connected in an instant. Fortunately, it was also possible to enjoy theatre and concert performances on an electroscope; public entertainment given in any city in the world was available. The occupation of mediocre artist, so common in the 1890s, had thus disappeared. The public was used to only the best and would stand for no less. This did not improve the status of artists, whom Bellamy classed with players, singers, and courtesans—"all who had pleasure to sell."[37]

THE CONCEPTION OF THE TELHARMONIUM

In 1891 Arthur T. Cahill graduated from Oberlin High School at the age of 19 and, although he was offered a baseball scholarship to Harvard University, moved immediately to Washington to work in his elder brother's laboratory. There the latter sought new piano attainments with his next patent, granted that same year. He designed a power action, utilizing a rotating friction-driven shaft, to increase the loudness and reduce the exertion by the performer. The instrument's newly powerful tone permitted faster execution, he promised, and required less wearisome technical practice. It would now be possible for a hammer to drive more than three strings; hence, the number of strings could be increased in accordance with the size of the auditorium. *Any* number of strings could be activated, he asserted, producing a volume and grandeur of tone never before known.[38]

Cahill was third in a class of more than a hundred when he graduated (Fig. 1) from Columbian University Law School with the degree of LL.B. in 1892. He was among five who received honorable mention from the faculty, of which Justices Harlan and Brewer of the U.S. Supreme Court were members. The following year he received his LL.M. degree.[39]

Fig. 1. Thaddeus Cahill, Probably a Graduation Portrait, 1892. (*American Monthly Review of Reviews,* April 1906, **XXXIII**:4, 421)

In 1892 or 1893 Thaddeus Cahill also slowly began to research and formulate the ideas that resulted in the Telharmonium. Some reports[40] put the conception as early as 1891, but these are passing mentions with no concentration on the details of how the work commenced and proceeded. Others give 1894 or 1895, not for the idea itself but as the inception of "unremitting"[41] "laboratory work"[42] or "ceaseless toil and experimentation"[43] when he became "devoted to the invention"[44] or "devoted to experimentation."[45] Several accounts,[46] however, devote energetic interest to the evolution of Cahill's concepts, and these name or imply 1892 or 1893 as the time of conception.

Cahill inaugurated his search for the perfect instrument by exhaustive research into the principles of sound, primarily as demonstrated by Helmholtz. His guiding vision was twofold: a machine that could produce scientifically perfect tones, and absolute control of these tones to a mathematical certainty by mechanical means. Such fine control should allow the player to express all his spellbinding emotion with the surging power and intensity of a violinist—with as little mechanical impediment as possible. The tone should be sustained indefinitely, like an organ, but should yield willingly to the musician's touch with absolute sympathy and sensitivity. The instrument must of course retain the chord capacity of the piano or organ. Thus could the defects of the three great domesticated musical instruments—piano, organ, and violin—be consigned to oblivion.[47]

Cahill concluded that some form of telephone receiver could serve as a vibrating body to produce the sound, so all he needed to contrive was an electrical current containing the various notes. He soon arrived at the dynamo or electric generator.[48] To make an absolutely pure tone from a ponderous, costly, elaborate generator was theoretically within the realm of possibility. However, there would have to be numerous generators, one for each pitch, so they would have to be of simple and inexpensive construction. A dogged exploration and development began, one which would last nearly 12 years.[49]

In 1892 the brothers completed an electric typewriter model; a patent on a nonelectrical mechanism was granted the following year. It featured a movement device that allowed a small number of piano-style keys to be struck together in various combinations to produce all the letters, figures, and other characters. The idea bears some analogy to the Telharmonium using a small number of harmonics in various loudness combinations to produce all the musical timbres. He called his mechanism a "synthesizer." By this time his other brother, George F., had also joined him in Washington; both signed the patent drawings as witnesses.[50]

Cahill continued to labor on the piano power action and patented improved designs in 1894 and 1896. His father and two of his older sisters, Mary H. and Eleanor, moved to Washington; the sisters also began to witness the patent drawings. Only sister Margaret escaped the family obsession with Thaddeus's inventions, having moved to New York to teach at the Wadleigh High School in 1893. It was an exciting and glamorous time for the five young brothers and sisters living in the capital; they met Bell and Edison, there was even a White House invitation, the future was filled with promise.[51]

In 1894 Cahill was admitted to the bar and began to practice law.[52] In his spare time he also began to construct a set of dynamos, each generating a different pitch. It dawned on him that if the output currents could be transmitted by wire to a telephone receiver, they could be transmitted wherever wires might be run. He believed it might be possible to convey the music to thousands of buildings in scores of cities. He also awoke to the realization that it was not enough for the new instrument to produce a fixed timbre. In order to surpass the capabilities of other instruments, it should be able to generate any timbre desired.[53] Not only would a separate dynamo be required for each fundamental pitch, but additional dynamos would be needed to produce harmonics. With the basic concepts in place, but without having constructed a complete instrument, Cahill began to compile an application for patent protection.

Typewriter work progressed as Cahill earned two patents in 1895. One provided for two successive letter-characters to be printed simultaneously, by arranging the type-printing mechanism to incorporate numerous compound- and double-letter characters.[54] The other accomplished the same goal by means of two separate but coacting printing mechanisms and keyboards, one for each hand.[55]

Cahill harnessed electricity around 1895 to improve and simplify his idea of printing successive letters by striking two keys simultaneously. He patented his first electric typewriter. There were two symmetrical keyboards side by side, again similar to a piano keyboard. Each had twelve keys. These keyboards were not fixed: a key could be assigned to any desired letter. Cahill recommended single keys for the most common letters, and combinations of two keys produced the remainder. Electrically the two were jumpered together to control only one printing mechanism powered by a dynamo or a battery. The left-hand keyboard, however, was prevented from closing the circuit by an electromechanical obstructing mechanism. This was removed only when a right-hand key had already closed the circuit and was released. (If the operator preferred, he could select the left-hand keyboard to have priority.) Thus, the operator could strike one or two keys of each keyboard simultaneously, and the mechanism would print two letters in rapid succession.[56]

LATER TELEPHONE CONCERTS AND THE TELEFON-HIRMONDÓ

In 1889 a telephone concert demonstrating Edison inventions was transmitted simultaneously to 14 different locations in the states of New York, Massachusetts, New Jersey, and Pennsylvania.[57] Two or three years later, telephone concerts had become quite common, and commercial telephone concert systems began to appear. London theatrical performances were transmitted to Birmingham and also to pay receivers in London hotels—ten minutes for a shilling in the slot. The Théâtrophone in Paris signed up numerous subscribers. Telephone concerts traversed longer and longer distances—more than 900 miles from New York to Chicago, then back to New York, for a bidirectional concert in 1892. The next year a New York pianist auditioned over the telephone for a job at the Columbian Exposition in Chicago. She played into a receiver with "an immense sheet-iron horn, wrapped in oiled linen . . . with a mouth as large as the head of a flour barrel."[58] There was no report of whether she got the job. The Crystal Palace opened in London in 1893, complete with a telephonic music room that received transmissions from theatres and concert halls in London, Birmingham, Manchester, and Liverpool. Nearly 60,000 people visited the facility during its six-month run. As a result of this success, the Electrohome Co. began regular distribution in 1895 of musical performances, public speeches, and church services to standard telephones. By the end of the first year there were 47 subscribers.[59]

In 1896 the Paris Théâtrophone and the London Electrohome were connected in an experiment, and the Paris Opéra and Opéra Comique were heard at Pelican House, headquarters of the Electrohome. The male voices, brass instruments, and oboe came through quite clearly; the female voices and violins were less audible. Difficulties in maintaining clear long-distance connections prevented the establishment of commercial service from Paris to London.[60]

Meanwhile, the largest system of telephonic broadcasting had been established by Théodor Puskás, proprietor of the Budapest Telephone Service. In 1892 he had filed for patents on his method of telephonic news distribution. Permission was granted from the Ministry of Commerce to inaugurate service, and the Telefon-Hirmondó ("Telephonic Herald") sent out its first program on February 18, 1893. The service cost about 75¢ per month and at first consisted only of news reports. Service began at eight or nine o'clock in the morning and ran anywhere from midafternoon to nine in the evening. News reports were supplemented by stock prices and editorials.[61]

A month after service was inaugurated, Théodor Puskás died, and shortly thereafter François also died. Their younger brother Albert continued the operation briefly, then sold it to Étienne Popper, a Budapest engineer, in 1894. Popper was able to infuse the Telefon-Hirmondó with considerable capital, and subscribers flocked to sign up. They swelled from 497 in 1893 to 6,185 in 1896. By this time there were 168 miles of wire in service, the company having secured the same rights as the telephone and telegraph companies to run wires through the streets of Budapest. Besides the news, an abundance of additional programming was supplied 12 hours daily—the Royal Opera of Budapest, plays, vocal and instrumental concerts, lectures on music, art, and literature, even the names of strangers staying at Budapest hotels. Twenty-eight news reports were given each day, delivered by strong-voiced men called "stentors." The Telefon-Hirmondó presented its offerings according to printed schedules. Although the low fidelity of musical transmissions left much to be desired, the service was well received by the public, and would peak at 9,107 subscribers in 1930.[62]

The Théâtrophone also continued well into the twentieth century. In 1925 its circuitry was finally converted to vacuum-tube amplifiers.[63]

THE FIRST TELHARMONIUM PATENT

Thaddeus Cahill filed his first patent application for the *Art of and Apparatus for Generating and Distributing Music Electrically* on August 10, 1895. It was not accepted. The National Archives, which retains successful applications and related correspondence, does not possess this first application or a copy of the offical examination of the Patent Office. Later correspondence reveals that his problems were three-fold: (1) the plan contained principles and practices found in other patented devices; (2) in making his claims as broad and numerous as he could, he trespassed on other inventions; and (3) some of the objections voiced by the examiners at the Patent Office were irrelevant.

Cahill set out again with an application filed February 10, 1896, which opened the long road to his goal. To the examination of the Patent Office, not preserved, Cahill responded strenuously with a protracted set of amended claims[64] and an even wordier 134-page letter[65] to justify them and rebut the examination.[66]

In the amendment Cahill explained that his original 1895 application had been quite complicated because the proposed apparatus would produce music similar to that of an organ. In the 1896 application, however, he had now simplified the design to produce music more like that of a piano. Cahill proclaimed his intention to prosecute the two designs in separate applications with clear divisions between them. He was careful to point out that, although his invention resembled an electric piano, its processes could be used for other types of electric music-generating instruments.[67]

In his letter accompanying the amendment, Cahill analyzed each of his 108 claims[68] in the light of the exhaustive Patent Office examination of his 1895 application. He admitted that his idea of distributing music from a central station was not new, referring to Clément Ader's patent no. 257,453 of 1882. Ader had proposed to pick up the sounds of acoustic instruments with microphones and transmit them to subscribers. The difficulty with this system, Cahill pointed out, lay in the very weak amplitude of the signal. It could only be heard if a telephone receiver were held directly to the ear. Cahill's system differed in several important ways. It called for the direct generation of electrical signals, combining them into various notes of different timbres, controlling their expression by means of various inductive and resistive devices, and then transmitting the music thus produced at high power to a receiver that could be heard at some distance from the ear.

Cahill next confessed that his idea of generating music electrically was not new. Elisha Gray's patent no. 173,618 of 1886 for an electrical organ had disclosed a system of pitched vibrating reeds, one per key, each of which created a note by periodically interrupting and connecting its own battery circuit. This converted the battery dc to a rough ac signal. Its shortcomings, according to the acerbic Cahill, were legion. First, the metal reeds had to be made very tiny in order to escape electrical arcs across their contact points. The resulting low power of the instrument put it in the same feeble class as Ader's idea. Second, the reeds generated harsh waveforms, and Gray had made no provision to smooth them out. Cahill, on the other hand, was able to filter his waveforms by passing them through successive transformers. Third, Gray's device could not manufacture sine waves. Fourth, it had no method to synthesize notes of various timbres out of the sine waves it was unable to generate. Gray knew of sound synthesis and in fact had devised two systems of synthesizing tones, primarily for use in multiple-pitch telegraphy (patent no. 205,378 of 1878; patent no. 233,345 of 1880). Here a number of telegraph transmitters, tuned to different notes, were operated independently; at the other end of the single multiplex wire, each transmitted note activated only its own tuned receiver. In Gray's patent description this harmonic telegraph had not been designed or intended as a musical instrument. Fifth, Gray's organ had no stipulation for expression. Cahill claimed "expression devices practically perfect . . . just as in the common piano-forte."[69] He held Gray's rattletrap invention to be "practically useless. No person of taste or culture could be supposed to derive any enjoyment from music rendered in poor, harsh tones, with uneven power, and absolutely without expression or variation."[70]

The Patent Office examiner had cited no fewer than 15 prior patents upon which Cahill had trespassed. Some of these were for inventions that used "rotatory rate-governors," or tone wheels, to produce specific pitches for one purpose or another, not always to do with music. But Cahill could prove the uniqueness and efficacy of his arrangement. His idea to put 12 sets of rotors on 12 separate shafts was genuinely new; it permitted each rotor to move at the exact

angular velocity necessary to create a precise pitch in equal temperament. Singer's patent no. 501,540 of 1893 had described a piano
sostenuto device using rotors mounted on a single shaft. In a devastating critique of Singer's patent, Cahill showed that it provided no
means of synchronizing the vibrations of the strings with the signals
emitted by the rotors, "resulting in ruinous beats."[71] Furthermore, in
order to sustain the strings without phase cancellations, the insulating and conducting sections of Singer's rotors must of necessity not
produce any fractional cycles over one complete revolution of the
rotor. Building rotors with such integral-numbered sections would
require a circumference of 38 feet to produce just the seven-note
diatonic scale. Should the twelve-note chromatic scale be of interest,
a rotor 3800 feet in circumference would not be sizable enough to
avoid fractions.

The examiner had also cited two British patents issued to
Mercadier, no. 10,363 of 1888 and no. 13,322 of 1889, describing a
harmonic telegraph system. In addition to covering a "non-analogous
art," so greatly different as to make its citation invalid in a case
involving musical devices, Cahill observed that its scattered keys
were designed to be operated independently, each by a different
operator.

Turning to synthesis of sounds, musical or otherwise, the examiner
had cited Gray's patent no. 205,378 of 1878. This evoked his
harmonic telegraph: metal reeds, here tuned to the fundamental and
other harmonics; each reed connected to its own battery circuit; a key
for each reed-circuit; and a set of common (not tuned) receivers.
(Recalling Helmholtz's one-note synthesizer, Gray had analyzed the
vowel *a* as part of the patent specification. Using different keys,
sounds of various timbres could be synthesized.) The impediment
here, Cahill charged, was that the device required a separate battery
circuit and a separate key for each harmonic of each note. For the
range of a piano, that exceeded 500 batteries and 500 keys: "for every
single note we must depress six or more keys. Many full chords of
frequent occurrence would require for their production the depressing of half a hundred keys."[72] Furthermore, Gray's vibrating reeds
"do not produce undulations of current; they produce sharp, violent
pulsations."[73] The device "unavoidably adds to the partials desired
many which are injurious—so many that his patent . . . seems . . . to
wholly break down."[74]

Gray had understood the defect and surmounted it by using tuned receivers in his next synthesizing device, patent no. 233,345 of 1880. As in the earlier harmonic telegraph, it employed a tuned receiver for each partial. The design of the receiver, in attenuating extremes of frequency, could thus in some measure compensate for the roughness of the waveform that drove it. Cahill scathingly countered that this dubious design called for hundreds of tuned receivers to enable the reception of the range of the piano. Furthermore, since the signal for one note would wend its way through all these receivers, their combined impedance would be so enormous as to throttle the loudness output to the faintest remnant. Add to these problems the practical difficulty of keeping a large number of receivers, in different places at different temperatures, in tune with their corresponding reeds, and Gray's improved atrocity was undeniably "devoid of any practical or commercial use whatsoever."[75]

In a recent patent cited by the examiner, no. 492,563 of 1893, Singer had claimed some synthesizing capability in an improved *sostenuto* piano, providing "facilities for playing which are afforded to the organist, in respect of varying the quality of the sounds produced, or of combining those qualities, and the production of octaves and harmonics of the initial note, on the depression of one key."[76] Four sets of strings, tuned in octaves, served as "stops" for a single note. Each string could be sustained in vibration by switching on an electromagnet driven by a rotor (all rotors were mounted on a single shaft as in Singer's other patent).

Cahill retorted that he had already proven the device practically inoperative because of its rotor arrangement. Furthermore, Singer did not deliver electrical signals to be converted into music. He merely generated signals to sustain the vibrations of piano strings, whose sounds already contained a rich palette of harmonics. Sustaining and combining the sounds of these strings would make "the tones sharp, thin and metallic—the very faults which builders use the greatest pains to avoid . . . supposing it to work, it still has no utility; for it makes the instrument to which it is applied a much poorer instrument than it would otherwise be."[77]

"Notwithstanding the manifest inutility"[78] of Gray's and Singer's patents, Cahill and Ellis Spear, his attorney, thought it best to formulate patent claims whose terms avoided these prior patents. In so doing, and in striving to protect each separate part of his invention, they found it necessary to arrive at the conspicuous quantity of 107 claims.

Turning to the matter of expression mechanisms, Cahill asserted that his movable-coil loudness control was the first use of this type of device to govern loudness in any musical instrument. He admitted that the principle was already in use in electrotherapeutic apparatus and in electric lighting, but such nonanalogous arts could not be cited against him. The examiner, however, had cited two patents in telephony, both of which resembled Cahill's device to an intriguing degree. One was no. 371,557 of 1887 to Drew; the other no. 477,870 of 1892 to Pollak. Each consisted of (1) a coil which carried the audio signal, (2) another coil which could pick up the audio signal, and (3) a means for adjusting or varying the inductance between the two coils. The purpose of these inventions was to suppress extraneous noises caused by inductive interference, then a common problem in telephone systems. Cahill's objective, however, was to regulate the sounds belonging *to* the system, not to eliminate outside interference. Furthermore, he complained that Drew's and Pollak's devices were installed on receivers for use by listeners. Cahill's device was installed at the transmitting point and operated by the performer: "a root difference, which serves to mark the total dissimilarity of the systems."[79]

The examiner had cited another expression device, patent no. 501,543 of 1893 to Singer. It was a resistance box containing powdered carbon. The force, exerted as the musician pressed the key, squeezed the carbon in the box, varying the resistance of the circuit in which the box was inserted. Cahill countered that the carbon device was better suited to infinitesimal pressure variations (as the carbon microphone used in telephones responds to air pressure) than to "great differences, such as the government of expression requires."[80] Furthermore, Singer's resistance box was supremely irrelevant in design to Cahill's induction coils, besides being intended for a *sostenuto* piano and not electrical synthesis.

Having thus defended and explained the claims covering his apparatus, Cahill turned to his claims for method and process.

He acknowledged that in his first application of 1895, some of the claims had in fact been broader than required for the protection of his invention. They had included "other and different arts, where the present claims are suitably limited."[81]

Now that he had sampled a light amount of crow, Cahill focused on the examiner's stated opinion of the earlier claims. It made up the core of the examiner's resistance to the application:

All there is of due process in this application is clearly stated in applicant's claim 1. That is to say, the process herein consists in generating simple electrical undulations corresponding in periodicity, amplitude and vibration [form] with the sound vibrations which it is desired to produce, and then translating such undulations into audible aerial vibrations. Whether this be done by induction, whether it be done in one circuit or in several circuits, whether it be done with one system of apparatus or another, is all manifestly immaterial, so far as the method is concerned. Now, this method is old and well known, and was fully described by Gray in several of his patents . . . [which] show all of proper process disclosed in this application. Each method claim is therefore rejected, either as being old in the reference to Gray, or as covering over Gray the mere function of the apparatus specified in the rejected claims.[82]

Cahill retorted warmly:

That is to say, Gray having invented one mode of combining partials electrically, and that a very inferior one, as we have already seen, . . . no one after him can invent any method or process whatever, having any relation to the subject. . . . the law, it is submitted, rewards as well the producing of an old result in a new and better way, as it does the producing of a result never produced before.

. . . The differences between applicant's process and Gray's are more marked than, and full as important as, the differences between Reiss [sic] and Bell, which were held sufficient to sustain the Bell patent.[83]

And finally, to illuminate a very telling aspect of the first application and the manner of its rejection:

This action, it must be borne in mind, was taken by the examiner on the first view of a very complicated case, without having had the opportunity, it is understood, to himself read the whole of the very lengthy specification. Moreover, the specification in that case . . . *did not explain at length, if at all, the peculiar physical considerations and elemental electrical actions involved in the operation of applicant's apparatus,* and which prove it to involve true process subject matter. And the action of the examiner was taken according to the usual practice, it being a first action, without argument or explanation on the part of the applicant.[84]

There were three root points of difference in the processes of the opposing systems:

Gray	*Cahill*
Generated signals by current interruption.	Generated signals by induction.
Used make-and-break circuits.	Used closed circuits.
Produced abrupt and harsh pulsations.	Produced smooth waveforms.

The examiner had held the use of a sine wave instead of a make-and-break wave to be the substitution of equivalents. Cahill agreed that such may be the case in harmonic telegraphy, where tuned receivers (reeds, tuning forks, or strings) could be activated by waveforms of various shapes, yet emit essentially a constant timbre as determined by their physical characteristics and construction. There remained the impediment of the famous patent to Alexander Graham Bell, no. 174,465 of 1876, which had described the advantages of combining "undulations" over pulsations for transmission along a telegraph system. These undulations were not sine waves but electrical reproductions of acoustic waveforms. Bell had pointed out that his system might well be used as a general method for transmitting music, noises, or sounds of any kind. Cahill argued that this was very different from his own system—Bell had been endeavoring to send as many signals as possible over a single wire and found that undulations served the purpose better than pulsations. Cahill asserted that he was not trying to "claim broadly the process of synthesizing composite undulations out of smooth electrical undulations."[85] Furthermore, Bell had confined his method to a single circuit (as had Berliner in a similar method, patent no. 258,356 of 1882), whereas Cahill was working with many closed circuits. This design enabled him to install a separate tuned filter for each note. It was clearly new:

> There is no patent, so far as known, and no publication in which this tempering effect of different circuits on different electrical tones, has ever been considered or proposed for practical use in a music-generating system. The physical principle on which it rests, is of course as old as the universe; but the first practical application of it, in the production of music, appears to be new with the applicant. It certainly involves process.[86]

In addition to the filtering capability, the multiple closed circuits afforded more flexible control over expression. This enabled not only the control over harmonic proportions, but also permitted the performer "to accent the leading parts and subdue the accompaniment, according to the requirements of expression."[87] This was also clearly new: "There is not, so far as known, a particle of evidence that the expression of a musical composition has ever been controlled in this way, or that any one has ever appreciated the fact that it might be thus controlled."[88]

The series of operations, summed up Cahill, was his invention. There was no claim for each operation alone. Together they constituted an elegant new method for musical purposes exquisitely superior to any known.

Cahill also strove to justify his process of filtering notes by successive inductive transfers, even though transferring signals in this way from one circuit to the next was well known in other fields. He believed that such a method, when used to purify tones, was new and patentable. The examiner had cited Mercadier's British patent no. 13,322 of 1889; Cahill countered that it had nothing to say on the subject of filtering musical notes. Mercadier's device was a harmonic telegraph, about which Cahill would have a few words to say at the end of his lengthy letter.

The arguments neared conclusion with a vivid and stinging critique of the impracticalities of attempting to employ the insipid, two-bit patents cited by the examiner to create music of the scope and scale allowed by Cahill's application. With Gray's first system, combining hundreds of circuits in parallel would decrease the power output to uselessness; in Gray's second system, hundreds or even thousands of batteries would be required and would wear out faster than they could be replaced; in Bell's and Mercadier's systems, the large number of coils in series (one for every harmonic of every note) would choke the output to next to nothing; in Berliner's system (improving on Bell's and Mercadier's by closing the circuits of unused coils), the shorted coils would overheat, and the constantly varying numbers of coils in use would continually mangle the waveform beyond repair.[89]

As Cahill had promised, his concluding thrust was an assault, biting yet lawyerly in tone, on the relevance of harmonic telegraph patents:

The incidental or unintentional formations of separate groups of vibrations out of elemental vibrations, and the formation of resultant vibrations out of the groups of composite vibrations, by separate groups of telegraph instruments, located at different points and acting on the same line, but acting each independently of the others, and with no common physical purpose of object in view to be accomplished by their joint action; with no designed coaction, and no physical result which is the joint product of all, is surely a very different thing from the designed and controlled coaction of a multiplicity of vibration generators cooperating in the production of the same composite undulations, the production of which is the conscious object and the joint effect of their separate actions.[90]

There Cahill rested his case. Five weeks later he heard from the examiner.

Charles H. Lane, Head Examiner, was used to grappling with stubborn and tenacious applicants. Indeed, he displayed conspicuous traces of mulishness himself in his letter to Cahill. He did not capitulate:

The invention is a simple one, and there is no difficulty in understanding it, except that, in the words of Judge Coxe— ". . . he has obscured his real invention in a multitude of fuliginous and attenuated claims . . . he has claimed it indistinctly, to the annoyance of the public."

Applicant in his letter refers to only a few of the most elementary and clearest patents, and entirely fails to examine others, one of which, Van Rysselberghe, anticipates more than half the claims in this case.[91]

Lane first pointed out that a number of devices to filter signals were well known, and Cahill's selection of a suitable method was not an invention. After lodging numerous complaints against the unsystematic wording, he held that only Cahill's overall organization was patentable, not the components or details. He summarized patent no. 363,188 of 1887 to Van Rysselberghe, a reed telegraph with (1) rheotomes tuned to the first and second harmonics, (2) signals synthesized in closed circuits, (3) successive inductive filtering, (4) adjustable resistance and induction devices, both operated at the transmitting station, to control the volume, and (5) a common (not tuned) receiver. All of these components could be found in Cahill's apparatus.[92]

Again on the matter of filtering, Lane bristled that it is inevitable in every case of induction. He noted that Cahill had filled several pages to describe filtering results whose amplitude relationships could well be expressed in a single line. Furthermore, in not disclosing any quantitative frequency or induction data of his filtering method, Cahill appeared to be attempting to patent merely a principle.[93]

Lane also cited the patent of Hutin and Leblanc, no. 552,564 of 1884. Here a telephone system was dependent upon the generation of a number of pure sine waves in an accurate harmonic series, just as Cahill was doing.[94]

Of the 108 claims Cahill had submitted, Lane allowed only 34. These were sufficiently close to describing a complete operative device, or a major portion of its elements; 55 of the 74 rejected claims were ascribed to Van Rysselberghe.[95]

"The patentable novelty in this case," wrote Lane, "resides in applicant's organization, and not in any of the details thereof."[96]

Within two months Cahill countered with Amendment B, which does not survive. A few weeks later, Charles H. Lane rebuffed again those claims that had been transferred from remote patents. Van Rysselberghe was entitled to all the uses of his patent, even those the inventor did not contemplate. Cahill's loudness expression device could not be patented because it was no more than a resistance box with a new name. Cahill had managed to reduce the number of objectionable claims to 36; 35 of these were again ascribed to Van Rysselberghe.[97] That same month Cahill countered with Amendment C; redoubling his already spirited efforts, he filed four more amendments during the first three months of 1897. He reorganized his claims, emphasizing the idea that each rotor was tuned to a particular frequency by driving it at a particular angular velocity, so that any desired temperament could be produced.[98]

Thus was the unflagging inventor finally able to shatter the resistance of the Patent Office. Residing in Washington, D.C., he could and did prosecute his claims in person. His last amendment was a lengthy revision accepted almost wholesale by the examiner.

The descriptions were well etched and succinct, and conveyed the heart of Cahill's design elements as a new and different art. The keys of the instrument were not included in the main output circuit, in order that each could be operated independently without interrupting the output. The same was true of the expression devices, so that a number of these could also work separately without disturbing each other or the output. His expression devices included not simply resistance boxes, but inductive vibration-emitting and vibration-receiving devices. These provided for greater isolation and independent action of the expression control. He described the essence of the sound generating design—a separate circuit for generating each component, or harmonic, of one composite tone, with devices out of the main circuit which served to bring each harmonic independently into the main line by induction. Furthermore, the circuit for generating each harmonic was driven by a rotor tuned to the frequency of the harmonic. One rotor could be tapped for more than one harmonic: the second harmonic of one note is the same frequency as the fourth harmonic of the note an octave below. Two tuning systems were encompassed in the Telharmonium: one in the pure harmonic series (just intonation) for building the timbre of each note, the other in equal temperament for combining the individual notes into a scale. He also described the distribution system as having numerous receivers of the music located in different places.[99]

The application was accepted and the cornerstone patent for electric music granted on April 6, 1897.[100]

The essence of it was

> to generate music electrically with tones of good quality and
> great power and with perfect musical expression, and to
> distribute [this] music . . . from a central station to translating
> instruments located at different points and all receiving their
> music from the same central point.[101]

The apparatus was depicted as a mainframe that supported twelve physically identical pitch-shafts, one for each frequency of the equal-tempered scale (Fig. 2). Each shaft was belt driven by a drive-pulley of different diameter, causing it to rotate at the rate proportional to its desired frequency. The twelve drive-pulleys were all mounted on a single driveshaft powered by an electric motor.[102] Mounted on the pitch-shafts were "rheotomes," rotating cylinders with alternate sets of longitudinal conducting and insulating sections (Fig. 3). Each rheotome had six sets of brushes bearing upon it, which would make and break connections with it as it revolved. The lowest note of a shaft was generated by a compound rheotome-cylinder consisting of six simple rheotomes, one for each of the first

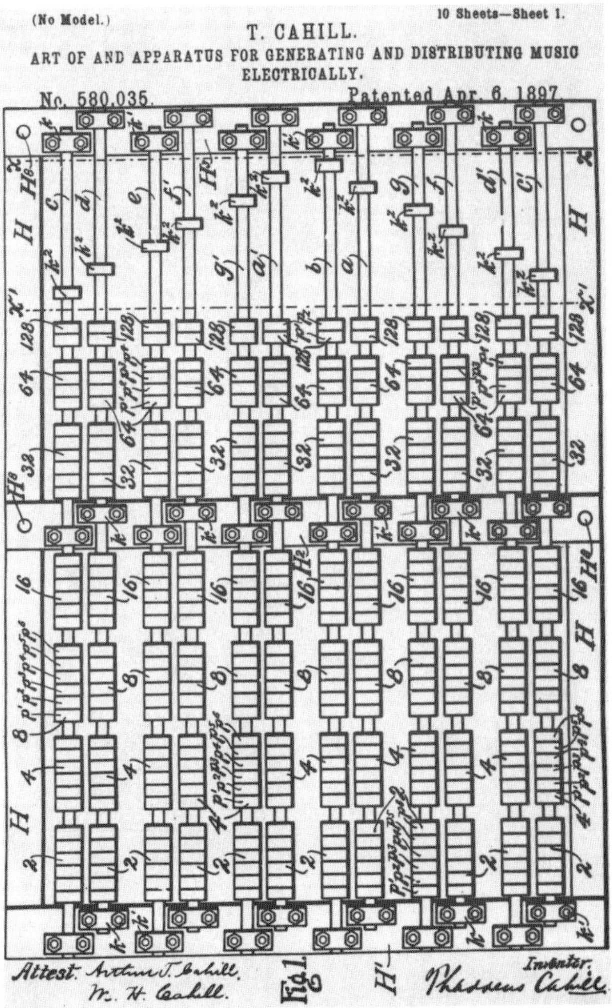

Fig. 2. Overhead Schematic View of Twelve Pitch-Shafts. (U.S. Patent 580,035 [1897] drawings sheet 1.)

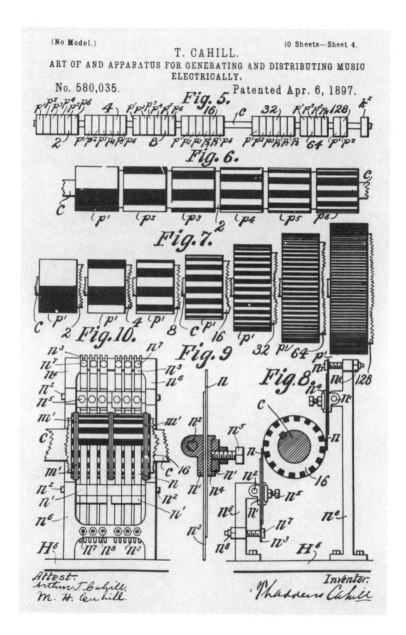

Fig. 3. Details of Rheotome, Brush, and Rheotome-Cylinder Designs (U.S. Patent 580,035 [1897], drawings sheet 4)

six harmonics of that note. Each shaft had seven rheotome-cylinders. The highest cylinder had only two rheotomes, the one below that had four, and the remaining five had all six rheotomes. As with many acoustical instruments, a richness of harmonics was unnecessary in the upper register. Consequently, the seven notes on a shaft spanned a compass of six octaves of fundamental tones, with the harmonics extending another octave above this range.[103] The apparatus had a "hot chassis" supplying current from a large dynamo through all the shafts into the rheotomes. When a key was depressed, the current would flow out of its rheotome through the brushes into a coil (where the sound would be tapped), then to the key-circuit, and back to the dynamo. The sound quality of the electrical signal was harsh and biting, with many strong high harmonics. (This was a basic design characteristic of rheotomes, since they formed signals through abrupt make-and-break switching of the current. Rheotomes were cheap and easy to construct, but their mechanical limitations rendered them unsuitable for high-power applications; Cahill would turn to alternators in the future.) As the current flowed through the coil, it induced a current in a neighboring secondary coil. This induced secondary signal was purged of some of the harshness imbued in the primary signal. This arrangement was repeated several times, with four successive inductive transfers serving to smooth out each harmonic of each rheotome to something approximating a sine wave. The last coil in the series was connected to the line output of the instrument.[104]

Two of these coils were arranged as components of an expression device, based in part on Cahill's 1894 patent no. 520,667 for a piano friction-driven power action. When a key was struck, a proportional force was transferred to a metal hammer, amplified by a rotating sympathetic friction-driver (Fig. 4). The hammer struck the bottom of a vertical sliding shaft, atop which was mounted a primary coil carrying the signal. Some distance above this coil was a secondary coil wound around a hollow bobbin. If the key were struck very forcibly, the primary coil traveled completely into the bobbin, and maximum signal level was transferred into the secondary coil. If the key were struck weakly, the greater distance between the two coils reduced the transfer of current, keeping the sound softer. A blow of intermediate force moved the shaft only part of the distance, providing a moderate sound level. As soon as the shaft had traversed its distance, it was gripped in place by an electromagnetically

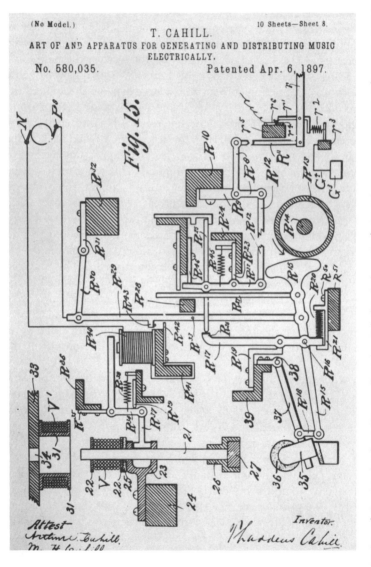

Fig. 4. Design of Key Mechanism: Key (r), Rotating Friction-Driver (R14), Metal Hammer (R15, 35, 36), Vertical Sliding Shaft (21), Primary Coil (V), Clutch (R37), Secondary Coil Wound Around Hollow Bobbin (V1). (U.S. Patent 580,035 [1897], drawings sheet 8)

controlled clutch, thus continuing to maintain a consistent sound volume as long as the key remained depressed.[105]

The patent was supplemented by 22 well-made drawings that clearly displayed the construction and features of the instrument. On the same date the patent was granted, Cahill applied for patents in Great Britain, France, Germany, Austria-Hungary, and Belgium.[106] To these applications he appended the substitution of ac alternators for rheotomes. Their toothed armatures rotating in magnetic fields easily generated sine waves.[107] He also offered minor improvements in the clutch of the loudness expression device and a hollow rheotome filled with a resistant fluid to effect a more gradual current variation.[108] He managed to avoid calling his invention an "electrical pianoforte," a term that had crept into the U.S. patent text. The French patent was granted in a scant three months, the British patent one month later. The German patent, which had identical drawings and a much-abbreviated list of claims, was not granted for nearly four years.[109]

CONSTRUCTION, DEMONSTRATION, AND LICENSING OF THE TELHARMONIUM

Until the age of 30, Cahill weighed only about 115 pounds. Always small, but not noticeably thin, people said he seemed to be larger than he really was. There was an expression and charisma in his face that attracted people. This distinctiveness was not captured on film, and family members regretted that Cahill never took a satisfactory photograph.[110]

His ladylove was a Miss Mary C. Fairchild, eldest daughter of a Sullivan County, N.Y., lawyer. His attentions, clearly more devoted to his work than to her, went unrequited; perhaps she was unwilling to become the first electric-music widow. In 1898 Cahill drew up his will and ardently left Mary his prayer book, hymnal, and a box of other books. He never married or changed the bequest. His physical welfare was excellent, even though walking was the only exercise he engaged in. His pulse was very slow, but Cahill's only weakness was an occasional cold. He possessed prodigious endurance and working power, and rarely took even half a day off. He was just beginning the most difficult work of his life and would need all the stamina and narcissism he could muster.[111]

In 1898 construction of a small working model of the Telharmonium at Cahill's Washington laboratory began in earnest. The keyboard came from a superannuated organ purchased from a Virginia church once attended by George Washington.[112] The nascent efforts went slowly. Cahill was also studying for a doctoral degree in law and operating the Cahill Writing-Machine Manufacturing Co. with his brothers, which they had incorporated in 1896. Then in 1899 their father, who had come to live with them in Washington, died at the age of 63 from congestive heart failure. By 1900, as Cahill received his D.C.L. from Columbian University, the instrument reached a rudimentary state of completion.[113] However, it was not yet ready for demonstration to investors, much less the public. Cahill transmitted music over telephone lines within Washington, from his laboratory in one part of the city to his home and office in another. Over the next two years, he experimented with different designs of alternators, developing plans for a much larger instrument. He was aided by his two brothers, a superintendent, an electrician, and a draftsman.[114]

At the century's turn, Cahill also more or less perfected his electric typewriter. The key action was very different from the Remington, the Smith, and other common machines of the day. On the Cahill Universal Electric No. 2, Model P, a key had to be depressed only $1/4$ inch for the typebar to strike the paper and then drop back into position. It was unnecessary to wait for one key to return to its original position before striking the next. This enabled an easy *legato* touch. Additionally, the last letter of a word and the spacebar could be struck together. These improvements enabled an operator to increase average typing speed by one-third. One typist reportedly blazed through a single familiar sentence at the rate of 200 words a minute. The typewriter was exhibited at the Pan-American Exposition at Buffalo in April 1901, by and at the expense of the U.S. government. The unusual machine was hailed as an "epoch-making invention"[115] and an outstanding proof of the value of the patent system. Nonetheless, the company would fold in 1905, three years after the Cahills moved away and permitted it to continue on in Washington. The brothers later blamed "dissension and trickery"[116] for the demise; however, their questionable judgment in becoming absentee owners, while expending their energies in other endeavors, may have led to this perhaps paranoid assessment. Ultimately, the company produced a total of 40 machines at a cost of $157,000.[117]

By 1901 Cahill had sufficiently developed the working Telharmonium model to seek investment backing. He approached Oscar T. Crosby (Fig. 5), a pioneer developer of electrical railroads and a prominent Washington capitalist. Crosby had graduated from West Point, followed by five years of service in the Army Corps of Engineers. In 1887 he had resigned his army commission to become chief electrical engineer of local railway installations for the General Electric Co., first in Richmond, Va., then Baltimore, Md. He was hired by inventor and engineer Frank J. Sprague, at whose wedding he had been best man six years earlier. Sprague admired Crosby for his grit and cool nerve. Electrical railroad operation was then a young industry, and Crosby went on to co-author one of the earliest books on the subject.[118] He later worked as general manager of the railway department of the General Electric Co., then left to become a partner with James G. White. They formed the White Crosby Co., electrical engineers and constructors, but broke apart after several years. White would go on to establish one of the largest engineering and construction companies in the world, while in the late 1890s Crosby once again headed local railways and utilities, this time in Washington. Crosby was also becoming interested in world travel and visited Abyssinia and the Sudan in 1899 and 1900, the first of many extensive trips to remote lands.[119]

Crosby took a spirited interest in the Telharmonium. He brought in a partner, Frederick C. Todd, an electrical engineer who managed the Baltimore office of the General Electric Co. Todd was an avid hunter and sportsman. He owned a log cabin festooned with antlers, moose and other animal heads, trophies, and antique guns. A refuge from this carnage was his houseboat, "Peeker".[120] The partners furnished Cahill with funds to improve the model so they could demonstrate it and raise capital from other investors.[121]

In 1902 Cahill was 34 years old. His electric typewriter business was foundering, and he had little money of his own. The need for substantial funding for the Telharmonium was dire, yet he was unwilling to secure this by losing his only asset, his patent. Testing the waters, Crosby and Todd organized a dinner of bankers and prominent businessmen at the Maryland Club, a private club in Baltimore. In the dining room was an ordinary telephone receiver attached to a small horn. The investors listened in rapt awe as the

Fig. 5. Oscar T. Crosby, ca. 1940. (Courtesy of Dr. John T. Hornblow)

eloquent strains of Handel's *Largo* filled the large room. The music was being performed long-distance on the Telharmonium in Washington by Paul W. Fishbaugh, a young businessman who was also a skilled musician. Before leaving the table the men agreed in principle to put up $100,000 for the Telharmonium.[122]

Arduous negotiations ensued. Cahill was determined to retain the rights to his invention. He was fortunate to have a calm and certain personality and no little salesmanship. He never seemed to hurry or be nervous or flustered. The discussions were not concluded in a burst of impulsive enthusiasm; they took more than three months. In the end the vanquished businessmen yielded to the inventor on almost every point. The $100,000 they had agreed to pay him would be only the first installment for the license to distribute Telharmonic music in New York and New England. It was payable in advance; there would be substantial continuing payments. They also agreed to cover all costs of every kind to construct the first commercial Telharmonium, which were understood to be undetermined, but probably would amount to several hundred thousand dollars. Cahill retained his present and future patents. Finally, they left the writing of the elaborate and comprehensive contracts to the inventor, which took another three months. Cahill had managed to hold his own virtually alone against the entire group. This was all the more remarkable when one realizes that no large-scale Telharmonium had ever been built, that few if any besides Cahill and Crosby thoroughly understood the instrument, and that $300,000 to $400,000 was then an immense sum.[123]

The license was signed on June 19, 1902; it would run ten years. Although the one patent already granted to Cahill was solely in his name, the wisdom of joint title was now apparent. Should any misfortune befall Cahill, should he become unable to manage his affairs, protecting and enforcing the valuable license would be jeopardized. Cahill granted the license, therefore, as a consortium of five trustees: the three Cahill brothers and two attorneys, Ellis Spear and E. Hilton Jackson.[124]

Ellis Spear had assisted Cahill in obtaining the first Telharmonium patent. He was a respected 68-year-old patent attorney who had served with great distinction in the Civil War, having risen from a captain of Maine volunteers in 1862 to brigadier general in 1865. Immediately after the war he entered the civil service, starting out as an assistant examiner of railway and civil engineering in the

Patent Office. He rose to become commissioner of patents in 1877; Spear resigned the post nearly two years later to enter private patent law practice.[125]

E. Hilton Jackson had been a classmate of Cahill's throughout the 1890s at Columbian University. They had received their law doctorates together two years earlier. Now 32, he was already the author of a text on legal Latin and had been practicing law for seven years.[126]

Another Columbian law graduate, Pickens Neagle of North Carolina, was one of fellow Southerner Oscar T. Crosby's lawyers. The 40-year-old Neagle was named as a license assignee. His legal experience had begun as a law clerk with the secretary of the navy some 15 years earlier.[127]

The contracts established the three Cahill brothers as the Cahill Music-Patents Trust. The brothers and their lawyers became the trustees, who were given legal powers to prosecute applications in the Patent Office, to hold title to the patents, to license local companies, to sue infringers, and to administer any income of the trust. The trust was also empowered to sell shares. Frederick C. Todd acquired 635 shares at $100 each; it is probable that Crosby held an interest of at least a like amount.[128]

The contracts stipulated that licensee companies were to be charged a royalty of 4% of gross receipts per year, plus

> $50 per year on each diaphragm used in the parlors, dining rooms, bar rooms, billiard rooms, porches, or other public rooms or places of any hotel, restaurant, cafe, saloon, billiard room, lodge, club, store, shop, depot, or other public place, in towns of more than 100,000 inhabitants.[129]

The diaphragm fee decreased to $25 per year in smaller towns, and fell to only $10 for a private room in a hotel or residence. But before the trustees could remit any of this largess to the Cahill Music-Patents Trust, Thaddeus Cahill was entitled to collect $5 per diaphragm personally right off the top.[130]

The contracts also provided for the interests of the Cahill Music Machinery Manufacturing Co., as yet unincorporated. Whenever organized, it would have sole license to manufacture the music-generating and -distributing apparatus to be leased to local companies all over the U.S. The unformed company's first obligation, to be fulfilled within 30 days of incorporation, was to issue 10,000 shares of stock at a par value of $50 each, free of charge, to Thaddeus Cahill. Furthermore, the trustees were compelled to order Telharmonic devices and instruments exclusively from this company, unless the firm should prove unable to make delivery within 18 months.[131]

License in hand, Crosby set out to form the first Telharmonic corporation. The wisdom of the day dictated a New Jersey charter.

Proximate to the great financial centers of New York and Philadelphia, but with scant investment capital of its own, New Jersey had set out to attract industry by assuming national primacy in chartering corporations. The legislature had enacted some of the most liberal and forward-looking yet respectable incorporation laws in the land. Nowhere else could reputable corporations issue mortgage bonds, convert bonds to stock, guarantee bonds of other corporations, pay bond yields exceeding usury limits, hold stock in other corporations, and issue stock in exchange for property.[132] Furthermore, the incorporation fee was only 1/50 of 1% (20¢ per $1000) of the par value of the authorized capital stock. Only one director had to be a New Jersey resident. The amount of stock that could be issued was limitless, as was company indebtedness.[133] The natural result of such leniency was that New Jersey had become midwife to the "trust" movement of the late nineteenth and early twentieth centuries.[134]

Oscar T. Crosby and his financial partners formed the New England Electric Music Co. on June 28, 1902, in Jersey City. Outside the state the company was permitted by its charter to own and generate telephone, telegraph, and electric light plants. These did not necessarily have to possess any connection with electric music. The company was capitalized at $200,000.[135]

Crosby set up Frederick C. Todd as president and himself as vice president. The officers and directors were all Baltimoreans, save one Jersey City lawyer. In its first annual report, filed when the corporation was not yet a month old, the amount of stock issued— $1,000—had not increased from that given in the incorporation papers.[136]

Cahill was kept busy demonstrating the Telharmonium to assist his licensees and their financing.[137] He also transmitted the instrument to the home of George Westinghouse, inventor of the air brake.[138] Westinghouse was then 55 and at the height of a flourishing career. It had begun shortly after the Civil War when he made high-speed rail travel safe with his engineer-operated brake system, replacing the method of tightening brakes on each railway car individually. He developed numerous patents in rail, natural gas, and electrical power, and organized large companies for the creation and manufacture of inventions and equipment. His second great achievement was developing high-voltage alternating-current power transmission and ac motor design.[139]

Westinghouse owned three permanent homes. He and his wife had a great interest in wiring them with electrical conveniences. In 1888 their home in Lenox, Mass., became the first building in the world fully lighted indirectly. More than 1500 custom-designed lamps were installed in specially designed mouldings. All the Westinghouse homes had private wires installed, connecting them with his business offices. When at home he could reach his subordinates promptly and confidentially; when at work he could reach his wife without delay. Even though Westinghouse declined any business involvement with the Telharmonium, he took a great interest in the machine. He had developed a warm friendship with Britain's Lord Kelvin, and in April 1902, Mr. and Mrs. Westinghouse brought Lord and Lady Kelvin to Cahill's laboratory.[140]

William Thomson, Baron Kelvin of Largs, was one of the most respected and honored scientists of the nineteenth century. He was one of the founders of thermodynamics, having proposed its second law. By 1855, at the age of 31, he had published 96 papers and had reached the end of his career in pure research. He devoted the remainder of his life to applied physics, particularly electricity, and developed much equipment, including stranded conductors. His work was particularly valuable to the design and laying of the transatlantic cables. He was also something of a musician, having delighted his students at the University of Glasgow by illustrating his lectures on sound with demonstrations of pitch change on the French horn. Kelvin was now nearly 78 and on his third and last visit to America.[141]

Lord Kelvin described Cahill's work to Mr. and Mrs. Westinghouse as "one of the greatest accomplishments of the brain of man."[142] He offered to read a paper himself to the Royal Society of London, of which he was a past president, if Cahill would send him one on electrical music. Cahill never did so, considering it more important to press ahead with research and construction.[143]

Cahill was entering the most difficult period of his life. He would have to assemble and deliver his machine on a scale never before attempted. For the next few years he would average less than four hours of sleep a night. He would develop a prodigious appetite, consuming twice as much food as his brothers and sisters. Yet his digestion never troubled or failed him.[144]

The Baltimore businessmen with whom Cahill had contracted to build a Telharmonium selected the site of this endeavor for him: Holyoke, Mass.[145] In the early summer of 1902, Cahill went there to establish a laboratory with his brother Arthur, who became its superintendent. The next year Cahill closed his Washington laboratory and moved it to Holyoke.[146]

NOTES

1. Elliot N. Sivowitch, "Musical Broadcasting in the Nineteenth Century," *Audio,* June 1967, 51:6, 19; David L. Woods, "Semantics Versus the 'First' Broadcasting Station," *Journal of Broadcasting,* Summer 1967, XI:3, 200; Telephone interview with Bill Massa, Manuscripts and Archives Department, Sterling Memorial Library, Yale University, September 25, 1989.

2. Sivowitch, 19.

3. Sivowitch, 20; "Music by Telegraph," *New York Times,* July 10, 1874, 2; Sivowitch, "A Technological Survey of Broadcasting's 'Pre-History,' 1876-1920" (hereafter "A Technological Survey"), *Journal of Broadcasting,* Winter 1970–71, XV:1, 2; Woods, 200.

4. Sivowitch, "Musical Broadcasting in the Nineteenth Century," 21; Sivowitch, "A Technological Survey," 2.

5. "Music by Telegraph," *New York Times,* April 3, 1877, 5.

6. "Telephone Concerts," *Steinway Hall Programme,* April 2, 1877, I:94, B.M.I.A., 1–2; "Music by Telegraph," April 3, 1877, 5; Harold C. Schonberg, "When Music Was Broadcast by Telephone," *New York Times,* May 11, 1975, D17.

7. Sivowitch, "Musical Broadcasting in the Nineteenth Century," 21.

8. Sivowitch, "A Technological Survey," 2; Woods, 201–202.

9. Woods, 202, 200; Sivowitch, "Musical Broadcasting in the Nineteenth Century," 22; Antony Askew, "The Amazing Clément Ader," pt. 1, *Studio Sound,* September 1981, 23:9, 48.

10. Askew, 45, 48; Askew, pt. 2, *Studio Sound,* October 1981, 23:10, 67, 68; Askew, pt. 3, *Studio Sound,* November 1981, 23:11, 101.

11. Askew, pt. 3, 100; Askew, pt. 2, 68.

12. Askew, pt. 3, 102; Askew, pt. 1, 45; Woods, 201.

13. Woods, 200–202.

14. George F. Cahill, "Thaddeus Cahill (June 18, 1867–April 12, 1934): A Preliminary Paper," New York?, 1934?, typewritten, C.R.L.C. E-1488, Cat. C, L609.214, C115, 1; Personal interview with Margaret Eleanor Cahill Schwartz, Rochester, Vt., August 29, 1990; Declaration of Timothy Cahill for Original Pension of an Invalid, sworn before Joshua S. Sloan, Clerk of the District Court, October 11, 1872, N.A.F.T.B., SC-127-969, 1; Robert Moore, Assistant Marshal, "Schedule 1.—Free Inhabitants in Ward 5, City of Nashua, in the County of Hillsborough, State of New Hampshire, enumerated by me, on the 15th day of June, 1860," in *Population Schedules of the Eighth Census of the United States, 1860,* Roll 673, New Hampshire, vol. 5, Washington: National Archives Microfilm Publications, National Archives and Records Service, General Services Administration, 1967, 113; Harvard University, "Cahill, Timothy," Record of Attendance, Harvard University Archives, 1; Affidavit of Evan B. Hammond, M.D., sworn before Bernard B. Whittemore, Notary Public, September 16, 1872, N.A.T.F.B., SC-127-969, 1; Michael Donohoe, Certificate of Disability for Discharge, Army of the United States, Timothy Cahill, Hospital Steward, November 10, 1862, N.A.F.T.B., Timothy Cahill, 10th N.H. Inf., 1; Collector of the 1st Collection District, State of Rhode Island, Internal Revenue License no. 7552, granted to Timothy Cahill, May 1, 1865, M.C.S.; Louise Margaret Jamieson Cahill, "Arthur Timothy Cahill," 1963?, typewritten, M.C.S., 1–2; Rules of the Senate and House of Representatives of the State of New Hampshire, Concord: Amos Hadley, State Printer, June 1864, M.C.S., 13, 29; Asa McFarland, George Edwin Jenks, and Henry McFarland, *The Statesman: Political Manual for the State of New Hampshire,* Concord: McFarland and Jenks, 1864, M.C.S., 25, 30.

15. Affidavit of John Bell, M.D., sworn before M. D. Snyder, Clerk of the District Court, September 30, 1872, N.A.T.F.B., SC-127-969, 1; Affidavit of Mary Cahill, sworn before Joshua S. Sloan, Clerk of the District Court, October 9, 1872, N.A.T.F.B., SC-127-969, 1; Affidavit of C. N. Cooper, M.D., sworn before Joshua S. Sloan, Clerk of the District Court, October 4, 1872, N.A.F.T.B., SC-127-969, 1–3; Affidavit of William Crady, M.D. [not sworn], October 2, 1872, N.A.T.F.B., SC-127-969, 1–2; Letter from Ramona [Mrs. Eugene M.] Clark, Stockport, Iowa, September 13, 1983, 1; Chester F. Ralston, "Noted Inventor Who Dies Boy Here 50 Years Ago," Oberlin *News-Tribune,* November 5, 1935, O.C.A. 28/1, Box 38; Declaration of Timothy Cahill for the Increase of an Invalid Pension, sworn before Robert Hunter, Clerk of the District Court, September 26, 1879, N.A.F.T.B., SC-127-969, 1; Government Printing Office, *List of Pensioners on the Roll, January 1, 1883,* vol. III, Washington: The Office, 1883, 195.

16. Cahill, 2; "Dr. Thaddeus Cahill," *Electrical World,* March 31, 1906, XLVII:13, 656.

17. Cahill, 2.

18. Ray Stannard Baker, "New Music for an Old World," *McClure's Magazine,* July 1906, XXVII:3, 298.

19. John Grant, "The Electrical Generation of Music," *American Telephone Journal,* October 27, 1906, XIV:17, 268.

20. Cahill, 2; Baker, 298.

21. Baker, 298; A. B. Easterbrook, "The Wonderful Telharmonium," *Gunter's Magazine,* June 1907, 3:5, S.C., 566, 568; "Dr. Thaddeus Cahill," 656.

22. Cahill, 2; "Dr. Thaddeus Cahill," 656.

23. Letter from W. E. Bigglestone, Archivist, Oberlin College Archives, Oberlin, Ohio, June 29, 1982, 1.

24. "Dr. Thaddeus Cahill," 656.

25. U.S. Patent 345,028, *Organ,* Thaddeus Cahill, Oberlin, Ohio, patented July 6, 1886, 1–2.

26. Henry Margenau, "Introduction," in Hermann Ludwig Ferdinand Helmholtz, *On the Sensations of Tone,* 1885, reprinted, New York: Dover Publications, 1954, 1–5.

27. Hermann Ludwig Ferdinand Helmholtz, *On the Sensations of Tone,* second English edition, translated and conformed to the fourth German edition of 1877 with notes by Alexander J. Ellis, 1885, reprinted with an introduction by Henry Margenau, New York: Dover Publications, 1954, 120–126.

28. *Ibid.,* 398–400.

29. *Ibid.,* 204–211.

30. U.S. Patent 359,557, *Piano-Action,* Thaddeus Cahill, Oberlin, Ohio, patented March 15, 1887, 1–4.

31. U.S. Patent 359,842, *Organ,* Thaddeus Cahill, Oberlin, Ohio, patented March 22, 1887, 1–2.

32. Thomas Commerford Martin, "The Telharmonium: Electricity's Alliance with Music," *American Monthly Review of Reviews,* April 1906, XXXIII:4, 423; "Dr. Thaddeus Cahill," 656.

33. Baker, 298; "Dr. Thaddeus Cahill," 656.

34. "Edward Bellamy Dead," *New York Times,* May 23, 1898, 7; Edward Bellamy, *Looking Backward: 2000–1887,* with an introduction by Heywood Brown, Boston: Houghton Mifflin Company, The Riverside Press, 1887, 1926, 50, 56, 226–227.

35. *Ibid.,* 110–115, 138–140, 273.

36. Ludwig A. Geissler, *Looking Beyond,* London: William Reeves, 1891, reprinted, New York: Arno Press and The New York Times, 1971, 15, 22, 24, 28–29.

37. Edward Bellamy, *Equality,* D. Appleton and Company, reprinted, New York: Greenwood Press, Publishers, 1969, 157, 204–205, 295, 347–348, 291.

38. Louise Margaret Jamieson Cahill, 2; U.S. Patent 458,219, *Piano-Forte Action,* Thaddeus Cahill, Oberlin, Ohio, patented August 25, 1891, 1–2.

39. "Dr. Thaddeus Cahill," 656; Baker, 298.

40. E. E. Higgins, "A Wonderful Musical Instrument," *Success Magazine,* May 1906, 9:144, N.Y.P.L. *MKY Box, n.p.; "Century's Musical Wonder," *Holyoke Daily Transcript,* March 21, 1906, 8.

41. "Dr. Cahill's Telharmonium," *Talking Machine World,* April 15, 1906, II:4, 42.

42. "Electrically Made Music—Its High Possibilities Viewed Commercially," *Musical Age,* March 2, 1912, LXXVII:6, 94.

43. Easterbrook, 566.

44. "Telharmonic Demonstration," *Music Trade Review,* January 19, 1907, XLIV:3, 11.

45. Baker, 297.

46. George H. Picard, "Music for the Million," *Amsterdam* [N.Y.] *Recorder,* July 13, 1907, S.C., 9; Edwin Hall Pierce, "A Colossal Experiment in 'Just Intonation,' " *Musical Quarterly,* July 1924, X:3, 327; "Magic Music from the Telharmonium," *New York Times,* December 16, 1906, pt. 3, 3.

47. Baker, 297–298; Picard.

48. Picard.

49. Pierce, 327.

50. Louise Margaret Jamieson Cahill, 2; U.S. Patent 502,700, *Type-Writing Machine,* Thaddeus Cahill, Washington, D.C., patented August 8, 1893, 1–2, 28, drawings sheet 1.

51. U.S. Patent 520,667, *Pianoforte-Action,* Thaddeus Cahill, New York, N.Y. ["residing temporarily at Washington"], patented May 29, 1894; U.S. Patent 554,108, *Pianoforte-Action,* Thaddeus Cahill, New York, N.Y. ["residing temporarily at Washington"], patented February 4, 1896, 1, 31; U.S. Patent 554,109, *Pianoforte-Action,* Thaddeus Cahill, New York, N.Y. ["residing temporarily at Washington"], patented February 4, 1896, 1, 6, drawings sheet 1; personal interview with Margaret Eleanor Cahill Schwartz.

52. "Dr. Thaddeus Cahill," 656; "Dr. Cahill Dies at 66; Inventor of Telharmony," *New York Herald Tribune,* April 13, 1934, 19.

53. Picard.

54. U.S. Patent 531,904, *Type-Writing Machine,* Thaddeus Cahill, Washington, D.C., patented January 1, 1895, 1.

55. U.S. Patent 541,222, *Type-Writing Machine,* Thaddeus Cahill, New York, N.Y. ["temporarily residing at Washington"], patented June 18, 1895, 1, 2.

56. U.S. Patent 566,442, *Type-Writing Machine,* Thaddeus Cahill, New York, N.Y. ["residing temporarily at Washington"], patented August 25, 1896, 1–22, drawings sheets 1–5. The piano-style keyboard was no

innovation. It had been employed in writing machines as early as 1867. Cynthia Monaco, "The Difficult Birth of the Typewriter," *American Heritage of Invention and Technology,* Spring/Summer 1988, 4:1, 12–13.

57. "The Telephone: A Remarkable Experiment in Phonographic and Telephonic Transmission Between New York and Philadelphia," *Phonogram,* February 1891, 1:2, 48.

58. "Time and Car Fare Saved," *New York Times,* February 28, 1893, 5.

59. Woods, 201; "The Telephone: The Long-Distance Telephone Concert in Philadelphia," *Phonogram,* February 1892, 2:21, 50; "Phonograph Concert," *Phonogram,* February 1892, 2:21, 51; "A Novel Phone," *Phonogram,* February 1892, 2:2, 49; "A Concert Through Nine Hundred Miles of Wire," *Phonogram,* January 1893, 3:1, 307; Sivowitch, "Musical Broadcasting in the Nineteenth Century," 23.

60. "Music," *New York Times,* June 7, 1896, 10.

61. Woods, 202–203; "Hungarian Telephonic News Service," *Phonogram,* March, April 1893, 3:3–4, 387.

62. Woods, 202–205; Miklós Szabó, "A Telefon Hírmondó jelentősége," *Jel-Kép,* 1983, no. 2, M.R., 133–134; "The Telephone Newspaper," *Scientific American,* October 26, 1895, LXXIII:17, 267; Sivowitch, "Musical Broadcasting in the Nineteenth Century," 22–23.

63. Lloyd Espenschied, "Early Experiments in the Electrical Transmission of Music," October 12, 1944, typewritten, A.T.T.B.L.A. Espenschied 60.10.01.03, 2.

64. Amendment A from Thaddeus Cahill and Ellis Spear, Counsel, to the Commissioner of Patents, April 7, 1896, N.A. 241, 580,035.

65. 131 pages plus pages 45a, second 80, 90a.

66. Letter from Thaddeus Cahill and Ellis Spear, Counsel, to the Commissioner of Patents, April 7, 1896, N.A. 241, 580,035.

67. Cahill and Spear, Amendment A, 1, 1a, 1b.

68. 107 claims with two numbered "86."

69. Cahill and Spear, Letter, 14.

70. *Ibid.,* 15.

71. *Ibid.* 18.

72. *Ibid.,* 41.

73. *Ibid.*

74. *Ibid.,* 43.

75. *Ibid.,* 44.

76. *Ibid.*

77. *Ibid.,* 45a.

78. *Ibid.,* 46.

79. *Ibid.,* 71–72.

80. *Ibid.,* 73.

81. *Ibid.,* 80.

82. *Ibid.,* 80–81.

83. *Ibid.*, 81.

84. *Ibid.*, 83 (italics added).

85. *Ibid.*, 88.

86. *Ibid.*, 90.

87. *Ibid.*, 113.

88. *Ibid.*, 109.

89. *Ibid.*, 119–126.

90. *Ibid.*, 129–130.

91. Letter from Charles H. Lane, Head Examiner, U.S. Patent Office, to Thaddeus Cahill, May 12, 1896, N.A. 241, 580,035, 1–2.

92. *Ibid.*, 3–6.

93. *Ibid.*, 6–8.

94. *Ibid.*, 6–7.

95. *Ibid.*, 9–13.

96. *Ibid.*, 5.

97. Letter from Charles H. Lane, Head Examiner, U.S. Patent Office, to Thaddeus Cahill, August 4, 1896, N.A. 241, 580,035, 1–5.

98. Amendment D from Thaddeus Cahill to the Commissioner of Patents, January 27, 1897, N.A. 241, 580,035, 1; Amendment F from Thaddeus Cahill to the Commissioner of Patents, February 13, 1897, filed March 13 1897, N.A. 241, 580,035, 1–3.

99. Amendment G from Thaddeus Cahill to the Commissioner of Patents, February 2, 1897, filed March 2, 1897, N.A. 241, 580,035, 1–23.

100. U.S. Patent 580,035, *Art of and Apparatus for Generating and Distributing Music Electrically,* Thaddeus Cahill, New York, N.Y. ["residing temporarily at Washington"], patented April 6, 1897, 1.

101. *Ibid.*, 1.

102. *Ibid.*, 5–6.

103. *Ibid.*, 4–7.

104. *Ibid.*, 7–9.

105. *Ibid.*, 9–11.

106. Oath of Thaddeus Cahill, sworn before Henry E. Cooper, Notary Public, February 10, 1902, N.A. 241, 1,107,261, 1.

107. British Patent 8725, *Art of and Apparatus for Generating and Distributing Music Electrically,* Thaddeus Cahill, New York City, Robert Alexander Sloan, Patent Agent, Liverpool, application April 6, 1897, patented August 21, 1897, 4, drawings sheet 11.

108. *Ibid.*, 13, 16–17, 24.

109. Brevet d'Invention 265721, *Procédé et appareil pour engendrer et distribuer de la musique électriquement,* Thaddeus Cahill, application April 6, 1897, patented July 16, 1897; Kaiserliches Patentamt Patentschrift 115631, *Verfahren und Vorrichtung zur Erzeugung und übertragung von Musik auf elektrischem Wege,* Thaddeus Cahill in New-York, application April 7, 1897, patented January 3, 1901.

110. George F. Cahill, 13.

111. Thaddeus Cahill, Last Will and Testament, October 13, 1898, filed at Surrogate's Court, New York County, New York, N.Y., January 3, 1935, recorded in "Record of Wills, Liber 1563," 43; George F. Cahill, 14.

112. Arthur T. Cahill, "The Original and Scientifically Priceless Cahill Electric Music Instrument: The First Instrument That Created Music from the Electrical Waves of Alternating Current Generators," n.d. [rubber stamp: "AUG 31 1951"], mimeographed and typewritten, A.T.T.A. M-l, 1; "Music and Musicians," *New York Evening Sun,* January 12, 1907, 5.

113. Affidavit of George F. Cahill, In the Matter of Proving the Last Will and Testament of Thaddeus Cahill, December 17, 1934, filed at Surrogate's Court, New York County, New York, N.Y., 2; Cahill Writing-Machine Manufacturing Company, Certificate of Incorporation, December 5, 1896, and June 17, 1897, received and recorded at the Office of the Hudson County Clerk, Jersey City, N.J., June 18, 1897, filed and recorded at the Office of the Secretary of State, Trenton, N.J., June 18, 1897, 3; Letter from Harry C. McLean, Chief Clerk and Deputy Health Officer, Commissioners of the District of Columbia, Health Department, to Dr. W. W. Foster, May 22, 1911, H.U., 1; "Dr. Thaddeus Cahill," 656.

114. Baker, 298; George F. Cahill, "Thaddeus Cahill (June 18, 1867-April 12, 1934): A Preliminary Paper," 5.

115. George F. Cahill, "Thaddeus Cahill (June 18, 1867-April 12, 1934): A Preliminary Paper," 3.

116. *Ibid.*

117. Wilfred A. Beeching, *Century of the Typewriter,* New York: St. Martin's Press, 1974, 176; "Expert Electric Typewriter," *Holyoke Daily Transcript,* n.d., H.P.L.; George F. Cahill, "Thaddeus Cahill (June 18, 1867-April 12, 1934): A Preliminary Paper," 3; Louise Margaret Jamieson Cahill, 2; The Cahill Writing-Machine Manufacturing Company, *The Cahill Electrical Typewriter,* Washington, D.C.: The Company, 1900?, M.C.S., 2.

118. Oscar Terry Crosby and Louis Bell, *The Electric Railway in Theory and Practice,* New York: W. J. Johnston Co., 1892.

119. "Electric Music Generating System," *Talking Machine World,* July 15, 1906, II:7, 34; Baker, 298; "Crosby, Oscar Terry," *The National Cyclopaedia of American Biography,* vol. XXXV, New York: James T. White and Company, 1949, 83–84; "Crosby, Oscar Terry," *Who Was Who in America,* vol. 2, Chicago: The A. N. Marquis Company, 1950, 36; "Oscar Crosby Dies; Treasury Ex-Aide," *New York Times,* January 3, 1947, 21; John Hammond, "Reminiscences of Frank J. Sprague," n.d., typewritten, H.H.F., John Hammond File, H-73.

120. Oscar T. Crosby, *New York Electric Music Company* [Stock Prospectus], New York: April 1906? [penciled on cover: "W. J. Hammer, Aug. 17-'06"], S.L., 3; William M. Dabney, M.D., Certificate of Death of Frederick Charles

Todd, November 10, 1918, filed at the Maryland Department of Health, Annapolis, Md., certificate no. 42445, Maryland State Archives; George Fauth and James S. Whedbee, appraisers, Frederick Charles Todd: Inventory: Personal Estate, December 10, 1918, filed and recorded at Baltimore County Orphans Court, Baltimore, Md., "Baltimore County: Inventories, WJP #42," Maryland State Archives CR 9107, 537–538.

121. "Electric Music Generating System," 34.

122. George F. Cahill, "Thaddeus Cahill (June 18, 1867-April 12, 1934): A Preliminary Paper," 6, 14; Arthur T. Cahill, 1.

123. George F. Cahill, "Thaddeus Cahill (June 18, 1867-April 12, 1934): A Preliminary Paper," 5, 12, 14, 15; Arthur T. Cahill, 1.

124. John W. Crawford, Pickens Neagle, Robert E. Logan, Ellis Spear, E. Hilton Jackson, George F. Cahill, Arthur T. Cahill, and Thaddeus Cahill, Indenture, June 20, 1902, recorded in "Records of Transfers of Patents, Liber S65," June 20, 1902, P.T.O., 40.

125. "The Commissioner of Patents," *New York Times,* January 18, 1877, 1; "The Commissioner of Patents," *New York Times,* March 24, 1878, 7; "In the Five Forks Woods," *New York Times,* May 28, 1880, 3; "Spear, Ellis," *Who Was Who in America,* vol. I, Chicago: Marquis-Who's Who, 1966, 1160; "Spear, Ellis," *National Cyclopaedia of American Biography,* vol. XIII, New York: James T. White and Company, 1906, 364; "Spear, Ellis," *Appleton's Cyclopaedia of American Biography,* vol. V, New York: D. Appleton and Company, 1898, 625; "General Ellis Spear Dies in Florida," *New York Times,* April 6, 1917, 13.

126. "Jackson, E(rnest) Hilton," *Who Was Who in America,* vol. 3, Chicago: Marquis–Who's Who, 1960, 441; "President Sets Up Peace Objectives and Bides His Time," *New York Times,* January 10, 1940, 6.

127. "Neagle, Pickens," *Who Was Who in America,* vol. 2, Chicago: The A. N. Marquis Company, 1950, 393; "Neagle for Navy Law Post," *New York Times,* August 31, 1921, 15.

128. John W. Crawford *et al.,* 43–45; Fauth and Whedbee, 538.

129. *Ibid.,* 46.

130. *Ibid.,* 46, 57.

131. *Ibid.,* 65, 71.

132. John W. Cadman, Jr., *The Corporation in New Jersey,* Cambridge: Harvard University Press, 1949, 440, 441, 438.

133. Ralph W. Hidy and Muriel E. Hidy, *Pioneering in Big Business 1882–1911: History of Standard Oil Company (New Jersey),* New York: Harper and Brothers, 1955, 308.

134. Cadman, 416.

135. New England Electric Music Company, Certificate of Incorporation, June 28, 1902, received and recorded at the Office of the Hudson County Clerk, Jersey City, N.J., June 30, 1902, filed and recorded at the Office of the Secretary of State, Trenton, N.J., July 1, 1902, 2, 3.

136. New England Electric Music Company, Annual Report for 1902, July 24, 1902, filed at the Office of the Secretary of State, Trenton, N.J., July 31, 1902, 1.

137. George F. Cahill, "Thaddeus Cahill (June 18, 1867-April 12, 1934): A Preliminary Paper," 5.

138. Baker, 298.

139. "Mr. George Westinghouse," *New York Times,* November 30, 1902, pt. 2, 17; "Westinghouse—Inventor and Human Dynamo," *New York Times,* November 3, 1907, pt. 5, 3; Orestes H. Caldwell, "Westinghouse, George," *Dictionary of American Biography,* vol. X, New York: Charles Scribner's Sons, 1936, 16–18; "Westinghouse, George," *American Biography: A New Cyclopedia,* vol. II, New York: The American Historical Society, 1918, 348–354; "Westinghouse, George," *Who Was Who in America,* vol. I, Chicago: Marquis–Who's Who, 1966, 1324.

140. Francis E. Leupp, *George Westinghouse: His Life and Achievements,* Boston: Little, Brown, and Company, 1919, 259–273; George F. Cahill, 8; Marion Melius, "Music by Electricity," *World's Work,* June 1906, XII:2, 7662.

141. E. Scott Barr, "Kelvin," *The McGraw-Hill Encyclopedia of World Biography,* vol. 6, New York: McGraw-Hill Book Company, 1973, 161–162; "Lord Kelvin Dead, Years a Sufferer," *New York Times,* December 18, 1907, 4; "Lord Kelvin," *New York Times,* December 19, 1907, 8; "Prof. Gray's Life of Lord Kelvin," *New York Times Book Review,* August 15, 1908, 446; "Life of Lord Kelvin," *New York Times Book Review,* April 2, 1910, 177.

142. George F. Cahill, "Thaddeus Cahill (June 18, 1867-April 12, 1934): A Preliminary Paper," 8.

143. *Ibid.,* 17.

144. *Ibid.,* 14.

145. "Wonder Musical Machine Invented by Holyoke Men," *Boston Post,* March 18, 1906, 29; "Century's Musical Wonder," *Holyoke Daily Transcript,* March 21, 1906, 8.

146. George F. Cahill, "Thaddeus Cahill (June 18, 1867-April 12, 1934): A Preliminary Paper," 3; "Dr. Thaddeus Cahill," 656; Baker, 298; Martin, 423.

CHAPTER II

HOLYOKE

HOLYOKE AND THE CABOT STREET MILL

Seven miles north of Springfield, Mass., at Hadley Falls, the great Connecticut River drops nearly 60 feet. To harness this vast untapped power, a group of Boston capitalists had formed a company in 1847. Many were owners of the cotton mills at Lowell. Seeking to build greater textile mills, they began to acquire property and water rights at Hadley Falls. At the driest time of year, the flow over the falls was found to yield a robust 550 mill powers. (One mill power is provided by the fall of 38 cubic feet down a drop of 20 feet in one second. The largest mills at the time drew about 5 mill powers.) It offered the grandest potential for mill development in New England.[1]

Thus was the town of Holyoke (Fig. 6) created from a section of West Springfield in 1850. The canal system design was superb; no adjustment or reconstruction has ever been necessary. The river was dammed and the water diverted to an upper canal more than 6,000 feet long. A second canal, 20 feet lower, was dug parallel to the first. Mills were erected between the two canals, and the water surged from the upper canal through the mill waterwheels into the lower canal. The water was then exploited a second time, as it flowed through another set of mills built between the lower canal and the river. The owners charged an annual rental per mill power, but the mill power rights were treated like real estate. They were leased in perpetuity and conveyed with titles to the land used for mill sites.[2]

The Boston investors had overestimated industrialization and the demand for water power. Furthermore, their enterprise was not only absentee owned but absentee managed. It never made money and the

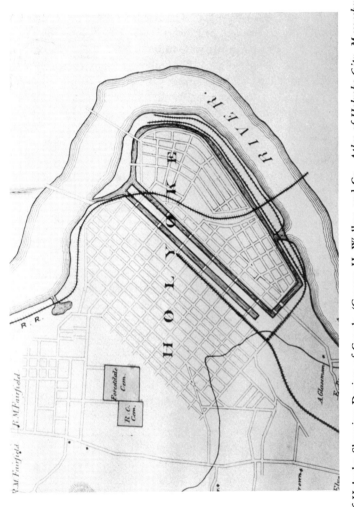

Fig. 6. Map of Holyoke Showing Design of Canals. (George H. Walker and Co., *Atlas of Holyoke City, Massachusetts*, Boston: The Company, 1884, unpaginated)

venture finally went bankrupt in 1859. The real estate and water power rights were quickly snapped up by the newly formed Holyoke Water Power Co., headed by men who, although they generally did not live in Holyoke, were directly involved in the local scene. Then, at the end of the Civil War, paper manufacturers became attracted to the combination of ample, cheap water power and chemically pure wash water. Seven paper mills were built in little more than a year, and the number eventually swelled to more than two dozen. In contrast to the cotton and wire mills, these were family concerns, largely developed by local capital.[3]

Favorable transportation rates resulted from the completion of a second railroad in 1872. The competition forced down freight charges as well as cartage costs on the Connecticut River.[4]

The industrial boom of the era afforded growing opportunities to rent space to new ventures. In 1881 the Water Power Co. directors voted to erect a large mill on the upper-level canal to house infant enterprises. Dubbed the Cabot Street Mill, it was later to be occupied by the laboratory and machine shop of Thaddeus Cahill. The companies that rented inexpensive space here repeatedly grew large enough to occupy mills of their own, and the room was again rented to newcomers. By this time Holyoke had 23 paper mills turning out 150 tons of paper daily. Nearly all the permanent water power rights had been sold. Even with rate raises, its cost was still attractively low—about one-third the cost of steam or coal.[5]

Holyoke had also become a machine manufacturing center, a direct outgrowth of the need of its mills for such equipment. As early as 1860, the town had a large textile machine shop employing 250 men, and a number of small machine companies. Others soon set up to produce castings, turbines, waterwheels, and additional mill machinery. All were formed by local capital. New inventions were developed and manufactured—a steam pump, machine parts, and switchboard signaling devices after the Bell telephone was established in 1876. By 1890 there were 13 machine shops and foundries, with a total capital investment valued at nearly that of the woollen mills. Of the more than 13,000 manufacturing employees in Holyoke that year, 837 worked in the machine industry.[6]

This pool of intelligent, skilled labor was basically conservative. Unionization made but a few tenuous beginnings that soon disappeared. Many new immigrants were still arriving, often from Quebec or Ireland; their low standard of living and the competition for jobs usually kept aggressive wage demands in check.[7]

In 1902 Thaddeus Cahill moved to Holyoke to avail himself of the expert machine labor, good rail transportation, and plentiful power. As had so many fledgling industries earlier, he set up shop in the Cabot Street Mill (Fig. 7). At first Cahill divided his time between Washington and Holyoke. He gradually established his laboratory for the announced manufacture of electrical machinery, joining a number of small industries at that location. His quarters were on the ground floor facing Cabot Street.[8] Thaddeus and his brother Arthur lived at the Hotel Hamilton that first year. In 1903 the two moved to a house at 270 Walnut Street and were joined by Mary, Eleanor, and George, all single.[9]

In 1904 the Cabot Street Mill with its ten permanent mill powers was bought from the Water Power Co. by Clifton Crocker and Frank McElwain, who were breaking away from the American Writing Paper Co. This combine of 25 mills—16 in Holyoke—had been established

Fig. 7. The Cabot Street Mill, Holyoke, 1984. Cahill's laboratory was in the right-hand section, facing Cabot Street.

in 1899 in an attempt to control the paper industry in the U.S. Unlike other trusts of the day, however, it was a forced marriage put together by investors who had made no provision for management unity.[10]

Cahill's new landlords did well, even through the Panic of 1907. By the time he finally left in 1911, Crocker and McElwain's business was booming; they even purchased another mill two years later.[11]

CROSBY GOES ABROAD

By April 1903, Oscar T. Crosby's New England Electric Music Co. had issued $160,500 in stock to fund Cahill's efforts in Holyoke.[12] The next month Crosby left to explore Central Asia. He undertook a journey from the Caspian Sea to Bombay, through Turkmenistan (then known as Turkestan), Uzbekistan, and Tajikistan, then through China, Tibet, and Kashmir. Crosby was a veteran of numerous travels and had previously explored Abyssinia, Alaska, and Egypt.[13] He wrote *Tibet and Turkestan,* a book about his experiences. In the overstuffed prose of the day, he presented his accounts and views of agricultural practices, religion, social customs, history, and political institutions. There was no dearth of travel anecdotes, but he projected in general a serious outlook, particularly on foreign policy. He displayed considerable erudition, and his cultural insights bespoke a sensitivity to other values, a wide and deep appreciation of other points of view.

Crosby, who had married the daughter of a New Orleans cotton planter in 1886, and had fathered four daughters, was much taken with polygamy: "It is a proof of a certain largeness of nature that a man's heart should go out to many women, willing, wanting to be loved."[14] He also showed that his priorities in life were sound and sensible, his "chief elements of general life" being "women, art, and ambition."[15] He claimed to travel with a library of Kant, Spinoza, Descartes, the Koran, the Bible, and Buddha's Meditations.[16] Crosby confessed that he was no stranger to situational ethics, vouching that the popularly presumed "5% ratio of corruption in the U.S. Congress is substantially correct. . . . Circumstances required that I should know the number, names, and prices of 'approachable' members."[17] This was no doubt in connection with his building of utilities in Washington in the 1880s.

Upon his return from Asia, Crosby met the press in Paris. He predicted the British takeover of Tibet, which did not happen, and the Russian acquisition of Turkmenistan (then part of China), which did. He returned to New York in February 1904.[18]

THE WORK IN HOLYOKE

Activity meanwhile was humming in Holyoke, and Thaddeus Cahill's employees often worked long into the night. As the machine was being developed and tested on local wires, the telephone company received numerous complaints of interference.[19] The ensuing curiosity, coupled with Crosby's decision to introduce an incorporation bill in the Massachusetts legislature, led to the first flurry of press coverage. Crosby needed a new statute to permit the incorporation of a company to operate an electric music plant in Boston, an intent not even remotely contemplated by Massachusetts law. It would be known as the Cahill Telharmonic Co. of New England, a subsidiary of the New England Electric Music Co. (Crosby's focus later shifted to New York and the proposed corporation was never actually brought into existence.) The breaking news report, in the *Boston Evening Transcript* of March 30, 1904, cited the praise of Lord Kelvin and other leading scientists. The writer attempted a halfhearted technical description, promised service to Boston within two years, and explained the proposed rates. The cost to an individual subscriber would begin at $50 per year, later to be considerably reduced. A subscription to a particular type of music was pegged at $100. To their discomfiture, the article disclosed the names of all the New England Electric Music Co. officers and stockholders. The local press immediately picked up the story. One paper reported that Cahill's "musical telephone" was being built for installation in Boston, where it would serve some 2,000 subscribers in less than six months. A successful test transmission from Holyoke to New Haven had already been conducted. Great popularity was predicted, to match that of moving pictures. The first distribution would be to hotels, clubs, and vaudeville houses, where it would replace salaried musicians. Later, private residences would be able to subscribe, renting the music just like a telephone.[20]

Cahill had given a lengthy interview, promising that "it will be possible to secure the very best musicians to play the best music written for many hours of the day or evening . . . for a charge of not over $5 a month at such hours of the day or night as may be desired."[21] The awestruck reporter said of the Washington Telharmonium, which was utilized for tests and demonstrations as the new commercial Telharmonium was being constructed, "the notes were clear and vibrant, and admitted of as much expression as the best-played instrument."[22]

Two obstacles occupied Cahill. One was the mixing circuit, in which a number of different signals were combined into a single signal. The problem, which was never totally overcome, was that signals added together had a tendency to cancel.[23] The other was solved, if not fully, at least to a sufficient degree—the creation of a relatively simple and inexpensive dynamo that would produce a reasonable approximation of a sine wave.[24] Cahill then turned to working out a system of intonation and the construction of the keyboard.[25]

William Hogan, then a telegraph boy of 15 in Holyoke, delivered a great many telegrams to the Cahill home on Walnut Street (Fig. 8).

Fig. 8. A House Filled with Crackling Music: The Cahill Residence at 270 Walnut Street, Holyoke, 1984.

He later wrote: "When I rang the door bell, and came in, the house was wired, with phonographs, all wires and hornes [sic], with some noise like crackling muisic [sic]."[26] The Cahills were, he said, "very fine people, like Quakers."[27] The Cahills were not particularly churchgoers, but were enthusiastic teetotalers and nonsmokers. Hogan soon become an ironmolder and worked with the heavy castings for the Telharmonium being made at a small foundry several blocks from Cahill's factory.[28] As a youth of 17, Hogan's brother Patrick worked as a mechanic for Cahill, along with 15 others. He later recalled: "Mr. Cahill was a very fine gentleman. Every day he would go through the shop and speak to the men in a friendly way."[29]

THE NEW YORK ELECTRIC MUSIC CO.

As of April 1904, Oscar T. Crosby had sold no further stock in the New England Electric Music Co.,[30] but prior issues totaled only $39,500 below its chartered limit. His company would eventually be required to remit far vaster sums than that to Thaddeus Cahill for constructing the firm's instrument. Accordingly, Crosby moved to increase the capital stock authorization from $200,000 to $300,000, at the usual par value of $100 per share. There were 27 stockholders assenting to the change; most had purchased 25 or 50 shares.[31]

Crosby next determined that further investment capital ought to flow into a separate company dedicated to service in New York. The New England Electric Music Co. would accordingly limit its Telharmony to Boston.[32]

The New York Electric Music Co. was incorporated in Jersey City on August 10. The capitalization was set at a heady $350,000. Along with its sister company, this corporation was chartered to operate telephone, telegraph, and electric light utilities in any state except New Jersey. Crosby assumed the presidency this time; Frederick C. Todd became vice president. Within two days of the incorporation, no less than $301,000 in stock was already issued.[33]

The following month Crosby and Todd incorporated a third concern. The Pacific Coast Telharmonic Co. was established in Seattle, Wash., to distribute electrical music in California and nine other western states. Capital was authorized at $400,000. Todd took 190 3/4 shares at a par value of $100; Crosby likely acquired a similar amount. However, the company never undertook to do any business, at least as a distributor of Telharmony.[34]

In December, Crosby approached Frederick P. Fish, president of the American Telephone and Telegraph Co. He announced that the first complete Telharmonium was almost ready for operation. He proposed that the Telharmonic companies do business under the A.T.&T. franchises, all the expenses to be met by the former. A.T.&T. would be able by its franchises to obtain any necessary conduit space to run electric music wires, and would in essence adopt Telharmonic music as a part of its own business without being at financial risk. Crosby noted that physically connecting the wires of the two enterprises was unnecessary; the electric music cables would be separate, run in separate ducts, to separate receivers. The present purpose was simply to allow Telharmonic music to be transmitted without obtaining its own franchise. The future, added Crosby, would determine the "wisdom of closer physical and financial connection between two great functions which, by nature, have much in common."[35] The basic question, of course, was whether A.T.&T. had the legal right to deliver music through telephone receivers.[36]

Frederick P. Fish was in the midst of an unprecedented building and financing campaign. He had become head of A.T.&T. in 1901, just after it had taken over the American Bell Telephone Co. to dominate the Bell system. Fish's background was in patent and corporation law, and after 25 years of litigation experience, he had achieved a formidable reputation. He was now supervising the vigorous expansion of A.T.&T., as thousands of exchanges were being built all over America, fueled by the sale of numerous issues of stocks and bonds. The number of messages transmitted annually by the Bell system was approaching four billion.[37]

In spite of his "broad human sympathies and a warm and generous heart,"[38] Fish was cold to the Telharmonium. He passed the question on to the general managers of the operating companies—the New York Telephone Co. and the New England Telephone Cos.—remarking that he could foresee great difficulties in the use of telephone lines for the purpose Crosby suggested.[39]

Nevertheless, fruitful negotiations ensued with Charles F. Cutler, president of the New York Telephone Co. Its legal department soon

concluded that one of the branches of telephony indeed was Telharmony—that a legitimate function of a telephone company was to
transmit music by wire—and that their company was thus fully
empowered by charter to provide such service. Hence, the parties
signed a contract on April 21, 1905, allowing lines to be drawn in
the streets of New York by the telephone company for service to the
New York Electric Music Co.[40]

INCREASES IN CAPITAL STOCK

As the contract negotiations with the New York Telephone Co.
neared conclusion, the New York Electric Music Co. was approaching the legal limit of its capitalization. Stock worth $349,000 had
been issued; the chartered maximum was $350,000. All but ten of
the shares had been issued in the names of Crosby, Todd, and two
other partners as syndicate managers. Sales were made from this
block of stock to outsiders, but the names of these investors did not
appear on the books of the corporation. Clearly, Crosby was keeping
tight voting control of this company. It was also apparent that, as the
instrument was nearing completion, a great deal more money could
be raised, whether needed or not. Hence, Crosby moved to augment
the capitalization to a cool $600,000.[41] Meanwhile, the New
England Electric Music Co. had attracted an additional $23,500 in
investment capital, raising its total outstanding stock to $184,000.[42]

Now that real money was involved, the mighty endeavor of
electric music would soon be deployed and promulgated to the
public. Hordes of additional investors would doubtless clamor for the
opportunity to place their funds with the Telharmonium. The
climate of optimism was intoxicating: 1905 ended a banner year,
setting records in iron production, crop values, railroad earnings,
stock exchange values, and bank clearings. This rising tide was,
however, accompanied by a nettlesome stringency in the money
supply. Vast demands for funds sprang from the new commercial
trade, including a massive buildup of orders for railroad cars, steel
rails, and an all-time record 6,300 locomotives. Borrowings by
Russia and Japan, whose war had recently been concluded, placed
further strain on the money markets. A foreboding sign indeed was

the rise of interest rates on call money (overnight loans by stockbro-
kers for purchases on margin) toward the end of the year to 28%,
briefly touching 125% just at the close of 1905.[43]

EDWIN HALL PIERCE

In spite of the principals' disinterest in publicity before the Telharmonium for New York was completed, another local newspaper
account was published in 1905. The apparatus was reported as
"about completed." Referring to the 70-mile test transmission from
Holyoke to New Haven over leased telephone wires, the account
claimed that tone quality was unchanged whether transmitting half
a mile or 100 miles.[44]

In 1905, Cahill and an associate were on a streetcar in downtown
Holyoke, discussing how they might find someone to translate
German to English, and vice versa. Their conversation was overheard
by Edwin Hall Pierce (Fig. 9), a musician who introduced himself
and told them he could do such translations.[45] Pierce, a violinist,
pianist, and organist, born in 1868, had studied at the Royal
Conservatory of Music in Leipzig from 1890 to 1892, afterward
filling a variety of teaching posts at Wooster, Ohio, Auburn, N.Y.,
and Champaign, Ill.[46] He moved to Holyoke in 1901 to become
organist at St. Paul's Church and director of the "Holyoke College of
Music," assisted by a faculty of four.[47] In his Holyoke debut, he
"delighted everyone" by playing an organ suite by Arthur Foote
"from memory with good tone, quality and considerable refinement."[48] By 1903 he was teaching on his own.[49] Whenever he felt
the need of a change, Pierce would move back to his birthplace in
Auburn, N.Y. He did so shortly after meeting Cahill, but took the
translating work with him. He became very interested in the
Telharmonium, so the absence from Holyoke was brief. He moved
back to a new address and went to work full time for Cahill, whose
instrument was nearing completion and required skilled performers.[50]

At that time Pierce had six children. The eldest, Roderic, had been
on the streetcar when the meeting with Cahill took place. He was
followed by James (Fig. 10), who was then about nine or ten years old

Edwin H. Pierce,

Teacher of

Piano, Violin, Harmony and Composition.

Also Sight=reading for Singers.

Residence and Studio. 16 Seminary St..

Auburn. N. Y.

TERMS ON APPLICATION

Fig. 9. Front Cover of Edwin Hall Pierce's Brochure, ca. 1898. (Courtesy of James Edward Pierce)

Fig. 10. James Edward Pierce in the Pierce Family Living Room, 8 Cottage Ave., Holyoke, ca. 1905. (Courtesy of James Edward Pierce)

(born November 8, 1895). On several occasions, the boys were taken by their father to the Cahill factory, where Pierce played the pilot model of the Telharmonium for them. To James the tone was somewhat organlike, although he could detect distinctions as the various instruments were imitated on a two-manual keyboard. They also watched the machinists cutting the teeth of the rotors for the new instrument to be installed in New York. The huge rotor mechanism seemed to James to be at least 40 or 50 feet long, and about four feet high and wide. The boys' most vivid memory of Cahill (who, recalled James Pierce, pronounced his name CaHILL) was not the Telharmonium, however, but their very first automobile ride. Cahill had expended some of his license income on a 1902 Cadillac and took the Pierce children for a ride one Sunday afternoon.[51]

Cahill's work on the system of tuning for the Telharmonium was a zealous quest for combining the perfection of just intonation—with its pure thirds and fifths—with the practicality of equal temperament, which facilitates modulation to any key. The enormous funds being sunk into the instrument allowed the extensive development and construction necessary to combine these two systems into one, a dream of keyboard instrument builders for many years.

The basic design of one long shaft for each scale tone allowed the shaft to be mounted with a full range of alternators (Fig. 11) in absolutely pure intonation—not only the scale tones in their octaves, but also beat-free fifths, thirds, even the harmonic seventh. The shafts were geared to run together in equal temperament.[52]

As the large instrument neared completion, Pierce's primary task was to devise a system of fingering on the new keyboard. The plan was to provide up to 36 keys to the octave in 3 sets, or banks—12 for the basic equal-tempered tones, 12 slightly sharp, and 12 slightly flat. (Since 4 of the projected 12 pitch-shafts were never installed, an accurate equal-tempered scale actually never became available. Yet the complication of a fourth keybank was later added to each of the two manuals to produce the very flat scale tones derived from the seventh harmonic.) The two extra keybanks were used to compensate for the mistuned thirds of equal temperament. Cahill and Pierce found that the mistuning of the fifth in equal temperament was so very slight that it could be safely accepted, and they concentrated their attention on the rendering of the various thirds in just intonation. This was effected by playing the major third of a triad on the slightly flat key, since all major thirds in the tempered scale are too sharp. Thus, when playing a major triad in root closed position on the Telharmonium, the second and fifth fingers would be on the middle keybank, and the thumb would reach down to play the middle note on the lower keybank. Minor chords were rendered by letting the third stand and lowering the tonic and fifth. Here the Telharmonist's first and fifth fingers played notes on the lower keybank, while his third finger reached up to the middle keybank. By combining tones from different keybanks, it became possible to transcribe well-known music written in equal temperament, of a slow or sustained character, into just intonation so that the charm and power of the pure intervals would be readily apparent for the first time. And in accompanying singers, the Telharmonium could thus provide them with a more surefooted base. Pierce's system provided for equal temperament to be represented by ordinary notation. He added grave or acute accents to notes to indicate that they were to be lowered or raised. One of the first pieces to be so transformed was Beethoven's *Trio in C Major* for two oboes and English horn, which

Fig. 11. Young Mill Worker with Rotor of Eight Alternators, Cabot Street Mill. (*McClure's Magazine,* July 1906, XXVII:3, 293)

"proved to be one of the most beautiful and effective pieces ever played on the new instrument"[53] and became part of the standard repertoire of the Telharmonium.[54]

Since the instrument had only eight of its twelve originally intended pitch-shafts, there were four keys, and their relative minors, in which it was impossible to play. Financial constraints and the pressure to place the instrument in service to begin generating income forced this compromise in construction.[55]

There was further experimentation with the seventh harmonic in the dominant seventh chord. The equal-tempered flatted seventh is considerably sharper than the natural harmonic. Pierce found that the use of the latter sounded so smooth and well blended as actually to forfeit the need for any resolution. The equal-tempered dominant seventh gave a much stronger pull to the tonic third. Pierce began to add the tonic seventh harmonic to the final tonic chord, to enrich the timbre without detracting at all from the sense of rest and closure. As long as the timbre of the seventh was kept simple, and not too low in register, this worked very effectively.[56]

Pierce's first purpose in experimenting with harmonics was to devise methods of creating the tone colors of the various instruments. Early in 1906 as the instrument neared completion, it was sufficiently developed to allow the blending of tonal pigments to begin. That was an exciting moment for Pierce and his assistant musicians, who had recently been employed to acquire a performance technique on the new machine. As they already knew, the simplest tone was the flute, for which the fundamental sine wave alone served quite well. The clarinet was first imitated by a first and third harmonic, and later made more brilliant by the addition of a trace of the fourth harmonic. The oboe tone was developed by one of the assistants, Karl W. Schulz, who found that the upper harmonics were required to be very strong. There was only the slightest trace of first harmonic, a weak second harmonic, and a very robust third harmonic. The violin tone was not successfully synthesized and would continue to remain elusive. A reasonable approximation of the upper cello register was eventually achieved, though. The musicians easily produced a characteristic Telharmonium tone, consisting of the first eight harmonics blended in nearly equal amounts. They also developed clangorous chimes, achieved by combining harmonics of various fundamentals.[57]

In one respect the tuning of the Telharmonium proved to be too perfect. The octaves, not being tempered, were absolutely in tune. Mechanically mounted and locked to the same shaft, their phase did not vary so much as the tiniest fraction of a degree. These relentlessly perfect octaves did not sound like octaves at all. The upper note merely brightened the lower, and the two voices blended as one.[58] It is not for nothing that pianos, organs, and other instruments are tuned with slightly "stretched" octaves, which expand slightly as they extend to extremes of range.

THE COMPLETION OF THE SECOND TELHARMONIUM

The first Telharmonium, which Cahill had completed in Washington, remained in active service at Holyoke as the second instrument was being finished. It was much smaller, of course, the alternator section being only about 42 inches square and 14 feet long (Fig. 12). The entire apparatus weighed approximately 14,000 pounds. Unlike the new instrument, it had absolutely just intonation, scale-tone fifths included; however, it could be played only in a few keys.[59] It was still being used to test designs for the larger machine; it was also now impressed into fairly continuous service as a dependable demonstration instrument (Fig. 13)—Oscar T. Crosby was beginning to seek public display and press coverage.

It was this first experimental prototype that was displayed to the anonymous author who initially revealed the principles of Telharmony to a waiting world. This witness appears to have been Addams S. McAllister. He was 31 years of age and had served as an electrical engineer with Westinghouse Electric and several other companies; he had recently received a Ph.D. in electrical engineering from Cornell University. Already a prolific author of technical articles, McAllister was just completing *Alternating Current Motors,* which would become a standard textbook in the field and go through four editions. In 1905 he had become associate editor of *Electrical World,* a leading weekly technical journal. Apparently he had no musical skills or critical ability to speak of.[60]

The dazzling announcement was delivered in the pages of *Electrical World* on March 10, 1906. The Telharmonium was officially

Fig. 12. The Dynamos of the Washington Telharmonium, Cabot Street Mill.
(*McClure's Magazine,* July 1906, **XXVII**:3, 292)

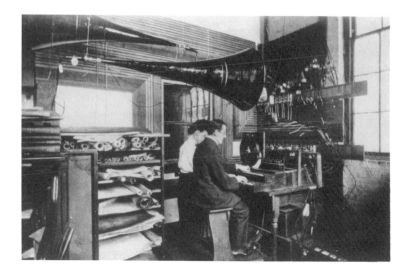

Fig. 13. Probably Mary H. Cahill with Edwin Hall Pierce at the Washington Telharmonium Keyboard, Cabot Street Mill. (*World's Work,* June 1906, 12:2, 7663)

christened, technically described, and pronounced ready for immediate commercial application. In a title-page editorial, the journal was duly appreciative of its privilege in describing the birth of the new art. Cahill's invention was trumpeted as the fulfillment of Edward Bellamy's dream in *Looking Backward:* "the music may be heard wherever a wire can be stretched."[61] Furthermore, the Telharmonium would also afford a finer, more delicate control than possible on any known instrument. Here spouted the first effervescent trickle of what would become a torrent of hyperbole. In three months, it was promised, the great central station instrument would be installed in New York, ready to supply 5,000 customers—restaurants, hotels, theatres, and so on. Smaller instruments would be manufactured for home use. Cahill had done more for the art of music than anyone since Pythagoras. It was hoped, the editor concluded abjectly, that those controlling the patents would exercise their rights moderately, so the public might benefit from a lowering of the costs of music.[62]

The article appearing elsewhere in the same issue of *Electrical World* reported few hard details of the Washington Telharmonium's construction, except that it had two keyboards and possessed a range of five octaves. Several types of mixing transformers were briefly described. "The tones are remarkably pure and beautiful,"[63] exulted the author. There was no difficulty to his ear in imitating all the instruments, violin included: "the auditor felt sure he heard the bow gliding across the string."[64] The expression devices on the instrument were enthralling, with the touch-control movable inductor and the various hand-operated dynamic controls serving to facilitate adroit attacks, *tremoli, crescendi* and *diminuendi*. The shafts of the instrument, which had originally been connected by belts, were now joined by steel gears, rendering the tuning "as permanent as it is perfect."[65] It seemed as if the instrument's response to the performer's feelings was superior to any instrument in existence except the violin, viola, and cello.[66]

A few tantalizing details of the new musical power plant destined for New York were also disclosed. There were eight 11-inch steel shafts bearing 145 alternators. The 60-foot mainframe was built of 18-inch steel girders set on brick foundations. Ten switchboard panels contained nearly 2,000 switches. The weight was 200 tons; the cost, $200,000. It was said to be for use by the New England Electric Music Co., which had been formed to install service in Boston. A second, identical machine was also reportedly under construction, and would be completed in several months.[67] The idea of constructing Telharmoniums for both Boston and New York would persist[68] until a machine was finally installed in New York. At that point, it would be all the promoters could do to run one.

The article had an immediate impact and was liberally quoted in the *New York Times* the next day.[69] A few periodicals lifted large portions of the text.[70]

The first exhibitions of the new, large machine were given the following week in the huge ballroom of the Hotel Hamilton (Fig. 14) in Holyoke. There, half a mile from Cahill's factory, were two telephone receivers with six-foot horns. Visitors could stand more than 100 feet away and listen to the demonstrations transmitted over ordinary telephone wires.[71] Reporters were welcome to savor the music, but found the Cahill brothers disinclined to divulge publicly the full particulars of their still-evolving invention. However, they proffered assurances that it was indeed quite ready for the market.

Fig. 14. Hotel Hamilton, Dwight Street between Race and Main Streets, Holyoke. (H. R. Page and Co., *Holyoke Illustrated,* Holyoke: The Company, 1891, unpaginated)

Furthermore, they pledged that their establishment would remain in Holyoke, despite the recent importunings of other communities for them to relocate, and in spite of the greater appreciation of their achievements in cities larger than the mill town.[72]

By this time Cahill employed about 50 workers, operating all manner of turret lathes, grinders, reamers, assemblers, and other forms of electrical manufacturing machinery. He contracted out rough castings, but all remaining work was done on the premises. Music was sent to an aggregation of 400 receivers right there in the shop to test the apparatus.[73] These receivers were partially buried in a long box filled with sawdust, from which they could be pulled and unmuffled to verify transmission.[74]

One reporter was awed at how the instrument "with absolute faithfulness produces the sound of bows on the strings, the clear bell tones of the brass instruments and the marvellous harmony of perfect orchestration, or the rare tones of an organ."[75] He further noted that Edward Bellamy's dream of telephone music in *Looking Backward* had become realized only a mile or two away from where the author penned his predictions 20 years ago, just across the Connecticut River at Chicopee. Another observer was impressed with the beauty of the flute tones, but felt the apparatus was "rather crude and the operation not as rapid as an organ."[76] Some of the reporters did not understand the machine in the slightest.[77]

At a demonstration for local and national reporters on the evening of March 20, a complete program was presented. Edwin Hall Pierce was assisted by Karl W. Schulz and H. Franklin Harris (Fig. 15):

Adagio from Trio, Op. 87 . . . . Beethoven
Mazurkas in B-flat and C . . . . Chopin
    Mr. Edwin H. Pierce, of Holyoke
Overture to William Tell . . . . Rossini
Träumerei . . . . Schumann
    Karl W. Schulz, of Springfield
Prelude to Ratcliff . . . . Mascagni
Narcissus . . . . Nevin
    Franklin Harris, of New York
Duet—First Violin Concerto . . . . Bériot
Duet—Violin Duet, Op. 39, No. 2 . . . . Spohr
    Messrs. Pierce and Schulz[78]

The music came "sweet and clear over the wires."[79]

George F. Cahill was willing to disclose a few impressive technical measurements. Some of the alternators had outputs of 15 to 19 horsepower (11,190 to 14,714 watts),[80] and the current at the receivers averaged one-twentieth of an ampere, sometimes growing as large as one ampere. This was far greater than that used or needed for the telephone, in which a receiver would respond to currents as low as six ten-trillionths (.00000000000006) of an ampere. As the flute, piano, horn, trumpet, and violin were paraded in "tones beautifully strong and clear,"[81] the "singular attack" of the Telharmonium was also noticed—and compared to "a hammer on a string."[82]

There was a buzz of speculation about the implications of the new invention. For the first time, anyone, anywhere would be able to have music cheaply. The Telharmonium would mark the age of musical democracy. It was yet another benefit of electricity, that great unifying force on which Americans had spent a billion dollars the previous year—for information, communication, light, heat, loco-

Fig. 15. Probably Karl W. Schulz and H. Franklin Harris at the Keyboard of the Washington Telharmonium, Cabot Street Mill. (*McClure's Magazine,* July 1906, **XXVII**:3, 294)

motion, and so on. Now music was to be added. It would not be the thin, raspy echoes of telephone concerts,[83] distant and unsatisfying novelties, but original production of strong and powerful tones of clear, sweet purity. Future Paderewskis would no longer appear in concert, but would labor in seclusion at central stations for electric music. And what would become of second-rate musicians when only the best were at the Telharmonic keyboard and could be dispensed at any time? What of the instruments now rendered obsolete? Was the piano doomed to join the clavichord and the harpsichord?[84]

THE STOCK PROSPECTUS OF THE NEW YORK ELECTRIC MUSIC CO.

The claims for the Telharmonium grew and multiplied. *Any* sound of *any* instrument, regardless of timbre, could be accurately synthesized by the central station instrument. Furthermore, a single performer at the keyboard could blend and combine these tones into the sound of a full band or orchestra. Such puffery was the siren song that lured investors in the prospectus of the New York Electric Music Co., which appeared in April.[85]

This prospectus, by Oscar T. Crosby, announced that the company was exclusively licensed to exploit the Cahill patents in New York State and had made "satisfactory arrangements for street subway [underground cable conduit] space in New York City."[86] It proposed to divide the state into six territories, each to be supplied with electric music by a separate operating company: New York, Buffalo, Rochester, Syracuse, Albany, and Newburgh. The new subsidiary companies would be organized once the company had demonstrated that the operation of the central station was practicable with music of good quality and in commercial demand. This would be done in New York, located at "a desirable Broadway situation, at a rental of about $30,000 a year."[87] The New York Electric Music Co. would retain control of the subsidiaries via majority stock ownership.[88]

Of the expanded $600,000 capitalization established the previous year, the company had raised $426,000 to date. Of liabilities, $200,000 had been earmarked for the Telharmonic machine. Another $326,000 would be required for license rights to Cahill, for payments to the New York Telephone Co. for the line it would soon lay on Broadway down to 23rd Street and up Fifth Avenue, and for other organizational expenses. The prospectus estimated that a total of $600,000 would be required to cover the central station and connections to customers. This was exclusive of the building and the distibuting wires, both of which were to be rented. Operating expenses would "probably be covered by the receipts from paid admission to the Central Station Concert Hall,"[89] and would safely amount to no more than 25% of gross receipts.[90]

The prospectus extrapolated estimates of profits from statistics on the sums of money expended on music in New York City in 1905. The general market was demonstrated by the employment of more than 25,000 musicians at a union rate of $5 per day.[91] At 300 working days per year, their annual pay exceeded $37,500,000. While not all musicians would be displaced, the implication that the Telharmonium would expropriate a considerable slice of their pie was clear. Furthermore, at least one-fourth of the 13,009 saloons and restaurants with liquor licenses would become direct paying customers or install coin-operated receivers. Present mechanical music slot machines averaged $1 per day in revenue. Deflecting these payments to the Telharmonium in, say, 3,252 saloons and restaurants per year would rake in $1,075,600. Such devices as automatic banjos and pianos were earning $900,000 per year, much of which would doubtlessly fall to the electric music system, which was greatly superior. Other flourishing musical industries would also lose revenue to the Telharmonium. The Edison company was selling 75,000 records a day at 30 cents, and the Victor Talking Machine Co. had sales in 1905 exceeding $7,500,000. Rented pianos were available from more than 200 companies in the New York area, and the largest firm had more than 8,000 in circulation, at an annual rental of $60 apiece.[92]

Crosby anticipated that some churches would purchase their own small Telharmoniums, along with a few theatres and private homes. The number of such customers was conservatively put at 200 annually for the first ten years, generating a profit of $1,000 each: "The number of pianos and organs now sold in New York City is very great. The Telharmonium will give a wider range of music than either."[93]

As a clincher, the prospectus then offered a list of probable customers, with the average rate per day to be anticipated:

	Rate per day
2827 Restaurants	$ 3.00
9350 Saloons	1.00
556 Hotels	10.00
1068 Churches	
657 Schools	.50
276 Hospitals, Sanitariums, Asylums, etc.	1.00
125 Theatres	
633 Boarding Houses	.50
1575 Dentists	.50
5070 Barber Shops	.50
5960 Doctors' Waiting Rooms	.30
624,000 Residences, including Apartments	.20[94]

In conclusion, the prospectus blared:

> These figures suggest a profit so enormous that there is a
> natural inclination to doubt them. However, when it is
> considered that this Company occupies toward the Telhar-
> monic art the same relation that the original Bell Telephone
> Company occupied towards the art of the telephone, and when
> the known results to the stockholders are born in mind, it
> would seem that these figures are not really extravagant.[95]

As a final reassurance, it was suggested that only a "small fraction"
of the indicated income would be necessary to ensure "annual dividends
of several hundred per cent on the entire authorized capital stock."[96] At
that time, $300,000 in stock was offered, and the right was reserved to
reduce or reject individual subscriptions. Only 20% of the price had to
be paid with the subscription.[97] Money was tight, after all, and the
company did not require all of the funds immediately.

Although otherwise inactive while Telharmonic attentions were
being focused on New York, the New England Electric Music Co.
had continued to raise money. Its outstanding stock now totaled
$206,500.[98]

While investment in the New York Electric Music Co. had swelled from $349,000 to $426,000 during the past year, Crosby and Todd had put $95,200 worth of shares in their own names. The block of stock controlled by the four syndicate managers had decreased to $249,000. The small remainder of shares was held by seven other investors.[99] One more time the company amended its charter to increase the authorized capital stock. The new limit was a stupendous $750,000, again at a par value of $100 per share.[100]

REPORTS ON THE TELHARMONIUM

Fulsome tributes to the Telharmonium continued to flow. Only rarely noted was its unique feature of equal temperament with the option of just intonation. Most writers, even those who were musicians, were inconversant with the young science of acoustics. Those who understood the issue realized that the public would have little patience for perplexing discourse on the relative merits of different systems of tuning. One reporter tackled the issue with the assertion that the equal-tempered scale was a "cheap compromise."[101] The substantial difference between F-sharp and G-flat was always brought out by violin virtuosi. So it was on the Telharmonium, enabling the recovery of more than one "lost chord," intervals whose absolute purity had been sullied by equal temperament. This restoration would be "as nearly so as is desirable,"[102] a necessary disclaimer in view of the fact that just intonation was available only for certain intervals in certain keys on the instrument.

The musically sensitive also noticed that, contrary to earlier reports, there was no "rasping of the bow, or *noise* of the piano 'hammer.' "[103] The very novelty of these sounds encouraged the judgment by some that the disappearance of such noise components imbued greater musical eloquence. Others missed the sound of "resin and catgut" and did not assert their absence necessarily as an advantage. Walter Damrosch, the great conductor of the New York Symphony Orchestra, journeyed to Holyoke to hear for himself. He complained that the tone was thin and needed further development.[104]

Predictions for growth soared. In the mistaken belief that Telharmonic currents were as small as, and compatible with, the telephone, residents as distant as Buffalo or Washington were promised long-distance access to the music through their telephone systems. Soon there would be not one but four separate circuits: ragtime, dance music, operatic or classical music, and sacred music.[105]

After several months' touting to the world the expressive delicacy of the instrument remained a wonder to some. Its sympathy to the performer's soul was perhaps exceeded only by the violin. The three musicians practicing at the new machine—Pierce, Schulz, and Harris—confided their delight to one reporter that "all the varying meanings and emotions of classical music may be brought out artistically."[106] This machine was truly "as sensitive to moods and emotions as a living thing."[107] After all, the individual touch of each player could be detected at a receiver many miles away.

RAY STANNARD BAKER

Of all the glowing reports of the Telharmonium, one in particular captured public notice and attention as did no other. The description by Ray Stannard Baker in the July 1906 issue of *McClure's Magazine* fixed the machine firmly on the horizon.

Journalist Ray Stannard Baker had begun his career with the *Chicago News-Record* by following and reporting on Coxey's Army as it marched in 1894 from Massillon, Ohio, all the way to Washington, D.C. He then covered the Pullman strike and riots south of Chicago. His clear, vivid prose limned more than social problems, however. Amid many other assignments in the 1890s, he was given a daily column to write, "Shop Talk on the Wonders of the Crafts." This was designed to appeal to the workers in Chicago's mills and factories. Having received a good education in science and mathematics (where he learned the importance of careful observation, so valuable to the reporter), Baker was able to write scores of 1,500-word articles on every possible industrial subject: saws and saw making, wood pulp and paper, drop forging, Bessemer steel, and many others. These were later compiled into Baker's first book, published by the *News-Record* without his knowledge, consent, or byline.[108]

Baker continued to write occasionally on science and invention after he joined the sensation of the magazine publishing world, *McClure's Magazine,* in New York in 1898. This bright, fresh periodical of interviews, biography, and fiction made others look stodgy by comparison. Most of the contributors were young— Stephen Crane, Jack London, and William Allen White were all in their twenties. Late in 1901 Baker covered Marconi's experiments in St. John's, Newfoundland. He witnessed the first wireless telegraph transmission, the letter *S* received from Cornwall, England.[109]

In 1903 *McClure's Magazine* became a leading muckraking journal, scathingly exposing political and social evils. Baker, along with staff authors Ida M. Tarbell and Lincoln Steffens, launched this crusade against corruption, in which public interest eventually began to dwindle around 1906.[110]

In the spring of 1906 there was a falling out between the editor, S. S. McClure, and some of the staff, including Baker. They left and took over the *American Magazine* in July. That same month appeared "New Music for an Old World," the last article Ray Stannard Baker would ever write for *McClure's.*[111]

After expressing wonder at its astonishing physical construction, so unlike any other musical instrument, Baker marveled at how there was no suggestion of musical sounds from the whirring dynamos themselves. Switchboard clicks could be heard, even the pop of a flashing spark, but no notes emanated from the noisome machinery.[112]

What appealed above all to Baker was the prospect that no longer would the best music be limited to the rich. Baker predicted that this new means of sending music to the people would usher in the democratization of music. Museums and printing had done much to bring great art to Everyman, and free libraries had placed the best books in the hands of any citizen who wished to read them. But the very best music, so intangible and so expensive to produce, had been until now the province of the wealthy. Poor music could be heard anywhere, but grand opera was a social pastime pumped up by the rich. Its lack of accessibility to all accounted for the regrettably glacial development of musical taste in America. But now even a benighted sod farmer 100 miles from the Telharmonic central station would have the ideal standard of the finest music. Small towns would be given the same high-class concerts available in the big cities.[113]

Baker did not hesitate to predict the effect on musicians. The Telharmonium would reduce the danger of strikes, since ten or twenty performers would be able to supply thousands with music. Today it required that many musicians just to fill the violin section of the Boston Symphony Orchestra. It would not, however, seriously endanger the present employment of musicians. Rather, it would generate greater public appreciation of music, encouraging more to enter musical careers. After all, the automobile had not displaced the horse, and neither had the electric light obliterated the use of kerosene lamps and candles. Furthermore, Baker noted with rare perceptiveness for a nonmusician, these "peculiar and beautiful tones may in their very sweetness and perfection fail to please every one. As artists and architects know, there is a certain appeal to the senses in that which is imperfect and irregular."[114] People would never give up the old, especially since observing the humanity of performing musicians was so very charming and appealing.[115]

Baker had gone to Holyoke, where he was given a demonstration of the Washington Telharmonium. He was taken to the Hotel Hamilton: "When the music began, it seemed to fill the entire room with singularly clear, sweet, perfect tones."[116] It was enthralling indeed that the notes flowed from a paper horn, much like that of a phonograph, but without a trace of the scratching and scraping of that machine. Even more miraculous, there was no discernable sonic element of the noisy revolving dynamos Baker had seen back at the Cahill laboratory half a mile away. It was pure music and it seemed to spring from nothingness—just a pair of wires.[117]

Baker listened to selections for an hour, ranging from Bach and Schubert to *The Arkansas Traveller* and ragtime. Of this last, he pronounced the music less than a success. Here was no great flaw, since it was more important that the machine be fitted to the higher classes of music. He was duly impressed with the close imitations of instruments, except that the piano and violin were not yet perfect. He was able to detect the subtle shift in character when H. Franklin Harris replaced Edwin Hall Pierce at the keyboard. Baker was struck most by the difference in quality of the Telharmonium from any other instrument "in the fullness, roundness, completeness of its tones."[118]

Cahill admitted to Baker that he was not fond of the popular name "Telharmonium" and preferred to call his instrument the "Dynamophone."[119] At the interview, the inventor sat for a photographic portrait (Fig. 16). Another was taken of his brother Arthur (Fig. 17).

Fig. 16. Thaddeus Cahill in His Office at the Water Power Building Near the Cabot Street Mill. (*McClure's Magazine,* July 1906, XXVII:3, 296)

Fig. 17. Arthur T. Cahill with a Final Tone Mixer, Cabot Street Mill. (*McClure's Magazine,* July 1906, XXVII:3, 295)

Summing up Cahill's accomplishments, the journalist was appreciative of their breadth, although his understanding of Cahill's limited financial role was imperfect:

> and few inventors have so combined the genius to produce a machine, with the legal knowledge to protect it with patents, and the business acumen to raise the very great sums of money necessary to carry on the experiments, which have cost a fortune, and to build a commercial plant which has cost $200,000 more.[120]

Plans for disassembling the second Telharmonium and moving it to New York had begun. Baker disclosed the news that the machine was being installed near the Metropolitan Opera House,[121] which was located at the northwest corner of Broadway at 39th Street. The plan was to increase the Telharmonic cables from one pair to four, to offer classical, operatic, sacred, and popular music.[122] A further genre to be developed was "sleep-music," which Cahill felt to have been unduly neglected by composers. The inventor dreamed of the day when all might fall asleep to lullabies and be awakened by stirring music the next morning. Baker confirmed that the Telharmonium was "indeed, peculiarly adapted to the sweet, soft strains of sleep-music. It would be difficult to produce more exquisite effects than Dr. Cahill gets in such selections as 'Träumerei.' "[123]

OFF TO NEW YORK

The Cahill laboratory employees and a few guests celebrated the completion of their new Telharmonium at the ballroom of the Hotel Hamilton on June 8. The machine gave its last recital in Holyoke, "of an exceedingly high class,"[124] before being dismantled and shipped to New York.

The transport and reassembly of the machine took most of the summer. Press reports continued to herald the tremendous new supply of music, which would flow freely as gas or water.[125] The site selected was the Broadway Building, at the northeast corner of Broadway at 39th Street. Directly across 39th Street was the glittering Casino Theatre, one of the leading establishments on the

Great White Way. The flamboyant stretch along Broadway from 37th Street to 42nd Street was known as the Rialto, the heart of the theatre district. The finest hotels and fanciest bars drew a constant surge of crowds, cars, and lacquered carriages.[126]

Public interest in the Telharmonium was fanned by the spokesmen for the New York Electric Music Co. It was already a "proven proposition," they said. After flooding all the city's theatres, hotels, and homes with Telharmony, the open air was next: contracts would be secured for furnishing the parks and piers with music of all styles any time after nine o'clock in the morning.[127]

Meanwhile, the stringing of the cables through the streets of New York began in July. Using the conduits (Fig. 18) and poles of the New York Telephone Co., in accordance with the contract that had been signed a year earlier, separate wires for the Telharmonium were run alongside the telephone lines.[128]

In a bid to temper the mounting expectations of the public, Oscar T. Crosby cautioned that the musicians would at first be hampered by a difficult new keyboard with no fewer than 48 keys to the octave. There was only one such keyboard and the musicians were not used to it. Nevertheless, the machinery installation was nearly complete, and a few private recitals would probably be given about the beginning of August in the "beautifully fitted"[129] music room.[130]

THE EASTERN CAHILL TELHARMONIC CO.

On August 2 the fourth corporation devoted to the exploitation of electrical music was formed in Maine. The stated purposes of the Eastern Cahill Telharmonic Co. were as follows: to acquire rights to Cahill's inventions; to acquire equipment for generating music electrically; to run such a business at a profit; and, to acquire telephone lines, conduits, and poles. The corporation declared it would not conduct a telephone business in the state of Maine, but reserved the right to do so elsewhere where permitted. Furthermore, the corporation proposed to acquire franchises in order to do business.[131]

With the apparent success in New York so near at hand, the new corporation was created to offer investors a vehicle to get in on the ground floor at other eastern locations—conveniently unnamed in

Fig. 18. Laying Telephone Conduits Underground. (Herbert N. Casson, *The History of the Telephone,* Chicago: A. C. McClurg and Co., 1911, f. 238)

the incorporation documents. There was plenty of stock authorized for sale—$3 million worth, of which nine shares at $100 par had been spoken for by the three directors. Frederick C. Todd spoke for 993 shares; Crosby presumably acquired a like amount.[132] The president was Charles McHenry Howard, a prominent Baltimore lawyer and great-grandson of Francis Scott Key.[133]

The new corporation proudly took its place with the College of Physiognomy and Sublime Wisdom of Life, the Conscience Law Corporation, and other new Maine corporations. They were forming at the rate of hundreds per month. The ventures covered all bases—mining, amusements, women's wear, mussel raising, oil, patent medicines, synthetic coal, the propagation of cats, even the development of two republics. Maine had cornered the market on freak corporations, with the lowest charter fees and annual franchise taxes in the nation. Almost no questions were asked. Most paid their assessments for the first year and then let their charters expire for want of unpaid taxes, generally less than $25. The annual bite for the Eastern Cahill Telharmonic Co. would nearly double to $175 after the legislature raised the rates in 1907.[134]

The birth of the new company was reported in the press,[135] immediately after which the corporation increased its board of directors from three to nine. The new directors would thus be shielded from disclosure and public view, at least until the annual report was filed a year later.[136]

As the opening in New York neared, reaction to the Telharmonium reports began to come in from overseas. The invention was admired if not always understood. One correspondent in London wished for Cahill to install the Telharmonium at Covent Garden, from which the hugely popular opera *Eugene Onegin* could thus be transmitted to people's homes.[137]

NOTES

1. Constance McLaughlin Green, *Holyoke, Massachusetts: A Case History of the Industrial Revolution in America*, New Haven: Yale University Press, 1939, 1, 19–22.

2. Ella Merkel DiCarlo, *Holyoke—Chicopee: A Perspective*, Holyoke: Transcript-Telegram, 1982, 163; Green, 24–26, 38–39.

3. Green, 62–64, 66, 73.

4. *Ibid.,* 96–97.

5. *Ibid.,* 151–153, 174.

6. *Ibid.,* 68, 80, 145, 164–165, 174.

7. *Ibid.,* 232, 224.

8. "Music First Transmitted by Wires in Holyoke," *Holyoke Daily Transcript and Telegram,* April 11, 1931, 4.

9. Transcript Publishing Company, *Holyoke City Directory, 1903,* Holyoke: Price and Lee Company, Publishers, The Company, 1903, 68–69; Transcript Publishing Company, *Holyoke City Directory, 1904,* Holyoke: Price and Lee Company, Publishers, The Company, 1904, 70.

10. Green, 228, 192–193.

11. *Ibid.,* 229.

12. New England Electric Music Company, Annual Report for 1903, April 17, 1903, filed at the Office of the Secretary of State, Trenton, N.J., n.d., 3.

13. Oscar Terry Crosby, *Tibet and Turkestan,* New York: G. P. Putnam's Sons, The Knickerbocker Press, 1905, 127.

14. *Ibid.,* 12.

15. *Ibid.,* 48.

16. "Crosby, Oscar Terry," *The National Cyclopedia of American Biography,* vol. XXXV, New York: James T. White and Company, 1949, 84; *ibid.,* 99.

17. *Ibid.,* 163.

18. "American Explorer Visits Central Asia," *New York Times,*" January 31, 1904, pt. 1, 4.

19. Ruth Douglass, "Hogan Brothers Knew Thaddaeus [*sic*] Cahill," Worksheet for article published in *Holyoke Daily Transcript-Telegram,* May 8, 1968, R.W., 1.

20. "Music by Wire," *Boston Evening Transcript,* March 30, 1904, 7; "Bostonians May Soon Have Music 'Delivered by Wire' at Their Homes," *Boston Post,* March 31, 1904, 12; "A Bellamy Dream Realized," *Springfield Republican,* April 3, 1904, 17; "Music for the Million," *Holyoke Daily Transcript,* April 4, 1904, H.P.L. Biography; n.p.

21. "A Bellamy Dream Realized," 17.

22. *Ibid.*

23. George H. Picard, "Music for the Million," *Amsterdam* [N.Y.] *Recorder,* July 13, 1907, S.C., 9.

24. Edwin Hall Pierce, "A Colossal Experiment in 'Just Intonation,'" *Musical Quarterly,* July 1924, X:3, 327.

25. *Ibid.*

26. Letter from Wm. J. Hogan to Ruth Douglass, March 7, 1968, R.W., 1.

27. Personal interview with Margaret Eleanor Cahill Schwartz, Rochester, Vt., August 29, 1990; Douglass, 1.

28. Letter from Wm. J. Hogan, 1.

29. Douglass, 1.

30. New England Electric Music Company, Annual Report for 1904, April 21, 1904, filed at the Office of the Secretary of State, Trenton, N.J., April 27, 1904, 3.

31. New England Electric Music Company, Certificate of Increase of Capital Stock, May 23, 1904, filed and recorded at the Office of the Secretary of State, Trenton, N.J., May 24, 1904, 2, 4.

32. Letter from O. T. Crosby, President, New York Electric Music Company, to F. P. Fish, President, American Telephone and Telegraph Co., December 16, 1904, A.T.T.A. 520155, 1.

33. New York Electric Music Company, Certificate of Incorporation, August 10, 1904, received and recorded at the Office of the Hudson County Clerk, Jersey City, N.J., August 10, 1904, filed and recorded at the Office of the Secretary of State, Trenton, N.J., August 10, 1904, 4, 2; New York Electric Music Company, Annual Report for 1904, August 12, 1904, filed at the Office of the Secretary of State, Trenton, N.J., August 12, 1904, 3.

34. Pacific Coast Telharmonic Company, Articles of Incorporation, September 3, 1904, filed and recorded at the Office of the Secretary of State, Olympia, Wash., September 12, 1904, 1, 3; George Fauth and James S. Whedbee, appraisers, Frederick Charles Todd: Inventory: Personal Estate, December 10, 1918, filed and recorded at Baltimore County Orphans Court, Baltimore, Md., "Baltimore County: Inventories, WJP #42," Maryland State Archives CR 9107, 538.

35. Letter from O. T. Crosby, 3.

36. *Ibid.*, 1–3.

37. "Fish, Frederick Perry," *The National Cyclopaedia of American Biography,* vol. XXVI, New York: James T. White and Company, 1937, 202; "Frederick P. Fish, Noted Lawyer, Dies," *New York Times,* November 7, 1930, 25; Charles W. Price, "Remarkable Progress in Electrical Development," *New York Times Annual Financial Review,* January 8, 1905, 22.

38. "Fish, Frederick Perry," 202.

39. Letter from F. P. Fish, President, American Telephone and Telegraph Co., to O. T. Crosby, December 24, 1904, A.T.T.A. 520156, Pres. L. B. 37/86, 1.

40. Letter from Oscar T. Crosby, President, New York Electric Music Co., to Charles F. Cutler, President, January 27, 1907, A.T.T.A. 16878, L. B. 46/427, 2, 3.

41. New York Electric Music Company, Certificate of Increase of Capital Stock, April 25, 1905, filed and recorded at the Office of the Secretary of State, Trenton, N.J., May 2, 1905, 1, 2, 4; New York Electric Music Company, Annual Report for 1905, April 25, 1905, filed at the Office of the Secretary of State, Trenton, N.J., n.d., 3; "Incorporations 1905," *Presto,* January 4, 1906, 47.

42. New England Electric Music Company, Annual Report for 1905, April 27, 1905, filed at the Office of the Secretary of State, Trenton, N.J., n.d., 3.

43. "1905—A Retrospect of the Year," *New York Times Annual Financial Review,* January 7, 1906, 2; Robert L. O'Connell, "Post Haste," *American Heritage,* September/October 1989, 40:6, 82.

44. "Uperfected [*sic*] Invention," *Holyoke Daily Transcript,* May 25, 1905, 3.

45. Letter from Rod[eric Pierce] to Jim [James Edward Pierce], June 12, 1974, J.E.P., R.W., 1.

46. Edwin Hall Pierce, *Edwin H. Pierce, Teacher of Piano, Violin, Harmony and Composition; Also Sight-Reading for Singers,* Auburn, N.Y.: The Author, 1898?, 4; "Pierce, Edwin Hall," *The Macmillan Encyclopedia of Music and Musicians,* New York: The Macmillan Company, 1938, 1429.

47. Transcript Publishing Company, *Holyoke City Directory, 1902,* Holyoke: Price and Lee Company, Publishers, The Company, 1902, 320, 665.

48. "304th Organ Recital," *Holyoke Daily Transcript,* April 25, 1901, 3.

49. Transcript Publishing Company, *Holyoke City Directory, 1904,* Holyoke: Price and Lee Company, Publishers, The Company, 1904, 343.

50. Personal interview with James Edward Pierce, Echo Lake Farm, Great Spring Road, Smithfield, Va., April 23, 1983.

51. James Edward Pierce, "James E. Pierce and Frances Hall Married July 11, 1866, in Auburn, N.Y.," List of family birthdates, April 23, 1983, R.W., 1; James Edward Pierce, "Item Regarding Pioneer Inventor of Electric Music and His Association with the Pierce Family," August 1970, typewritten, J.E.P., S.I., 1; Letter from James E. Pierce to Cynthia Hoover, Smithsonian Institution, May 25, 1974, S.I., 1; Letter from James E. Pierce, Smithfield, Va., n.d., postmarked March 30, 1983, 1; Personal interview with James Edward Pierce, April 23, 1983.

52. Edwin Hall Pierce, "A Colossal Experiment in 'Just Intonation,' " 328.

53. *Ibid.,* 329.

54. *Ibid.,* 328–329; Thaddeus Cahill?, "The Cahill Electrical Music," 1906?, typewritten, M.C.S., 2; Daniel Gregory Mason, "Electrically Generated Music," *New Music Review,* March 1907, 6:64, 240–241.

55. E. H. Pierce, 328, 331.

56. *Ibid.,* 329–330; Mason, 241.

57. E. H. Pierce, 328; Mason, 239–240.

58. E. H. Pierce, 330.

59. Arthur T. Cahill, "The Original and Scientifically Priceless Cahill Electric Music Instrument; The First Instrument That Created Music from the Electrical Waves of Alternating Current Generators," n.d. [rubber stamp: "AUG 31, 1951"], mimeographed and typewritten, A.T.T.A. M-l,

1; E. H. Pierce, 329; Thaddeus Cahill?, "The Cahill Electrical Music," supplement, September 21, 1910, typewritten, M.C.S., 6.

60. "McAllister, Addams Stratton," *The National Cyclopaedia of American Biography,* vol. XV, New York, James T. White and Company, 1916, 75–76, f. 75; "McAllister, Addams Stratton," *Who Was Who in America,* vol. 2, Chicago: The A. N. Marquis Company, 1950; "Addams S. McAllister," *New York Times,* November 27, 1946, 25.

61. "The Art of Telharmony," *Electrical World,* March 10, 1906, XLVII:10, 509.

62. *Ibid.,* 509–510. There are published reports that Leopold Stokowski signed this editorial, but he did not. He was a 24-year-old church organist in New York at the time; he did see the Telharmonium, according to Otto Luening. However, there are no traces of anything written by Stokowski on the instrument. Herbert Russcol, *The Liberation of Sound: An Introduction to Electronic Music,* Englewood Cliffs, N.J.: Prentice-Hall, 1972, 33; William Ander Smith, *The Mystery of Leopold Stokowski,* Rutherford, N.J.: Fairleigh Dickinson University Press, 1990, 198–199; Telephone interview with Otto Luening, New York, N.Y., September 21, 1992; Letter from Edwin E. Heilakka, Curator, Stokowski Collection, Curtis Institute of Music, Philadelphia, Pa., September 28, 1992, 1.

63. "The Generating and Distributing of Music by Means of Alternators," *Electrical World,* March 10, 1906, XLVll:10, 520.

64. *Ibid.*

65. *Ibid.*

66. *Ibid.,* 519–520.

67. *Ibid.,* 520–521.

68. "Dr. Thaddeus Cahill," *Electrical World,* March 31, 1906, XLVII:13, 656.

69. "To Manufacture Music by Electrical Device," *New York Times,* March 11, 1906, 4.

70. "The Generating and Distributing of Music by Means of Alternators," *Musical Age,* March 17, 1906, LIII:7, 596–597; Century's Musical Wonder," *Holyoke Daily Transcript,* March 21, 1906, 8; "Electrical Music," *Scientific American,* March 31, 1906, XCIV:13, 268–269.

71. "Electrical Music," *Holyoke Daily Transcript,* March 13, 1906, 4.

72. "Makes Electric Music," *Springfield Evening Union,* March 13, 1906, 4.

73. "Wonder Musical Machine Invented by Holyoke Men," *Boston Post,* March 18, 1906, 29; "Electrical Music," *Scientific American,* March 31, 1906, XCIV:13, 268.

74. Marion Melius, "Music by Electricity," *World's Work,* June 1906, XII:2, 7661.

75. *Ibid.*

76. "Death of Inventor Recalls Odd Machine," *Springfield Republican,* April 14, 1934, 4.

77. "Music First Transmitted By Wires in Holyoke," *Holyoke Daily Transcript and Telegram,* April 11, 1931, 4.

78. "Century's Musical Wonder," *Holyoke Daily Transcript,* March 21, 1906, 8; William Hand Browne, Jr., "Orchestral Music from a Dynamo," *Harper's Weekly,* 50:14, 493.

79. *Ibid.*

80. 1 hp = 748 w.

81. "Cahill Company Gives Concert," *Springfield Republican,* March 21, 1906, 8.

82. "Electrical Music," *Scientific American,* March 31, 1906, XCIV:13, 268; Thomas Commerford Martin, "The Telharmonium: Electricity's Alliance with Music," *American Monthly Review of Reviews,* April 1906, XXXIII:4, 422.

83. Telephone concerts continued to be presented and spark interest. On April 6, the opera *Faust* was performed in Cheyenne, Wyo., and transmitted to a convention of electricians in Salt Lake City. "Audience 600 Miles Away," *New York Times,* April 8, 1906, pt. 2, 1.

84. Martin, 420–423; "Science and Invention: Electrical Music," *Literary Digest,* April 14, 1906, XXXII:15, 566–567.

85. "Dr. Cahill's Telharmonium," *Talking Machine World,* April 15, 1906, II:4, 42.

86. Oscar T. Crosby, *New York Electric Music Company* [Stock Prospectus], New York: April 1906? [penciled on cover: "W. J. Hammer, August 17-'06"], S.L., 6.

87. *Ibid.*

88. *Ibid.*

89. *Ibid.,* 7.

90. *Ibid.*

91. The best orchestras paid $35 to $40 or more per week, an enviable salary protected from foreign invasion by union regulations that forbade membership until six-months' residence had been completed. With rehearsals and extras for section leaders and the conductor, the cost of a full orchestra concert ran from $600 to $1,000. "Orchestras Divide Spoils," *New York Evening Mail,* November 19, 1906, 6.

92. Crosby, *New York Electric Music Company,* 7–8.

93. *Ibid.,* 8.

94. *Ibid.*

95. *Ibid.,* 9.

96. *Ibid.*

97. *Ibid.,* 9, 11.

98. New England Electric Music Company, Annual Report for 1906, April 20, 1906, filed at the Office of the Secretary of State, Trenton, N.J., n.d., 3.

99. New York Electric Music Company, Annual Report for 1906,

May 8, 1906, filed at the Office of the Secretary of State, Trenton, N.J., n.d., 3.

100. New York Electric Music Company, Certificate of Increase of Capital Stock, May 7, 1906, filed and recorded at the Office of the Secretary of State, Trenton, N.J., May 18, 1906, 4, 1.

101. E. E. Higgins, "A Wonderful Musical Instrument," *Success Magazine,* May 1906, 9:144, N.Y.P.L. *MKY Box, n.p.

102. *Ibid.*

103. *Ibid.*

104. "The Telharmonium," *Outlook,* May 5, 1906, 83:18, 10; "Miss Terry Here Again," *New-York Daily Tribune,* January 27, 1907, pt. IV, 6.

105. *Ibid.*; Melius, 7662.

106. Melius, 7661.

107. *Ibid.*

108. Ray Stannard Baker, *American Chronicle,* New York: Charles Scribner's Sons, 1945, 6–44, 50–53; Robert C. Bannister, Jr., "Baker, Ray Stannard," *Dictionary of American Biography,* supp. 4, 1946–1950, New York: Charles Scribner's Sons, 1974, 46.

109. Baker, 73, 84, 77–78, 85, 99, 148; "Marconi Hailed on 80th Anniversary of Radio Message," *New York Times,* December 19, 1982, pt. 1, 56.

110. Bannister, 46–47; "Ray S. Baker Dead; Noted Biographer," *New York Times,* July 13, 1946, 15.

111. Baker, 211, 220; Bannister, 47.

112. Ray Stannard Baker, "New Music for an Old World," *McClure's Magazine,* July, 1906, XXVII:3, 291.

113. *Ibid.,* 291, 293–294.

114. *Ibid.,* 301.

115. *Ibid.*

116. *Ibid.,* 295.

117. *Ibid.,* 295, 297.

118. *Ibid.,* 297.

119. *Ibid.,* 301.

120. *Ibid.,* 298.

121. *Ibid.,* 291, 295.

122. *Ibid.,* 300.

123. *Ibid.,* 293.

124. "Machine Goes to New York," *Holyoke Daily Transcript,* June 9, 1906, 4.

125. "Electric Music Factory to Open Soon," *Musical Age,* June 23, 1906, LIV:8, 389.

126. "Electric Music Generating System," *Talking Machine World,* July 15, 1906, II:7, 34; Byron, "Every day scene . . . ," photograph, November 1906, P.C.M.M.L. G. NEW YC Broa; Lloyd Morris, *Incredible New York,* New York: Random House, 1951, 182.

127. "Electric Music Generating System," 34.

128. *Ibid.*

129. "Electro-Music Ready on August First," *Musical Age,* July 14, 1906, LIV:11, 486.

130. *Ibid.*

131. Eastern Cahill Telharmonic Company, Certificate of Organization of a Corporation, August 2, 1906, received and filed at the Office of the Secretary of State, recorded in vol. 56, p. 537, Augusta, Me., August 3, 1906.

132. *Ibid.,* 4–5; Fauth and Whedbee, 538.

133. "Chas. M'H. Howard, Baltimore Lawyer," *New York Times,* May 20, 1942, 20.

134. "Maine the Birthplace of Freak Corporations," *New York Times,* June 23, 1907, pt. 5, 9; "Costs More to Incorporate in Maine," *Music Trade Review,* June 8, 1907, XLIV:23, 9.

135. "Telharmonic Incorporates in Maine," *Musical Age,* August 11, 1906, LV:2, 33; "Incorporation Filed in Maine," *Music Trade Review,* August 18, 1906, XLIII:7, 11; "1906 Incorporations Reached into Billions," *New York Times,* January 6, 1907, pt. 5, 20.

136. Eastern Cahill Telharmonic Company, Certificate of Change, August 6, 1906, received and filed at the Office of the Secretary of State, recorded in vol. 5, p. 351, Augusta, Me., August 7, 1906.

137. "The Trade in England," *Talking Machine World,* August 15, 1906, II:8, 17.

CHAPTER III

THE TECHNOLOGY OF THE SECOND TELHARMONIUM

Thaddeus Cahill's continuing efforts to patent his electric music inventions were protracted and arduous. They resumed in 1901 and did not cease until 1919. The details of these applications, and the lengthy responses, are given in Appendix 1: "The Four Later Telharmonium Patents." The often theoretical elements and legal considerations bore little direct or causal connection to the practical, everyday events that marked the establishment of the Telharmonium as a working instrument.

In this chapter a familiarization with the underpinnings of Telharmonium design and technology will illuminate the narrative to follow. A limited amount of information taken from the extended patent descriptions is included here as helpful in understanding basic design concepts. The first problems Cahill tackled were gearing the pitch shafts, producing virtual sine waves, fabricating receivers, and wiring the alternators. By early 1902 he had arrived at suitable methods.

TOWARD PERFECT PITCH: TOOTHED GEARING

In the earlier design the instrument was liable to get out of tune due to belt slip. Cahill now resorted to a system of toothed gearing connecting the driveshaft with the pitch-shafts, making them impossible to drift. The inventor contrived numerous and elaborate gearing systems and combinations, endeavoring to cover all possible arrangements, even an instrument in just intonation. He found that it was desirable to reduce the speed of rotation of the higher-frequency pitch-shafts by constructing the alternators on them with more teeth. They could then be geared down to be driven at a slower speed and still generate the required upper frequencies. This also helped to bring some of the pitches closer to those of ideal equal temperament—something that could be attained with twelve absolutely identical sets of alternators only by driving some with impractically large gears having some 400 teeth. Numerous tooth and gearing variations were possible even as the relative angular velocities were kept the same.[1]

Cahill's original 1902 gearing design, likely employed for the second Telharmonium, is shown in the upper portion of Fig. 19. The twelve pitch-shafts (1a, 1b, 1c, etc.) were driven in four groups of three, by two gears (9, 10) mounted on each end of the driveshaft (8), powered in the center by an electric motor (11). A number followed by "T" indicates the number of teeth on the gear. In Case A, corresponding alternators among all pitch-shafts were identical, hence their production of different frequencies was accomplished solely by a considerable difference in the number of teeth on the two drive gears. In Case B, the six higher (right-hand) pitch-shafts had alternators with 50% more teeth than the lower shafts, requiring very little difference. In Case C, the six higher shafts had $1/3$ more teeth, also requiring a relatively small difference. Cahill came to prefer Cases B and C for large machines.[2]

The lower portion of Fig. 19, a later design, became Cahill's ideal arrangement for large machines.[3] All twelve pitch-shafts were driven directly by the driveshaft. Connecting several pitch-shafts in series through intermeshing gears degraded the tuning of sensitive intervals, especially the perfect fifth.[4] Gears with small teeth and high speeds of rotation caused insuperable difficulties and had to be avoided at all times.[5] It was fortunate that the pitch-shafts of a large machine demonstrated a considerable stabilizing, or fly-wheel, effect. If the drive motor were well built to run at a constant speed and powered by a stable, constant voltage, then the "variations in angular velocity will not be noticed by the average listener."[6]

Cahill was careful not to claim the approbation of the unaverage, professional musician. In discussing the matter of pitch variations in

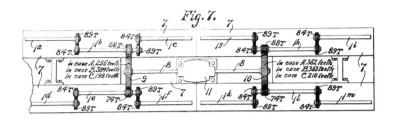

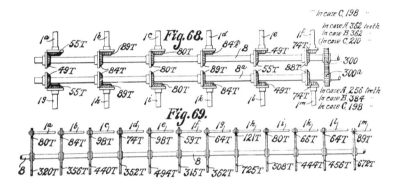

Fig. 19. Toothed Gearing Arrangements. TOP: Cahill's original design, likely used for the second Telharmonium. BOTTOM: the ultimate preferred design, all pitch-shafts driven directly by the driveshaft, probably employed for the third Telharmonium. (U.S. Patent 1,295,691, drawings sheets 12, 43)

his third patent, he indicated that the degree of perfection attained was not unassailably perfect: "I have not found the changes in speed sufficiently great to affect the quality of the notes or chords, nor indeed to be discoverable with the unaided senses, by the average man."[7] The unaided ear of a trained musician, however, can detect very, very slight pitch changes indeed, a facility that would bedevil synthesizer makers 60 years later.

TOWARD THE PERFECT ALTERNATOR: VIRTUAL SINE WAVES PRODUCED DIRECTLY

In early designs the rheotomes had produced waveforms that varied greatly from the ideal sine wave. They had been filtered by four successive inductive transfers into an approximation of a sine wave. In designing the commercial machine, Cahill turned to alternators that generated waves very nearly sinusoidal, such that no purifying circuitry was necessary. While they may not have been perfect sine waves, they were at least so nearly devoid of upper odd-numbered harmonics as to render filtering devices unnecessary. He learned that it was highly important for the teeth and pole pieces of the alternators to be equally spaced. Otherwise the waveforms would have unequal periodicity, causing frequency changes. He was able to cut rotor teeth successfully using a large, well-built gear-cutting machine with an extremely accurate indexing mechanism, worm-wheel, and worm.[8]

The signals were found to suffer a shift in waveform as they were transmitted to distant receivers: the higher harmonics were lost to some extent. With good lines this was not so serious a difficulty as to prevent practical distribution. By 1904 he could successfully distribute sounds almost as loud as those of an orchestra along a circuit of more than 100 miles in length. Just as for the toothed gearing, the inventor developed lengthy and elaborate details of alternator construction. He was careful to disclaim, however, the invention of any improvement in the alternator. All the means he had employed were well known in the art, and he had merely selected the most suitable of these techniques for his purposes.[9]

TOWARD THE PERFECT RECEIVER: A TELEPHONIC VIBRATION-TRANSLATING DEVICE

Earlier designs had specified a soundboard driven by electromagnets as a receiver of the musical vibrations. This arrangement had two drawbacks: it suffered from changes in response due to temperature and humidity variations, and it drew considerable power to operate.

In an improved version, developed by 1902, Cahill fitted an ordinary telephone receiver with a large horn. The diaphragm of the receiver was made of soft iron, but only about $1/100$ of an inch thick—thinner than those customarily used in receivers of the day. This bettered the bass response, as did the use of a horn at least five or six feet long.[10]

TOWARD IDEAL VOICING: INDEPENDENT WIRING OF ALTERNATOR ELECTROMAGNETS

Cahill had first wired the field electromagnets of alternators in series, with no provision for varying the intensity of excitation of the electromagnetic field. The power output of each alternator was thus fixed. Cahill began in the early 1900s to wire each electromagnet independently and put a rheostat control in the circuit. Hence, the intensity of excitation could be altered, enabling the instrument to be voiced. Each alternator could be set for an ideal power output to compensate for the tendency of receiver diaphragms to produce some tones at different volumes.[11]

THE SECOND TELHARMONIUM AS COMPLETED IN 1906

As the full-size commercial Telharmonium was constructed from 1902 to 1906, portions of its technology evolved as markedly distinct from Cahill's patent designs. But whatever the provenance of its components, upon its completion the second Telharmonium was undeniably a remarkable accomplishment.

THE ALTERNATORS

The alternating current dynamos, or alternators, employed by Cahill were of the inductor variety. As an iron tooth moved past an electromagnetic field, it generated an alternating current in the armature of the inductor. The stator, or stationary portion, was constructed to carry both the electromagnetic field windings, or coils, and the armature windings, as shown in Fig. 20. The number of north and south pole pieces in the stator corresponded to the number of rotor teeth. Since the pole pieces were interspersed with armatures, the stators had to be cut with twice as many teeth as the rotors. The pole pieces were maintained in a state of constant excitation by a 185-hp constant-speed dc motor, which also rotated the pitch-shafts bearing the massive alternators. As one rotor tooth would approach and recede from the position shown in Fig. 20, a current wave would be induced in the opposite armature coil. The current would rise continuously from zero to maximum positive value, then fall through zero to maximum negative value, and finally rise again to zero. Consequently, as the tooth would pass completely across the gap between pole pieces of opposite polarity, and through the electromagnetic field created between the poles, a complete sine wave would be induced in the armature coil. All the armature windings were in series, so the sum of currents generated at all the teeth in the alternator would be available at the output.[12]

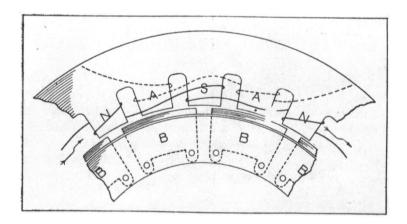

Fig. 20. Diagram of Field Windings (*solid line*) and Armature Windings (*dashed line*) in Inductor Alternator. N = North Pole, S = South Pole, A = Armature, T = Rotor Tooth. Only one turn of coil is illustrated, for simplicity's sake. (*American Telephone Journal,* October 27, 1906, XIV:17, 269)

In order to produce a sine wave, the teeth of the rotating inductors had to be most carefully curved. This was common practice in the construction of alternators, but was difficult to achieve in the fabrication of the high-pitched units with their numerous small teeth. After cutting the teeth of an alternator, Cahill ran it and measured its wave shape. He could then further mill the teeth to attain more nearly the exact voltage curve desired.[13] He also found that simpler dish alternators, in which the armatures and pole-pieces (instead of teeth) were circumferentially mounted on rotating disks, were preferable to the toothed-cylinder type of inductor to produce the two lowest fundamentals.[14]

THE DEPLOYMENT OF THE ALTERNATORS

In the original patent design, each of the twelve pitch-shafts carried seven fundamental alternators, six third-partial alternators, and five fifth-partial alternators. The frequency relationships were as shown in Table 1.[15]

In the patent design, each key had up to ten separate electrical contacts for the various harmonics of its note—to connect the keys to various alternators, all on the same pitch-shaft, as shown in Table 2. The pitch of a single alternator could, of course, be routed to more than one key. The pitches of the alternators may be seen in Table 3.[16]

Insofar as the dearth of harmonics in upper pitches was concerned, Cahill asserted that this was not objectionable, since their presence would make the notes "sharp and cutting."[17] Furthermore, some weak third and fifth harmonics would still be present, the sine waves of the higher frequencies not being perfectly pure. He admitted that mechanical and electrical difficulties militated against their production and limitations in receivers against their proper transmission.[18]

Only eight of the projected twelve pitch-shafts were eventually built (C, D, E♭, E, F, G, A, B♭), owing to their huge expense and the pressure to put the machine into service.[19]

Cahill had executed all of his original patent designs specifying a span of seven fundamentals covering six octaves on one pitch-shaft. The massive shafts were milled to accommodate 18 alternators each

Table 1
Vibration Frequencies of All Alternators
on One Pitch-Shaft

Hz	Fundamental	Third-Partial (Perfect Fifth)	Fifth-Partial (Major Third)
3072		96n (288)	
2560			80n (240)
2048	64n (192)		
1536		48n (144)	
1280			40n (120)
1024	32n (96)		
768		24n (72)	
640			20n (60)
512	16n (48)		
384		12n (36)	
320			10n (30)
256	8n (24)		
192		6n (18)	
160			5n (15)
128	4n (12)		
96		3n (9)	
64	2n (6)		
32	n (3)		

Note: n is the lowest in pitch of the fundamental alternators. The number of cycles per revolution of the shaft, which also equals the number of teeth or pole pieces on each alternator, is shown in parentheses.

and no more, except for one shaft that could hold an additional dynamo. After they were fabricated, the indispensability of the seventh harmonic for brass synthesis surfaced.[20] In order to avoid constructing longer shafts to hold added seventh-harmonic alternators (which would have necessitated a new mainframe, a more powerful motor, additional switchboards—essentially a substantially rebuilt Telharmonium), three existing alternators were divested from each shaft in order to make room for three fresh seventh-harmonic alternators. One of those discarded was the lowest alternator, thereby decreasing the range bridged by the pitch-shaft from six to five octaves (see Table 4).

If each pitch-shaft encompassed only five octaves, and an octave be

Table 2
Deployment of 18 Alternators on the C-Shaft

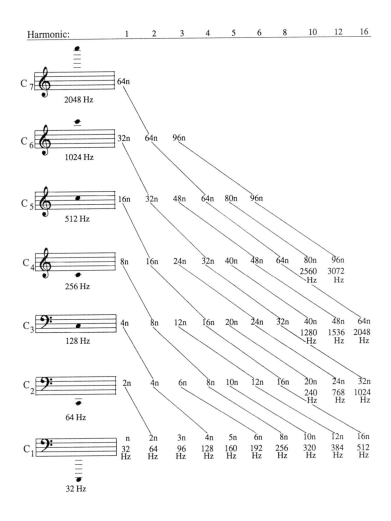

Harmonic:	1	2	3	4	5	6	8	10	12	16
C_7 2048 Hz	64n									
C_6 1024 Hz	32n	64n	96n							
C_5 512 Hz	16n	32n	48n	64n	80n	96n				
C_4 256 Hz	8n	16n	24n	32n	40n	48n	64n	80n / 2560 Hz	96n / 3072 Hz	
C_3 128 Hz	4n	8n	12n	16n	20n	24n	32n	40n / 1280 Hz	48n / 1536 Hz	64n / 2048 Hz
C_2 64 Hz	2n	4n	6n	8n	10n	12n	16n	20n / 240 Hz	24n / 768 Hz	32n / 1024 Hz
C_1 32 Hz	n / 32 Hz	2n / 64 Hz	3n / 96 Hz	4n / 128 Hz	5n / 160 Hz	6n / 192 Hz	8n / 256 Hz	10n / 320 Hz	12n / 384 Hz	16n / 512 Hz

Note: Alternators are numbered n, 2n, 3n, 4n, 5n, 6n, 8n, 10n, 12n, 16n, 20n, 24n, 32n, 40n, 48n, 64n, 80n, 96n. The lower C-keys are connected to ten harmonics. Over a range of five octaves, a single alternator could be employed for as many as five harmonics, as shown by the connecting lines.

Table 3
Pitches and Frequencies Produced by Each of the 18
Alternators on the C-Shaft

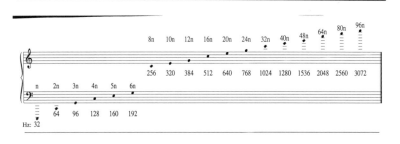

Note: All thirds and fifths are in just intonation, and can be tapped as fundamental pitches on keys adjacent to those for the twelve equal-tempered tones, in addition to their simultaneous employment as harmonics of C.

added to cover the scale, the result is a six-octave range. Yet, in describing the machine in 1906, the science writer A. S. McAllister stated: "The frequencies obtained vary from 40 to 4,000 cycles."[21] That is very nearly seven octaves. Furthermore, Cahill long afterward implied the instrument had a seven-octave range: "experience shows that eight octaves are much preferable to seven."[22]

The missing octave is at the low end of the range, since Cahill stated that the highest A-alternator of the instrument was tuned to 3480 Hz.[23] That would place the frequencies of the five A-alternators below at 1740 Hz, 870 Hz, 435 Hz, 217.5 Hz, and the lowest at 108.75 Hz, more than an octave above the instrument's putative stretch to 40 Hz.

How could a phantom octave be cajoled from a five-octave pitch-shaft? There was indeed a way, pointed by McAllister's careful disclosure: the frequencies of 40–4000 Hz were only *obtained,* not necessarily all *generated directly,* by alternators tuned to those frequencies.

A glance at the scheme of alternators on a shaft (Table 2) shows that the lowest seven alternators possessed teeth in increments of 2 (4, 6, 8, 10, 12, 14, 16). In addition to their employment as various lower-order harmonics, these alternators also constitute the second through eighth harmonics of the frequency of a nonexistent two-toothed alternator. That fundamental frequency, an octave below the

Table 4
Number of Teeth on Each Alternator

	Hz	Fundamen-tals, 2nd, 4th, and 8th Harmonics	3rd and 6th Harmonics	5th Har-monics	7th Har-monics
C	4138.4	128			
G	3103.8		96		
E	2586.5			80	
C	2069.2	64			
B♭	1810.6				56
G	1551.9		48		
E	1293.3			40	
C	1034.6	32			
B♭	905.28				28
G	775.96		24		
E	646.31			20	
C	517.31	16			
B♭	452.64				14
G	387.98		12		
E	323.32			10	
C	258.65	8			
G	193.99		6		
C	129.33	4			

Note: Tooth count and vibration frequencies of eighteen alternators on the C-Shaft. Note variances from the design described in Cahill's patents (Table 1): the range has been truncated and the seventh harmonic added. "Magic Music from the Telharmonium," *New York Times*, December 16, 1906, pt. 3, 3; Daniel Gregory Mason, "Electrically Generated Music," *New Music Review*, March 1907, 6:64, 239.

four-toothed alternator, could be formed as a difference tone. Any two or three adjacent harmonics, especially toward the lower compass of the series, sounded louder than *mezzo forte,* will create the sound of their fundamental. This is generated by simple arithmetical addition and subtraction, in the reproducing system as well as directly in the ear. In fact, *all* of the harmonics in the series will be produced as sum and difference tones, or combination tones, reinforcing the sound of the fundamental. With up to seven adjacent harmonics as the generating set, and with their amplitudes carefully regulated to progressively diminish upward, a reasonably convincing two-toothed fundamental would result. The individual pitches would more or less blend although not disappear, and would cause a brand new phantom low note to appear. Organ builder Robert Hope-Jones wrote of the Telharmonium: "It is interesting to observe how the resultant C [fundamental] is still heard when the ground tone has been practically all shut off and nothing but a chord of harmonics is left sounding."[24]

Cahill's patent descriptions make no mention of this technique. It must be remembered, however, that it was getting to be an old and familiar scheme acoustically. Helmholtz mentioned the phenomenon, which was particularly evident on the harmonium. Builders of this small reed organ even installed tuned resonators to enhance the effect.[25]

One pitch-shaft had a five-toothed alternator installed.[26] Exactly which shaft was not reported, so there is uncertainty about the pitch supplied. Such a tooth count would yield a major third above the lowest alternator. The second octave had no F#, G#, or C# (see Table 5), and the first of these cavities was probably the most painful. A 19th alternator on the D-shaft brought the total complement (18 times eight, plus one) to 145 alternators. The numbers 144 and 145 were constantly both reported as the full count throughout the instrument's entire tenure at Telharmonic Hall in New York from 1906 to 1908.

As may be seen in Table 5, a complete twelve-tone *tempered* scale was never available on the Telharmonium. The first, second, and sixth octaves did not even possess the full chromatic scale. However, there was great flexibility of pitch selection in the midrange: four separate frequencies could be tapped for the notes G and D, and three for each E, F, A, B♭, and C.

THE KEYBOARD

Table 5 also helps to clear up the mystery of the key count on the keyboard. The Washington Telharmonium, in use at Holyoke for many demonstrations in 1906, had two ordinary black-and-white manuals. The keyboards on the large commercial Telharmonium constructed for New York were more complicated. Performer Edwin

Hall Pierce, who was associated with the Telharmonium until early 1907, mentioned a 36-key-to-the-octave manual;[27] other reports stipulated 48.[28] Photographs of the keyboards at the central station in the spring of 1907 appear to indicate four banks of about 84 alternating black and white keys for each of two manuals (Figs. 21 and 22).[29] The black keys are not grouped in twos and threes, but alternate consistently with the white keys. Pitches and octave divisions are difficult to decipher, but 84 keys do span precisely seven octaves at twelve tones per octave. Had there been a full complement of twelve pitch-shafts, 48 keys to the octave would have been required. That was the capacity of the four 84-key banks comprising each manual. They had been installed in anticipation of four more pitch-shafts, to be ordered once the requisite riches began to pour in. Hence, the promoters could display and ballyhoo two 48-tone-to-the-octave, 336-key manuals, even though only 153 keys produced notes (145 alternators plus eight for the phantom octave); the remaining keys had to be dummies. Pierce, on the other hand, spoke of a 36-key count closer to the actual 32 pitches generated in the inner octaves. He was more likely referring to a keyboard fitted to the original pitch-shaft design described in Cahill's patents, probably an earlier and more familiar prototype keyboard he had used at Holyoke and during the first presentations in New York in 1906. This could well have been three banks of standard black-and-white keyboards for each manual. With twelve such pitch-shafts (containing tonics, major thirds, perfect fifths, but no flatted sevenths), a maximum of precisely 36 keys per octave would have been required.

THE GEARING

The gears connecting the pitch-shafts were cut in Cahill's laboratory in Holyoke; the job had been turned down by several of America's leading gear-cutting shops, since the train of gears was so complicated and fast-running as to menace the required stability. The temperature of the gears, along with that of the alternators, was controlled by a water cooling system.[30]

Table 5 145-Note Tuning Scheme of the Telharmonium

1st (Phantom) Octave 8 notes

36.291　38.449　40.735　43.157　48.443　54.375　57.608　64.663

2nd Octave 13 Notes

72.582　76.898　81.470　86.315　90.727 (D)　96.885　108.75 (D)　108.87　115.22　115.35 (Eb)　122.21 (E)　129.33 (E)　129.47 (F)

3rd Octave 24 Notes

145.16　145.33 (G)　153.80　162.94　163.13 (A)　172.63　172.82 (Bb)　181.45 (D)　192.24 (Eb)　193.77　193.99 (C)　203.68 (E)

215.79 (F)　217.50　217.75 (D)　230.43　230.69 (Eb)　242.21 (G)　244.41 (E)　254.04 (D)　258.65　258.94 (F)　269.14 (Eb)　271.88 (A)

4th Octave 32 Notes

285.15 (E)　288.04 (Bb)　290.33　290.66 (G)　302.10 (F)　307.59　323.32 (C)　325.88　326.25 (A)　339.10 (G)

345.26　345.65 (Bb)　362.91 (D)　380.63 (A)　384.49 (Eb)　387.54　387.98 (C)　403.26 (Bb)　407.35 (E)　431.57　435.00

435.49 (D)　452.64 (C)　460.87　461.39 (Eb)　484.43 (G)　488.82 (E)　508.07 (D)　517.31　517.89 (F)　543.75 (A)　558.29 (Eb)

continued

Table 5, cont.

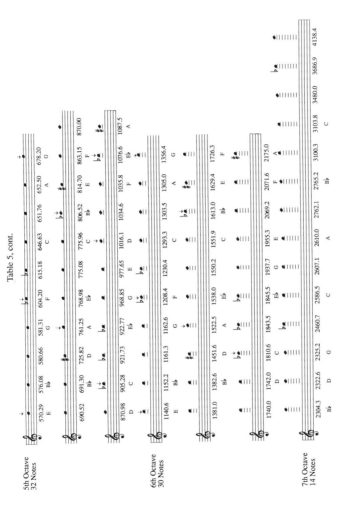

Note: A note from a pitch-shaft of the same name is in equal temperament. Other notes, in just intonation of various keys, are indicated by the source pitch-shaft named below the frequency (Hz). Notes derived from the seventh harmonic, hopelessly flat as scale tones, are shown with an arrow. Tuning is based on A = 435 Hz.

Fig. 21. Musician at Keyboards A and B, Telharmonic Hall. (*Gunter's Magazine*, June 1907, 3:5, S.C., 563)

Fig. 22. Detail of Fig. 21: Keyboards A and B, Telharmonic Hall. (*Gunter's Magazine*, June 1907, 3:5, S.C., 563)

THE MOTOR

While all the alternators were run simultaneously, most of them at any given time were on open circuit. Hence, the load on the 185-hp motor averaged only about 100 hp. The same motor was used to turn the rotors and to supply current to the electromagnetic field excitation coils.[31]

THE RELAY SWITCHES

In order to lighten the keyboard action, the alternators were switched in and out of circuit by electromagnetic relays on separate switchboards. The tiny contact switches mounted on each key (Fig. 23) merely closed low-voltage dc circuits, which in turn actuated the

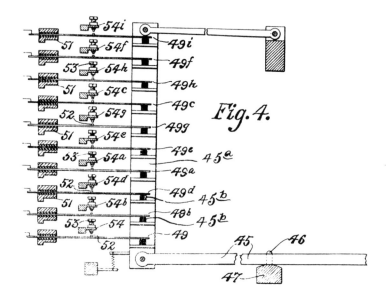

Fig. 23. Electrical Key Contacts for Actuating Relay Switches on Switchboards. (U.S. Patent 1,295,691, drawings sheet 5)

relays. As a result, the mass of the key was not burdened by heavy switches. Pushing down the key (45) would raise the contact springs (49) up against the contact bars (54). Also seen in Fig. 23 are the insulating bars (51), the platinum contact points (52), and the contact screws (53). Although this patent design shows ten switch contacts on a key, Cahill ultimately employed eleven. On the massive switchboards, 30 feet in length (Fig. 24), a plunger-type relay lifted a vertical strip of wood with eleven knife-switch contacts that closed eight circuits of harmonics and three line circuits. The wooden strip was light and counterbalanced by a lever weight, so that it ascended readily when the relay was energized.[32]

THE TIMBRE-CONTROL SWITCHES

The timbre control was effected by routing the harmonics of each order through individual bus-bars; all the fundamentals went into

Fig. 24. Switchboards and Tone-Mixing Transformers in the Basement of Telharmonic Hall. (New York Electric Music Co., *Telharmony*, New York: The Company, late December 1906, 6)

one circuit, all the second harmonics into another, and so on. The bus-bar circuit of a particular harmonic then entered the primary of an iron-core transformer that was controlled by an iron-core impedance rheostat, or "stop," operated by the performer. The rheostat had seven or eight induction coils wired in parallel, with smooth contact surfaces of alternate strips of copper and mica. Each coil had a different amount of induction and was connected by a knife switch to the output. Several redundant contact blades were employed for one switch, each spring-loaded, so that the possibility of an open circuit was very remote. A row of knife switches operated by the musician connected a number of the separately insulated sections of coils in parallel, varying the impedance of the circuit and thereby the amplitude of the harmonic. By closing the switches, singly or in combination, a performer could regulate the volume level of each harmonic and obtain a wide variety of timbres. It was possible to vary the attack and sustain of a single chord by operating the levers during these portions of the tone. Generally, however, the levers were set at the beginning of each phrase, in the fashion of organ stops.[33]

In Fig. 25 the timbre-control knife switches (55, 55a) may be seen at the left of the keyboard. The rightmost switch (55a) in each group connected the signal at full volume; the others (55) attenuated the signal to one degree or another. A side or sectional view of vertical line 21, 21 is seen at upper left. At middle left is a front view of the switches and at lower left an aerial view.[34] Cahill later added draw switches for timbre control; these may be seen below the music rack in Fig. 21 and Fig. 22.[35]

THE EXPRESSION DEVICES

Of Cahill's expression devices on the second Telharmonium, the most important was an electrical swell connected to a foot pedal. The signal passed through a series of 48 induction coils connected to contact plates; as the foot-controlled brush passed over the plates, the

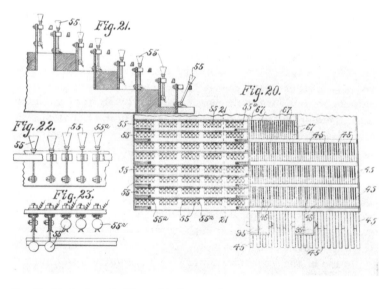

Fig. 25. Early Console Plan with Detail of Timbre-Control Switches. (U.S. Patent 1,295,691, drawings sheet 19)

coils were cut in or out of the circuit, making the signal gradually softer or louder. The brush had four fingers so that at any position there would be certain contact.[36]

Another expression device, for sudden volume changes, was the dynamic manual. Here the signal again passed through a series of induction coils, but each coil was connected to a key, similar to that on a pitch keyboard. It required a *legato* touch so as not to break the circuit, but afforded the performer the means of dramatically changing the volume virtually instantaneously. When the performers' hands were not free to operate the manual, a weight had to be used to hold down one key.[37]

THE OUTPUT TRANSFORMERS

The outputs of the four circuits, one for each manual, were induced into the several primaries of another transformer, which had one secondary yielding the final composite signal (Fig. 26). This was not sent out directly, but entered an air-core transformer that filtered out undesirable partials, and whose secondary was tapped at several points so that different transmission voltages could be selected. The primary of this last transformer contained several impedance rheostats, allowing the overall loudness of the signal to be controlled.[38] In fact there were only two working manuals when the instrument was put into service in 1906. In New York the music was transmitted not as a composite signal but as two separate signals, one for the melody or treble, the other for the accompaniment or bass.[39] This permitted more volume to be conveyed and furnished the flexibility of balancing and adjusting receivers.

OVERVIEW: THE COMPLETE ELECTRICAL WORKINGS

A basic electrical schematic of the instrument, for one keyboard and one harmonic, is seen in Fig. 27. The dynamos (2 c, c#, d, etc.) were mounted on the twelve pitch-shafts and were constantly rotating.

Fig. 26. The Output Transformers in the Basement of Telharmonic Hall. (New York Electric Music Co., *Telharmony,* New York: The Company, late December 1906, 7)

Here a symbol for only one dynamo is shown for each scale tone. In Cahill's Fig. 2 (left), the signal traveled from a single dynamo (2) to a single key contact spring (49). When the key (45) was depressed, the signal flowed into the bus-bar (54), then through one or more of the timbre-control switches (55, 120) (more than shown in the drawing, typically seven or eight), then into a primary coil (56), where it was induced into a secondary coil (58) (transformer no. 1). The circuit was completed as the current traveled into the common return line (48). In Cahill's Fig. 1 (center), the circuit of the primary coil (56) is illustrated once again. Here it is shown that the circuit containing the secondary (58) of transformer no. 1 also possessed the volume-control impedance coils (60); the number of coils employed

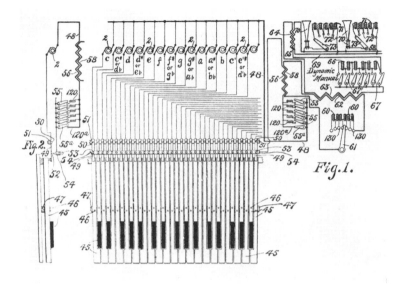

Fig. 27. Simplified Electrical Schematic for One Keyboard and the First Harmonic Only. (U.S. Patent 1,295,691, drawings sheet 1)

(they actually totaled 48) was determined by the position of the brushes (61) of the foot-operated electrical swell control. The output of this circuit was a primary coil (62), and the signal was induced into a secondary coil (63) (transformer no. 2). The circuit of the latter coil contained the volume-control dynamic manual with its impedance coils (66) controlled by keys (67). The output primary (64) then passed into a secondary (65) (transformer no. 3), which sent the signal to the receivers (70). There the volume could be controlled by rheostats (71, 72, 73).[40]

A more developed electrical schematic of the instrument appears in Fig. 28. All the dynamos on one pitch-shaft are connected in multiple routings to various of the ten individual harmonic buses. Every main dynamo furnishing an octave of C is labeled "2"; each is additionally labeled with a frequency designation (n, 2n, 4n, etc.). There are seven octaves of C. Every supplemental dynamo furnishing a third partial or harmonic (perfect fifth in its octaves) is labeled "3"; each is additionally labeled with a frequency designation related to the fundamental, n (3n, 6n, 12n, etc.). Every supplemental dynamo

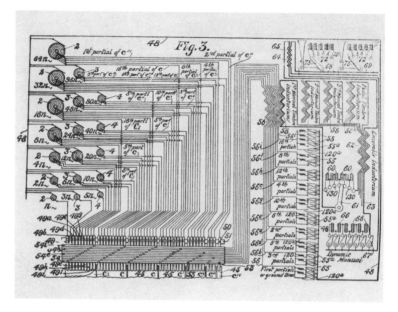

Fig. 28. Electrical Schematic for Successive Octaves and Other Harmonics of the Note C Only. (U.S. Patent 1,295,691, drawings sheet 3)

furnishing a fifth partial or harmonic (major third in its octaves) is labeled "4" and also with a frequency designation (5n, 10n, 20n, etc.). The dynamos with their frequencies are the same as shown in Table 1. These 18 alternators comprised the components of the C pitch-shaft. The concentric circles represent multiple windings, or outputs, so that the signal of one alternator could be tapped by different keys. For example, dynamo 64n had five windings, since its frequency was employed, respectively, as a first, second, fourth, eighth, and sixteenth harmonic of various octaves of C, each of course actuated by its own key. The keys (45) here have different widths; strictly speaking, the representation is not of the key, but of the strip of wood attached to the end of the key that bore the contact springs (49). The lowest key (C1) was connected with ten alternators (left to right, lines going from the dynamos down to 49, 49a, 49b, etc.: n, 3n, 5n, 2n, 6n, 10n, 4n, 12n, 8n, 16n); the highest key (C^{iv}) with but one (64n). When a key was depressed, the signals of as many as ten dynamos would flow into the ten metal bus-bars (54, 54a, 54b, etc.). Each bus-bar served respectively for one harmonic (1st, 2nd, 3rd,

4th, 5th, 6th, 8th, 10th, 12th, 16th). All of the first harmonics of every note on the keyboard went through bus-bar 54, all of the second harmonics through 54a, and so on. Each bus had its own primary coil (56, 56a, 56b, etc.) and its own set of switches (55, 55a) to regulate the loudness of that harmonic. The outputs of all ten primaries were taken up by one secondary (58). In the upper-right section of the schematic are shown primary and secondary coils (56h, 58) from the other two keyboard manuals and the pedalboard, whose entire circuits replicated this figure. All sent signals through successive primary coils (62) mixed into one secondary (63).[41]

PLAYING THE INFERNAL CONTRAPTION

A performer's nightmare come true, the Telharmonium must have been one of the most hair-raisingly complicated instruments to play in all the history of music. Thaddeus Cahill blithely prescribed that two performers divide their labors as follows: the first performer to operate the four pitch manuals (three keyboards and one pedalboard), the other to operate the dynamic manual (Fig. 25, keys 67) and the timbre-control switches, and each to operate two of the four swell pedals.[42]

With a single manual containing four banks of 84 keys each—336 keys, of which 153 were working—it was all a performer could do to play one manual of the keyboard. Insofar as the bass line and accompanying chords demanded less production of just-intonation thirds on different banks, Musician A was free to take on the operation of setting the timbre-control switches for his and his partner's keyboards. He would still have to operate the electrical swell pedal for his manual and the dynamic manual as well. Musician B, performing the melody and treble harmonies, was continually stretching his hands to create just-intonation thirds, constantly shifting and slipping his fingers among the upper and lower keyboard banks—and sometimes over to the fourth bank when a flatted seventh was required. Musician B had to operate his swell pedal in addition, plus control a smaller share of the timbre-control switches and draw switches when possible, and perhaps move the little lead weight depressing a key on the dynamic manual, which both frazzled musicians were too preoccupied to perform properly. With black keys alternating constantly with white ones, instead of being grouped in twos and threes, the keys had to be labeled so the performers could find their way. Naturally, with four banks, four notes had the same label on each manual. Eyes off the music to find a key, a page turn coming up, and the instrument suddenly drifting down in pitch necessitating a quick adjustment on the master tuning rheostat . . . ! A musically mediocre Telharmonic presentation could still be visually captivating.

NOTES

1. Application of Thaddeus Cahill for letters patent to the Commissioner of Patents, February 16, 1904, filed February 17, 1904, N.A. 241, 1,213,803, F4, F34, F36, F39, F41-F42, F49.

2. U.S. Patent 1,295,691, *Art of and Apparatus for Generating and Distributing Music Electrically,* Thaddeus Cahill, New York, N.Y.: Applications January 19, 1901, February 26, 1903, February 17, 1904, June 26, 1915, Renewed May 8, 1918, Patented February 25, 1919, 6, 10, 11, 43.

3. *Ibid.,* 46.

4. Application of Thaddeus Cahill, F44-F45.

5. *Ibid.,* F48.

6. *Ibid.*

7. *Ibid.,* F53.

8. *Ibid.,* F4-F5, F17.

9. *Ibid.,* F29-F30, F33.

10. *Ibid.,* F5, F28.

11. *Ibid.,* F6, F52.

12. John Grant, "The Electrical Generation of Music," *American Telephone Journal,* October 27, 1906, XIV:17, 269; Addams Stratton McAllister, "Some Electrical Features of the Cahill Telharmonic System," *Electrical World,* January 5, 1907, XLIX:1, 22.

13. Application of Thaddeus Cahill for letters patent to the Commissioner of Patents, April 26, 1915, filed April 27, 1915, N.A. 241, 1,213,804, B15.

14. *Ibid.,* B16, B17.

15. *Ibid.,* B11-B12.

16. *Ibid.,* B20-B22.

17. *Ibid.,* B22.

18. *Ibid.*

19. "Magic Music from the Telharmonium," *New York Times,* December 16, 1906, pt. 3, 3.

20. Thaddeus Cahill, "The Electrical Music as a Vehicle of Expression," *Papers and Proceedings of the Music Teachers' National Association at Its Twenty-ninth Annual Meeting, Columbia University, New York City, December 27–31, 1907,* 1908, 209.

21. McAllister, 22.

22. Application from Thaddeus Cahill for letters patent to the Commissioner of Patents, April 26, 1915, filed April 27, 1915, N.A. 241, 1,213,804, B100.

23. Thaddeus Cahill, "The Electrical Music as a Vehicle of Expression," 208.

24. Robert Hope-Jones, "The Future of the Church Organ," *New Music Review,* February 1908, 7:75, S.C., 175.

25. Hermann Ludwig Ferdinand Helmholtz, *On the Sensations of Tone,* second English edition, translated and conformed to the fourth German edition of 1877 with notes by Alexander J. Ellis, 1885, reprinted with an introduction by Henry Margenau, New York: Dover Publications, 1954, 157.

26. "Magic Music from the Telharmonium," 3.

27. Edwin Hall Pierce, "A Colossal Experiment in 'Just Intonation,' " *Musical Quarterly,* July 1924, X:3, 328.

28. Telharmonic Securities Company, *Telharmonic Hall: Program, Week of December 30th,* New York: The Company, 1907 [stamped: "From the William J. Hammer Scientific Collection"], S.L., 1.

29. The largest and clearest is in A. B. Easterbrook, "The Wonderful Telharmonium," *Gunter's Magazine,* June 1907, 3:5, S.C., 563.

30. George F. Cahill, "Thaddeus Cahill (June 18, 1867-April 12, 1934): A Preliminary Paper," New York?, 1934?, typewritten, C.R.L.C. E-1488, Cat. C, L609.214, C115, 5.

31. McAllister, 22.

32. *Ibid.,* 22–23; U.S. Patent 1,295,691, 5, 15–16; Eastern Cahill Telharmonic Company, *Telharmony: The New Art of Electric Music,* New York: The Company, June?, 1907, M.C.S., 18.

33. Application of Thaddeus Cahill, April 26, 1915, B23-B24; McAllister, 23–24.

34. U.S. Patent 1,295,691, 6.

35. *Ibid.,* 34–35, drawings sheet 33.

36. Application of Thaddeus Cahill, April 26, 1915, B24-B25.

37. *Ibid.,* B26-B27.

38. McAllister, 23; Grant, 270.

39. Letter from Robert E. Chetwood, Jr., American Telephone and Telegraph Co., to G. M. Yorke, Assistant Engineer, American Telephone

and Telegraph Co., January 2, 1907, A.T.T.B.L.A., Boston File 500, 603822, 1–2.

40. U.S. Patent 1,295,691, 15–16, 21.

41. *Ibid.*, 8–9, 16–17, 19.

42. Application of Thaddeus Cahill, April 26, 1915, B27.

CHAPTER IV

PREVIEW CONCERTS AT TELHARMONIC HALL

THE FIRST NEW YORK CONCERT

More than 900 members of the New York Electrical Society presented their membership cards at the doors of Telharmonic Hall on the evening of September 26, 1906. The organization's first meeting of the season was being held at the new central station a few blocks south of Times Square (Fig. 29). The attendance bulged to three times normal.[1]

Now the miraculous machine would finally be heard by others besides a few selected members of the press. The Telharmonium, however, was not yet in shape for the general, much less the musical, public. So the frequently less-discerning ears of card-carrying electricians and physicists were relied upon to be duly impressed. Whatever quality of music might be heard, the engineering achievements embodied in the machine were undeniably substantial, and would encourage these listeners to sing all manner of Telharmonic praises to the outside world. Naturally, there were among the assembly at least a few well-trained musicians who could discount the promotion and the electromechanical triumphs to hear the Telharmonium as it really was.

The crush at the door was exacerbated by the occupancy limit of Telharmonic Hall. The 50-by-80-foot music hall on the street level, where the performance console was located, could accommodate only 250 people at best. Some relief was afforded by throwing the machinery rooms in the basement open to visitors, who wandered about prior to the concert inspecting the alternators, tone mixers, switchboards, and the "Duma." This last was the long sandbox in which several hundred muffled receivers were buried, christened after the recently dismissed Russian parliament.[2] The noisy dynamos

TIMES SQUARE

The Metropolitan Opera
House

Hotel Astor
The Times Building

Fig. 29. Across from Telharmonic Hall: West Side of Broadway, 40th Street to 44th Street. (A. Wessels Company, *New York Historic and Picturesque: A Calendar for 1906,* New York: The Company, 1905, 14)

had been set up in one subterranean room, while the switchboards and tone mixers were situated in another, an eerily silent basement chamber where only the ominous clicking of wooden and metal rods and electical relays could be heard.[3]

Before the music was revealed, Oscar T. Crosby delivered an extensive address extolling the invention and his plans for it. In no way was the Telharmonium a kind of mechanical music, which had recently been castigated by John Philip Sousa in a widely circulated and hotly debated article.[4] The Telharmonium could, of course, be operated by a mechanical attachment, just as a player piano, but in its intended and best form would be played by a live performer. This would afford the sensitivity of expression no "canned" music could possibly provide. As to the capacity of the music supply, Crosby asserted that no fewer than 15,000 to 20,000 receivers could be driven by the central station. Other keyboards would soon join the one keyboard now seen in the auditorium, to provide various styles of music over different circuits. In a few years, home Telharmoniums would be available for the same cost as a good grand piano, with the material advantage that the output could be wired to any place in the house, out on the lawn, even down the block. In conclusion, Crosby proclaimed the birth of a new art with so great a range of applicability for mankind that its utility superseded "the electric light, telephone, and the trolley."[5]

At last came the music: solos, duets, accompaniments to several songs delivered by a Miss Fiske, and a fife and drum corps among other imitations. The sounds issued from eight invisible telephone receivers fitted with paper horns. These had been artfully concealed about the hall, among ferns, hydrangea shrubs, trellises, columns, and furniture.[6] A music critic from the *Musical Age* was loath to judge the machine's ultimate worth: "the selections were mere scraps, and the technical difficulties were apparent."[7] Nevertheless, in spite of the performers' inexperience and the overcrowded hall, it became apparent that here was not a mechanical player but a real musical instrument with human control. Its predominantly woodwind sound most closely resembled an oboe, and the range of other effects was not nearly so great as an organ's.[8]

The difficulties of Cahill's unconventional keyboard attracted immediate notice. It seemed doubtful whether thereby attempting to give both just intonation and equal temperament their due simultaneously could ever be successfully negotiated in performance. The sonic semblance of a pipe organ was mitigated by good imitations of the cello, flute, piccolo, clarinet, oboe, horn, and bassoon. Until there could be some provision for variations in the manner of attack, however, it was unlikely that the Telharmonium might ever imitate plucked, struck, and the higher bowed instruments. Furthermore, the bass register was wanting in fullness, and the upper tones suffered from a dearth of brilliance. At present the instrument seemed best suited to small pieces of a gentle and unassuming character.[9]

The technical people were quite taken with what they heard, however. Albert F. Ganz, head of the electrical department at Stevens Institute of Technology and author of numerous technical publications,[10] "remarked that they had been listening to a new instrument which summed up all other musical instruments."[11]

GETTING READY

The street cable installation took a great deal of time, and during the fall connections from it were still underway up and down Broadway and Fifth Avenue. The New York Telephone Co. had its hands full with its own expansion and did not consider the work under the Telharmonic contract to be a priority.[12] There were test transmissions from the central station to the southern tip of Manhattan over regular telephone lines.[13]

Early in October the family of Edwin Hall Pierce made preparations to join him in New York. Pierce had moved there a month earlier. There were now seven children including little four-week-old Edith. The mother and younger children went in Cahill's automobile to stay at his house for a few days while the furniture was being moved to their sunny new third-floor flat on 131st Street. The older boys stayed with a neighbor. They all went to New York on October 8.[14]

ELLIOTT SCHENCK

The announcement was made in late October that the renowned composer and conductor Elliott Schenck had accepted a position "of great responsibility" with the New York Electric Music Co.[15] Schenck was to become music director of the Telharmonium. Just where Edwin Hall Pierce fit into this new picture is speculative. Pierce was an accomplished musician, but Schenck brought greater prestige. Born in Paris of American parents, Schenck had studied law for a year at Columbia College in 1900 and then turned to music. Upon his return from five-years' study in Dresden and Berlin, he had conducted Wagnerian operas in Boston and New Orleans to considerable acclaim and demand. He was at somewhat loose ends, having recently been looking for a production of his new opera and seeking bookings for a fall lecture tour.[16]

After the announcement, Schenck continued with other commitments. One was his highly praised conducting of offstage choruses for the oratorio *Children's Crusade* in December, produced by the New York Oratorio Society.[17]

SERVICE BEGINS AT THE CAFÉ MARTIN

As the lines were being laid and tested, the proprietor of the Café Martin, one of the finest Parisian restaurants in the city, urgently requested Telharmonic service. With comfortable banquettes and marble-topped tables, James B. Martin had transformed the former Delmonico's restaurant, bestowing upon it "an atmosphere of exotic impropriety: the foyer was hospitable to well-groomed ladies who seldom disdained invitations to an evening of diversion."[18] Martin would spend nearly half his time in Europe, where he acquired wines, recipes, and fetching appointments for his lavish and luxurious eatery. Every employee was required to speak good French; 150 waiters were hired to serve up to 1,800 guests daily and over 2,000 on Saturday. The establishment was situated near Madison Square, on the south side of 26th Street between Broadway and Fifth Avenue, about three-quarters of a mile from the central station. There were entrances to the Café Martin on all streets, each to a different dining room; that on Fifth Avenue led to the Empire Room, festooned with walnut, gold, mirrors, and an illuminated fountain of changing colors. Within a week of Martin's request, the first connection was made from the Telharmonic line running down Broadway. On

November 9 Oscar T. Crosby and eight directors of the New York Electric Music Co. celebrated the inauguration of business with a banquet and demonstration of the new product at the Café Martin. Press reporters were in attendance; the guests included former Governor Herrick of Ohio, Lady Cunard of London, and Charles A. Coffin, president of the General Electric Co.[19]

The company had installed the receivers with long horns in one of the eight private dining rooms. As two musicians labored upon the complicated keyboard uptown, with its 48 keys to the octave, the music flowed into the room like the tones of a distant organ. There was a flaw somewhere in the connection and the music was not so strong and clear as had been expected. Although the music was blessedly devoid of the rasp and scrape of the phonograph, the problem Cahill had misnamed "diaphragm crack" arose: all the notes were inaugurated "with little explosive puffs."[20] The first selection, *It's Nice to Have a Sweetheart,* was dismaying—the F-sharps blared shrilly at the guests. A defective diaphragm was quickly replaced, and the dining room became discreetly suffused with the strains of *Bill Simmons, Annie Rooney,* selections from *Tannhäuser* and *Carmen,* a Norwegian lullaby, chiming bells, and other sounds of instruments.[21]

Some reporters claimed that numerous instruments were distinguishable, that musicians there had declared the music to be the most perfect of all time.[22] Yet the overall resemblance to a church organ, "much softer and sweeter,"[23] did not fail to be drawn. Another listener heard only flutes and horns.[24]

One reporter recalled the first Holyoke demonstrations of this same central station, recollecting the limited musical qualities at that time. But then the new complex keyboard had been so unfamiliar to the musicians, and Cahill had not really completed all his development of the expression devices. Now the verdict at the Café Martin, energetically encouraged by company principals, was that the operators had become so skilled and "the instrument itself has been so improved in tone and power, as to place it in a commanding position as a purveyor of concert music for the million."[25]

After the concert and banquet, the directors and their invited guests repaired to the central station, where they could hear the music more clearly, from the flowers in the ceiling and the ducts in the floor. They heard a surprise as well. For many years electricians had spoken of the "singing" of the carbon arc lamp—each oscillated at its own individual note. At the suggestion of one of the younger employees the Telharmonic current was connected to an arc lamp. As the lamp glowed it resonated faintly in song: the Telharmonic "singing arc" (Fig. 30) was born.[26]

"Some of it was positively hair-raising because of its novelty . . . has it on either Mr. Edison's machine or the singing trees of Africa in the way of being something downright startling,"[27] commented one reporter. Another wrote that Herr Heinrich Conried and his Metropolitan Opera were in danger of being replaced by the central station just across the street, and might have to go back to Europe to find employment.[28]

The directors were flush with enthusiasm and exulted over their plans and prospects. Would not the labors of thousands of factory employees best be lightened and lighted by a highly profitable singing arc? At any rate, nightly concerts had now begun at the Café Martin. The central station was in business, and other subscribers would also be able to enjoy classical music. Various musical styles would soon follow.[29]

Fig. 30. The Singing Arc: Music and Light from Overhead Arc Lamps, Telharmonic Hall. (*Deseret Evening News,* July 13, 1907, S.C., 21)

It was fitting that the first connection was to a fine restaurant. Of all the utilizations envisioned, the most universal and lucrative, as well as the earliest, was by the great restaurateurs.[30] As their business had flourished, it had burgeoned to involve musical concerts to an amazing degree. As one wag put it:

> [Telharmonic] music is absolutely pure in pitch and of a remarkably grateful and soothing quality, and its introduction into some restaurants and dining rooms where now the inevitable orchestra is a source of pain and sadness would give welcome relief in the nerves of many a wayfaring diner-out.[31]

Restaurateurs were among the largest employers of musicians in the city. A repast at one of their establishments was truly an imposing event, gastronomically and musically.

SUPPER WITH A SONG: MUSIC COMES TO NEW YORK RESTAURANTS

In the New York of the early 1900s the powerful influence of the stomach, well fed or needy, upon the doings of mankind did not often go unacknowledged. For many the importance of a good meal as prelude or postlude to any endeavor was paramount. Several times a day the business of the world would simply cease. And in the finest restaurants of the city could be seen the modern pinnacle of an old science—ministering unto the needs of the moneyed appetite.[32]

Many sumptuous new restaurants had opened within the past ten years, as wealth had grown and more people turned to good eating as an antidote to business cares. The first-class hotel in New York invariably had a fashionable restaurant, something most fine hotels throughout the country were conspicuously lacking. The rival thoroughfares were Broadway, which had the Astor, Rector's, Shanley's, and the New Knickerbocker, while Fifth Avenue had the Holland, the Waldorf-Astoria, Sherry's, Delmonico's, the St. Regis, the Savoy, and a half-dozen other establishments. The Café Martin faced both on their intersection at Madison Square. The Broadway restaurants were a little more cosmopolitan than those on the Avenue. A planked fowl, for example, would be a curiosity at

Delmonico's, but was an artistic joy and luxury to be had for $4 at any house on Broadway.[33]

Beneath the splendidly gilded dining room the galley workers toiled to produce the feast. Between eight o'clock and eleven the restaurants were nearly idle. People were in the theatres, while the chefs, oyster openers, bartenders, dishwashers, silver cleaners, and laundrywomen busied themselves down below to prepare for the after-theatre onslaught. As the crowds burst in, the orchestra broke out and the bustle began.[34]

Tables beckoned the diners with flowered china, colorful bouquets, and tiny electric lights hidden in floral shades. They were set with a gleaming, lavish correctness that almost demanded something be served on them to break the fastidious perfection. The showy and assured assemblage that descended on these altars of gastronomy was dressed resplendently. Men were bedecked in full evening regalia, and jeweled women bloomed brightly in their loveliest gowns and prettiest feathered hats. As the glittering crystal and shining silver were lifted, they clattered merrily along with the orchestra, to form an enchanted environment of colorful lights and sounds.[35]

Menus bound like books featured hundreds of items. At least 500 selections could be found on most bills of fare, and some boasted twice that number. As James B. Martin, proprietor of the Café Martin, put it: "Rome in its palmy days could not hold a candle to New York. No feast of Nero or Lucullus was graced by so many rarities as one can buy at any of a dozen first-class hotels and restaurants in New York."[36]

Specialties and novelties, such as a truffled capon of Mans ($5), could be found at every establishment, at a price. That could easily exceed a princely $20 to $25 for a dinner for two, if money was no object. Most entrées were priced at $1 to $3; soups, salads, vegetables, and desserts cost anywhere from 20¢ to $1; wines averaged as high as $5 for good Piper Heidsieck dry champagne. A rare vintage could bring five times that sum. Prices were consistently identical among all the finest restaurants. One item rarely varied more than 10¢.[37]

The new dining fashion was simplicity, at least compared to former times. Instead of a banquet, a small dinner was the rule: women, especially, were fearful of gaining weight. And so, at the Café Martin, a light meal for two could be ordered in 1906 as follows:[38]

A clear, strained chicken gumbo with a dash of Madeira came first, chilled into jelly and served in a cup. Sherry was *de rigueur* with the soup, usually a pint of dry Amontillado. Either before or after the soup, a relish tray of small celery stalks, olives, etc., would appear. Salted almonds were also placed on the table. Hors d'oeuvres were next—a Canadian melon, some artichoke hearts, and herring. Then the fish course arrived, perhaps a kingfish with meunière sauce and potatoes. Now the white wine was brought in, for example, a Château Yquem—a most delightful if slightly sweet Bordeaux. The next course was the entrée, and here was a delicious choice—chops, sweetbreads, ham, filet of beef, or a novel specialty of the house, or simply a breast of chicken Marmotte, or preferably the sirloin Financière. The next part of the dinner was the roast. This could possibly be a planked steak or fowl, but was more often roasted or broiled poultry—squab, guinea hen, or capon—with three or four vegetables of the season. At the Café Martin, however, the special roast was *canard à la presse* (duck at the press). Two or three attendants were required to ceremoniously prepare and present the dish right in the dining room, to the envy of the entire clientele. A sauce for a roasted duck was produced by squeezing out all the juice from another cooked whole duck in a huge gleaming silver press. Burgundy and relishes augmented the sauce. The effort was triumphant and well celebrated by a bottle of champagne. Then the game and salad course arrived: truffled paté of game in aspic and a Russian salad. The final course of the modern light dinner was ices and dessert. A fruit ice in the form of a Parisian doll was very popular. Small cakes and three or four fresh fruits, including fresh green almonds, concluded the meal. It was topped off by coffee in Vienna glasses and yellow chartreuse liqueur.[39]

Well-to-do New Yorkers made up for the reduced size of the modern meal by eating a little more frequently. Four or five meals daily were not uncommon. As Theodore Dreiser described Sherry's in *Sister Carrie,* it was an

> exhibition of showy, wasteful, and unwholesome gastronomy as practiced by wealthy Americans, which is the wonder and astonishment of true culture and dignity the world over. The large bill of fare held an array of dishes sufficient to feed an army, sidelined with prices which made reasonable expenditure a ridiculous impossibility.[40]

SUPPER WITH A SONG: LISTENING TO MUSIC IN NEW YORK RESTAURANTS

> When Athens was a very intellectual, a truly civilized city, we had no music to disturb our conversation; now that Athens is full of rich foreigners who have no culture, we have music everywhere.
>
> —Socrates

Delmonico's, the first of New York's fine restaurants, was the lone holdout. The others had all entered the tea- and dinner-music wars, which by 1908 were being fought at a sum exceeding $1 million annually. This immense amount fell in decrements as high as $50,000 to $60,000, to the Waldorf-Astoria, where there were three or sometimes four orchestras, to the Plaza, where conductor Nathan Franko commanded an orchestra of thirty men, to Sherry's, to the Café Martin, which employed three orchestras, and to some dozen or more other establishments.[41]

Selections were a true mixed grill, as fashions rose and waned. At one point selections from Puccini operas reigned; later Viennese waltzes were all the rage. *Tales of Hoffman* was always popular, and there were frequent calls for music from new operas. Such fare was interspersed with bits of Chopin, Wagner, Victor Herbert, and ragtime. One or two of the restaurants presented a set program, which was actually printed and given to the patrons. The Plaza did so for both afternoon tea and dinner, offering on one occasion:

Butterfly's Enjoyment	Gung'l
Norwegian Dances	Grieg
Waltz—*Wine, Women, and Song*	Strauss
Fantasie—*La Bohème*	Puccini
Hymne Ste. Cécile	Gounod
Valse Lente—*Song d'Automne*	Joyce
Selection—*Our Miss Gibbs*	Monckton
Salut d'Amour	Elgar

Nathan Franko asserted that his audience craved only the very best music for dinner; his requests were principally for grand opera.

Franko did admit that the clientele also enjoyed a sprinkling of popular music and light airs. They were annoyed by noisy numbers, although the crowd was usually in the mood for lively selections by dinner's end. Nevertheless, he claimed that his public fairly demanded to be educated in classical music. Carlos Curti, who directed the orchestras at the Waldorf-Astoria, noted a marked improvement in public taste since the beginning of his tenure in 1904. No more than 10% of his listeners had called for classical music at that time, but by 1910 fully 30% of the diners desired the best. His programs were not set, though. If many Germans were present, he offered Wagner; to Italians, Verdi. It was important to maintain a large repertoire, so as to be able to satisfy the astonishing variety of requests from numerous nationalities. Mostly light selections were preferred, the principal object being to keep patrons in good humor. Hence, Curti avoided slow music since it seemed to sadden many customers. By 1910 Delmonico's had finally surrendered. It offered live music along with all the rest, a typical mix of classical and popular selections.[42]

The hours during which music was offered were numerous. It began with luncheon at twelve or one o'clock, continued during the tea hour of late afternoon, and then into dinner. A two-hour respite preceded the supper hours for the after-theatre crowd, which ended at midnight or one A.M.[43]

Many of the players were imported from among the best Europe had to offer. To keep up with the times Sherry's sent its red-jacketed Venetian musicians packing in 1908, and imported a new orchestra from the imperial palace in Vienna. These were 28 former court musicians to Emperor Franz Josef, formerly led by Johann Strauss. At the St. Regis, members of the Russian Symphony were employed. The Café Martin offered a thoroughly authentic French sextet to render the music of Paris. A Russian violinist at the Knickerbocker attracted huge crowds by his intense, theatrical performances, fiddling through the crowd as conversations fell silent. A rival French conductor-violinist, hired away from a London restaurant by another hotel, put up stiff competition with his Napoleonic yet gracious manner and his dramatic scrapings near the bridge. Tables were at a premium.[44]

Such musicians were required to possess considerable skill and artistry, since the clientele was among the most fastidious. They were paid comfortable salaries, about the same as those received by opera

and symphony musicians. The players were generally highly qualified graduates of the best conservatories, and felt very much on a par
with their colleagues at the Met. In fact, opera stars were among the
appreciative luncheon audience at one of the well-known hotels, and
such virtuosi as Mischa Elman led the applause for the hotel
orchestra. Despite the oft-heard comments on how dreadful it must
be to play in a restaurant instead of on the stage, the musicians were
glad of steady work at a good salary. Their hours were protected by
the musicians' union, and they further enjoyed the approbation of
many discriminating listeners.[45]

The first strategy in using musicians had been to shield them from
the public's gaze. They might have been concealed behind screens or
potted palms, or put away on an overhanging balcony. However, as
public appreciation improved, they began to be featured promi-
nently. The leaders' and soloists' personalities as well as their music
drew them attention, followings, gratuities, even weekend invitations.[46]

During the warm weather the hotels set up rooftop gardens with
restaurant service. The Waldorf-Astoria had twin roofs with an
orchestra on each. Lacking architectural acoustics to reinforce and
project the orchestral music, some orchestra leaders added huge
gramophones to increase the volume. On the roof of the Waldorf-
Astoria, Caruso would sing on a spinning disk while accompanied by
a 25-piece orchestra. Sometimes gramophones or other types of
music machines, such as the player piano or orchestrion, might even
be used to augment the orchestra indoors. However, when the
management of several restaurants tried to use these to provide music
between orchestral performances, the musicians threatened to walk
out. No use of mechanical music alone was allowed at fine restaurants.[47]

And how did the public reveal itself when confronted with this
grand new perquisite? Some assumed an affected air, swaying with
the music and sharply silencing any table companion who dared
break their reverie. Others evinced a genuine need for musical
education by asking for nonexistent operatic selections, or by failing
to recognize their requests when played. Occasionally someone
would become overanxious about when and whether a selection
would ever be heard, becoming virtually lost to food and compan-
ions. One particularly strange effect soon became happily noted by
pleased restaurateurs: certain selections caused the ordering of much

wine. *Amoureuse* and *Sourire d'Avril,* for example, created an over-powering desire for champagne. When either selection was heard, the cellar master called for extra help to meet the inevitable demand. It was speculated that a fortune awaited the composer who could write special dining tunes driving customers to various drinks. After an hour or two of this, the customers would have to be driven home in cabs. Naturally, the restaurant and taxicab people would pay handsome royalties for such music.[48]

A vocal and articulate minority despised the restaurant orchestra as the blaring enemy of conversation and wit. Men seeking to close an important business deal, or tired executives wishing to while away their troubles in a pleasant luncheon chat, felt rudely interrupted by the crashing chords of nearby musicians. To them it seemed that all the restaurants made a point of employing singers with abnormally penetrating voices, abetted by talking machines, in an effort to compel diners to eat mute. Furthermore, the lure of music and art, not food, now reigned supreme. All had to learn culture as they ate, gazing at masterpieces on the walls while their ears were assailed by musical classics. Perhaps restaurants could replace universities. They might begin by adding a house poet to the staff, to compose sonnets by the salad. Actors could be employed as waiters, spouting Shake-speare and Molière as they brought in courses. After all, the diner of the day lived on emotion and required a constant uplift to nurture the soul. And as the notes of a musical selection would fade away, the appreciative rattle of silverware tapping china augmented the noi-some *crescendo* of applause that swept over the room. For every selection seemed to nurture the soul equally, and the audience applauded each alike.[49]

The voluminous discussion boiled down to common sense: give the diner what he or she desired. Whether it be a wood fire, the evening paper, popular songs, or no music at all, such cravings satisfied would aid digestion and longevity. It must be borne in mind, however, that many persons were unable to eat to music without keeping time with their jaws. Thus, Sousa marches would not only impede thorough mastication but might even harm the dental apparatus. At any rate, the larger restaurants usually complied with the customer's wish by offering a choice of music or quiet, but the latter surroundings invariably provided fewer interesting people to observe.[50]

Once confined to expensive establishments, music began rapidly to spread to the 25¢-dinner restaurants. The numerous ethnic ensembles included picturesque Hungarian bands, Venetian mandolinists, German orchestras, and blackfaced minstrels. Luncheons were usually quiet in these cafés, but a spirited Bohemian atmosphere was affected at dinner:

> Here, in an uptown place, you find Irish waiters serving German beer to American diners-out, while a polyglot orchestra, dressed in Spanish costume, plays negro ragtime, or wants to know in voices that rise above the sound of their instruments has anybody here seen Kelly, which you may be sure, they haven't, as it is a Teutonic assemblage.[51]

The incongruities abounded, epicurean and musical, and really no greater than in the more ornate establishments. The cheap quick-lunch houses began to install the ubiquitous phonograph, having discovered that even their patrons appreciated popular records with hurried hamburgers.[52] Whether the musical strains were a joyous delight or tiresome and stupid was not nearly so important as the fact that they were free. The food was paid for, and supposedly the music was thrown in for no charge. The customers felt they were getting something for nothing, and that made most of them very delighted indeed.[53]

NEW YORK TELEPHONE HAS SECOND THOUGHTS

Around the end of November 1906, only several weeks after service to the Café Martin had commenced, the New York Telephone Co. began to explore the possibility of ineffectuating its contract with the New York Electric Music Co. Even though the comparatively huge currents of the Telharmonium were on two miles of separate lines, the wires of the two systems ran through the same conduits. They were parallel and proximate; hence, crosstalk into the telephone system could scarcely be avoided. It was as if a speaker line had been run next to a microphone cable, the former carrying many watts, the latter less than a milliwatt. The primitive shielding and grounding techniques of the day could not extricate the two systems from interference. Furthermore, the telephone company had on numerous occasions lent its regular connections and cables for Telharmonic music tests and transmissions to places where the electric music cable did not run. This brought the music right into the system where it could intrude on other telephone calls. Even worse encroachments ensued when the fascinated telephone company engineers performed tests using the permanent wires that delivered the Telharmonic signal to their laboratory. In its fight to protect its franchises, establish a monopoly, and beat back rate regulation, the last thing the telephone company needed was more complaints about service.[54]

Not only were there protests that melodic intrusions had thwarted business conversations, but also there were marital disruptions:

> In some instances the Telharmonium on the wires has caused no end of domestic trouble, and has even threatened to break up families. There is the case of a man who had to work late in his office one night, and called up his wife to tell her that instead of going home he would stay at a hotel.
>
> Just at the moment the merry strains of the "William Tell" overture came floating over the wires.
>
> "Where are you now?" his wife asked suspiciously.
>
> "In the office, of course," he made answer.
>
> "Indeed?" she replied. "Since when have you had an orchestra in your office? You're deceiving me. You're in some theatre. Don't try to deny it. I can hear the music."[55]

And so the second vice president with the New York Telephone Co., a Mr. Cahill (no relation), summoned Oscar T. Crosby to a meeting. He first raised the point that their contract did not compel New York Telephone to do any work and could be made effectively void if the company so chose. Crosby could only reply that this was indeed obvious but that he had no reason to assume anything but good faith on the part of New York Telephone—especially after having made so large an investment in the central station while depending wholly on the telephone franchise instead of securing a direct franchise. Vice President Cahill then questioned whether the telephone company had exceeded its authority in facilitating business through the public streets by the New York Electric Music Co. Crosby observed that this matter had been fully explored when the 1905 contract was negotiated. The telephone company's legal department had assured Crosby that it was fully empowered by franchise to run lines for Telharmony. The only impediments to the telephone company's actually doing the entire work of Telharmony itself were that the New York Electric Music Co. controlled the patents and had established the central station. Even though the contract was profitable for New York Telephone, Crosby got the message that a parting of the ways was in the offing. He assured Vice President Cahill that his company would soon apply for its own franchise. He asked only that the telephone company not "embarrass" the New York Electric Music Co. in the meantime by withholding service. The meeting ended with Crosby's clear impression that New York Telephone was uninterested in any further extensions of the cable system it was already supplying to the New York Electric Music Co. Crosby expressed the hope for some degree of mutual cooperation in his quest for a direct franchise, as it would effect an orderly cessation of the contract, if that was what was desired. Naturally, he understood that New York Telephone would be most interested and influential in any matter of wire franchises granted by New York City and would expect to be thoroughly consulted on any steps proposed by Crosby.[56]

FURTHER CONNECTIONS AND SCRUTINY

The next reported restaurant installation was at Louis Sherry's, on Fifth Avenue at 44th Street, which was noted for its many great banquets; the massive third-floor banquet hall, decorated in Louis XVI style, rose three stories high. With its impeccably correct appointments, Sherry's was regularly patronized by the Four Hundred—almost as their private club, with admission a matter of refinement and wealth. Amid baskets of ferns with concealed red lights, velvet hangings, crystal globes on the ceiling, and torches on the walls, Telharmony was savored on December 8. The occasion was the annual banquet of the then-very-exclusive Automobile Club of America. Six hundred persons dined to a long program, sixteen numbers of Telharmonic music, which accompanied a selection of motion pictures. Ten megaphones served up Telharmony, sweet and clear, to the diners. One reporter wrote, "It was a weird experience to realize that the performer, several blocks away, could not have had the remotest idea of the reception given to his music, or of the sensation it was causing."[57] One of the members, an executive of the Sierra Madre Land and Lumber Co., later reflected with rococo ripeness on his ecstasy:

> It was like invisible hands at the close of summer day striking from unseen harp strings unspeakable music to comfort, to solace, and to cheer. . . . Many days have passed since that eventful hour, and still there rings through all the corridors of memory, mystic, mysterious, majestic, that will abide until we pass beyond the veil of time and sense into the land of perpetual light and increasing harmonies.[58]

By this time, winter weather was prohibiting further work in the streets. The Telharmonium line had been laid along Broadway from 45th Street down to 23rd Street, thence turning up Fifth Avenue to 34th Street. Outlets had been run into various establishments, although unintentional delays by the New York Telephone Co. prevented lines from being brought to some customers who had requested service.[59]

By mid-December, there was intermittent service to Sherry's and the Café Martin. When it was supplied the music was sent out for luncheon from 12:30 to 2:00 and for dinner between 6:00 and 8:00. By now there were scores of daily visitors to the music room of the central station (Fig. 31)—press people, scientists, musicians, but not yet the general public. The music salon was no conventional proscenium auditorium. It bore more of a resemblance to an indoor arbor ornamented by hanging vines, potted ferns, and floral arrangements. There was a circular divan in the center. Easy chairs, some of wicker and others of wood, surrounded the divan. The console containing the two-manual keyboard, each with four banks, and the timbre-control switches, was on a raised platform against the wall at the far end of the room (Figs. 32 and 33). The visitor could approach the keyboard and ascertain that indeed no sound issued forth, save for a soft metallic click occasionally accompanied by a flashing spark. The music poured only from the receivers ensconced in the divan and the greenery.[60]

The increased notice taken of the new machine prompted a nearly full-page description in the Sunday *New York Times*. The writer found the "notes wonderfully like the reed tones of an organ, but sharper, clearer, sweeter, purer."[61] The obligatory instrumental imitations were presented. Cahill revealed that the expression devices

Fig. 31. The Music Room, Telharmonic Hall. (New York Electric Music Co., *Telharmony,* New York: The Company, late December 1906, 3)

were to be upgraded and that he was now at work on a touch-sensitive keyboard which could increase and decrease the volume by simply changing the pressure on a key.[62]

The article immediately attracted the attention of Mark Twain, who visited the music room of the central station the following Saturday afternoon:

> The trouble about these beautiful, novel things is that they interfere so with one's arrangements. Every time I see or hear a new wonder like this I have to postpone my death right off. I couldn't possibly leave the world until I have heard this again and again.[63]

Idling at the keyboard platform, his legs swinging languidly, he proposed great exploitations of the singing arc:

Fig. 32 (above). The Keyboard at Telharmonic Hall. (New York Electric Music Co., *Telharmony,* New York: The Company, late December 1906, 4)

> If a great princess marries, what is to hinder all the lamps along the streets on her wedding night playing that march together? [He had just listened to the wedding march from *Lohengrin.*] Or, if a great man should die—I, for example—they could all be tuned up a dirge.[64]

In December the Telharmonium principals requested the assistance of A.T.&T. in transmitting the Telharmonium long-distance to an electrical exhibition in Chicago. A.T.&T. agreed to perform some tests, making use of existing experimental circuits running from Telharmonic Hall to the New York Telephone Co. laboratory on Cortlandt Street.[65]

The usual transmission of Telharmonic music utilized two separate lines, one for the treble and the other for the bass. In general practice the former was represented by the melody and the latter by the accompaniment, with a separate keyboard dedicated to each. A.T.&T. engineer Robert E. Chetwood, Jr., recognized that two

Fig. 33 (above). Detail of Fig. 32, the Keyboard at Telharmonic Hall. (New York Electric Music Co., *Telharmony,* New York: The Company, late December 1906, 4)

circuits would be necessary to convey all the music to Chicago, but carried out his tests only on the treble circuit.[66]

Just after Christmas, Chetwood connected Telharmonic transmission from Cortlandt Street to A.T.&T.'s own New York laboratory. From there he sent it out over the main pole lines to Boston and back again, equivalent to the distance of the New York–Chicago line. As a result, he listened to the long-distance transmission right in his laboratory and compared it to the original.[67]

Chetwood found that the music made "but a very faint sound."[68] It did not much exceed the volume of a regular voice transmission over the same distance, in spite of the fact that New York Telephone was providing maximum possible current.[69] Apparently the very limited high-frequency response of the telephone system removed some portion of the musical signal; worse, optimally engineered as it was to transport low signal levels, the system could not help but attenuate a greater proportion of such high-power signals as Telharmony.

Chetwood then tested for crosstalk interference on other lines along the same telephone poles. He found that "the music was induced on practically every other circuit on the pole line and with a sufficient loudness to be considered extremely serious."[70]

Introduction into the circuit of a telephone repeater, an induction coil used to transfer a long-distance signal from one circuit into another without connecting them directly,[71] and capable of countering signal attenuation, did not boost the reception at all.[72]

Chetwood concluded that a much greater current level would be needed to transmit long-distance music to Chicago. If such current were available, which of course New York Telephone could not supply without encountering severe disturbances in its own adjacent circuitry, it would be necessary to remove from service the other long-distance circuits on the same pole line to Chicago.[73] His colleagues at A.T.&T. concurred with Chetwood: the interference was unacceptable, and the faintness of the music made transmission impracticable.[74]

The same engineers were, on the other hand, much taken with the horn used to amplify Telharmonic tones as they emanated from telephone receivers. They made a careful sketch of the horn for their files, duly noting its thickness ($^5/_{64}$ of an inch), its substance (papier mâché), and of course the dimensions of its orifices ($^5/_{16}$ of an inch; 2 feet) and of its length (4 feet, 9 inches).[75]

Telharmonic entertainment was next furnished along regular telephone circuits to the American Museum of Natural History, located on Central Park West between 77th and 81st Streets. At a reception there for the American Association for the Advancement of Science on December 29, the output of the central station supplied continuous music during the evening.[76]

The year 1906 closed, and it was clearly an occasion for self-satisfied appraisals. Mark Twain welcomed 1907 with the comment that he could exult over other dead people when he died, for he would have been the first person to turn "music on tap" on and off in his house like gas. He boasted of having been the first residential telephone subscriber some 30 years earlier, and of now being the first home Telharmonium subscriber as well. (Twain's house was on the southeast corner of Fifth Avenue and 9th Street, about three-quarters of a mile below the southern terminus of the Telharmonium line; a special wire had been arranged to establish the connection to the great humorist.)[77] The value of electrical apparatus manufactured during the year just ended had broken the record, exceeding $200 million. The Western Electric Co. was assembling a staggering 5,000 telephones each day. The Telharmonium was praised as the leading new electrical craft of 1906, an unbelievably wild fancy come true.[78]

The general prosperity was so unprecedented as to contain within itself the seeds of adversity. Commerce had stretched manufacturing, distribution, and banking facilities to their limits. Railroads had declared record dividends and proclaimed there was not money enough in all the world to build the tracks needed to relieve the traffic congestion sired by the rising prosperity. The money supply was totally inelastic; at harvest time and year end—the two periods of peak demand—interest rates on call money touched 40%. Money shortages were exacerbated by the losses in the San Francisco earthquake, which had wiped out $250 million in capital the previous April. Yet steel mills were booked through the closing months of 1907. Such unchecked heated expansion would put the money markets to a much severer strain in the coming year. Profit margins had narrowed as wages had risen in response to the greater demand for labor. Higher raw material costs were also putting the squeeze on earnings. It seemed as if productivity was on a collision course with the economic infrastructure, and each would disrupt the other in 1907.[79]

PREPARING FOR THE PUBLIC

The New York Electric Music Co. announced in the Saturday and Sunday papers of January 5 and 6 that the doors of the central station music room would finally be thrown open to the public on Monday, January 14. In these advertisements and press releases, the home of electric music was first dubbed "Telharmonic Hall." Two wonderful recitals daily at 3:00 and 8:30 were promised and "Hear the Singing Arc-Light, the Wonder of the Age"; admission was 50¢. Along with instrumental numbers there would be vocal selections featuring Telharmonic accompaniment.[80]

Out came the brochure *Telharmony* (Fig. 34) to plug the product. A one-page quotation from *Looking Backward* reminded the reader of

Fig. 34. Cover of *Telharmony* Brochure. (New York Electric Music Co.,
Telharmony, New York: The Company, late December 1906)

the Bellamy prophecy now being fulfilled. The new music would be
"subtle and entrancing beyond any harmony yet heard."[81] Most of
the pamphlet was devoted to a simple layman's explanation of the
technology. A close parallel to an electrical power station was drawn,
the two having similar equipment and service. The conclusion
praised Cahill as that rarity in the world of invention, the man who
had both conceived his idea and made it practicable. Most successful
inventions were the result of years of labor by many men before the
original proposal was realized—the telegraph, the electric arc light,
the dynamo, and the internal combustion engine. Cahill, however,
had brought his concept all the way to fruition, for it was "rapidly

being put into hotels, restaurants, and homes throughout New York."[82] This last assertion was echoed by Elliott Schenck's friends at the *Musical Courier,* who opined that "much of the success of the instrument is due to Mr. Schenck's directorship."[83]

Accompanying the brochure was a 1 $^1/_2$-by-2 $^1/_2$ foot broadside, *The Wonderful Telharmonic System.* The text was an edited version of Ray Stannard Baker's article in the July 1906 issue of *McClure's Magazine.* References to the musicians Karl W. Schulz, H. Franklin Harris, and Edwin Hall Pierce had been deleted, except for one mention of Pierce that remained undetected. Listed among the staff of the New York Electric Music Co. was Carl M. Pihl as manager.[84] Pihl had studied chemistry and engineering at Johns Hopkins University and in 1897, at the age of 23, became manager of his first utility plant—the telephone exchange at Holyoke. He supervised the installation of a new main exchange and eight branch exchanges, as the number of telephones swelled from 400 in 1897 to more than 1,200 in 1906. Nevertheless, when he cast his lot with the Telharmonium in the fall of 1906, and his successor took charge of telephone service, the Holyoke paper commented, "Subscribers may now look for a decided upward tendency in the character of service rendered."[85]

THE CASINO THEATRE

A few days before the public opening, the New York Electric Music Co. supplied its first theatrical connection. This did not travel far, only across 39th Street. There the huge, ornate Casino Theatre (Fig. 35), a center of finery and show, ringed with the carriages of the rich, put the music in its lobby. The elaborate Moorish facade and gleaming Oriental decorations, gilded with deranged expansiveness, outfitted a luxurious temple of musical comedies "of the Casino type, fluffy and frolicsome."[86] It was the prime gathering place for privileged youth to survey a showcase of feminine bloom. The Telharmonic concerts mystified patrons, whose searches failed to discover the musicians or the machine whence came the music. For an hour before the curtain rose on each performance of *Princess Beggar,* with its huge chorus, pretty and shapely women, and bubbling

Fig. 35. Across from Telharmonic Hall: East Side of Broadway, 39th Street to 38th Street, Casino Theatre. (Rand, McNally and Company, Publishers, *Greater New York Illustrated,* Chicago: The Company, 1901, 149)

gaiety, audiences were treated to electric music. Tunes were also supplied during the entr'actes. In honor of the new service, Telharmonist Karl W. Schulz added a tune from the show to the repertoire.[87]

THE GALA RECEPTION

The New York Electric Music Co. celebrated the inauguration of public service with a large formal reception held on Friday, January 11. The concern had distributed invitations (Fig. 36) to distinguished personages in science, business, and the arts to a late-afternoon recital at Telharmonic Hall. A dinner party in the evening followed at Sherry's and several other restaurants, where more of the music was given. In the auditorium Mendelssohn's *Song of Spring, Träumerei,* selections from *William Tell,* and ragtime syncopations delighted prominent New

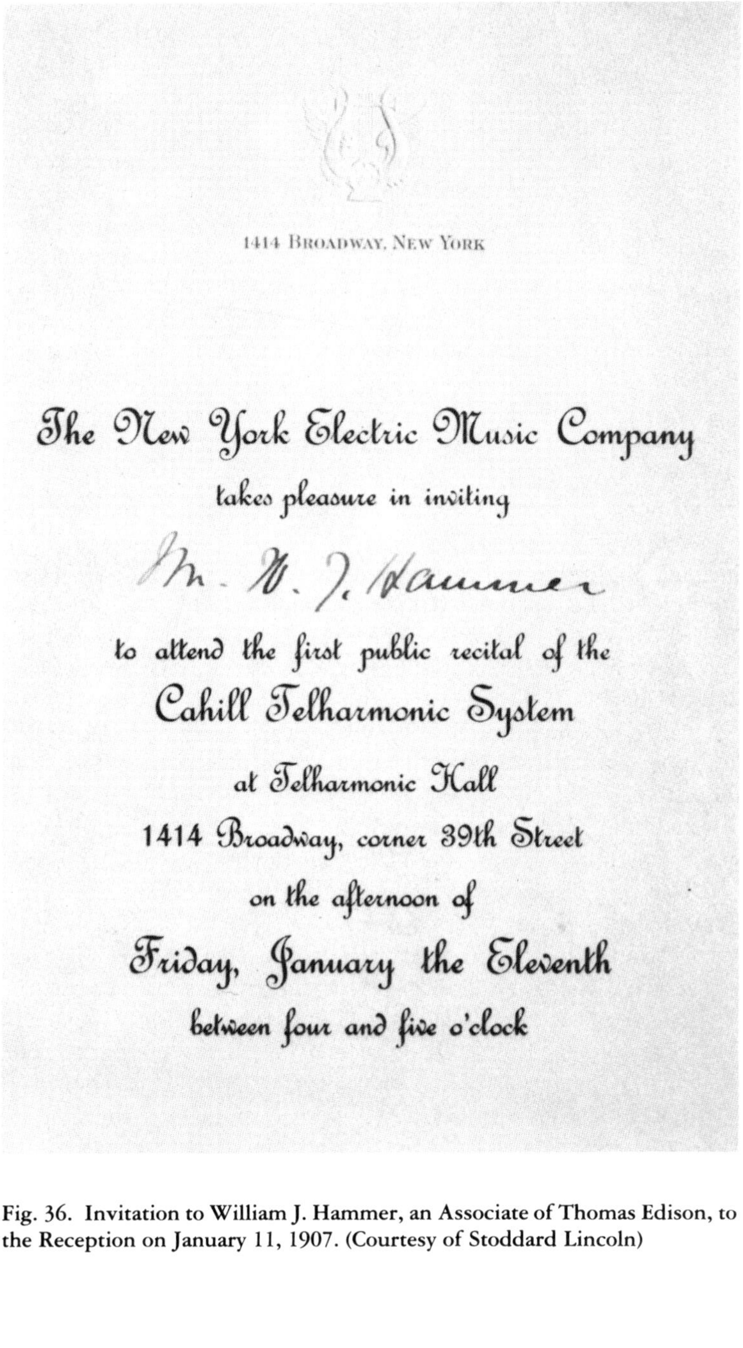

1414 BROADWAY, NEW YORK

The New York Electric Music Company

takes pleasure in inviting

Mr. W. J. Hammer

to attend the first public recital of the

Cahill Telharmonic System

at Telharmonic Hall

1414 Broadway, corner 39th Street

on the afternoon of

Friday, January the Eleventh

between four and five o'clock

Fig. 36. Invitation to William J. Hammer, an Associate of Thomas Edison, to the Reception on January 11, 1907. (Courtesy of Stoddard Lincoln)

Yorkers. One report compared its sound to "a peculiar combination of the oboe horn, the 'cello, and the violin, and at the same time the tones of which are fuller and more complete than those of any of these instruments."[88] In a fulsome tribute, the same reporter averred that Cahill had indeed succeeded in combining the best of all known musical instruments while eliminating their defects. The imitations of instruments—even the violin—were to him perfect, excepting only the piano. Appreciative audiences at the Café Martin and the Hotel Imperial on Broadway at 31st Street—whose renowned Palm Room attracted nightly a cosmopolitan after-theatre crowd of pleasure-seeking editors, writers, artists, theatrical stars, and titled foreigners—were treated to the same concert heard in Telharmonic Hall, which also featured a display of the singing arc. Further experiments were performed on an ordinary incandescent bulb, alternately dimming and brightening along with the musical currents. Many of those present were of the opinion that the music emanated directly from the Telharmonic keyboard. They were disabused of this notion when the receivers were hung up, the only remaining sound being a slight clicking of the keys. Listeners at the Café Martin and the Hotel Imperial, whose sound was not cut off, confirmed that the instrument indeed continued to function. There was talk at the reception of the company's plans to lay its own lines, and of the inadvisability of using those belonging to the telephone company, which the directors claimed were prone to interruption. The principals grandly announced that receivers had recently been installed at the Normandie Hotel on Broadway at 38th Street, and at the Waldorf-Astoria Hotel, on Fifth Avenue from 33rd to 34th Street. The Normandie was famed for its steaks and mutton chops; it had four conservative, quiet dining rooms, one featuring an immense carved mahogany mantel evoking an old English hall. The vast Waldorf-Astoria served 5,000 meals daily in its many rooms—the muraled Astor restaurant, the imperial Waldorf room, the two marbled and domed gardens, the oaken café, the numerous private rooms, the satin-paneled East Room, the grand ballroom (all ormolu over Pompeiian red), and the mahogany State Banquet Hall, its walls lined with cabinets of rare and beautiful china services. Orders for electric music were beginning to flow in from private residences. Oscar T. Crosby and his investors conveyed the impression of being willing to spend virtually unlimited funds to provide public Telharmonic service. The list of luminaries present read like a Who's Who in New York,[89] and included the following:

Spencer Trask,

62-year-old banker and backer of Edison's electric lighting enterprises from their earliest days. His Edison investments provided the capital that enabled him to gain directorships and control over various railroads and realty companies. Trask was beginning to wind down business activities, devoting more of his time to art patronage and philanthropy. His country estate, "Yaddo" at Saratoga Springs, N.Y., overflowed with art treasures. He permitted the public to wander about the 500-acre grounds.[90]

George Foster Peabody,

54-year-old recently retired banker and railroad financier. As a boy, Peabody found work in a Brooklyn dry-goods firm after his impoverished family had moved there to escape post–Civil War Georgia. He met Spencer Trask at the Reformed Church in Brooklyn Heights, and they became partners in 1881. Peabody specialized in the firm's railroad investments and became a director of numerous railroads and other corporations. Along with Trask, Peabody invested $10,000 in Edison's incandescent light experiments. At the peak of his career, in April 1906, Peabody retired to devote his time to philanthropy and radical causes. He felt his wealth to be the result of other men's labors, so he decided to become his own executor and administer his funds for the benefit of the people to whom he felt it rightfully belonged. He advocated Henry George's single tax, women's suffrage, free trade, and government ownership of railroads and public franchise corporations.[91] Upon receiving its own franchise, Peabody would have had the Telharmonium come under government control.

Robert Curtis Ogden,

70-year-old merchant and philanthropist, a partner of John Wanamaker, and manager of their mammoth retail store in New York. His formal schooling had ended at age 14, when he went to work in his father's Philadelphia dry-goods store. Ogden managed the entire Wanamaker concern from 1889 to 1893, while Wanamaker was serving in President Harrison's cabinet. Ogden devoted much effort to promoting education in the rural South, working for increased taxes and higher standards for both black and white schools. He encountered bitter opposition at first, but eventually gained so much public support that he became one of the favorite Northerners in the South.[92]

Walter Damrosch,

44-year-old conductor of the New York Symphony Orchestra. Son of the distinguished violinist and conductor Leopold Damrosch, he had been trained as a pianist and violinist. He had grown up in a home in Breslau that witnessed the visits of family friends Richard Wagner, Clara Schumann, Franz Liszt, Hans von Bülow, and Anton Rubinstein. In 1871, the family emigrated to America. Ten years later, at the age of 18, Damrosch received his first conducting appointment, with the Newark, N.J., Harmonic Society. In 1885 his father suddenly fell ill while conducting a series of German operas at the Metropolitan Opera House in New York. The son took his place, conducting opera for the first time and completing the season. The elder Damrosch died within a few weeks, and Walter Damrosch took over the opera company's tour. In those days, he recalled later:

> Wagner was a debated novelty, opera was considered exotic
> . . . . For the great mass of people not only opera but also
> chamber music was an unknown quantity. Comparatively few
> cities had orchestras; regimental bands rendered descriptive
> pieces in which anvils and cannon played important parts. . . .
> For the great majority "The Old Oaken Bucket" and "Sweet
> Adeline" meant music.[93]

That same year Damrosch accepted appointments at the Metropolitan Opera, the New York Symphony Orchestra, and the New York Oratorio Society. After several years he left the Met to concentrate on symphonic and choral concerts, with occasional presentations of German opera. He organized the New York Symphony Orchestra into a permanent organization in 1903.[94]

Victor Herbert,

47-year-old composer of light operas. Born in Dublin, Herbert had been educated in Germany and had later served as solo cellist in the Württemberg Court Orchestra at Stuttgart. In 1886, he became engaged to prima donna Augusta Forster, who was then hired by Walter Damrosch to perform at the Met. He could not bear to part with her, and so they married and emigrated to America. Herbert became solo cellist at the Met. In the ensuing years he was hired as soloist and conductor of various orchestras, including the Pittsburgh Orchestra. His composing career began in 1884 with theatre music, and ten years later he wrote the first of many light operas. Their popularity kept him so busy that he eventually gave up the cello. His greatest successes were *Babes in Toyland* (1903), *It Happened in Nordland* (1904), and the immensely popular *The Red Mill* (1906), which was enjoying a standing-room-only run on the night of the Telharmonium reception. He was now called "Lucky Victor," for there were fully ten shows of his playing to delighted audiences at the beginning of 1907. Two had just opened on Christmas Day, one featuring the song *Love by Telephone.* His sheet music sales were enormous. In addition to a talent for sparkling, bewitching melodies, Herbert was blessed with a jovial, kindhearted personality that won him countless friends. His capacity for work was prodigious. He sometimes worked on four scores at a time, walking from table to table to record incessant outpourings of music.[95]

Clarence Hungerford Mackay,

32-year-old capitalist. His father, John Mackay, was one of the four "Silver King" miners who exploited the Comstock Lode at Virginia City, Nev., in the mid-1870s. The bonanza had yielded $150 million worth of silver. When it abruptly ceased, the four had already sold off their worthless interests, bringing ruin to thousands. The younger Mackay was made a director of his father's telegraph and cable companies at the age of 22. He supervised the completion of the first transpacific cable to the Orient, after his father's death in 1902. He was fond of hunting and technology, and so a year before had had an

electric buck constructed on his 500-acre Roslyn estate. One of
Mackay's electricians built a miniature railroad with many sudden
turns and elevations. A buck with wool insides, a canvas skin, and a
magnificent pair of real antlers was mounted on a little electric
trolley. Guests took turns firing at the twisting, leaping target,
managing to knock off only a few antler prongs and the tail. The real
deer on Mackay's estate were left in peace. Mackay was also an ardent
amateur cellist and enthusiastic athlete, having captured the national
racquets championship in 1902.[96]

Clyde Fitch,

41-year-old playwright. Reared in affluence, Fitch roamed Europe
for several years after graduating from college, developing a keen eye
and ear for the foibles and comedies of life. He settled in New York
City in 1888, writing poetry and stories for children's magazines.
His first play, *Beau Brummel,* written and produced in 1890, was an
exhilarating success. Numerous witty, clever dramas followed at the
rate of two or three a year, most playing to packed houses. He was
widely regarded as a genius, the first great American playwright,
although critical response could be adverse: "Only occasionally . . .
has he dealt with emotions that are vitally of the strongest and
maintained the dramatic struggle between them."[97] Four days before
the Telharmonium reception, two of his plays had opened the same
night—*The Straight Road* and *The Truth.* The latter concluded as
follows:

> *Becky.* You can't forgive me!
> *Warder.* We don't love people because they are perfect.
> (*He takes her two trembling hands in his, and she rises.*)
> *Becky.* Tom!
> *Warder.* We love them because they are themselves.
> (*And he takes her in his arms close to him, as the final curtain falls.*)[98]

The press's reception of *The Truth* was tepid, while *The Straight Road,*
a melodrama of the slums of New York, received plaudits everywhere. A few days later, the critics would change their tune about
The Truth, but it soon closed under the force of their original
attacks.[99]

Peter Cooper Hewitt,

45-year-old millionaire inventor, son of former New York mayor Abram S. Hewitt and grandson of philanthropist and iron manufacturer Peter Cooper. He had inherited considerable mechanical ability from his grandfather, and those who watched him work "felt that a part, at least, of Hewitt's thinking apparatus was in his hands."[100] He had begun to work with electricity in 1898, and in 1903 invented the Cooper Hewitt lamp. This became the most efficient electric lighting instrument then available; it passed electric current through mercury vapor. The lamp was widely adopted in factories and motion picture studios. Other Hewitt inventions included an ac-dc rectifier, a high-frequency generator for wireless telegraphy, and a hydroplane that he was working on at the time of the Telharmonium reception. He expected it to travel at speeds of up to 100 mph. Hewitt was also an accomplished pianist and possessor of the largest musical instrument collection in New York.[101]

Colonel Robert Charles Clowry,

68-year-old president of the Western Union Telegraph Co. and also a director of the Telharmonium's supplier, the New York Telephone Co. He had begun as a telegraph messenger at the age of 14, working his way up slowly through managerial and supervisory posts. During the Civil War he was in charge of military telegraphs. Clowry became president of the 20,000-employee Western Union corporation in 1902, just as it was beginning its long, slow asphyxiation at the hands of telephone competition.[102]

Henry Herman Westinghouse,

53-year-old mechanical engineer and brother of inventor George Westinghouse, who had been interested in Cahill's work in Washington. Henry Westinghouse became involved with his brother's air brake company, but in 1883 invented a steam engine and then formed his own machine company and engineering firm. His steam

engine became a worldwide success, but he continued to serve as
officer and director with the George Westinghouse companies.[103]

Gustave Schirmer,

42-year-old son of the founder of the great music publishing house
G. Schirmer. Since the death of their father he had headed the firm
with his brother. Gustave Schirmer was widely admired in the music
world for his cultivated and knowledgeable musicianship and refusal
to publish low-quality popular music. He supported modern composers, particularly Charles Martin Loeffler, and took an interest in
new musical directions.[104]

Anna Farwell de Koven,

46-year-old author and socialite. She was the wife of Victor Herbert's
archrival, composer Reginald de Koven, whose most enduring legacy
was a ballad still often heard at the odd wedding, *O Promise Me*. Anna
de Koven had written several novels and had then begun to study the
life of John Paul Jones. A few months before the Telharmonium
reception, she had electrified the literary world with a detailed
critical exposé of the revered *Life of Paul Jones* (1900) by Augustus C.
Buell as a complete hoax. In two full newspaper pages de Koven
showed the biography to contain reports of imaginary committees,
false letters, nonexistent journals, and invented entries from known
diaries.[105]

TELEPHONE LINES

As Telharmonic Hall was undergoing final preparations for its debut
to the masses, Oscar T. Crosby telephoned Vice President Cahill of
the New York Telephone Co. He wanted to discuss the application
of the New York Electric Music Co. for its own franchise. The two
could lunch in Crosby's quarters, where Telharmonic music had
recently been installed. Cahill frostily refused to see him, stating that

Crosby was to submit his plans in writing. In due course any papers would be properly considered by the legal department of New York Telephone.[106]

The vice president was very likely preoccupied with the wide and strident criticism of the wretched phone service that prevailed throughout Manhattan. Angered by three years of fighting overcharges, slow service, and poor accounting, a local taxpayers' association had recently called a special meeting to appeal to the legislature. Especially infuriating were the frequent assertions by operators that a line was disconnected when the caller knew perfectly well that his or her party was at a working telephone awaiting the call. Subscribers who kept strict accounts of usage discovered overcharges. Telephone bills listed calls on nonexistent days. Nearly every subscriber had a litany of complaints, which went largely unheeded by the exchange managers. The burgeoning demand for telephone service had overburdened the system, much of which was antiquated and undergoing disruptive modernization.[107]

Another incursion that harassed telephone company officials had to contend with was the efforts of rival companies to crack open their monopoly. The Atlantic Telephone Co. was negotiating with the Board of Estimate for a franchise. It had recently received permission to install an experimental automated exchange in the Mulberry Street Police Headquarters.[108]

NOTES

1. "The First Public Telharmonic Concert," *Electrical World,* October 6, 1906, XLVIII:14, 637.

2. *Ibid.*; "Duma Dissolved; Army in Capital," *New York Times,* July 22, 1906, pt. 2, 1–2; "Dismissing the Duma," *New York Times,* July 23, 1906, 6.

3. "Music and Musicians," *New York Evening Sun,* January 12, 1907, 5.

4. John Philip Sousa, "The Menace of Mechanical Music," *Appleton's Magazine,* September 1906, VIII:3, 278–284; "The Day of 'Canned' Music," *New York Times,* August 24, 1906, 6; "Sousa Severely Roasted by Editors," *Musical Age,* September 15, 1906, LV:7, 168; Rupert Hughes, "The Place of Mechanical Instruments in Musical Culture," *Etude,* October 1906, XXIV:10, 672, 674.

5. "The First Public Telharmonic Concert," 637.

6. *Ibid.*

7. "Electric Music Demonstration," *Musical Age,* September 29, 1906, LV:9, 231.

8. *Ibid.*; "Dynamophone Music Heard," *New-York Daily Tribune,* September 27, 1906, 13; "Dynamophone Music Heard," *Talking Machine World,* October 15, 1906, II:10, 6.

9. James Francis Cooke, "Das Telharmonium: Ein neues Wunder in der Musikwelt," *Musikalisches Wochenblatt,* December 13, 1906, 37:50, 933–935, tr. Martin Wulfhorst.

10. "Prof. Albert F. Ganz Dead," *New York Times,* July 29, 1917, 15.

11. "The First Public Telharmonic Concert," 637.

12. *Ibid.*; Letter from Oscar T. Crosby, President, New York Electric Music Company, to Charles F. Cutler, President, New York Telephone Company, January 27, 1907, 3.

13. "Distributing Music," *Electrical World,* November 17, 1906, XLVIII:20, 949.

14. James Edward Pierce, "James E. Pierce and Frances Hall Married July 11, 1866, in Auburn, N.Y.," List of family birthdates, April 23, 1983, R.W., 1; Edna Leaf Woodruff Pierce, Diary, Auburn, N.Y., February 4, 1898, to March 6, 1908, J.E.P., 12; Letter from James E. Pierce to Cynthia Hoover, Smithsonian Institution, June 7, 1974, S.I., 1; Letter from James Edward Pierce, Smithfield, Va., May 11, 1983, 1; Personal interview with James Edward Pierce, Echo Lake Farm, Great Spring Road, Smithfield, Va., April 23, 1983.

15. "A New Position for Schenck," *Musical Courier,* October 24, 1906, LIII:17, 24.

16. "Elliott Schenck, Composer, Was 69," *New York Times,* March 6, 1939, 15; "Schenck's Success," *Musical Courier,* January 24, 1906, LII:4, 41; "Schenck for New Orleans," *Musical Courier,* July 18, 1906, LIII:3, 19; "Schenck Not for New Orleans," *Musical Courier,* August 1, 1906, LIII:5, 31; "A New Opera by Elliot [*sic*] Schenck," *Musical Courier,* August 8, 1906, LIII:6, 33; "Schenck to Lecture," *Musical Courier,* October 3, 1906, LIII:14, 41.

17. "Schenck Aids the 'Children's Crusade,' " *Musical Courier,* December 12, 1906, LIII:24, 29.

18. Lloyd Morris, *Incredible New York,* New York: Random House, 1951, 260.

19. "Distributing Music," 949; "Cafe Martin," display advertisement, *New York Times,* December 14, 1906, 10; Lewis, Scribner and Co., *Where and How to Dine in New York,* New York: The Company, 1903, 7–12; "Music Is on Tap Now over New York 'Phones," *New York Times,* November 10, 1906, 6; "Get Music by Telephone," *New York Sun,* November 10, 1906, 4; "Central Plant Sends Music over Wires," *New York Herald,* November 10, 1906, 5; "Arc Lights Shed Electrical Music," *New York World,* November 10, 1906, 6.

20. "Get Music by Telephone," 4; "Grand Opera by Wire," New York *Evening Sun,* November 10, 1906, 3.

21. "Get Music by Telephone," 4; "Grand Opera by Wire," 3; "Hear Electrical Music," *Musical America,* November 17, 1906, V:1, 13; "Music on Tap over 'Phone," *Music Trade Review,* November 17, 1906, LXIII:20, 3; "Get Music by Telephone," *Talking Machine World,* November 15, 1906, II:11, 43; "Music Is on Tap Now over New York 'Phones," 6.

22. "Get Music by Telephone," 43; "Music Is on Tap Now over New York 'Phones," 6; "Music on Tap over 'Phone," 3.

23. "Music on Tap over 'Phone," 3.

24. " 'Telharmonium' Works Well," *New-York Daily Tribune,* November 10, 1906, 16; "New Musical Instrument," *Denison* [Tex.] *Herald,* November 10, 1906, S.C., n.p.

25. "Concert Music by Wire," *New York Evening Mail,* November 12, 1906, 7.

26. "Hear Electrical Music," 13; "Music Is on Tap Now over New York 'Phones," 6; "Distributing Music," 949; "Get Music by Telephone," 4.

27. "Music Is on Tap Now over New York 'Phones," 6.

28. "Get Music by Telephone," 4.

29. "Music Is on Tap Now over New York 'Phones," 6; "Get Music by Telephone," 43; "Dr. Cahill's Invention," *Holyoke Daily Transcript,* November 10, 1906, 2.

30. "The Oracle," *Holyoke Daily Transcript,* October 23, 1906, 10.

31. "Concert Music by Wire," *New York Evening Mail,* November 12, 1906, 7.

32. "Behind the Scenes in a 'Smart' New York Restaurant," *New York Times,* July 15, 1906, pt. 3, 2.

33. " 'Covers for Two': A Gastronomic Study," *New York Times,* September 2, 1906, pt. 4, 2.

34. "Behind the Scenes in a 'Smart' New York Restaurant," 2.

35. "Behind the Scenes in a 'Smart' New York Restaurant," 2; " 'Covers for Two': A Gastronomic Study," 2.

36. "That Dreadful New York Appetite," *New York World,* January 20, 1907, Magazine Section, 6.

37. " 'Covers for Two': A Gastronomic Study," 2.

38. *Ibid.,* 2.

39. *Ibid.*

40. Theodore Dreiser, *Sister Carrie* [Doubleday, Page and Company, 1900], afterword by Willard Thorp, New York: The New American Library, 1961, 297–298.

41. "Ferrero Studies New York City in Its Nightly Pursuit of Pleasure," *New York Times,* December 20, 1908, pt. 5, 1; "Music at Meals and What It Costs," *New York Times,* August 30, 1908, pt. 5, 7; "Where Music

Soothes While Lobsters Broil," *New York Times,* April 24, 1910, pt. 5, 7; Lewis, Scribner and Co., 11.

42. "Music at Meals and What It Costs," 7; "Where Music Soothes While Lobsters Broil," 7.

43. "Music at Meals and What It Costs," 7; "Where Music Soothes While Lobsters Broil," 7.

44. "Music at Meals and What It Costs," 7; "Where Music Soothes While Lobsters Broil," 7.

45. "Music at Meals and What It Costs," 7; "Where Music Soothes While Lobsters Broil," 7.

46. "Music at Meals and What It Costs," 7.

47. "Music at Meals and What It Costs," 7; "Where Music Soothes While Lobsters Broil," 7; "Phonograph Music While You Eat," *Musical Age,* May 4, 1907, LVIII:1, 18.

48. "Music at Meals and What It Costs," 7; "Music as an Aid to Digestion," *Musical America,* May 11, 1907, V:25, 12; "Influence of Music on Dining," *Music Trade Review,* November 3, 1906, XLIII:18, 3.

49. "Where Music Soothes While Lobsters Broil," 7: "Music in Restaurants," *New York Times,* August 20, 1908, 6.

50. "Music as an Aid to Digestion," 12, "Always Eat to Slow Music," *Music Trade Review,* May 4, 1907, XLIV:18, 40: "Where Music Soothes While Lobsters Broil," 7.

51. "Where Music Soothes While Lobsters Broil," 7.

52. "Music as an Aid to Digestion," 12; "Phonograph Music While You Eat," 18.

53. "Where Music Soothes While Lobsters Broil," 7.

54. Letter from Oscar T. Crosby, 2; "The Telephone Fight Will Be Reopened," *New York Times,* July 15, 1906, pt. 2, 18; "Telephone Companies Bid for a Monopoly," *New York Times,* July 18, 1906, 14; "Hearing Before the Assembly Committee on General Laws on a Bill Introduced by Mr. Krulewitch, Entitled 'An Act to Regulate the Toll Charges for Local Telephone Communication,' " in *The Telephone System and Service Charges in New York City,* Report of the Committee on City Affairs of the Republican Club, New York: The Committee, 1906, 1–7, 12–13, 20–21; "Music on Wires," *New York Globe and Commercial Advertiser,* January 31, 1907, 4.

55. "Music on Wires," 4.

56. Letter from Oscar T. Crosby, 2–3.

57. Lewis, Scribner and Co., 125–127; "Telharmonic Music at a Public Function," *New York Globe and Commercial Advertiser,* December 10, 1906, 5; "Electric Music for Diners," *Musical America,* December 15, 1906, V:5, 6; New York Electric Music Company, *Telharmony: A New Art,* New York: The Company, early January 1907?, N.Y.P.L. *MKY Box, 3–4; "Music over the Wire," *New York Evening Mail,* December 11, 1906, 4.

58. Winthrop E. Scarritt, in Eastern Cahill Telharmonic Company, *Telharmony: The New Art of Electric Music,* New York: The Company, June? 1907, M.C.S., 13.

59. Addams Stratton McAllister, "Some Electrical Features of the Cahill Telharmonic System," *Electrical World,* January 5, 1907, XLIX:1, 24; Letter from Oscar T. Crosby, 3.

60. "Magic Music from the Telharmonium," *New York Times,* December 16, 1906, pt. 3, 3; New York Electric Music Company, *Telharmony,* New York: The Company, late December 1906?, N.Y.P.L. *MKY Box, S.L., 3–4.

61. "Magic Music from the Telharmonium," 3.

62. *Ibid.*

63. "Twain and the Telephone," *New York Times,* December 23, 1906, pt. 2, 2; "Twain and the Telharmonium," *Music Trade Review,* December 29, 1906, XLIII:26, 14; "Twain at the Telharmonium," *Electrical World,* December 29, 1906, XLVIII:26, 1233.

64. *Ibid.*

65. Letter from Robert E. Chetwood, Jr., American Telephone and Telegraph Co., to G. M. Yorke, Assistant Engineer, American Telephone and Telegraph Co., January 2, 1907, A.T.T.B.L.A., Boston File 500, 603822, 1.

66. *Ibid.,* 1–2.

67. *Ibid.*

68. *Ibid.,* 2.

69. *Ibid.*

70. *Ibid.*

71. Edwin J. Houston, *Electricity in Every-Day Life,* vol. 3, New York: P. F. Collier and Son, 1905, 163.

72. Chetwood, 3.

73. *Ibid.*

74. Letter from Chief Engineer [n.n.], American Telephone and Telegraph Co., to C. H. Wilson, General Superintendent, American Telephone and Telegraph Co., January 2, 1907, A.T.T.B.L.A., Boston File 500, 603822, 1.

75. Letter and Drawing from Assistant Engineer [n.n.], American Telephone and Telegraph Co., to E. S. Warren, American Telephone and Telegraph Co., January 3, 1907, A.T.T.B.L.A., Boston File 500, 20.03.01.02, 1–2.

76. "Telharmonium Demonstration," *Electrical World,* January 5, 1907, XLIX:1, 8.

77. "Music and Musicians," *New York Evening Sun,* January 12, 1907, 5; Eastern Cahill Telharmonic Company, 13.

78. Thomas Commerford Martin, "Electrical Arts Output $210,000,000," *New York Herald,* January 2, 1907, 48; "Living by Electricity," *New-York Daily Tribune,* January 19, 1908, pt. V, 3.

79. "1906–1907," *New York Times Annual Financial Review*, January 6, 1907, 2.

80. "Telharmonium Will Play," *New York Globe and Commercial Advertiser*, January 5, 1907, 9; "Telharmonic Hall," display advertisement, *New York Times*, January 6, 1907, pt. 4, 4; "Telharmonic Hall," display advertisement, *New York Herald*, January 6, 1907, sec. 3, 15. Both pages also carry advertisements for "Horszowski, the Wonderful Polish Child Pianist;" Mieczyslaw Horszowski, 100 years old in 1992, does not recall the Telharmonium. Tim Page, "Music: Horszowski and Orchestra of St. Luke's," *New York Times*, February 2, 1986, pt. 2, 51; Telephone interview with Mrs. Mieczyslaw Horszowski, Philadelphia, Pa., May 13, 1986.

81. New York Electric Music Company, *Telharmony*, 5.

82. *Ibid.*, 11.

83. "Elliott Schenck's Latest Successes," *Musical Courier*, January 9, 1907, LIV:2, 31.

84. Ray Stannard Baker, *The Wonderful Telharmonic System*, broadside, edited text of Ray Stannard Baker's "New Music for an Old World," *McClure's Magazine*, July 1906, XXVII:3, 291–301, New York: New York Electric Music Co., late December 1906?, S.L.

85. "Long Illness Takes Life of Colonel Pihl," *Jacksonville* [Fla.] *Times-Union*, May 1, 1933, 9; "Jaxon Is Dead," *Jacksonville Journal*, May 1, 1933, 3; "Telephone Improvements," *Holyoke Daily Transcript*, April 3, 1906, 3; "New Manager Here," *Holyoke Daily Transcript*, October 11, 1906, 7.

86. Roy L. McCardell, "What the Casino's Twenty-fifth Birthday To-Morrow Means to Broadway's History Explained by McCardell," *New York World*, June 30, 1907, Metropolitan Section, 2.

87. "Clyde Fitch Again," *New-York Daily Tribune*, January 6, 1907, pt. IV, 6; "Electric Music for Theatre Patrons," *Musical Age*, January 12, 1907, LVI:11, 330; "The Telharmonic System Installed," *Music Trade Review*, January 12, 1907, XLIV:2, 33; Lloyd, 183, 189.

88. "It's Magical Music," *New York Globe and Commercial Advertiser*, January 12, 1907, 9.

89. New York Electric Music Company, Invitation from the Company to Mr. W. J. Hammer, January 1907?, S.L., copy S.I.; Letter from H. E. Mitchell to Wm. J. Hammer, January 3, 1907, S.L.; "Musical Items," *Etude*, February, 1907, XXV:2, 135; "Telharmonium Concerts," *Electrical World*, January 19, 1907, XLIX:3, 136; "Telharmonic Demonstration," *Music Trade Review*, January 19, 1907, XLIV:3, 11; "Music Heard by Wire," *New-York Daily Tribune*, January 12, 1907, 7; Lewis, Scribner and Co., 25–26, 94–95, 133–135; "It's Magical Music," 9.

90. "Trask, Spencer," *Who's Who in New York City and State*, third edition, New York: L. R. Hamersly and Company, 1907, 1285; "Trask, Spencer," *Who Was Who in America*, vol. I, Chicago: Marquis–Who's Who,

1966, 1251; "Mr. Trask Notable in Varied Fields," *New York Times,* January 1, 1910, 2.

91. "Peabody, George Foster," *Who's Who in New York City and State,* third edition, New York: L. R. Hamersly and Company, 1907, 1025; Louise Ware, "Peabody, George Foster," *Dictionary of American Biography,* vol. XI, supp. 2, New York: Charles Scribner's Sons, 958, 520–521; "Peabody, George Foster," *The National Cyclopaedia of American Biography,* vol. XV, New York: James T. White and Company, 1916, 140–141; "Peabody, George Foster," *The National Cyclopaedia of American Biography,* vol. XXVII, New York: James T. White and Company, 1939, 64–65; "George F. Peabody Retires," *New York Times,* May 1, 1906, 1; "G. F. Peabody Dead: Philanthropist, 85," *New York Times,* March 5, 1938, 17.

92. "Ogden, Robert Curtis," *Who's Who in New York City and State,* third edition, New York: L. R. Hamersly and Company, 1907, 995; William Bristol Shaw, "Ogden, Robert Curtis," *Dictionary of American Biography,* vol. VII, New York: Charles Scribner's Sons, 1962, 641–642; "Ogden, Robert Curtis," *The National Cyclopaedia of American Biography,* vol. XIV, New York: James T. White and Company, 1917, 415; "Mrs. R. C. Ogden Dies of Pneumonia," *New York Times,* December 4, 1909, 11; "R. C. Ogden Dies at Maine Home," *New York Times,* August 7, 1913, 7.

93. "Walter Damrosch Dies at Age of 88," *New York Times,* December 23, 1950, 16.

94. "Damrosch, Walter Johannes," *Who's Who in New York City and State,* third edition, New York: L. R. Hamersly and Company, 1907, 374; "Damrosch, Walter (Johannes)," *The National Cyclopaedia of American Biography,* vol. XLIII, New York: James T. White and Company, 1961, 8–9; "Walter Damrosch Dies at Age of 88," *New York Times,* December 23, 1950, 1, 16.

95. "Herbert, Victor," *Who's Who in New York City and State,* third edition, New York: L. R. Hamersly and Company, 1907, 659; "Victor Herbert Dies on Way to Physician," *New York Times,* May 27, 1924, 1; "Victor Herbert's Life as Shown in Anecdotes," *New York Times,* June 1, 1924, 12; "Victor Herbert's 'Red Mill,' " *Music Trade Review,* December 29, 1906, XLIII:26, 50; "Personal Briefs," *Music Trade Review,* January 5, 1907, XLIV:1, 49; "Successful Musical Comedies," *Music Trade Review,* January 5, 1907, XLIV:1, 48; "Victor Herbert," *New York Times,* May 28, 1927, 22.

96. "Mackay, Clarence H.," *Who's Who in New York City and State,* third edition, New York: L. R. Hamersly and Company, 1907, 883; "Sold by Clarence Mackay," *New York Times,* July 20, 1903, 1; "Mackay, Clarence Hungerford," *The National Cyclopaedia of American Biography,* vol. XXXI, New York: James T. White and Company, 1944, 24; "Mackay, Clarence Hungerford," *The National Cyclopaedia of American Biography,* vol. XIV, New York: James T. White and Company, 1917, 85; "Mackay, Clarence Hungerford," *American Biography: A New Cyclopedia,* vol. VI, New York:

The American Historical Society, 1919, 7–8; "Clarence H. Mackay Has Electric Buck," *New York Times,* April 16, 1905, pt. 1, 9; Wayne Andrews, "Mackay, Clarence Hungerford," *Dictionary of American Biography,* vol. XI, supp. 2, New York: Charles Scribner's Sons, 1958, 415–416; "Mackay, Clarence Hungerford," *Webster's American Biographies,* Springfield: G. and C. Merriam Company, Publishers, 1974, 672.

97. "Topics of the Drama: Mr. Fitch and His Shortcomings," *New York Times,* January 18, 1903, 34.

98. Clyde Fitch, "The Truth," in John Gassner and Mollie Gassner, eds., *Best Plays of the Early American Theatre,* New York: Crown Publishers, 1967, 510.

99. "Fitch, (William) Clyde," *Who's Who in New York City and State,* third edition, New York: L. R. Hamersly and Company, 1907, 499; "Fitch, (William) Clyde," *The National Cyclopaedia of American Biography,* vol. XV, New York, James T. White and Company, 1916, 192–193; "Fitch, Clyde," *The National Cyclopaedia of American Biography,* vol. XIII, New York: James T. White and Company, 1906, 452; Virginia Gerson, "Fitch, William Clyde," *Dictionary of American Biography,* vol. III, pt. 2, New York: Charles Scribner's Sons, 1959, 430–431; "Clyde Fitch Dead After an Operation," *New York Times,* September 5, 1909, pt. 2, 1.

100. Michael Pupin, in "Hewitt, Peter Cooper," *Dictionary of American Biography,* vol. IV, New York: Charles Scribner's Sons, 1960, 607.

101. "Hewitt, Peter Cooper," *Who's Who in New York City and State,* third edition, New York: L. R. Hamersly and Company, 1907, 664; "Hewitt, Peter Cooper," *Who Was Who in America,* vol. I, Chicago: Marquis–Who's Who, 1966, 558; "Hewitt, Peter Cooper," *The Cyclopaedia of American Biography,* vol. VIII, New York: The Press Association Compilers, 1918, 169–170; "Hewitt, Peter Cooper," *Dictionary of American Biography,* vol. IV, New York: Charles Scribner's Sons, 1960, 607; "Hewitt, Peter Cooper," *The National Cyclopaedia of American Biography,* vol. XIV, New York: James T. White and Company, 1917, 470; "P. Cooper Hewitt Dead in Paris," *New York Times,* August 26, 1921, 13; "Hewitt's Patent Granted," *New York Times,* April 20, 1910, 6; "To Aid Wireless Telegraphy," *New York Times,* February 20, 1903, 5; "Hewitt, Peter Cooper," *American Biography: A New Cyclopedia,* vol. XIII, New York: The American Historical Society, 1923, 253–254; "Our Musical Millionaires," *Music Trade Review,* November 30, 1907, XLV:22, 50.

102. "Clowry, Robert C.," *Who's Who in New York City and State,* third edition, New York: L. R. Hamersly and Company, 1907, 229; "Clowry, Robert Charles," *The National Cyclopaedia of American Biography,* vol. XIII, New York: James T. White and Company, 1906, 119–120; "Telegraph Strike Is Now Threatened," *New York Times,* May 20, 1907, 1.

103. "Westinghouse, Henry Herman," *Who Was Who in America,* vol. I,

Chicago: Marquis–Who's Who, 1966, 1324; "H. H. Westinghouse Dead at Age of 80," *New York Times,* November 19, 1933, pt. 1, 34.

104. "G. Schirmer," *Etude,* September 1907, XXV:9, 618; "In Memory of Gustave Schirmer," *New Music Review,* February 1908, 7:75, 162.

105. "de Koven, Anna Farwell," *Who Was Who in America,* vol. 3, Chicago: Marquis–Who's Who, 1960, 218–219; "Reginald de Koven Dies at a Dance," *New York Times,* January 17, 1920, 11; "Anna F. de Koven, Author and Poet," *New York Times,* January 13, 1953, 27; "De Koven, Anna Farwell," *The National Cyclopaedia of American Biography,* vol. XVI, New York: James T. White and Company, 1918, 290; Mrs. Reginald De Koven, "A Fictitious Paul Jones Masquerading as the Real," *New York Times,* June 10, 1906, pt. 3, 1; "The True Paul Jones," *New York Times,* June 11, 1906, 6.

106. Letter from Oscar T. Crosby, President, New York Electric Music Company, to F. P. Fish, President, American Telephone and Telegraph Co., January 25, 1907, A.T.T.A. 16878, L.B. 46/427, 1; Letter from Oscar T. Crosby, January 27, 1907, 4.

107. "Plan Legislation For 'Phone Evils," *New York Herald,* January 14, 1907, 7.

108. "To Exhibit New Telephone," *New York Evening Post,* January 15, 1907, 4.

CHAPTER V

THE FIRST SEASON AT TELHARMONIC HALL

TELHARMONIC HALL OPENS

A few days before the gala reception, press notices began to herald the forthcoming public opening of Telharmonic Hall. At last the people would have access to the new sensation. On January 14, more than a hundred years earlier than predicted, Edward Bellamy's system of electric music would become a reality for anyone to hear. The advertisement for Telharmonic Hall in the Sunday papers promised two concerts, at 3:00 and 8:30.[1]

The first response at the opening was amazement that music could for the first time be made to emanate from any object in the room—the ferns, the divan, the ceiling, even an urn. Retorting to Cahill's claim that by electrical vibration, he "could get music out of almost anything,"[2] one critic groused, "He should begin on Brahms' symphonies."[3] People missed the violin sound from the Telharmonic palette, and company spokesmen claimed it would be produced soon, when the number of harmonics was increased from eight to twenty.[4]

The ultimate response was a realization that the Telharmonium had not quite yet ushered in a musical Utopia:

> At the present moment the telharmonic music is rather crude and lacking in variety; also certain tones are over-accented. Time, no doubt, will remedy these defects. The usual sound of the electric music is that of a blend of woodwind and brass, with a peculiar tang of its own.[5]

The presentations went reasonably well, however, and public curiosity was great enough that later the same week the concerts were expanded to four each day: at 3:00, 4:15, 8:30, and 9:45.[6]

The New York Electric Music Co. immediately targeted the newly admitted general public for investment capital. The company published *Telharmony: A New Art,* an eight-page pamphlet subtitled "A Golden Dream Come True." Largely a compendium of glowing testimonials and paeans to the exquisite perfection of the music (by Mark Twain, some electrical writers, and exclusively out-of-town music critics), the circular concluded with a blatant hustle:

> There is no reason to suppose that a profit similar to that obtained from the development of the telephone industry may not be had from the distribution of Electric Music over telephone wires.[7]

FIGHTING FOR A FRANCHISE

Once the public concerts at Telharmonic Hall were running smoothly, Oscar T. Crosby countered Vice President Cahill's rebuff by seeking friendly telephone company cooperation at higher levels. Crosby had realized early on that A.T.&T. and New York Telephone would block him at once if he applied for any sort of a telephone franchise. His only hope was to obtain a New York City franchise specifically for generating and distributing music. However, any company that wished to secure such a franchise would have to be a New York corporation authorized by its certificate of incorporation to do a music generating and distributing business. A new corporation would thus have to be organized, since the three existing Telharmonic companies had been incorporated in New Jersey and Maine. Understandably there existed no clear section of the state code permitting a corporation to be formed for this purpose, so the first step was to get such a statute passed by the legislature in Albany. It was vital that the telephone companies understand that the proposed bill was not intended to threaten their interests, or they would throttle it summarily. Crosby therefore went straight to the top and wrote to Frederick P. Fish, head of A.T.&T.[8]

Crosby complained of Vice President Cahill's lack of approachability, and assured Fish that he would keep A.T.&T. fully aware of the movements of the New York Electric Music Co. Crosby had no wish to be challenged by the telephone interests. He hoped Fish would join him for dinner sometime in a restaurant where the Telharmonium was now heard.[9]

Two days later Crosby wrote Charles F. Cutler, 65-year-old president of the New York Telephone Co. Cutler was also president of its subsidiary, the Empire City Subway Co., which installed and controlled the electrical utility conduits throughout the steets of New York. Cutler had been in the telephone business from its very beginnings and had formed the original New York and New Jersey Telephone Co. in Brooklyn. He was a director of eight other telephone companies throughout the East and widely respected as one of the great builders of telephone service in the United States.[10]

Crosby told Cutler that his company intended to have a bill passed by the New York State Assembly and Senate to amend the Telephone and Telegraph Incorporation Act, recognizing the existence of Telharmony as a separate endeavor. This would be followed by an application to the New York City Board of Estimate for a franchise, strictly limited to "the generation and distribution of music electrically."[11] He assured Cutler that no interference would be made with existing telephone companies and hoped that none would urge objection. Crosby expected the application to be made in the name of the New York Cahill Telharmonic Co., to be organized as soon as the proposed bill became law. He mentioned the doubts of Vice President Cahill over the legality of their 1905 contract as an indication that it was time to give Telharmony its own lawful existence. Crosby warned that he did not feel bound to await the response of New York Telephone's legal department and would be in Albany next week to lobby for his amendment.[12]

Fish took a rain check on the dinner and music invitation and claimed to leave the remaining questions to Cutler:

> I am sure that Mr. Cutler intends to deal fairly and in an entirely proper spirit with your enterprise. He knows his own situation, however, so well that I cannot think of undertaking to influence him one way or the other.[13]

Fish urged Crosby to show Cutler the text of the amendment.[14]

Crosby reported to Fish that since writing to him last he had "had a very satisfactory interview with Mr. Cutler. In taking the field, it will not be necessary to deal at arm's length as it seemed at first to be the case."[15] He offered to supply Fish's Boston office with music whenever the telephone lines could be turned over to the New York Electric Music Co. for half an hour or so to make the connection.[16] He attached the text of his amendment, which had to be one of the most succinct on record: "This article is hereby made applicable to corporations for the generation and distribution of music electrically."[17]

His course cleared, that same day Crosby wrote to the New York City Board of Estimate, confidently announcing publicly that he expected to apply for a franchise. He suggested that the board designate an engineer to examine the unfamiliar new art of electric music.[18]

Fortunately Crosby had an important ally in Albany. The state superintendent of public works, Frederick C. Stevens, was an old Washington crony of Crosby. Stevens had been a banker there and had invested in Crosby's street railway and utility enterprises. Having recently sunk his money into the Telharmonium, Stevens was ready to wield a little pressure on the legislature. The bill was introduced by press conference at the end of January and in the assembly the next week as an amendment to the Transportation Corporations Law.[19]

The bill spelled trouble from the start. It would amend Article VIII, which provided for "the incorporation of telegraph and telephone corporations, the construction and extension of their lines, the transmission of their dispatches, consolidation of corporations, and the appointment of special policemen."[20] Special policemen for electric music? The proposed new law would award any company incorporated under its authority the same powers as a telephone company. With a franchise in hand, the corporation could condemn rights of way, erect poles and wires, and string cables in the streets.[21] Opposition developed and became understandably widespread; this bill would have to be revised.

EDWIN HALL PIERCE LEAVES

"The Season's Wonder," avowed the Sunday Telharmonic Hall advertisements on January 20: "See the Singing Arc-light, the 145

Dynamos."[22] Horns were then mounted on the facade of Telharmonic Hall to inflict musical advertising upon the thousands who passed by Broadway and 39th Street. Inside, the loudness of the singing arc had just been improved so that it could be heard more clearly throughout the hall; the management then announced that soon Telharmonic selections would emanate from the streetlights outside the auditorium. Besides transmitting hourly chimes to announce the time to subscribing hotels and homes, the musical works included Mendelssohn's *Song of Spring,* Brahms's *Hungarian Dance No. 7,* Paderewski's *Menuet in G,* Chopin's *Nocturne in D-flat,* the *Allegretto* from Beethoven's *Symphony No. 8,* and the *Overture* to Rossini's *William Tell.*[23] The following week's newspapers announced that, effective immediately, Sunday evenings would be added to the current schedule.[24] Program No. 1 for the next few weeks showed nine selections for each of the four daily and two Sunday programs, mostly short classical numbers: the Bach-Gounod *Ave Maria,* Schumann's *Träumerei,* Chopin's *Nocturne in E-flat* and *Prelude in E Minor, Det Förste Möde* and *Solvejg's Song* by Grieg, *Norwegian Folk Song* by Ole Bull, Godard's *Canzonetta* and *Second Valse,* Rossini's ubiquitous *William Tell,* Field's *Nocturne in B-flat, Intermezzo* from *Cavalleria Rusticana* by Mascagni, *Andante* from a Goltermann cello concerto, Simonetti's *Madrigale, Romanze* by Sivori, Czibulka's *Love's Dream After the Ball, The Letter of Manon* and *Loin du Bal* by Gillet, and Paderewski's *Menuet in G.* A few of the pieces were repeated in more than one daily concert. With such an extensive and varied schedule, sufficient time for undisturbed practice became a problem. An announcement printed in the program assured listeners that soon the system would "provide for the production of every musical tone or tone quality known to the human ear, besides many new tones."[25] When more keyboards were installed, six musicians would render music equivalent to an 85-piece orchestra.

The program listed Elliott Schenck as musical director, Karl W. Schulz as assistant musical director, and four staff musicians: Henry W. Geiger, Harold O. Smith, Christian Schiott, and Otto Scheda. Schulz was now the only Holyoke musician remaining in the employ of the New York Electric Music Co. There was no mention of H. Franklin Harris or Edwin Hall Pierce. Performer Christian Schiott (Fig. 37) was a 24-year-old Norwegian who had begun to give piano recitals in Oslo when he was eight years old.[26]

Staff musician Otto Scheda was a 43-year-old Viennese violinist

Fig. 37. Christian Schiott, Berlin, ca. 1912. (Courtesy of Jeanbett Schiott)

whose considerable talent had never propelled him past an alarming business naiveté and a general propensity to ill fortune. Scheda had just abandoned a grueling two-year cross-country tour playing five shows per day. His act was called "Paganini's Ghost." His manager retained 50% of the gross; Scheda covered all his expenses from the remainder. As a youth he had served in the Austrian Forest Service, joined the circus, and toured five continents as a violin soloist. He settled in America, played orchestral and hotel jobs, and then dyed his skin and even his eyes to tour London as the "World's Only [American] Indian Violinist." He now sought steady employment with the New York Electric Music Co., playing his violin and then the Telharmonium to demonstrate their similarities. Plaudits from Enrico Caruso, who would visit Telharmonic Hall after rehearsing at the Met, helped ensure Scheda a job during that first season.[27]

Edwin Hall Pierce ostensibly fell victim to financial difficulties experienced by Oscar T. Crosby and Frederick C. Todd. Matters came to a head around the end of January. A promoter or an associate was said to have embezzled some of the stock proceeds and fled the country with the money. The ensuing financial stringencies seemed to preclude a keyboardist whose salary must support and maintain a wife, a mother, and seven children in New York. There were plenty of younger performers in New York with fewer attachments and responsibilities. As to the difficult keyboard, with its extra keys that required special technique, the prevailing performance practice among Telharmonists had slowly drifted more and more toward ordinary equal temperament. This was not through negligence or laziness, but out of the musicians' growing realization that the pure intervals of just intonation were too insipid, too tame for most music. Pure thirds and fifths were all very well for tranquil and placid selections, but did not seem nearly bracing and energetic enough for music with more movement and flow. Thaddeus Cahill, as may be imagined, was severely annoyed and offended by this development, but the actions of employees of the New York Electric Music Co. were beyond his control or influence. At any rate, the predominant use of a single bank on each manual now permitted the employment of any ordinary pianist or organist at Telharmonic Hall, so Pierce was no longer needed. By the middle of February Pierce had gotten his family back to Auburn, N.Y.[28]

The last connection Pierce had with the Telharmonium was to demonstrate the instrument to the celebrated young composer

Daniel Gregory Mason, who was writing a magazine article. When it appeared in March Pierce was credited with this assistance, and his association with the enterprise was mentioned in the past tense.[29]

THE HEYDAY OF THE TELHARMONIUM

Widespread demands for Telharmonic music burgeoned in January. Electric tunes were supplied for a reception at the Waldorf-Astoria honoring Baron Mayor des Planches, the Italian ambassador. Telharmonic selections also graced the Kappa Alpha Alumni Association at the Hotel Imperial and a Women's Press Club reception at the Waldorf-Astoria. Next the Worcester Polytechnic Alumni dinner at the Normandie Hotel on January 29 featured Carl M. Pihl as one of the speakers. His talk on the details of the Telharmonium was accompanied by popular and classical selections.[30] The instrument even provided accompaniment to the former students' college songs. After Pihl's address, motion pictures of a performer at Telharmonic Hall were shown to the audience while they listened to selections transmitted from the central plant. This combination of images and sound was called a *"tour de force"*[31] that "literally brought down the house."[32]

Two days later, the press demanded that Pihl explain the growing Telharmonic interference with telephone conversations. By this time hundreds of New Yorkers had noticed music in the wires. "It's not our fault," protested the hapless manager. "The telephone company is responsible. It is using two pairs of wires from our place to the laboratory for test purposes, and sometimes they get crossed with lines that are being used for the regular telephone service."[33]

The next promotion encouraged dramatically close scrutiny of the Telharmonium. Perhaps it became downright uncomfortable, for it was not retained as a standard feature of the demonstrations. The Hall hired various musicians on cello, oboe, and other instruments to join Otto Scheda on violin. After each played his instrument, the Telharmonist bravely played the corresponding timbre for all to compare. This was the daring instigation of Elliott Schenck, who also decreed another program change: the Sunday concerts would henceforth present only sacred music.[34]

Notable visitors to Telharmonic Hall in late January included Walter Damrosch, who pronounced the musical tone and performers' expression much improved, and composer Giacomo Puccini. Andreas Dippel, a Metropolitan Opera tenor, had visited repeatedly and was now ready to reveal a direct involvement with the enterprise. His early experience in Germany had included five-years' employment in a bank, and he was known to be financially skilled. Dippel was the highest paid, most versatile artist at the Met. Master of 150 roles, he frequently consented to substitute when others were indisposed. He had had a costume for every role until 96 were destroyed in the San Francisco earthquake and fire the previous year. The plan, announced by Dippel and Cahill, was for Dippel to install the instrument in the chief cities of Austria-Hungary.[35]

"Tone building" was celebrated by the press as the newest amazement to be shown at Telharmonic Hall, beginning the first Monday in February. Sounds of the oboe, flute, violin, French horn, and clarinet would be built up from scratch.[36] Attendance was large; hundreds filled the hall each day (Fig. 38).[37] In the enthusiastic

Fig. 38. A Gathering at Telharmonic Hall. (*Gunter's Magazine,* June 1907, 3:5, S.C., 567)

words of Metropolitan Opera conductor Alfred Hertz: "You have a system that can do anything you want in music. It is wonderful, and I believe in Telharmony as an art of music."[38] Press reports multiplied and appeared nearly every day of February 1907 in the New York papers. Much virtually identical wording attested to the energetic efforts of the publicity staff at Telharmonic Hall. "As amazing as it is delightful," went a typical judgment.[39]

Plans were laid for a two-channel transmission featuring the voice of Miss Isabelle Winlocke. This addressed the last glaring defect of the Telharmonium, that even with all its potential for perfection fully realized, it would remain dumb and mute as a surrogate human voice. Fortunately, Miss Winlocke possessed an "exceedingly rich"[40] mezzo-soprano, one that could travel along an ordinary telephone line with some power even as electric music traversed its own separate lines. For $400, she permitted her voice to be recorded singing three selections. The records were to be played back and distributed from the central station with Telharmonic accompaniment.[41]

In addition to tone building, Telharmonic Hall presented an electrical imitation of the violin. It was given with an acoustic piano accompaniment to heighten the illusion of realism. The operators also demonstrated the volume-control resistance box installed with every Telharmonic receiver, so that the room-filling sounds could be stopped down in the bedroom to the faintest faraway level as an aid to sleep.[42]

The New York Electric Music Co. added another hotel, the Victoria, on the little block bounded by Fifth Avenue, Broadway, and 27th Street, to its expanding roster of hostelries. The Victoria's restaurants, run by a Parisian chef, were luxurious and quiet. Outfitted with tapestries, lace, and candelabras, the atmosphere attracted such clients as Grover Cleveland and William Jennings Bryan. Should the hotel clientele have spiritual needs as well, these were attended to by New York's unofficial "hotel chaplain," the Reverend Henry Marsh Warren.[43] He had become interested in the new device that was supplying music to so many of the important constituents of his "parish." He devised plans for a totally new kind of service on the first Sunday in Lent. The showpiece would be Telharmonic hymns transmitted simultaneously to all the hotels.[44]

Warren qualified as New York's leading electric media evangelist. Every day he conducted a service at ten o'clock A.M. over the telephone to the office of Mrs. J. Alden Gaylord, Wall Street's only female broker. As he prayed, Mrs. Gaylord covered her eyes with her right hand, bowed her head, and repeated the Reverend Mr. Warren's words to those members of the financial community gathered in her office. The prayer by wire was followed by a Scripture reading, including such comforting verses as "A little that a righteous man hath is better than the riches of the many wicked" (Psalm 37). Warren's mission was to provide consolation to those who were financially troubled, depressed, and contemplating suicide.[45]

As preparations for the hotel service went forward during the week preceding Lent, the tone-building demonstration was revamped. Instead of building each instrument up from the first harmonic, the sounds were transformed from one instrument across to another. Thus, the flute became the oboe, and so on, ending with the violin tone.[46] Another novelty that week was the "silent number," the sound only of clicking keys. The receivers at Telharmonic Hall were shut off, but the audiences at hotels and restaurants heard the selection at full volume. Recent visitors included tenor Enrico Caruso again, pianist Ossip Gabrilowitsch, restaurant conductor Nathan Franko, and Rear Admiral Charles Dwight Sigsbee. The admiral had commanded the battleship *Maine* when it was blown up in Havana harbor, precipitating the Spanish-American War.[47] He now had a few dollars to invest in the Telharmonium.

The Reverend Mr. Warren led his Telharmonic Lenten revival service in the new assembly hall of the Hotel Imperial (Fig. 39) on Sunday evening, February 17. As he announced the hymns the performer at Telharmonic Hall was cued by telephone to begin. The worshipers did not hesitate to join in singing. Several solos were rendered by Mrs. Karl W. Schulz, wife of the Telharmonist. The halls at both the hotel and the central station were packed.[48]

The successful presentation of Telharmonic motion pictures at the Normandie Hotel three weeks earlier led to their inevitable introduction at Telharmonic Hall. On the first week of Lent, audiences were not shown some scene encouraging spiritual self-denial, but a new consummation of sybaritic self-indulgence: a depiction of the actual process of telephoning for a musical selection and getting it played instantly. Another film, screened while the music was being performed, showed the alternators and other machinery running in the basement. Audiences were warned that the full explanation of the

Fig. 39. The Reverend Henry Marsh Warren Leads the Telharmonic Gospel Service at the Hotel Imperial, February 17, 1907. (*Gunter's Magazine,* June 1907, 3:5, S.C., 564)

process would soon be eliminated from the program, so all New Yorkers interested in this revolutionary information should visit Telharmonic Hall at once.[49]

Weekly advertisements for Telharmonic Hall were still running in the Sunday papers. "The Music of A.D. 2000" was the banner in mid-February.[50] Admission remained at 50¢; top Broadway theatre seats went for $1.50, while vaudeville establishments were charging 25¢.

A new keyboard was again promised for Telharmonic Hall, so that four players could produce more complicated music and provide a closer equivalent to the violin tone. The operators said they would put in more dynamos as well. The cost of the improvements was estimated at $60,000.[51]

Thousands of visitors were drawn by Telharmonic Hall that week. A revised Program No. 1 was published, and Elliott Schenck's musical staff gave recitals presenting the usual Rossini and Bach-Gounod with many new selections: the folk song *Marechiare, La Cinquantaine* by Marie, Godfrey's *Andantino, Gavotte* from Thomas's comic opera *Mignon,* the Italian folk songs *O Sole Mio* and *Maria e Mari,* the *Allegro Assai* and *Rondo* from *Sonatina in F* by Beethoven,

Delibes's *Pizzicati* from the ballet *Sylvia; or, The Nymph of Diana* and *Le Pas des Fleurs Valse* from his *Naila, Melodie* and *Serenade* by Moskowski, *Nocturne for Viola* by Kalliwoda, Hauser's *Dorflied, Berceuse* and *Det Förste Möde* by Grieg, *Allegretto* by Macbeth, Chopin's *Waltz in A Minor,* and a concluding improvisation. To the film program was added images of distant audiences listening in amazement. The singing arc continued to excite delight and wonder in the visitors. Giacomo Puccini was again among them. The throngs included not only public figures but ordinary seekers of entertainment as well. By the end of February, the seventh week of public Telharmony, the astonishment at the purest tones ever produced, from the most expensive musical instrument ever made, continued unabated. It seemed the greatest instrument in history.[52]

LEE DE FOREST BROADCASTS THE TELHARMONIUM

The inventor Lee de Forest had been working on devices to improve the transmission of wireless telegraphy since 1900. Competing with Marconi, he had developed an improved radio wave detector and then made advantageous use of the newspaper publicity to gain wireless contracts from the U.S. Navy. In 1906 he had patented the triode, or audion, one of the greatest and most seminal electrical inventions of the twentieth century. Despite de Forest's extensive training in theoretical physics—Yale had awarded him one of the first Ph.D. degrees in electrical physics—he had no idea what he had wrought. He viewed the audion as another wireless detector and believed that it had to be filled with gas in order to operate. Not until 1912 would he understand the most important properties of his three-element vacuum tube: its capabilities to oscillate and to amplify.[53]

Attracted by the reams of publicity streaming from Telharmonic Hall, de Forest carried a small arc transmitter to the offices of the New York Electric Music Co. He persuaded the management to let him broadcast their music. De Forest ran a wire from the transmitter up to a flagpole on the roof. His diary entry the next day read:

> February 28, 1907: Radio Telephony and Teleharmony
> [*sic*]—new, epoch marking, crowding one upon the other so

rapidly, and with such bewildering complexity of possibilities that my mind cannot realize with what wonders I am toiling.

There is Music, dearest of the soul's pleasures, created in largesse, broadcast like some merchandise, owned and distributed by a new art, unknown until yesterday.

Leaving all its mysteries—physical, electrical, commercial, half-realized, dimly comprehended, I rush forward still another bound into the radical future, and seek to transmit these glorious vibrations of sound made by the new electricity, without a medium save that intangible, viewless, bodiless mystery of mysteries, the ether.[54]

The rebuff by New York Telephone of the Telharmonium and the pending efforts to secure a franchise were well known, so de Forest "was hoping to show the Cahill brothers that their fine, synthetic, electric music could be widely distributed without wires."[55] This would be "throughout the New York City area, by means of my radio telephone system."[56] De Forest's attitude toward electric music was not to remain so tolerant, however. Some years later, experimenting with the audion oscillator in 1915, he found he could create

sounds resembling violin, cello, wood winds, muted brasses— and other sounds resembling nothing ever heard from an orchestra or by the human ear up to that time—of the sort now so often heard in the nerve-racking [sic], maniacal cacophonies of a lunatic swing band. Such tones led me to dub my new musical instrument the "squawk-a-phone."[57]

De Forest installed his receiving apparatus on the roof of the towering, eleven-story Yale Club, at 30 West 44th Street. A Telharmonic concert had already been scheduled there for March 1 and would be given by wireless if possible, otherwise by wire.[58]

The experiments were of particular interest to Frederic Thompson, manager of Luna Park at Coney Island. He was willing to pay handsomely for hourly Telharmonic concerts at a special theatre to be constructed at the park. The theatre would be a quadruplex design, simultaneously presenting grand opera, comic opera, orchestral, and popular music. The problem was whether use of ordinary telephone wires would be permitted by New York Telephone. Furthermore, the distance of some 13 miles to the south shore of Brooklyn would no doubt attenuate much of the power needed to fill the concert rooms with sound. If de Forest could accomplish the transmission by wireless, he would create a huge popular success.[59]

De Forest next put his receiving equipment on top of the Normandie Hotel, located a block south of Telharmonic Hall. Through a wireless receiver connected to a telephone, the music was easily pulled in and heard. The experiments at this new location had been kept secret, but on the evening of March 5, a man burst into Telharmonic Hall and demanded to know, "How are you putting this music on the wireless?"[60] The staff tried tactfully to deny that any such activity was in progress. He replied: "That won't do. You can't fool me. I'm G. S. MacDonald, chief electrician in charge of the wireless station in the Brooklyn Navy Yard, and I know I heard 'Wilhelm [sic] Tell' and 'Ave Maria' over my wireless, and it could not come from anywhere except here."[61] Blended with naval orders, the astounded operator had recognized the Telharmonium on a broadcast five miles distant.[62]

The next day, music, speech, and telegraphic signals from an incoming steamship in the bay were all heard in a public demonstration in the receiving room atop the Normandie Hotel. The selections were announced into a telephone at Telharmonic Hall; these comments, and the operator's sundry questions about when the music should be started and stopped, and how the audience was feeling, were transmitted by wireless right along with the music. Since the room at the Normandie was not equipped with a transmitter, the queries thus remained unanswered. In order to be clearly understood, the operator was compelled to speak loudly and separate his words. The steamer signals, being transmitted miles away on a similar frequency, were accidentally received and mixed in with Mendelssohn's *Song of Spring*, the inescapable *William Tell*, and other airs from the next block.[63]

Now de Forest was ready for some *real* publicity, and so he quickly removed his listening apparatus to the roof of the New York Times tower at Broadway and 43rd Street the following day, March 7. That evening, spoken messages were followed by Telharmonic music, all clearly heard on the 24th floor of the Times building. De Forest also picked up more Morse code interference from wireless telegraph stations at 42 Broadway, the Brooklyn Navy Yard, and even Bridgeport, Conn. De Forest was well rewarded with a lengthy article explaining his process in the next day's *Times*. He told the reporter that with further experimentation the radio frequency could be changed so that telegraph signals would no longer intrude on the reception.[64]

The use of the Times building to further the interests of wireless telephony spurred the rival *New-York Daily Tribune* to denigrate the doings. In a lengthy editorial, the paper sniped that perhaps no more than six or eight broadcast frequencies could ever be used simultaneously, at great disadvantage to wired telephony. Too, the same conductor—the ether—had to be shared with wireless telegraphy, an unwanted interloper at de Forest's recent demonstration. Furthermore, the distance spanned at the Times exhibition—less than a quarter of a mile—was insignificant. Even if it could be extended, experts agreed that wireless telephony could never cover more than half the range of wireless telegraphy. The latter's superiority would thus garner to it most of the business, rendering a truly discouraging future for wireless telephony. "There are many things that are feasible which are not profitable."[65]

The transmissions proceeded for several months, and were picked up and logged at New York harbor by amateur wireless enthusiast Francis Arthur Hart.[66] On March 20, he noted "music at 5:27 from De Forest's good twice,"[67] then added "3rd,"[68] then on April 27: "De Forests [*sic*] music strong."[69] Other entries in the log book—"weak . . . static fierce . . . pretty fair . . . grew weaker . . . extremely weak . . . breaks everything up as usual . . . very heavy magnetic storm whole evening no regular . . . just readable"[70]—attest to the difficulty of receiving wireless dots and dashes through the fickle ether, let alone uncluttered music.

Many other amateurs around New York reported hearing the Telharmonium, as did the wireless operator on the steamship *Bermudian*. De Forest speculated that soon passengers on ocean liners 100 miles out to sea would be able to enjoy musical selections. The public on land could also have music simply by installing a receiver and antenna. With a transmitter of sufficient voltage, the sound could be heard throughout the room, provided a megaphone was employed. To him the music sounded "perfect and clear."[71] He tried to do business with Cahill's backers, and found them "without imagination."[72] Only after de Forest's company or some other corporation had established and perfected the wireless would they discuss commercial arrangements. "And be refused the use of the ether,"[73] retorted de Forest sullenly. But to the New York Electric Music Co. reliability was paramount. With atmospheric disturbances, frying noises, and a metallic sound quality, the undependable and unsteady transmissions proved to be below commercial standards.[74]

BUSINESS DEVELOPMENTS

William Skinner of the famed Skinner silk mills of Holyoke became a director of the Eastern Cahill Telharmonic Co. He was prominent in the business world as a director of life insurance concerns, banks, and many railroads. Skinner and his brother Joseph, who headed the silk concern together, had invested considerably in Telharmonic stock, along with a few other Holyoke industrialists. Since William Skinner worked at the firm's New York sales office, he would be able to attend meetings of the board.[75]

Elliott Schenck continued to garner plaudits from the *Musical Courier* for his supervision of the keyboard artists at Telharmonic Hall. Schenck pursued other musical interests concurrently, including conducting an advanced student orchestra at the School of Musical Art and a series of pop concerts. In March he was elected conductor of the prestigious Schubert Glee Club of Jersey City. Plans were put forth to present concerts with the New York Symphony Orchestra of which Schenck had been assistant conductor.[76]

The display advertisements for Telharmonic Hall grew slightly smaller in March, although they conveyed undiminished enthusiasm: "Sensation, Education, Orchestration and Revelations by Electrical Music." The film screenings continued to attract interest. A notable event was the annual banquet of the Indiana Society of New York at the Waldorf-Astoria; the entire assemblage sang Indiana songs with Telharmonic accompaniment.[77]

Oscar T. Crosby spent some time in Albany working on his amendment and saw Frederick P. Fish there. The prospects of the Telharmonium were bright and alluring. The front-cover illustration of the new *Scientific American* was a sequence of Telharmonium vignettes (Fig. 40).[78] It seemed as if the endeavor would flourish to become a massive enterprise. Crosby next went to see Thaddeus Cahill in Holyoke, and after several long and energetic discussions, succeeded in wresting the manufacture of Telharmonic devices from him. Cahill's 50-man machine shop lacked the required capacity.[79]

Vol. XCVI, No. 10   NEW YORK, MARCH 9, 1907.   10 CENTS A COPY
$3.00 A YEAR.

THE TELHARMONIUM—AN APPARATUS FOR THE ELECTRICAL GENERATION AND TRANSMISSION OF MUSIC [See page 210]

Fig. 40. Cover of *Scientific American* (March 9, 1907, XCVI:10, 205)

Crosby opened discussions with the General Electric Co. about manufacturing the heavy dynamos. He preferred not to start his own factory if it could be avoided. Similarly he wrote and offered Fish the manufacture of receivers, outlets, and other smaller equipment. Crosby was aware that A.T.&T.'s Western Electric factories were already running at full capacity, but perhaps its purchase of a new factory at Rochester would open room for manufacturing a line of Telharmonic apparatus. Crosby opined that his subscribers would require more materiel than the ordinary telephone customer and invited Fish to send his experts to make a full report on the nature and magnitude of the equipment to be produced.[80]

For the second week in March, a new business policy was adopted at Telharmonic Hall. Now there were three prices of seats: 25¢, 50¢, and $1.00. The number of daily concerts dropped from four to two, although their length doubled to two hours. Continuous daily recitals ran from 3:30 to 5:30 P.M. and from 8:30 to 10:30 P.M.[81] Audiences thronged the auditoriums, and business was brisk enough that the next week all 25¢ seats were omitted. The central station then offered a free view of the basement dynamos and machinery all day and announced that soon audience members would be given a chance to control the music via apparatus carried throughout the aisles.[82] Karl W. Schulz was still with the enterprise, but several of the staff musicians had been replaced. The hit of the week was Schulz's Telharmonic oboe solo with Henry W. Geiger's Telharmonic flute *obbligato,* supported by Harold O. Smith's accompaniment on an actual piano. By this time a dozen leading hotels and restaurants were receiving transmissions from Telharmonic Hall. Two huge switches had been placed on the stage to emphasize the outside connections to distant audiences. The singing arc remained popular on the programs, which now were attracting numerous school classes.[83]

Unexpectedly, another momentous wonder joined the Telharmonic catalogue of achievements. Several prominent hearing specialists had been experimenting at Telharmonic Hall with deaf persons. At the end of March they reported their startling yet conclusive results: persons unable to perceive any other kind of music were actually able to discern sensations of Telharmonic sound. It was done by placing a telephone receiver against the forehead or some other portion of the skull. They also applied wires carrying the musical currents directly to the body. The hard of hearing took immediate note of the Telharmonium, which now seemed as promising as recent French experiments in passing musical currents through the human body. Perhaps music could bypass disabled ears altogether. The hopeful deaf and their doctors thronged the Hall.[84]

Elliott Schenck's importation of the New York Symphony Orchestra to Jersey City for a concert with the Schubert Glee Club was a celebrated success. He decided that here was his endeavor of preference, and suddenly ended his association with the Telharmonium.[85]

Frederick P. Fish finally acknowledged Oscar T. Crosby's letter at the end of March. He pleaded overwork and promised to write to Crosby in a few days.[86] Then he turned the letter over to his chief engineer, Hammond V. Hayes.

Also near the end of March, a version of Crosby's electric music incorporation amendment was finally approved by the New York State Assembly. It had worked its way through the requisite three readings and had been amended. Any electric music company was now deprived of the rights of condemnation proceedings and eminent domain, but otherwise was permitted to erect poles and string wires. The bill passed by 131 ayes to one nay and would now go to the state senate.[87]

THE FIRST SEASON ENDS AT TELHARMONIC HALL

Toward the end of March, the New York Electric Music Co. mounted its fourth program of the season. There were 16 selections plus an opportunity to view the basement machinery room before the presentation commenced. After the opening number, *Serenade* by Macbeth, an introductory announcement put forth the significance of Telharmony. Patrons were then directed to note the large numerals visibly posted on objects about the hall, as they listened to Karl W. Schulz perform *Carnival of Venice:*

1 and 2. Ceiling Jardinieres, *Flute Quality.*
3. Right Front by Door, *Oboe Quality.*
4 and 5. Long Horns, R. and L. Front, *Tuba Quality.*
6. Hydrangea Bush, L. of Platform, *Violoncello Quality.*

7. R. Front Corner, *French Horn Quality.*
8 and 9. Urns on Pedestals, R. and L., *Clarinet Quality.*[88]

Fourth came another cello imitation with the *Andante* from a Goltermann *Concerto for Violoncello.* Then two assistants each picked up a horn affixed to a receiver, connected to a flexible wire, and carried the sounding assemblages throughout the audience.

The music could thereby be admired at close range. This demonstration was then repeated while the receivers were opened up, thus proving that the sound was indeed produced by electric current. Seventh on the program was a selection illustrating the use of resistance boxes for volume control. During a fife and drum imitation the boxes were carried throughout the audience. Patrons were invited to operate the controls themselves. With the eighth selection came a special highlight: motion pictures showing outside hotel and restaurant audiences supposedly listening to wired Telharmonic music. Other films displayed the procedure of requesting a selection by telephone and some scenes of the basement machinery in action. This was followed by a Norwegian folk song fed into incandescent lamps producing light to accompany the music. Then, after *Le Pas des Fleurs Valse* from Delibes's ballet *Naila,* came the long-awaited singing arc lamps lit up to the strains of Paderewski's *Menuet No. 2.* The twelfth number of the evening was billed as "Minor Approximations—*a*) Scotch Bagpipes; *b*) Intoned Bells and Chimes."[89] Then came Karl W. Schulz's own contribution to slumber music: *Cradle Song.* Another address to the audience followed, explaining and demonstrating tone building, and playing the wonderful pure tones now available for the first time as musical elements. Rousing performances of a selection from Rossini's ever-present *William Tell*—a Telharmonic oboe solo with flute *obbligato,* accompanied by piano—and Beethoven's *Polonaise* concluded the evening's electric music entertainment.[90]

As the flabbergasted concertgoers left the Hall, they could muse on the announcement printed on the back of the program. It promised that soon no fewer than six Telharmonic musicians would render programs equivalent to music now heard from an 85-piece symphonic orchestra.[91] The press reported enthusiastic comments from Enrico Caruso, Johanna Gadski, and other noted Metropolitan Opera celebrities who visited Telharmonic Hall in early April.[92]

Although Telharmonic Hall advertised at the end of March that seats were selling four weeks in advance, the thirteenth and final week of public Telharmony was announced in the Sunday newspaper advertisements the first week of April. The building would be closed indefinitely to enable the installation of additional keyboards and dynamos. And so the last of the public concerts was purveyed on Saturday, April 13, at the usual schedule and prices.[93]

The complexion of appraisals shifted markedly during those few months in force. "The purity of its 'intonation' is extraordinary and delightful,"[94] wrote the knowledgeable musician Daniel Gregory Mason early on. Swayed by the new sound sensation, he and other critics reveled in the exquisite obsolescence of "perverse human fingers,"[95] lips, and lungs for tone production. The new purity was "like stroking velvet and eating ice-cream at the same time."[96] The prevailing impressions of most appraisers were limited to mystification and delight.[97] Mason was one of the few in those first days to temper such judgments with a glimpse at the obverse of so suave a timbre: "This absence of brilliancy, mordancy, incisiveness, makes the Telharmonium but a sorry substitute for an orchestra—even a small one."[98] He expressed the forlorn hope that the promoters would not damage the instrument's prospects by exaggerated claims.

Another early critique, unusually perceptive in its anticipation of an uncertain future, complained of its capacity to reproduce only "the dignified music of the great masters. It is lacking in ability to manage perfectly the light popular airs, the lively music whose charm, if ephemeral, is strong while it lasts."[99] Without improvement in this respect the instrument could hardly be expected to flourish.

A few romantics continued to lavish unrestrained plaudits into April and May. A boys' story told of hearing the music issuing from the arc lamp at Main Street and Myrtle Avenue. Little Thomas Brown hurried home to find the piano closed and Telharmonic music emanating from the great fronds of the Boston fern in the living room. When Paderewski would play on the instrument, little Thomas's ecstatic family could hear him at home, 50 miles from New York. The moral of the story: "Yes, my son," said Mr. Brown. "It is a great thing to be a boy in nineteen hundred and seven."[100]

Another pundit fancifully proclaimed the coinage of the "harmel," a new parameter of electrical harmony and melody. Telharmonic music would soon be measured and charged for by such units.[101] The conspicuous success of the central station made him "wonder that nature wasted so much ingenuity in devising the human throat equipment, when all it is capable of doing can be duplicated by a little iron plate about the size of a silver dollar and worth perhaps two cents."[102]

Nevertheless, others began to hear the Telharmonium with some of its glow worn off. It did run perfectly in tune with itself, but frequently the whole machine ran too slow, drifting down in pitch. The difficulties of performing on two four-bank manuals, along with operating numerous stops and expression devices, degraded the excellence of the presentations. Coordination of the loudness articulation devices played by one hand with the pitch keys played with the other could be achieved in rapid passagework only with stunning skill and virtuosity. The dearth of such a standard was exacerbated by personnel replacements and the very limited time available for uninterrupted practice by the musicians. In their inexperienced if valiant efforts to attain at least some musical credulity, the potential of the instrument remained unrealized. The instrument's other limitations—"robbing," where adding voices depleted the volume, so that a many-toned chord could be softer than a single note; "diaphragm crack," where each *staccato* note sounded like the rap of a metal mallet; the impossibility of producing more than two, and later three, timbres simultaneously; the exaggerated "growling" of bass notes close together, a defect of the receivers rather than the instrument; the softness of output above 1,000 Hz; and the instrument's own unique, pervasive timbre that eventually became downright annoying to some—all these limitations militated against success.[103]

In particular, all the performers agreed among themselves that the timbre of the Telharmonium had grown to irritate them greatly. They were already under company constraint to acknowledge no criticism of the instrument to the public or the press. Now they had to be doubly careful not to express their opinions even to their own management.[104]

It must have seemed rash for the operators to close the season by decorating the windows of their resplendent Telharmonic Hall with a full display of the instruments now consigned to imputed oblivion. A flageolet, piccolo, fife, flute, clarinet, bassoon, saxophone, bass saxophone, cornet, French horn, tuba, snare drum, and violin were proudly marshaled to claim the natural sounds of the Telharmonium.

It was too much for the *Music Trade Review,* which until now had enthusiastically reported the development of the new invention:

> It is a fine array and no doubt creates admiration; but, as a matter of fact, only the usual organ tones are perceptible to the musically informed.[105]

As the first season closed on Telharmonic Hall, the gulf between aspiration and ability seemed to widen and to manifest itself to more than just a few. The glow of freshness would be absent at the next hearing of the Telharmonium. It had better be good.

HAMMOND V. HAYES REPORTS ON THE TELHARMONIUM

Hammond V. Hayes, the head of the A.T.&T. Engineering Department, spent the first two weeks of April investigating the Telharmonium. Frederick P. Fish had given him Crosby's letter and had wanted to know whether there was any possibility that the device could be profitably utilized as a component of the A.T.&T. system.[106]

Hayes was nearing the end of his 22-year tenure with A.T.&T., having joined the telephone company in 1885 upon receiving his Ph.D. in science from Harvard.[107] He had no training as a musician, but there was no doubt of his ability to assess the apparatus from a technical standpoint.

The chief engineer first did some background research by securing a copy of the report made by New York A.T.&T. engineers four months earlier on the proposed long-distance transmission from New York to Chicago.[108] Then Hayes went to Telharmonic Hall to see the central station and to listen to the music. He assigned two assistants to test and measure the transmission of the signal over the telephone company lines.[109]

In his report to Fish, Hayes praised the purity of its tone, but could not perceive any similarity of the Telharmonium to the sounds of the musical instruments it was supposed to imitate. Any claim of representing a full orchestra seemed farfetched. At Telharmonic

Hall, he was told he would hear the sounds of the flute, oboe, tuba, cello, French horn, and clarinet. It seemed to Hayes that, without the promoters' spoken suggestions, it was doubtful that he would have recognized any similarity. It seemed that many missing overtones would be needed to form these timbres completely. In sum, the music was marvelous and novel enough to maintain public appeal for a time, but in no way would it commercially replace orchestras or musicians.[110]

The apparatus itself, reported Hayes, was extraordinarily experimental, complex, and expensive. Great sums would be required for building models to arrive at a simple, practical machine. It would demand expertise of the greatest magnitude.[111]

Furthermore, the tests of Hayes's assistants showed that the music at present could not be transmitted over regular telephone lines. New inventions would be required to provide "special balancing of circuits."[112] Even with the installation of special circuits, the music would probably disturb regular telephone conversations.[113]

Hayes concluded that any investment in the Telharmonium would be enormously expensive and unprofitable for many years. The present massive efforts of the A.T.&T. companies to develop and simplify telephone service had already strained energies to the limit. The problems of legitimate telephone service were legion, and the companies could scarcely "afford to assist in the development of such an extraordinarily difficult problem as that of electrical music."[114] Hayes's report, which certainly served to preserve his own posterior, was supplemented by a brief letter from the A.T.&T. legal department, describing Cahill's exhaustive U.S. and British patent protection.[115]

Oscar T. Crosby was now on his own. Two years of cooperation by A.T.&T. were at an end, and the simple disapprobation of the telephone interests would wreak far more havoc than their refusal to build his equipment. As word got around, for the first time the Telharmonium had to bear a public humiliation.

The spurned suitor, Lee de Forest, was still transmitting from Telharmonic Hall, in hopes that now Crosby would be forced to adopt wireless. Upon learning of Hayes's fears of service disruptions, de Forest helped disperse the ominous tidings. He knew that the telephone system was built to accommodate only a fraction of an ampere at 24 volts and gleefully heralded "the induced current from this heavy charge spreading all over the lines, burning out ringing coils and disrupting the work of years."[116] But de Forest still could not secure the business of the New York Electric Music Co.

THE NEW ENGLAND AND NEW YORK ELECTRIC MUSIC COS.

Over the past twelve months, only $4,000 in additional capital had been put into the New England Electric Music Co. Its investment now stood at $210,500.[117] The New York Electric Music Co., however, had attracted the substantial infusion of $253,900. It had now sold a total of $679,900 in stock.[118]

THE NEW YORK CAHILL TELHARMONIC CO.

The second defeat for the Telharmonium was widely reported scarcely a week later. Although it had been passed by the state assembly, on April 18 the state senate defeated Crosby's proposed amendment, 23 to 14, authorizing the creation of corporations to generate and distribute music by wire. The senator who led the opposition declared that the amendment would permit a corporation formed under its aegis to engage in other types of telephone business besides music by wire. Since it was patently untrue, the objection could be overcome; "honest graft" might do. Crosby's sponsor in the senate had the bill tabled and vowed to offer it again.[119] Once more, however, the Telharmonium interests had endured the sting of a public reversal.

Crosby was not dead yet. Some boom talk would resuscitate prospects. Seventy tons of additional machinery had just been installed in Telharmonic Hall, went the press release, enabling the instrument to produce music on a much larger scale. Thanks to new keyboards and switchboards, orchestral effects would now be possible. The new transmissions would also reach many points outside the city. Other central plants were already being planned, and soon there would be Telharmony on tap in Chicago, Philadelphia, Denver, San Francisco, and Los Angeles. A new factory was to be built in France, to supply central station apparatus to Great Britain, Germany, France, Austria-Hungary, Belgium, and Spain.[120]

Crosby managed to ransom his amendment from the recalcitrant state senate. Barely a week since the bill had been defeated, it was again put to the senators—with no change in wording. Somehow there were sufficient changes of heart to permit passage: it sailed through by 37 ayes over 8 nays. The senate returned the bill to the assembly, whose clerk delivered it to the governor. At long last, on May 6, Governor Charles Evans Hughes signed Oscar T. Crosby's bill into law. The ink was barely dry on the amendment to Article VIII of the Transportation Corporations Law when it was used to authorize the birth of the fifth and newest Telharmonic corporation. The very next day Crosby signed the certificate of incorporation to create the New York Cahill Telharmonic Co. The document laid out an elaborate route of lines to be installed by the enterprise, from New York to (1) Albany, Syracuse, Rochester, Buffalo, and intermediate cities; (2) Connecticut, Massachusetts, Rhode Island, Vermont, New Hampshire, and Maine; (3) Montauk Point, Long Island, and intermediate cities.[121]

The authorized stock was $500,000, of which 16 shares at $100 each had been paid in. Crosby owned ten shares, and the other six directors each took one share.[122]

Aside from Crosby, the most illustrious director of the new company was 23-year-old Oliver C. Reynolds, who was just about to graduate from law school. He was a grandson of Oliver Charlick, the first president of the Long Island Railroad.[123]

THE FRANCHISE

Soon after the incorporation papers were issued, Crosby petitioned the Board of Estimate and Apportionment of the City of New York for a franchise to lay wires in the streets of the city. Crosby pointed out that his central station at 1414 Broadway was ready to send music to many points throughout the city. He requested a franchise "in the form of a contract, in accordance with the provisions of the Greater New York Charter."[124] The charter had just been amended in 1905, greatly revising the process of granting franchises.[125]

Crosby had originally contacted the Board of Estimate at the beginning of February, indicating his intention to apply for a franchise, and requesting that the board's engineer examine the central station. Engineer Harry P. Nichols had then inspected the Telharmonium and held several discussions with company officials over possible terms and conditions for a franchise. With this part of the investigation already completed, Nichols stated in May that he would be able to submit a report together with a proposed contract within a week or two. He suggested that the public hearing on the matter be held on June 7, which would allow sufficient time to issue and circulate his report.[126] At the meeting of May 24 the board adopted this course, ordering the petition to be published in the daily newspapers at the expense of the New York Cahill Telharmonic Co.[127]

Several months earlier the engineering department of the Board of Estimate had been expanded and reorganized, creating a separate division of franchises for the first time. The rapid expansion of the city, with its new water, sewer, and subway lines, had greatly overburdened the work of the engineering staff. The question of franchises had come under considerable discussion and scrutiny of late. The subject was not new, but an understanding of its vital importance was so recent that no legal text on franchises as yet even existed. Franchises were originally granted by the State of New York or by municipal legislatures given special authority by the state. There was but tenuous realization of the enormous value of these privileges, especially in densely populated cities like New York. Early franchises were blithely handed out in perpetuity and with little or no compensation to the city or the state. In the wake of ensuing scandals, franchise control was placed in the hands of the Board of Estimate, with new grants allowed only for limited periods. It was impossible to recover what had already been lost to the city, but the watchful eyes of those who had earlier been outdone were going to ensure that such fleecings did not happen again.[128] At last a separate division of franchises was a reality, manned by experienced administrators who would stop the giveaways. A rational franchise policy was about to be developed. These gentlemen set out to make a public example and model of their skill and expertise in dealing with one of the first applicants to their new division, the New York Cahill Telharmonic Co.

Nichols began his report with a technical description of the

Telharmonium. He noted that company representatives stated it had cost $300,000 "and is being operated at a very large expense."[129] He mentioned the plans to add more keyboards within a few weeks. He also gave the number of subscribers as "ten or twelve places outside of the central station."[130] As to the wires leased from New York Telephone, "the company states there are a number of inconveniences involved in this arrangement."[131]

This application was vastly different from any other franchise question that had ever been presented to the board. There were similarities to a telephone, but the music furnished was no necessity. It possessed no money value that subscribers could calculate. It was an amusement, and its income would depend on public approval rather than on any intrinsic commercial worth.[132]

Nichols then proposed a number of conditions for the franchise. Naturally the compensation should be based on gross receipts, with a security fund also required to ensure that the company would carry out its contract. Since the company's costs of delivering music were not fully determined, customer rates should be left unfixed, but the board should retain authority to reduce rates if found excessive at any time. In order to show good faith the company should be required to install 4,000 music outlets within three years, or else the franchise would cease. (This would prevent an unused franchise from being held for many years and then sold, a common abuse of previous years.) The franchise should be limited to Manhattan and the western part of the Bronx, in which a few companies had already installed street conduits that could be leased by any other company with a valid franchise. This would prevent the company from tearing up the pavements elsewhere in New York to install wires, a right that should never be granted when the commodity was not a necessity. Oscar T. Crosby had stated he was agreeable to such a limitation, provided the right to construct a line immediately to Coney Island was added. The company should be required to provide free installation and service to the charity wards of Bellevue and Allied Hospitals. The company should also furnish music to the assembly halls of the public schools at one-third of consumer rates; however, it need not connect more than ten schools per year, or extend its wires greater than 2,500 feet to effect a school connection.[133]

On the matter of compensation, Nichols suggested an initial fee of $25,000, half payable within 30 days, the remainder within one year. This was in addition to a security bond of $10,000.[134]

The full scale of annual compensation was proposed as follows:

Within 30 days, initial fee installment	$12,500
Within 13 months, remainder of initial fee	12,500
During the first five years, 1% of the gross receipts, not less than $5,000 per year	25,000
During the second five years, 2% of the gross receipts, not less than $10,000 per year	50,000
During the third five years, 3% of the gross receipts, not less than $20,000 per year	100,000
During the fourth five years, 4% of the gross receipts, not less than $35,000 per year	175,000
During the remaining five years, 5% of gross receipts, not less than $60,000 per year	300,000
Total minimum compensation over 25 years	675,000[135]

It is probable that Crosby was beginning to regret being at the mercy of his glorious profit projections. He had submitted an optimistic memo on estimated gross receipts, but the minimum payments were way out of proportion with the percentage of gross receipts required. The usual city policy had been to make the two amounts equal.[136] Certainly the city could not have driven so hard a bargain several years earlier, before the central station and its publicity had created the lure of a gold mine.

The report was followed by a complete proposed contract, which required the company to begin construction within six months after it was signed by the mayor.[137] The company would be required to file an annual map of connections, keep all of its account books open to the city comptroller, and submit to the board an annual financial report on its stock, debt, dividends, damage payments, and operational expenses.[138]

The public hearing was duly held on June 7. Only one person, Oscar T. Crosby, appeared at the hearing.[139] In addition a letter from one H. Taylor Cronk, M.D., was received in support of the franchise.[140] Dr. Cronk had gained considerable notoriety five years earlier for having shot the husband of the woman who cleaned his office; the man had tried to strangle Cronk for refusing to give opium to his 12-year-old son, whom the doctor had just operated on for an abscess. The case was dismissed.[141]

The application was referred to a select committee consisting of the president of the Board of Aldermen, the comptroller, and the president of the borough of Brooklyn. It was not given a high priority; these officials were also serving on numerous other such committees to consider 26 more pressing applications of companies furnishing public necessities—telephone, railway, gas, and electric service.[142]

With a franchise almost in hand, Crosby did not press ahead financially. It was the ethically elastic day when "honest graft" was the rule of business with the city, and a well-placed generous infusion of funds for "entertainment"[143] would assuredly have liberated the application from the select committee. But then the $10,000 bond and $12,500 initial fee installment would have been due immediately, to say nothing of the staggering expense of running miles of new wires and installing 4,000 receivers at $10 to $15 apiece.[144]

Current revenues at Telharmonic Hall amounted to a mere $800 or $900 weekly from the 12 hotels and restaurants paying $10 per day, plus perhaps another $1,000 to $1,500 in weekly ticket sales for the public concerts during their brief season. Clearly the operation was not covering expenses; there were substantial salary expenses for musicians and technicians over and above the $30,000 annual lease for Telharmonic Hall. An abundance of investment capital had already been expended for license fees to Cahill, purchasing the Telharmonium, and conducting the enterprise thus far, and now substantial new investments were required to ransom the business from the city.

Meanwhile the general money squeeze was becoming calamitously pinched. Nervous markets dreaded the demands of the fall harvest, which would drain banks already sharply depleted by the record commercial financing of the past several years. Stocks were sinking in value; even the railroads could not raise money.[145] How would it ever be possible to secure sufficient funds for electric music? And could Cahill's electric music, so complicated and expensive and yet now revealed as so humble a threat to acoustic instruments, realistically be expected ever to repay such a vast investment?

Crosby took time out in June. He received an honorary LL.D. degree from Thaddeus Cahill's alma mater, George Washington University (formerly Columbian University).[146] And he waited. Unable to raise money from others, he seems to have become suddenly unwilling to throw his own good money after bad. Yet it must have been bitter gall indeed that by now the Telefon-Hirmondó of Budapest had put in over 1,100 miles of wire, that the service was reaching nearly 7,000 subscribers, and that the Electrohome service in London was broadcasting telephone concerts to 600 homes. Though it could not fill entire rooms with sound, the Telefon-Hirmondó was exuberantly broadcasting news, parliamentary proceedings, political speeches, police reports, weather forecasts, lectures, and of course opera and concerts, from 8:00 A.M. to 10:00 P.M. daily. The cost of the service had dropped to 2¢ a day; advertising cost 50¢ for 12 seconds.[147]

Crosby's self-imposed stringencies were not known, and it was predicted that he would have his franchise within the year.[148] One newspaper commentator remarked that it was "somewhat startling to find [music by wire] removed from speculative fiction to the serious province of speculative finance, engineers' reports and government regulation."[149] Other press reports gave wide coverage to the remarkable new franchise, drawing on the minutes of the Board of Estimate to disclose full details of the proposed contract.[150]

THE FINAL CHORUS OF PRAISE

> I was seated at my desk enjoying an after-luncheon smoke, when my thoughts were rudely interrupted by a timid knock upon the door of my office.
>
> "Come in," I responded, rather gruffly.
>
> It was Jimmy, the office-boy. His usually solemn face lighted up as he ejaculated: "Say, Mr. Easterbrook, has yer seen the latest wonder?"
>
> "No," I answered, abruptly. "What is it?"
>
> "It's music what comes outen an arc lamp the same time what it gives out light," was the rather surprising reply.[151]

So began one of the last odes of Telharmonic wonderment. The effusion of acclaim had dwindled and the last installments were now on the press. The short-story format of this droll little office drama was quickly subsumed by an earnest essay on the "sweet and rounded music."[152] Ten prominent hotels, it was revealed, subscribed to the service. The author mentioned de Forest's wireless transmissions of the Telharmonium and disclosed that 150 people had attended the Reverend Mr. Warren's gospel service at the Hotel Imperial. Once the entire plant was completed, seven musicians would render the sounds of an 85-piece orchestra.[153] The author terminated with the claim, "the music can be heard and appreciated by persons who are comparatively deaf to ordinary melody."[154] The reason, "as explained by a prominent aurist, is the great penetrating power of the sound waves of the Telharmonium, as well as its long sustained, perfect tones."[155] Included with the article was a photographic representation of the dinner of the future, displaying the hypnotic effects of Telharmonic music from an overhead arc lamp upon three enchanted diners and two servants (Fig. 41).

A syndicated Sunday-supplement article appeared in papers across

Fig. 41. The Dinner of the Future: Telharmonic Music and Light from an Arc Lamp. (*Gunter's Magazine,* June 1907, 3:5, S.C., 560)

the nation in July, hailing the dawning of a new age of electric music. Musicians everywhere were admitting that it was time for a fundamental readjustment of our understanding of music. For the first time, perfect uniformity of tone was available indefinitely. And its real value, according to the emphatically changed tune of inventor Cahill, was not in imitating existing instruments, but in the origination of entirely unique tones never made by any other instrument. Even now, new wiring was being installed all over New York, great hotels were putting it in all their guest rooms, and soon it would be in all the department stores.[156]

The bloom was passing from the central station, and it was becoming time to mute the perfervid predictions and see if the machine could substantiate the initial popular estimation. It was getting to be old news. One of the final published hymns appeared in June 1907, a celebration of the attainment of musical democracy. Thanks to the player piano, the talking machine, and the Telharmonium, "No longer is the world of music barred from those who are unable to pay the tribute of the rich."[157] Echoing Ray Stannard Baker, the author deplored that until now 98% of music lovers had been prevented from ever hearing 98% of all the great music. Lack of musical knowledge had ushered in a sorry substitute, "the childish adulation of the performers."[158] But now the player piano was as good as if the artist were sitting there himself, and the talking machine so perfected that even an expert could scarcely detect the difference from another room.[159] More revolutionary still was the Telharmonium. Its only shortcoming, the complicated keyboard requiring years of practice, was now being simplified by the inventor so that great pianists would be able "to control at once the soul of this many-mouthed musical giant."[160] Then the destinies of music and the Telharmonium would intertwine triumphant:

> When the musical redeemer comes he will be able by means of the Telharmonic System to draw unimagined harmonies from the caves of sound, and create a music of the future differing as radically from the music of to-day as a performance of the Metropolitan Opera House differs from the strains that fell monotonously from the rude reed of a Grecian shepherd. Rich and poor will partake of the riches he brings. Thus the democracy of music will triumphantly be established.[161]

THE ANNUAL REPORT OF THE EASTERN CAHILL TELHARMONIC CO.

Such glorious approbation may have reassured anxious stockholders, but was unlikely to have soothed the troubled nerves of Oscar T. Crosby. However, a few more encomiums like that might nimbly loosen the purse strings of some fresh investors.

Putting the best face on the state of Telharmonic affairs, the Eastern Cahill Telharmonic Co. issued its annual report at the end of June. This corporation was now declared to be the holding company of the New York Electric Music Co. The report listed Crosby as president and Todd as vice president. The directors included some familiar names (William Skinner and James G. White) and several new ones. Rear Admiral Charles D. Sigsbee, who had been recorded as a Telharmonic Hall visitor some months ago, was now among the directorate. Sigsbee was also an inventor, and his deep-sea sounding machine had been much admired by Lord Kelvin at the 1876 Centennial Exposition.[162] More new blood emerged in the persons of Frederick W. Lord, head of a large New York electrical contracting company, and Edwin G. Baetjer, who shared Crosby's fondness for world travel. Baetjer, another Baltimore lawyer, was also a big-game hunter with his own personal preserve in the South.[163]

The report stated that about 20,000 people had attended the public recitals at Telharmonic Hall during the past winter. The successful transmissions to hotels and restaurants were noted with satisfaction. The company then outlined detailed plans for much broader service in New York, to be followed by the establishment of branch companies in various cities across the United States. Delivered with the report was a revised and liberally illustrated *Telharmony* brochure splattered with glorious testimonials from Ray Stannard Baker, Mark Twain, Metropolitan Opera musicians, journalists, a clergyman, and a doctor. It promised continuous music from noon to midnight, from separate wires connected to five different music rooms: general, popular, classical, dance, and special. Each would have its own set of musicians. The "special" circuit would provide selections rendered by request. Basic service would be charged at 20¢ to $1 an hour, depending on the type of premises. Home reception would end up costing but a cent or two for each selection. To justify wiring expenses, the company demanded a minimum New York

City subscription of $60 for the first year only, payable in install-
ments. That would entitle a subscriber to several hundred hours of
electric music. The lucky recipient could expect a printed program
every week in advance, and would also be furnished with an
ingenious clockwork mechanism attached to the receiver, enabling
the service to be turned on automatically at the same time each
day.[164]

THE NEW ENGLAND ELECTRIC MUSIC CO.

Despite the fact that it had attracted no new funds since its annual
report was issued the previous April, Crosby moved in September to
increase the capitalization of the New England Electric Music Co., of
which he was still vice president. The new authorization was no less
than $750,000, matching that of the New York Electric Music Co.
Virtually all stockholders assented by proxy to the change.[165]

NOTES

1. "Telharmonic Hall," display advertisement, *New York Sun,* January 6,
1907, sec. 3, 6; "Telharmonic Hall to Open," *New York Dramatic Mirror,*
January 12, 1907, LVII:1, 464, S.C., 11; "The Opera and the Play," *New
York Herald,* January 13, 1907, sec. 3, 13; "Telharmonic Hall," display
advertisement, *New York Times,* January 13, 1907, pt. 4, 3; "Telharmonic
Hall," display advertisement, *New York Evening Post,* January 14, 1907, 9.
2. "A New Mechanical Appliance . . . ," *Musical Courier,* January 16,
1907, LIV:3, 20.
3. *Ibid.*
4. "Electric Music," *New York Evening Post,* January 15, 1907, 9.
5. *Ibid.*
6. "Telharmonic Hall," display advertisement, *New York Evening Post,*
January 15, 1907, 9.
7. New York Electric Music Co., *Telharmony: A New Art,* New York:
The Company, early January, 1907?, N.Y.P.L. *MKY Box, 7.
8. Letter from Oscar T. Crosby, President, New York Electric Music
Company, to F. P. Fish, President, American Telephone and Telegraph Co.,
January 25, 1907, 1; Letter from Oscar T. Crosby, President, New York

Electric Music Company, to Charles F. Cutler, President, New York Telephone Company, January 27, 1907, 1–4; "Bill to Transport Music," *Music Trade Review,* February 2, 1907, LIV:5, 31; "New York Telharmonic Company," *Minutes, Meeting of Board of Estimate and Apportionment,* December 22, 1910, 5574.

9. Letter from Oscar T. Crosby, January 25, 1907, 1.

10. "Cutler, Charles Frederic," *Who's Who in New York City and State,* third edition, New York: L. R. Hamersly and Company, 1907, 369; "Charles F. Cutler's Death," *New York Times,* May 20, 1907, 9.

11. Letter from Oscar T. Crosby, January 27, 1907, 1.

12. *Ibid.,* 1–2, 4.

13. Letter from F. P. Fish, President, American Telephone and Telegraph Co., to O. T. Crosby, Esq., January 28, 1907, A.T.T.A. 16878, L.B. 46/463, 1.

14. *Ibid.,* 1–2.

15. Letter from Oscar T. Crosby, New York Electric Music Company, to Frederick P. Fish, President, American Telephone and Telegraph Company, January 29, 1907, A.T.T.A. 16878, 1.

16. *Ibid.*

17. *Ibid.,* 2.

18. Oscar T. Crosby, letter to the Honorable Board of Estimate and Apportionment of the City of New York, January 29, 1907, in "New York Electric Music Company," *City Record,* February 5, 1907, 1202.

19. "Stevens, Frederick C.," *Who's Who in New York City and State,* third edition, New York, L. R. Hamersly and Company, 1907, 1230; "Bill to Transport Music," 31; *Journal of the Assembly of the State of New York,* vol. I, Albany: J. B. Lyon Company, State Printers, 1907, 233.

20. "Bill to Transport Music," 31; "To Transport Music," *Electrical World,* February 9, 1907, XLIX:6, S.C., 296.

21. "To Distribute Music by Electric Corporations," *Albany* [N.Y.] *Argus,* February 6, 1907, S.C., n.p.

22. "Telharmonic Hall," display advertisement, *New York Times,* January 20, 1907, pt. 4, 3.

23. "Electric Music in the Street," *New-York Daily Tribune,* January 22, 1907, 14; "Salome Comes to Town," *New-York Daily Tribune,* January 20, 1907, pt. IV, 6.

24. "Telharmonic Hall," display advertisement, *New York Times,* January 27, 1907, pt. 4, 3.

25. New York Electric Music Company, *Program and Announcement: Telharmonic Hall, No. 1,* New York: The Company, January 27, 1907? [penciled on cover: "Gift of New York Electric Music Company, Feb. 16th, 1907"], N.Y.P.L. *MKY Box, 2.

26. *Ibid.,* 4; "Christian Schiott Dies," *New York Times,* December 30, 1960, 20.

27. Marion Knight, *A Comet Among the Stars,* New York: Pageant Press, 1953, 24–26, 35–36, 45–48, 51–52.

28. Personal interview with James Edward Pierce, Echo Lake Farm, Great Spring Road, Smithfield, Va., April 23, 1983; Letter from Rod[eric Pierce] to Jim [James Edward Pierce], June 12, 1974, J.E.P., 1; James Edward Pierce, "Item Regarding Pioneer Inventor of Electric Music and His Association with the Pierce Family," August 1970, typewritten, J.E.P., S.I., 1; Edwin Hall Pierce, "A Colossal Experiment in 'Just Intonation,'" *Musical Quarterly,* July 1924, X:3, 330; Edna Leaf Woodruff Pierce, Diary, Auburn, N.Y., February 4, 1898, to March 6, 1908, J.E.P., 12–13.

29. Mason, 238.

30. "Salome Comes to Town," 6; "Carl M. Pihl Spoke," *Holyoke Daily Transcript,* January 30, 1907, 3.

31. "Worcester Polytechnic Dinner," *Electrical World,* February 9, 1907, XLIX:6, S.C., 295.

32. *Ibid.*

33. "Music on Wires," *New York Globe and Commercial Advertiser,* January 31, 1907, 4.

34. "Dozen Grand Operas and Many Concerts," *New York World,* January 27, 1907, Metropolitan Section, 4.

35. "Miss Terry Here Again," *New-York Daily Tribune,* January 27, 1907, pt. IV, 6; "Tenor to Help Inventor," *Musical America,* February 2, 1907, V:12, 7; "Andreas Dippel Outlines His Plans for 'Musical America,'" *Musical America,* March 7, 1908, VII:17, 4; "Dippel, Tenor, Dies in Want on Coast," *New York Times,* May 14, 1932, 15; "'Send for Dippel!' Is the Cry When Caruso Strains His Voice," *New York World,* February 2, 1908, Metropolitan Section, M3.

36. "Strings, Wood Winds, and Brasses," *New York Evening Telegram,* February 2, 1907, S.C., 11; "'Tone building' will be . . . ," *New York Evening World,* February 2, 1907, S.C., n.p. [not found]; "The New Plays," *New York Evening Mail,* February 2, 1907, S.C., 7; "Telharmonic Hall, Broadway and . . . ," *New York American,* February 3, 1907, S.C., n.p.

37. "Musical News and Gossip," *New York Evening Post,* February 2, 1907, Saturday Supplement, 5; "Telharmonic Hall," *New York Press,* February 11, 1907, S.C., n.p.

38. "Musical Comedy Week," *New-York Daily Tribune,* February 3, 1907, pt. IV, 6; "Telharmonie als musikalische Kunst," *New York Morgen Journal,* February 3, 1907, S.C., n.p.

39. "Telharmonic Hall," *New York Press,* February 5, 1907, S.C., n.p.

40. "To Preserve Miss Winlocke's Voice," *New York Morning Telegraph,* February 5, 1907, S.C., n.p.

41. *Ibid.*

42. "Telharmonic Novelties," *New York Evening Mail,* February 5, 1907,

S.C., 12; "Musical News and Gossip," *New York Evening Post,* February 9, 1907, S.C., Saturday Supplement, 5.

43. "Minister Tells of Saving Many from Suicide," *New York World,* December 9, 1906, pt. II, 15; "Dr. H. M. Warren, Baptist Minister," *New York Times,* December 23, 1940, 19.

44. "Will Wire Music to Hotels," *New York Herald,* February 9, 1907, S.C., 8; Lewis, Scribner and Co., *Where and How to Dine in New York,* New York: The Company, 1903, 43–44.

45. "Will Baffle Despair with Aid of Prayer," *New York Globe and Commercial Advertiser,* January 10, 1907, 6.

46. "Among the new features . . . ," *New York American,* February 10, 1907, S.C., n.p.; "Das Haus-Orchester der Zukunst," *New York Morgen Journal,* February 11, 1907, S.C., n.p., tr. Martin Wulfhorst.

47. "Novelties at Telharmonic Hall," *New York Morning Telegraph,* February 12, 1907, S.C., n.p.; "At Telharmonic Hall the novelties . . . ," *New York World,* February 12, 1907, S.C., n.p. [not found]; "Henrietta Crosman Sustains 'All-of-a-Sudden Peggy,' " *New York Evening Mail,* February 12, 1907, S.C., 5; "At Telharmonic Hall, Thirty-ninth . . . ," *New York Dramatic Mirror,* February 23, 1907, LVII:1, 470, S.C., 16; "Admiral Sigsbee of the *Maine* Dies," *New York Times,* July 20, 1923, 13.

48. "Sunday Services in Greater New York," *New York World,* February 16, 1907, 8; "Attractions of the Theatres," *New York Evening Sun,* February 16, 1907, S.C., 2; " 'The White Hen' Lays for All at the Casino," *New York Evening Journal,* February 16, 1907, S.C., 9; "At Telharmonic Hall tomorrow . . . ," *New York Evening World,* February 16, 1907, S.C., n.p. [not found]; "The music of the future . . . ," *Brooklyn* [N.Y.] *Eagle,* February 16, 1907, S.C., n.p.; "Religious Music by Wire," *New York Herald,* February 16, 1907, S.C., 12; "The music of the future . . . ," *New York Press,* February 17, 1907, S.C., n.p.; "Among the features of the performances . . . ," *New York American,* February 17, 1907, S.C., n.p.; "Hymns by Electricity," *New York Herald,* February 18, 1907, S.C., 7.

49. " 'The music of the future' . . . ," *Brooklyn* [N.Y.] *Eagle,* February 16, 1907, S.C., n.p.; "Strings, Wood Winds and Brasses," *New York Evening Telegram,* February 16, 1907, S.C., 11; "Musical News and Gossip," *New York Evening Post,* February 16, 1907, S.C., Saturday Supplement, 5; "Busy Week of Rival Grand Operas, Concerts and Recitals," *New York World,* February 17, 1907, S.C., 4; " 'The music of the future' . . . ," *New York Press,* February 17, 1907, S.C., n.p., "Among the features of the performances . . . ," *New York American,* February 17, 1907, S.C., n.p.

50. "Telharmonic Hall," display advertisement, *New York Times,* February 17, 1907, pt. 4, 4.

51. "Tristan Hears Telharmonist," *Musical Age,* February 16, 1907, LVII:3, S.C., 54; "Telharmonium—America," *The American History and Encyclopedia of Music: Musical Instruments,* Toledo: Irving Squire, 1908, 222.

52. "Still Drawing Crowds," *New York Globe and Commercial Advertiser,* February 22, 1907, S.C., 2; "They are doing a very large business . . . ," *New York Dramatic News,* February 23, 1907, S.C., n.p.; " 'On Parole,' at Majestic, Play of Civil War," *New York Evening Journal,* February 23, 1907, S.C., 9; New York Electric Music Company, *Program and Announcement, Telharmonic Hall, No. 1,* New York: The Company, mid-February? 1907 [revised musical program No. 1], M.C.S., 4; "The Seventh Week of Telharmony," *New York Star,* February 26, 1907, S.C., n.p.; "Big Drawing Card," *New York Globe and Commercial Advertiser,* February 28, 1907, S.C., 14; "Musical News and Gossip," *New York Evening Post,* February 23, 1907, Saturday Supplement, 5.

53. Donald deB. Beaver, "De Forest, Lee," *Dictionary of American Biography,* supp. 7, New York: Charles Scribner's Sons, 1981, 175, 176; "The Audion Described," *New York Times,* October 27, 1906, 9.

54. Lee de Forest, "Diary," typewritten, Y.U., Lee de Forest Papers, CTYV84-A1065, Box 2, Folder 911, 328–329; cf. Lee de Forest, *Father of Radio,* Chicago: Wilcox-Follett, 1950, 225.

55. De Forest, *Father of Radio,* 225.

56. Lee de Forest, "Autobiographical Notes, vol. IV (1905–1911)," F.E.M., 435.

57. De Forest, *Father of Radio,* 331–332.

58. "Music by Wireless Now," *Holyoke Daily Transcript,* March 1, 1907, 10; "Grand Opera by Wireless," *New York Herald,* March 1, 1907, 8; "Make Way for the Blue and Gold," *New York Times,* July 9, 1989, Real Estate Section, 6R.

59. "Music by Wireless Now," 10.

60. "Wireless 'Phone Transmits Music," *New York Herald,* March 7, 1907, 8.

61. *Ibid.*

62. *Ibid.*

63. *Ibid.*; "Music by Wireless Telephone," *New-York Daily Tribune,* March 7, 1907, 4; "Cahill Music by Wireless," *Holyoke Daily Transcript,* March 7, 1907, 2; "Music by Wireless," *New York Globe and Commercial Advertiser,* March 7, 1907, 5; "Wireless Telegraph Music," *Musical America,* March 23, 1907, V:19, 13; Georgette Carneal, *A Conquerer of Space,* New York: Horace Liveright, 1930, 203.

64. "Music by Wireless to the Times Tower," *New York Times,* March 8, 1907, 16; "Music Now by Wireless," *Music Trade Review,* March 9, 1907, XLIV:10, 34.

65. "Wireless Telephony," *New-York Daily Tribune,* March 10, 1907, pt. I, 8; "Demonstration of Wireless Telephone," *New York Evening Mail,* March 7, 1907, 5.

66. Elliot N. Sivowitch, "A Technological Survey of Broadcasting's 'Pre-History,' 1876–1920," *Journal of Broadcasting,* Winter 1970–71, XV:1, 10.

67. Francis Arthur Hart, "Call Letters and Log Book of Francis Arthur Hart," 1906–1909, holograph, S.I., 23.

68. *Ibid.*

69. *Ibid.*, 34.

70. *Ibid.*, 22–23, 34–35.

71. Carneal, 209.

72. *Ibid.*

73. *Ibid.*

74. Samuel Lubell, "Magnificent Failure," *Saturday Evening Post,* January 24, 1942, 214:30, 38; "New Wireless Music," *Talking Machine World,* April 15, 1907, III:4, 9; "Sending Music Through the Air," *Talking Machine World,* May 15, 1907, III:5, 12; "Telephony Without Wires," *Talking Machine World,* August 15, 1907, III:8, 4.

75. "William Skinner," *Holyoke Daily Transcript,* March 7, 1907, 8; "William Skinner, a Silk Official, 90," *New York Times,* October 28, 1947, 15; "Skinner, William," *The National Cyclopaedia of American Biography,* vol. XXXVII, New York: James T. White and Company, 1951, 109; "Skinner, William," *Who's Who in New York City and State,* third edition, New York: L. R. Hamersly and Company, 1907, 1192; "Skinner, Joseph Allen," *The National Cyclopaedia of American Biography,* vol. XXXIV, New York: James T. White and Company, 1948, 555.

76. "Schenck and the Telharmonium," *Musical Courier,* March 6, 1907, LIV:10, 26; "Schenck Conducts School Orchestra," *Musical Courier,* February 27, 1907, LIV:9, 37; "Schenck 'Pop Concerts,' " *Musical Courier,* March 13, 1907, LIV:11, 29; "Schenck to Conduct Schubert Glee Club," *Musical Courier,* March 20, 1907, LIV:12, 19.

77. "Telharmonic Hall," display advertisement, *New York Times,* March 3, 1907, pt. 4, 4; "Musical News and Gossip," *New York Evening Post,* March 2, 1907, Saturday Supplement, 5; "Before the Footlights," *New-York Daily Tribune,* March 10, 1907, pt. IV, 6.

78. Charles Figaro, "The Telharmonium—An Apparatus for the Electrical Generation and Transmission of Music," cover illustration, *Scientific American,* March 9, 1907, XCVI:10, 205.

79. Letter from O. T. Crosby, New York Electric Music Company, to F. P. Fish, American Telephone and Telegraph Company, March 8, 1907, 1.

80. *Ibid.*, 1–2.

81. "Telharmonic Hall," display advertisement, *New York Times,* March 10, 1907, pt. 4, 4.

82. "Telharmonic Hall," display advertisement, *New York Times,* March 17, 1907, pt. 4, 4; "Musical News and Gossip," *New York Evening Post,* March 9, 1907, Saturday Supplement, 5; "Before the Footlights," 6.

83. "Oboe and Flute at Telharmonic Hall," *New York American,* March 21, 1907, S.C., n.p.; "Music Menu for Hotel Diners," *New York Press,* March 21, 1907, S.C., n.p.; "Music to Distant Hearers," *Music Trade Review,*

March 30, 1907, XLIV:13, 43; "The Wonder of the Age," *New York Irish-American,* March 23, 1907, 1.

84. "Many New Plays in Easter Week," *New York Evening Mail,* March 30, 1907, Supplement Section, 2; "New Plays This Week," *New-York Daily Tribune,* March 31, 1907, pt. IV, 6; "Converting Music into Electricity," *British Deaf Times,* September 1907, IV:45, 206.

85. "Music Across the Hudson," *Musical Courier,* March 27, 1907, LIV:13, 26C.

86. Letter from F. P. Fish, President, American Telephone and Telegraph Co., to O. T. Crosby, Esq., New York Electric Music Company, March 30, 1907, A.T.T.A., 604507, LB 47/410, 1.

87. "Music by Wire," *Musical Age,* March 23, 1907, LVII:8, 186; "Joker in Electric Music Bill," *Music Trades,* March 30, 1907, XXXIII:13, 33; *Journal of the Assembly of the State of New York,* vol. I, Albany: J. B. Lyon Company, State Printers, 1907, 612, 613, 643, 665, 834, 909, vol. II, 1083, 1162, 1199–1200.

88. New York Electric Music Company, *Program and Announcement: Telharmonic Hall, No. 4,* New York: The Company, late March? 1907, A.T.T.B.L.A., Boston File 500, 2.

89. *Ibid.,* 3.

90. *Ibid.,* 1, 2, 3.

91. *Ibid.,* 4.

92. "Concerts at Telharmonic Hall," *New-York Daily Tribune,* April 7, 1907, pt. IV, 7.

93. "Telharmonic Hall," display advertisement, *New York Evening Journal,* March 30, 1907, 2; "Telharmonic Hall," display advertisement, *New York Times,* April 7, 1907, pt. 4, 4; "Remodeling Telharmonic Hall," *Musical Age,* April 13, 1907, LVIII:11, 285; "Musical News and Gossip," *New York Evening Post,* April 13, 1907, Saturday Supplement, 5; "Telharmonic Hall," display advertisement, *New-York Daily Tribune,* April 13, 1907, 8.

94. Daniel Gregory Mason, "The Telharmonium: Its Musical Basis," *Outlook,* February 9, 1907, LXXXV:6, 297.

95. *Ibid.,* 298.

96. *Ibid.*

97. "Sothern and Marlowe in 'The Merchant,' " *New York Evening Journal,* February 19, 1907, S.C., 7.

98. Mason, 298.

99. "Buying Music by Meter Now—Just Like Gas or Water," *New York World,* January 27, 1907, Magazine Section, 7; "Buy Music by Meter Like Gas or Water," *Chicago Examiner,* February 3, 1907, S.C., n.p.

100. Charles Barnard, "Music Made by Electricity," *Saint Nicholas Magazine,* May 1907, 34:5, 638.

101. Carroll Brent Chilton, "Music by Wire," *Independent,* April 25, 1907, 62:4, 948.

102. *Ibid.*, 949.

103. Edwin Hall Pierce, 331–332; "Electrical Transmission of Music," *Electrical World,* April 28, 1910, LV:17, 1059–1060.

104. Edwin Hall Pierce, 326, 331.

105. "The Telharmonium Concerts," *Music Trade Review,* April 13, 1907, XLIV:15, 43.

106. Letter from Hammond V. Hayes, Chief Engineer, American Telephone and Telegraph Company, to F. P. Fish, President, American Telephone and Telegraph Company, April 12, 1907, A.T.T.A., 604507, 1.

107. "Hammond V. Hayes," *New York Times,* March 23, 1947, 60; "Hayes, Hammond Vinton," *Who Was Who in America,* vol. 2, Chicago: The A. N. Marquis Company, 1950, 243.

108. Letter from George M. Yorke, Assistant Engineer, American Telephone and Telegraph Co., to Hammond V. Hayes, Chief Engineer, American Telephone and Telegraph Co., April 5, 1907, A.T.T.B.L.A., Boston File 500, 20.03.01.02, 1.

109. Letter from Hammond V. Hayes, April 12, 1907, 1.

110. *Ibid.,* 1–2.

111. *Ibid.,* 2–3.

112. *Ibid.,* 3.

113. *Ibid.*

114. *Ibid.*

115. Letter from Thomas D. Lockwood to F. P. Fish, President, April 17, 1907, A.T.T.A.

116. Carneal, 207–208.

117. New England Electric Music Company, Annual Report for 1907, April 24, 1907, filed at the Office of the Secretary of State, Trenton, N.J., May 1, 1907, 3.

118. New York Electric Music Company, Annual Report for 1907, April 24, 1907, filed at the Office of the Secretary of State, Trenton, N.J., May 1, 1907, 3.

119. *Journal of the Senate of the State of New York,* vol. I, Albany: J. B. Lyon Company, State Printers, 1907, 579, 581, 843–844, 1018–1019, 1022, 1113–1114; "Telharmonic Bill Defeated," *Music Trade Review,* April 20, 1907, XLIV:16, 25; "Bill for Telharmonic Co. Failed to Pass," *Musical Age,* April 20, 1907, XLIV:16, 25.

120. "Electric Music Boom," *Holyoke Daily Transcript,* April 30, 1907, 7; "Electric Music Boom," *Music Trade Review,* May 4, 1907, XLIV:18, 13; "Tristan Talks of Coming Season," *Musical Age,* May 4, 1907, LVIII:1, 8.

121. *Journal of the Senate of the State of New York,* vol. I, 1220–1221; *Journal of the Assembly of the State of New York,* vol. III, 2472, 2475; "Chap. 310," *Laws of the State of New York Passed at the One Hundred and Thirtieth Session of the Legislature,* vol. I, Albany: J. B. Lyon Company, State Printers, 1907, 563; New York Cahill Telharmonic Company, Certificate of Incorpo-

ration, May 7, 1907, filed and recorded at the Office of the Secretary of State, Albany, N.Y., May 8, 1907, also filed and recorded at the Office of the County Clerk, New York, N.Y., May 9, 1907, A.C.C. 2757–1907, 1–2; "Hughes's Busy Day with Bills," *Albany Evening Journal,* May 7, 1907, 2; "Signed by the Governor," *New-York Daily Tribune,* May 8, 1907, 2.

122. New York Cahill Telharmonic Company, Certificate of Incorporation, 2–3.

123. "Reynolds, Oliver Charlick," *Who Was Who in America,* vol. VI, Chicago: Marquis Who's Who, 1976, 342; "Oliver C. Reynolds, Founded Law Firm," *New York Times,* May 29, 1970, 29.

124. "New York Cahill Telharmonic Company," *Minutes, Meeting of Board of Estimate and Apportionment,* May 24, 1907, 1628.

125. "New York Cahill Telharmonic Company," *Minutes, Meeting of Board of Estimate and Apportionment,* January 5, 1911, 49.

126. *Ibid.,* 1627–1628.

127. *Ibid.,* 1629.

128. Nelson P. Lewis, *Report of the Chief Engineer of the Board of Estimate and Apportionment of the City of New York for the Years 1906 and 1907,* New York: The Board, 1908, 7–8, 18–19; Richard C. Harrison, "Corporations and Franchises," in Francis G. Wickware, ed. *The American Year Book, 1911,* New York: D. Appleton and Company, 1912, 446.

129. Harry P. Nichols, *Result of Investigation by the Division of Franchises of the Application of the New York Cahill Telharmonic Company,* New York: Board of Estimate and Apportionment, Office of Chief Engineer, May 31, 1907, B.E., 4.

130. *Ibid.*

131. *Ibid.*

132. *Ibid.,* 5.

133. *Ibid.,* 5–8.

134. *Ibid.,* 20.

135. *Ibid.,* 9–10.

136. "New York Cahill Telharmonic Company," *Minutes, Meeting of Board of Estimate and Apportionment,* December 22, 1910, 5578.

137. Nichols, 18.

138. *Ibid.,* 18–20.

139. "New York Cahill Telharmonic Company," *Minutes, Meeting of Board of Estimate and Apportionment,* June 7, 1907, 1803.

140. *Ibid.*

141. "Physician Shoots a Man," *New York Times,* June 5, 1902, 6; "Dr. Cronk Discharged from Custody," *New York Times,* June 20, 1902, 3.

142. Lewis, 20–21, 219, 241, 251.

143. George F. Cahill, 9.

144. "New York Cahill Telharmonic Company," *Minutes, Meeting of Board of Estimate and Apportionment,* December 22, 1910, 5576.

145. "The Financial Situation," *New York Times,* September 9, 1907, 8.
146. "Crosby, Oscar Terry," *National Cyclopedia of American Biography,* vol. XXXV, New York: James T. White and Company, 1949, 84.
147. David L. Woods, "Semantics Versus the 'First' Broadcasting Station," *Journal of Broadcasting,* Summer 1967, XI:3, 204, 201; "Telephone Newspaper, Two Cents," *New York World,* June 30, 1907, Editorial Section, E3.
148. "Plan to Distribute Music Around Town," *Brooklyn* [N.Y.] *Times,* June 15, 1907, S.C., n.p.
149. "A Puzzle for the Board of Estimate," *New York Sun,* June 22, 1907, S.C., 6.
150. "Telharmonic Co. Wants a Franchise," *New York Times,* June 26, 1907, S.C., 7; "A select committee of the board . . . ," *New York Irish-American,* June 29, 1907, S.C., n.p.; "Franchise to Distribute Music," *Music Trade Review,* June 29, 1907, XLIV:26, 9; "Telharmonic Franchises," *Electrical World,* June 29, 1907, XLIX:26, 1298.
151. A. B. Easterbrook, "The Wonderful Telharmonium," *Gunter's Magazine,* June 1907, 3:5, S.C., 561.
152. *Ibid.*
153. *Ibid.,* 562, 565–566.
154. *Ibid.,* 568.
155. *Ibid.*
156. George H. Picard, "Music for the Million," *Amsterdam* [N.Y.] *Recorder,* July 13, 1907, S.C., 9, also *Deseret Evening News,* July 13, 1907, S.C., 21.
157. George Sylvester Viereck, "The Democracy of Music Achieved by Invention," *Current Literature,* June 1907, 42:6, 670.
158. *Ibid.*
159. *Ibid.,* 670–672.
160. *Ibid.,* 673.
161. *Ibid.*
162. "Admiral Sigsbee of the *Maine* Dies," 13.
163. "F. W. Lord, Leader of Electric Firm," *New York Times,* January 1, 1952, 25; "E. G. Baetjer Dies, Lawyer 54 Years," *New York Times,* July 22, 1945, 38.
164. "Electric Music Report," *Baltimore News,* June 28, 1907, S.C., n.p.; "Reports Progress Made," *Music Trade Review,* July 13, 1907, XLV:2, 7; "First Annual Report of Tel-Harmonic Co.," *Musical Age,* July 20, 1907, LVIII:12, S.C., 366; Eastern Cahill Telharmonic Company, *Telharmony: The New Art of Electric Music,* New York: The Company, June? 1907, M.C.S. 1, 4–8, 11, 12, 14.
165. New England Electric Music Company, Certificate of Increase of Capital Stock, September 11, 1907, filed and recorded at the Office of the Secretary of State, Trenton, N.J., September 16, 1907, 1, 3.

CHAPTER VI

THE SECOND SEASON AT
TELHARMONIC HALL

THE TELHARMONIC SECURITIES CO.

The distant thunder of the financial storm moved rapidly closer to drown out the optimistic claims for Telharmony and a legion of other endeavors. By September the value of stock exchange securities had plummeted by $3 billion, precipitating the failure of one of the country's largest investment firms. A $75 million bond offering by the Union Pacific Railroad went begging; it sold only 22%. Investors were defaulting on prior subscriptions to stocks and bonds. Currency began its annual harvesttime drain to the West. Money had all but dried up, and absolute convulsions seemed not far away.[1]

Oscar T. Crosby was inconvenienced but by no means ruined as the Panic of 1907 approached. He was actively occupied in building his large new home, "View Tree," in Warrenton, Va. Never particularly interested in music or the arts—he was almost amusical—he now simply decided to disengage himself from the Telharmonium business. The anticipation of radio and the pathetic inability of Cahill's electric music to displace orchestral instruments led Crosby to cut his losses. No longer would he lead the enterprise he had fashioned and nurtured so ardently.[2]

Control devolved to Frederick C. Todd, who became president of the sixth and final corporation organized during this period to advance the dwindling interests of Telharmony. The Telharmonic Securities Co. was incorporated in New Jersey as a breathtakingly unaccountable holding company. It was formed to operate and acquire the assets of the other corporations, by virtue of a two-member executive committee that could exercise all the powers of the board of directors. The stockholders had no right to examine the books of the corporation.[3]

A modest capitalization of $125,000 was sufficient, of which the three directors subscribed to ten shares at $100 each. John C. Rowe, a director of the New York Cahill Telharmonic Co., took eight shares. Oliver C. Reynolds, another director of the New York Cahill Telharmonic Co., took a share, as did a new recruit, John R. Turner. The latter was a 27-year-old New Jersey lawyer who assisted in the incorporation proceedings.[4] No officers were named in the document, but Frederick C. Todd was revealed as president when the firm applied several months later to do business in New York.[5]

THE PANIC OF 1907

By the beginning of October the depression in stock prices was disquieting all of Broadway. Announced productions were not opening, reported new theatres remained unbuilt, and an unusually high failure rate was evident. Outside capital had completely evaporated. Stocks selling at 60% of par necessitated a postponement in any unnecessary expenditures. The theatre was among the earliest businesses to feel the pinch as a noose. Salaries and employment were starting to diminish, eroding attendance at all but the very best and the very cheapest shows.[6]

The excess of prosperity had finally overwhelmed the tottering money supply, which was wholly rigid and could not expand to accommodate the creation of all the prodigious new wealth. In mid-October a collapse in the price of copper precipitated a bank failure, and the resultant inquiries revealed that about 20 banks were controlled by speculators allowed to lend to themselves. The prevailing spiritual diverticulitis deteriorated into raw terror, and runs on the banks set in. Soon all suspended payment and some closed their doors for good. By November so much currency had disappeared from the economy that banks were issuing substitute certificates.[7]

What currency remained in circulation went at a premium, as high as 4% in November. The government deposited huge sums with the paralyzed banks, reducing its own working balance to only

$3,500,000. Stock prices were decimated. By December business was devastated: thousands of employees were dismissed, factories reverted to part time, retail trade was severely curtailed, and many corporations went into receivership, notably the Westinghouse Co. New plays failing on Broadway had reached a record of 80%, and an estimated 8,000 actors were looking for work.[8]

TELHARMONIC HALL OPENS AGAIN

In spite of the economic commotion, Telharmonic Hall managed to restore service. The first sign of life was the sound of music from a manhole in the middle of Broadway at 25th Street one late October evening. Passersby speculated on the mystery. "A little German band is practicing in the sewer so that the usual bricks won't hit them,"[9] said a sternfaced man as *Lohengrin* streamed through holes in the iron cover. Then the strains of *Kiss Me Good-Bye and Go, Jack* floated out. "Some sentimental composer who is not appreciated has buried himself alive,"[10] said a young lady to her date. "He is playing his swan song."[11] The police had to disperse the crowd every once in a while to keep traffic moving. A few generous souls rewarded the concealed musicians by dropping coins into the holes of the manhole cover. This tiny accumulation of riches awaited the electricians of the Telharmonic Securities Co., who had left their receiving apparatus attached to the electric music cable running underneath Broadway. They had been repairing the wire when quitting time of five o'clock arrived. Musicians practicing into the night at the central station thus presented an unintended preview of the new season at Telharmonic Hall.[12]

The central station announced early in November that the wonderful new season would begin on Saturday the ninth— simultaneously at Telharmonic Hall, the New York Theatre at Broadway and 45th Street, and the last day of the Automobile Show in Madison Square Garden. The emphasis at the Hall was on publicity stunts. Arc lights and palm fronds were not enough: melodies would also issue from lily pads, rose bushes, doorknobs, and other objects.[13] The long-promised adjunct keyboards would finally materialize. A force of 12 soloists would execute the music by wire, and movies to demonstrate such service would be screened in the refurbished auditorium.[14]

Due to incomplete alterations, Telharmonic Hall stayed closed on opening night. However, outside transmissions did indeed go forth on the concluding day of the Auto Show, which was drawing huge crowds at the Garden—more than 10,000 daily. As a publicity coup, wiring the Auto Show was inspired. The Telharmonic tunes elicited constant favorable comment. The masses listened in mystification. From under the eaves around the hall, megaphones were delivering music with no apparent source. Regrettably, the press drew mixed conclusions. There were "still many improvements to be made in the tone and carrying power of the Telharmonium [but] the showing was good, and under proper management this method of transmitting music should have a bright future."[15] Part of the credit had to be awarded to Cahill's newly installed three-break circuit that largely eliminated the old "diaphragm-crack" static attacks on the notes.[16]

Later that week Telharmonic Hall advertisements finally appeared in the papers.[17] A "Grand Telharmonic Concert" with 145 dynamos and 12 soloists would work its musical magic four times daily, at 1:30, 3:00, 7:30, and 8:30. In a concession to hard times, the admission had dropped to only 25¢, the same price as vaudeville shows, cheap melodramas, and Eden's Wax Museum.[18] On opening night, postponed to November 11 and again to November 16,[19] ten of the twelve soloists materialized. They performed "a varied and picturesque program"[20] on a set of new keyboards "the length of three piano scales."[21] The next evening, Telharmonic high jinks made news when *The Merry Widow Waltz* was heard to emanate from a man's body. A soundboard driven by a receiver had been hidden under some fellow's coat.[22] The use of the Telharmonium for good music, he seemed to adumbrate, was about through. The *Times* concurred; instead of reporting central station doings under the heading "Music and Musicians," the intelligence was delivered as "Theatrical Notes" or "Vaudeville."[23]

Three days after the gala reopening of Telharmonic Hall, the frequency of concerts shrank to two—at 3:00 and 8:30.[24] The human soundboard was supplemented by fastening the receiver leads directly to the arms and other parts of the body. People tingled nervously as several thousand volts running through their systems caused their noses and fingers to vibrate. They were part of the new Telharmonic musical freak show. The management assured them it couldn't hurt. The press had a high old time telling of the new "Liver Gavotte."[25]

The ensuing attention improved business, and Telharmonic Hall restored its old ticket prices of 50¢ and $1.00 not long before it was forced to close Sunday nights.[26] Concerts and theatrical performances on the Sabbath were suddenly banned throughout New York. A group of ministers had been agitating against Sunday vaudeville, with the result that a long-neglected blue law to prohibit every form of Sunday entertainment was now being strictly enforced.[27]

Yet another novel application of the Telharmonium was broached in December. The central station announced that trolley cars could be supplied with music over their regular overhead power wires. Meriden, Conn., which perhaps not coincidentally was located on the railway between New York and Holyoke, promptly applied for Telharmonic service. Experiments were promised.[28]

At this time a few private houses were also taking Telharmonic music. They paid 25¢ per actual hour of music. There was no charge for installation of the receiver and the volume-control box.[29]

THADDEUS CAHILL DEMONSTRATES THE TELHARMONIUM

In November the Music Teachers' National Association had proudly revealed that the celebrated Thaddeus Cahill would bestow upon the society's members and guests a personal explanation and demonstration of his remarkable Telharmonium. The 29th annual convention was due to be held at Columbia University a few days after Christmas.[30] With the holidays drawing nigh, Cahill's impending talk at the meeting began to generate much interest. Until this occasion the inventor had consistently refused all invitations to speak in public from scientific as well as musical organizations. He preferred to devote his entire time to inventive designs, building and perfecting his instrument, and wrestling with the Patent Office. But now Cahill would make a special trip from Holyoke to meet the members at Telharmonic Hall and unravel its mysteries for them.[31]

Cahill stated that he would confine his remarks to an apparatus for equal temperament only, thus sacrificing an opportunity to promulgate some of his more interesting and radical designs. He set out by dissembling about the alternators, claiming a full chromatic set of twelve instead of the eight known to exist in the New York machine. On synthesizing instrumental tones, he recommended the first harmonic with a weak second harmonic for the flute, a third harmonic with a weak second and fourth for the clarinet, a prominent fifth harmonic for the oboe, strong seventh and eighth harmonics for the brass, and all but the seventh for the cello. Relative strengths of the timbre-control switches were graduated at six levels: *pp, p, mp, mf, f, ff.* This was a historic improvement over organ stops, which could be set only open or closed with no intermediate effect available. Interestingly, the musicians did not always concur among themselves over the proper recipes for synthesis: each had a different conception of which timbre was the most suitable to generate. Furthermore, the attack of a note, its dynamic control as it was sustained, and its release were all so crucial as to approach the importance of the harmonic mix itself in imitating orchestral intruments.[32]

Cahill emphatically disclaimed any responsibility for the fatuous claims that the New York Telharmonium was meant to imitate a full orchestra. Its new third keyboard manual and switchboard meant that it could presently create precisely three voices of different timbres and no more. Cahill had originally contemplated five manuals and switchboards for the instrument. Now, to do the work of an orchestra, he saw that no fewer than eight to twelve would suffice.[33]

At this point in Cahill's lecture the loyal Karl W. Schulz, last of the original Telharmonists, demonstrated the synthesizing of various timbres.[34]

Cahill admitted that the tones heard were not exactly identical to the instruments mentioned. Such similarity was "not indispensable, nor, indeed, is it always desirable."[35] In fact, the quality of electrical tones was often "purer and better."[36] The brass syntheses had none of the trombone's harshness, while the woodwind imitations could be created with a wider dynamic range at no change in timbre. Only the violin tones were "not as clear and incisive,"[37] but this would be rectified after a more complete harmonic series was installed.

Cahill exhorted the audience not to take the limitations of this Telharmonium as those of electrical music. This central station was the first of its kind. The designs were several years old now. Expense limitations had forced him "to make a simpler and less complete machine than he would have wished."[38] It should not be judged against existing instruments which had had many more years to develop, both in design and virtuoso performance technique.

Cahill then launched once more his well-worn tirade against the defects of the organ, piano, and violin. The organ had no expression; the piano had little tonal variation, no *sostenuto*, and limited volume; the violin lacked all capacity for full harmony, wide timbral variety, or majestic volume. The Telharmonium, on the other hand, promised that only an electrical system "would combine the widely different tone-colors, the great volume of tone, and the *sostenuto* powers of the organ with the vigorous movement that belongs to the pianoforte, and the grace and flexibility of the bowed instruments."[39]

On the future of musical synthesis, Cahill lucidly predicted:

> The composer of the past has been like the chemist or alchemist of ancient times, who could use in his combinations some few compound bodies only. The composer of the future will have in the sinusoidal vibrations of electrical music those pure elements out of which all tone-compounds can be built; not merely the known and approved tones of the orchestra, but many shades and nuances heretofore unattainable.[40]

Even more important than timbre was

> dynamic control, which, in an ideal instrument, should give the performer the power at every instant to control the loudness of each note; to attack it softly or vigorously; to sustain it with an even flow, or to increase or decrease it at will; to drop it suddenly, or by an almost imperceptible *diminuendo,* as his feelings require. In the electrical music the performer has this perfect control.[41]

With such an instrument, unquestionably better orchestral effects could be originated with steel-geared notes perfectly in tune by a far smaller number of performers than in an orchestra—perhaps ten instead of a hundred.[42]

Combining such forces with the capacity of propagation by wire should have

> the same important influence in disseminating a knowledge of and love for good music among the people, that the printing press had in spreading knowledge.[43]

Cahill's audience was not spared the singing arc or the musical ferns, to which they listened in surprised delight.[44] One questioner wished to know if the human voice could be reproduced by the central station. Cahill admitted that that was impossible on the present system, but claimed "vast improvements"[45] would develop and that "the versatility of electrical music was almost incomprehensible."[46]

PROGRAMS AND PROMOTIONS AT TELHARMONIC HALL

The week before Cahill's address, Mayor McClellan of New York had signed an ordinance permitting Sunday "sacred or educational vocal or instrumental concerts."[47] Telharmonic Hall restored Sunday concerts on the last Sabbath of the year[48] and did a brisk music teachers' convention business over the weekend.

The printed program for the following week listed two daily public performances plus two more concerts each day solely to outside subscribers. Held from 1:30 to 2:15 and 6:15 to 8:15, the two outside programs delivered the frothiest fare ever heard on the Telharmonium: a special *Telharmonic March* by Karl W. Schulz, several other marches including Hartz's *Indianola*, Holzmann's *Yankee Grit*, and Loftis's *Yankiana*, selections from Victor Herbert's *The Red Mill*, *The Fortune Teller*, and *Babes in Toyland*, a march and waltz from Herbert's *It Happened in Nordland*, Strauss's *Du und Du* waltz, Planquette's *Legend of the Bells*, Thorne's *Simple Aveu*, Czibulka's *Love's Dream After the Ball*, other romantic melodies including Eilenberg's *Schelm d'Amoure* and Eugene's *Cupid's Garden*, and two Irish folk songs. The few selections that could lay claim to a modicum of substance were Mendelssohn's *Song of Spring*, the march from Bizet's *Carmen*, Moszkowsky's *Bolero*, Thomas Thompson's *Serenade*, the *Andante* from a Goltermann cello concerto, and the obligatory excerpt from the dread *William Tell*. The New York Theatre, a leading vaudeville house, was proudly claimed as a subscriber; no others were listed. The programs would repeat exactly each day throughout the week before being changed.[49]

The exhibition concerts in the hall were held twice daily, at 3:00

and 8:30, as well as Sunday evening. The single program seemed to be designed primarily for promotion and elucidation rather than musical enjoyment. Most of the listings were demonstrations, *viz.*:

> *Introductory Announcement*, outlining the significance of the Telharmonic process as it is viewed by the leaders of thought of the world.
>
> *Selection*, illustrating how tone is produced wherever desired, in different tone qualities.
>
> *Selection*, Telharmonic equivalent of string quality. Andante from Concerto for 'Cello, Goltermann.
>
> *Selection*, during which the tone converter [receiver] is dissected, discussing the method of tone production direct from electric currents. Currents through the human body shown rendering music.
>
> *Selection* illustrating the use of resistance boxes, by which every one of thousands of users of Telharmonic Music can in his own premises control the volume of the music. Drum and Fife and Trumpet band.
>
> *View of the Music Currents* producing light in an ordinary incandescent lamp at the same time they produce sound. Selection. . . . Announced (accompanied by the light in the lamp).
>
> *The Musical Arc Lamps*, Selection played.
>
> *Minor Approximations—a.*) Scotch Bagpipes. *b.*) Intoned Bells and Chimes.
>
> *Address*, explaining the process, with an illustration of the marvelous capacity of the Telharmonic System to produce the partials or overtones which are the very elements of tone quality . . .
>
> *Selection*, "William Tell". . . Rossini.
>
> *Selection*, History of the Telharmonic enterprise and its proposed scope.[50]

A few unnamed "announced selections" were interspersed among the foregoing, but the only two composers actually specified in the auditorium program were Goltermann and Rossini.

The 24 divan seats went for $1.00; the remaining 273 seats were 50¢ (Fig. 42); "Special Rates to School Classes and Musical Organizations in Parties of Ten or More."[51]

Karl W. Schulz had finally reaped his reward for faithful service, or perhaps obduracy, and was now listed as the musical director. The

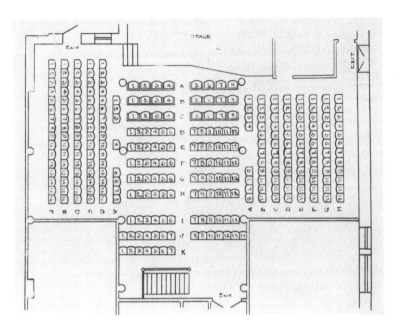

Fig. 42. Seating Diagram of Telharmonic Hall. (Telharmonic Securities Co., *Telharmonic Hall: Program, Week of December 30th,* New York: The Company, 1907, 1)

wandering H. Franklin Harris had returned to the fold and was given the post of assistant musical director. Four other Telharmonists were listed to complete the musical staff. The most prominent was 27-year-old Clarence Reynolds, who would later become city organist for Denver.[52]

The program invited the public to view "Machinery Hall" with its "half acre of dynamos and tone mixing and tone building mechanism"[53] (Fig. 43). Those who signed the guest book or filled out the visitors' cards handed out at every performance were promised "historical, musical, utilitarian and commercial"[54] information on Telharmony. Persons in quest of an investment trove might also visit one of the many offices of the Telharmonic Securities Co. in Rooms 120, 121, 122, 123, 124, 125, 126, and 127 of the Knickerbocker Theatre Annex Building across 39th Street next to the Casino Theatre, from 8:00 A.M. to 6:00 P.M.[55]

Fig. 43. The Dynamos in the Basement of Telharmonic Hall. (Telharmonic Securities Co., *Telharmonic Hall: Program, Week of December 30th,* New York: The Company, 1907, 1)

The program alleged 48 tones to the octave, a known exaggeration, and also affirmed that the 145 dynamos were split into 84 that produced the fundamental notes of the musical scale and 61 used to generate harmonics only.[56] Eighty-four chromatic notes encompass seven octaves, which the Telharmonium indeed spanned. However, the management could hardly concede that some of the twelve chromatic tones among the 84 could not be found in the instrument's extremes of range, owing to four nonexistent pitch-shafts.

Another misrepresentation in the program was a picture of four musicians seated side by side at four keyboards (Fig. 44). Recent press releases had even claimed five.[57] The central station had only three working keyboards at the time.[58]

The golden dream that franchise and funding would soon transpire led the Telharmonic Securities Co. to offer service by wire anywhere between 23rd and 59th Streets all the way from Madison Avenue to Eighth Avenue.[59] No delay was alluded to; the music could presumably be wired up immediately.

The company had also managed to inveigle testimonials from reputable musicians, insofar as that profession could be congruent with any rectitude. Arturo Vigna, the fiery Italian conductor at the

Fig. 44. Phony Publicity Photograph of Four Working Keyboards at Telharmonic Hall. (Telharmonic Securities Co., *Telharmonic Hall: Program, Week of
December 30th,* New York: The Company, 1907, 1)

Metropolitan Opera, averred that Telharmony "will eventually mean
the death of the present orchestral system."[60] Vigna was widely
esteemed by the public and musicians and had distinguished himself
with major premieres of Puccini and Sibelius.[61] The incomparable
Enrico Caruso prophesied, "It will bring a revolution into the
musical world, both through its artistic expression and by bringing
really good music to all kinds of people."[62] A few other Met
musicians similarly signed endorsements of the Telharmonium, as
did the conductor at the competing Manhattan Opera House.[63]

THE CONCERTS DWINDLE

As the economy constricted, Telharmonic Hall diminished its
concert offerings to one per day. Vigna's and Caruso's endorsements
appeared in the Sunday advertisements for Telharmonic Hall, but
business did not pick up.[64] An army of 250,000 unemployed was
swarming over New York, augmented by the daily influx of workers

from other parts of the country where factories and mills had shut down. Only pawnbrokers were enjoying bigger business. Around two million of the city's population were estimated to be near or at the precarious edge of utter destitution. Begging had reached unknown proportions, the homeless were everywhere, and tenements were stuffed by five or six persons living in each room.[65]

Panic psychology was epidemic. Thousands of fortunes had been diluted in the last few months, and many capitalists were now convinced they would never escape the poorhouse. To raise cash they pawned their jewels and forswore luxuries. Auto sales were down 50%; musical instruments had descended 75%, glutting the market with returned installment pianos. The premium on currency had barely disappeared, while call money was being charged at 20%. Hundreds of thousands of freight cars stood idle. Merchandise consumption had dwindled to a third of normal levels; thousands of jobless foreign workers were returning to Europe.[66]

Toward the end of January, Telharmonic Hall began to display enlarged photographs of stylus oscillographs depicting the various waveforms as they were built up on the Telharmonium. They also exhibited the three simplified new keyboards, which were identical to a standard twelve-key-to-the-octave piano and organ design.[67]

At the end of the month, the Sunday advertisements warned that these were the "last weeks of present wonderful lectures. Totally new form of entertainment in preparation."[68] The following week's ads strutted Mark Twain's revelation: "The Telharmonic System will be a greater benefactor to the human race than the telephone and the telegraph."[69]

THE LAST DAYS OF TELHARMONIC HALL

The final notice for Telharmonic Hall appeared on February 9, 1908. The second season would last only 14 weeks, one week longer than the first. The divulgence of the week was "A Veritable Miracle,"[70] plugged by Met prima donna Johanna Gadski. The statuesque blonde soprano was at 35 regarded as the greatest Brunhilde of the day.[71] The Telharmonium was not her maiden endorsement: several years earlier, her recommendation of Evans and Sons Antiseptic

Throat Pastilles, "having used them all last season at Covent Garden, London,"[72] was generously bruited about the music press. The energetic career of this Prussian-born opera star would later founder during World War I when she enthusiastically declared that she, herself, "would blow up American munitions factories to keep them from supplying Germany's enemies."[73] Gadski was not kidding. In 1916 her husband, a German naval officer, would be arrested for plotting to dynamite the Welland Canal in Canada.[74]

The final show at Telharmonic Hall was at 10:50 P.M. on February 16, an unscheduled minor mishap; the automatic electric shoeshine parlor in the Shubert Building next door caught fire. In the initial belief that it was the Metropolitan Opera House on fire, numerous engines answered the call and a crowd of hundreds assembled. In order to save the alternators in the basement the firemen used little water and many axes. The fire smoldered under the floor, much of which was chopped away to locate the source. The Telharmonium was saved. Fire Department officials rated the damage as "trifling," meaning less than $10.[75]

The New England Electric Music Co. managed to survive for one last annual report in April. Despite the earlier authorization to increase its stock, no additional capital had been secured. The company's final investment total stood at $210,500. Crosby and Todd were still listed as directors, but the report disclosed that there had been no recent directors' meeting. Hence, last year's officers had been held over beyond their term to the present. Oscar T. Crosby signed the report, his only documented act connected with the Telharmonium since September 1907, and the last as well.[76]

The New York Electric Music Co. simultaneously issued its final annual report that April. Not one dollar in new stock had been issued for a twelvemonth, so its grand total of capital invested remained $679,900. The report showed the company's affairs to be in chaos. Crosby and Todd were gone as directors and as officers. Telharmonium keyboardist H. Franklin Harris was now installed as a director, as were plant superintendent A. M. Paul Maschmeyer and engineer Percival C. Burgess. Furthermore, Harris had been put into the presidency! The only directors surviving from better days were New Jersey corporation lawyer John R. Turner, whose presence as a New Jersey resident was a legal formality, and Baltimore banker Harry Frey Stevenson, who had been secretary throughout the duration and was also now treasurer.[77]

In spite of the economic chaos of the Panic of 1907, the best artistic enterprises and entertainments had done well that season. Both the Metropolitan and Manhattan operas posted record patronages. The finer theatre offerings had no trouble selling $2.50 tickets.[78] At the other end of the ticket spectrum the motion picture craze had taken root across the nation during the past year.[79] From overseas came grating word that the Telefon-Hirmondó in Budapest continued its overwhelming success. At 8:55 A.M. began a full day of news, stock quotations, weather, and personals. The service switched over to military music from one of the cafés or gardens at 4:30, and in the evening came either the Royal Opera or a theatre program. The 6,200 subscribers were given two receivers to effect the choice.[80]

But the Telharmonic companies were beset by massive expenses and had no wires to reach their subscribers and hence no income. Without new investment capital, the franchise payments demanded by the city were staggering and impossible to meet. If only Oscar T. Crosby had been able to get a franchise quietly and inexpensively by 1905, before shoals of press reports had been mobilized to fuel great earnings expectations! Now even though the company safe was filled with contracts from hotels and restaurants for service running as high as $150 per week, there was no way to reach customers off the existing two-mile line. The new Hotel Plaza on Fifth Avenue at 59th Street, which had wired every room for Telharmonic music, now threatened to bring suit for nonfulfillment. Even though a number of subscribers had lost interest and canceled their orders, many still believed in the product and were willing to pay for it. Yet the Telharmonic backers had depleted their resources by lavishly building and running Telharmonic Hall as a cultural palace in the most extravagant location in the world. A fully operational enterprise might have been able to bear that burden. But now the money was gone, and in this depression no more would come in.[81]

The Telharmonic Securities Co. and its subsidiaries were totally paralyzed. Frederick C. Todd and the remaining investors closed the doors of Telharmonic Hall and walked away.[82]

The eight offices at the Knickerbocker Building across the street were vacated. For a while someone came around every day to collect the mail. Then on May 22 a judgment for $534.64 was entered in City Court against the New York Electric Music Co. by Jacob P. Muller and Emanuel Katz, advertising agents of upper Broadway. The next week, the secretary of state of Maine was duly informed that the Eastern Cahill Telharmonic Co. had ceased to transact business. In June the execution for the judgment was turned over to the New York sheriff. When a deputy visited Telharmonic Hall to make the levy, he found the premises bolted and deserted.[83]

NOTES

1. "The Financial Situation," *New York Times,* September 9, 1907, 8.
2. Telephone interview with Dr. John T. Hornblow, M.D., West Hartford, Conn., October 4, 1989.
3. Telharmonic Securities Company, Certificate of Incorporation, August 19, 1907, received and recorded at the Office of the Hudson County Clerk, Jersey City, N.J., August 19, 1907, 1–5.
4. *Ibid.,* 4, 6; "John R. Turner," *New York Times,* November 15, 1958, 23.
5. Telharmonic Securities Company, Application for a certificate to do business in the State of New York, November 19, 1907, and sworn Copy of Certificate of Incorporation, filed and recorded at the Office of the Secretary of State, Albany, N.Y., November 21, 1907, 4–5.
6. "Wall Street and the Drama," *New York Times,* October 6, 1907, pt. 6, 1.
7. "1907–1908," *New York Times Annual Financial Review,* January 5, 1908, 2; Francis W. Hirst, "The American Crisis—a Diagnosis and a Prescription," *New York Times Annual Financial Review,* January 5, 1908, 3; Paul Leroy-Beaulieu, "An Analysis of the American Crisis," *New York Times Annual Financial Review,* January 5, 1908, 5.
8. "Thousands of Actors Left Out of Work," *New York Times,* November 16, 1907, 4.
9. "A Manhole Spouts Music in Broadway," *New York World,* October 22, 1907, 1; reprinted as "Music Excites Broadway," *Music Trade Review,* October 26, 1907, XLV:17, 25; also reprinted as "Music from the Ground," *Talking Machine World,* November 15, 1907, III:11, 6.
10. *Ibid.*
11. *Ibid.*
12. *Ibid.*
13. "Telharmonic Hall Plans," *New York Times,* November 3, 1907, pt. 6, 1; "Telharmonic Hall Plans," *Music Trade Review,* November 9, 1907, XLV:19, 17; "Telharmonic Concerts," *New York Evening Mail,* November 11, 1907, 7.
14. *Ibid.*

15. "The Erring Sister Again," *New York Sun,* November 10, 1907, sec. 3, 6; "Telharmonium Makes Hit at Automobile Show," *Musical Age,* November 9, 1907, LX:2, 26.

16. Edwin Hall Pierce, "A Colossal Experiment in 'Just Intonation,'" *Musical Quarterly,* July 1924, X:3, 332.

17. "Telharmonic Hall," display advertisement, *New York Times,* November 15, 1907, 16.

18. "Telharmonic Hall," display advertisement, *New York Times,* November 17, 1907, pt. 6, 3.

19. "The Erring Sister Again," 6; "Telharmonic Hall," display advertisement, *New York Evening Telegram,* November 14, 1907, 4; "Telharmonic Hall Opens Tonight," *New-York Daily Tribune,* November 16, 1907, 7; "Telharmonic Hall," display advertisement, *New York Evening Telegram,* November 16, 1907, 7.

20. "Telharmonic Improvements," *Music Trade Review,* November 23, 1907, XLV:21, 3.

21. *Ibid.*

22. "Theatrical Notes," *New York Times,* November 19, 1907, 9.

23. *Ibid.*; "Vaudeville," *New York Times,* November 24, 1907, pt. 6, 1.

24. "Telharmonic Hall," display advertisement, *New York Times,* November 19, 1907, 16.

25. "New Play by Austin Strong," *New York Sun,* November 24, 1907, sec. 3, 6; "All Can Now Be Musical," *Music Trade Review,* November 30, 1907, XLV:22, 47.

26. Telharmonic Hall," display advertisement, *New York Times,* November 27, 1907, 16; "Telharmonic Hall," display advertisement, *New York Times,* December 8, 1907, pt. 6, 3.

27. J. I. C. Clarke, "New York City and the Ironclad Sunday Law," *New York Times,* December 8, 1907, pt. 5, 3; "Sunday Amusements Barred," *New York Dramatic Mirror,* December 14, 1907, LVIII:1,512, 2.

28. "Free Music on Meriden Trolleys," *Meriden* [Conn.] *Record,* December 16, 1907, S.C., n.p.

29. *Ibid.*; "Value of Telharmony," *Hoboken* [N.J.] *Observer,* December 6, 1907, S.C., n.p.

30. "Music Teachers' National Association," *New Music Review,* November 1907, 6:72, 785.

31. "Of Music and Musicians," *Springfield Republican,* December 22, 1907, S.C., 22; "Will Explain Invention," *New York Morning Telegraph,* December 27, 1907, S.C., n.p.; "Dr. Cahill's Interesting Talk," *Music Trade Review,* January 4, 1908, XLVI:1, 15.

32. Thaddeus Cahill, "The Electrical Music as a Vehicle of Expression," *Papers and Proceedings of the Music Teachers' National Association at Its Twenty-ninth Annual Meeting, Columbia University, New York City, December 27–31, 1907,* 1908, 207–209, 211, 213.

33. *Ibid.,* 210–211; "Electrical Transmission of Music," *Electrical World,* April 28, 1910, LV:17, 1059–1060.

34. Thaddeus Cahill, 211.

35. *Ibid.,* 213.

36. *Ibid.,* 214.

37. *Ibid.*

38. *Ibid.,* 212.

39. *Ibid.,* 216–217.

40. *Ibid.,* 219.

41. *Ibid.*

42. *Ibid.,* 220–221.

43. *Ibid.,* 222.

44. "May Send Music by Electricity," *New-York Daily Tribune,* December 28, 1907, S.C., 4.

45. "Dr. Cahill's Interesting Talk," 15.

46. *Ibid.*

47. "Sunday Ordinance Passed," *New York Dramatic Mirror,* December 28, 1907, LVIII:1,514, 5.

48. "Telharmonic Hall," display advertisement, *New York Times,* December 29, 1907, pt. 6, 3.

49. Telharmonic Securities Company, *Telharmonic Hall: Program, Week of December 30th,* hereafter *Telharmonic Hall,* New York: The Company, 1907, 1; "Vaudeville Notes," *New York Evening Mail,* April 20, 1907, 9.

50. Telharmonic Securities Company, *Telharmonic Hall,* 1.

51. *Ibid.,* 1, 2.

52. "Dr. Clarence Reynolds," *New York Times,* September 19, 1949, 23; "Reynolds, Clarence," *Who Was Who in America,* vol. VI, Chicago: Marquis Who's Who, 1976, 342.

53. Telharmonic Securities Company, *Telharmonic Hall,* 1.

54. *Ibid.*

55. *Ibid.*

56. *Ibid.,* 1, 2.

57. *Ibid.,* 2; "New Play by Austin Strong," 6.

58. Thaddeus Cahill, 210.

59. Telharmonic Securities Company, *Telharmonic Hall,* 1.

60. *Ibid.*

61. "Many Triumphs for Vigna," *Musical Courier,* January 24, 1906, LII:4, 45; "The Three Conductors of the Metropolitan Opera," *Musical America,* December 16, 1905, III:5, 1.

62. Telharmonic Securities Company, *Telharmonic Hall,* 1.

63. George F. Cahill, "Thaddeus Cahill (June 18, 1867-April 12, 1934): A Preliminary Paper," New York?, 1934?, typewritten, C.R.L.C. E-1488, Cat. C., L609, 214, C115, 6–7.

64. "Telharmonic Hall," display advertisements, *New York Times,* January 5, 1908, pt. 6, 3, January 12, 1908, pt. 6, 3.

65. "There Are About a Quarter of a Million People Trying to Get Work in New York," *New York Times,* January 5, 1908, pt. 5, 11.

66. "Luxuries Not in Demand Just at Present," *New York Times,* January 12, 1908, pt. 5, 3; "1908–1909," *New York Times Annual Financial Review,* January 10, 1909, 2.

67. "A Telharmonium Visit," *Electrical World,* January 24, 1908, LI:4, 173; "The Musicians Seated at the Keyboards," photograph, Telharmonic Securities Company, *Telharmonic Hall,* 1.

68. "Telharmonic Hall," display advertisement, *New York Times,* January 26, 1908, pt. 6, 3.

69. "Mark Twain," display advertisement, *New York Times,* February 2, 1908, pt. 6, 3.

70. "Mme. Johanna Gadski," display advertisment, *New York Times,* February 9, 1908, pt. 6, 3.

71. "Mme. Gadski," *Musical Courier,* April 11, 1906, LII:15, 34a; "In the Musical World," *Music Trade Review,* December 15, 1906, XLIII:24, 13.

72. "Gadski's Recommendation," *Musical Courier,* January 3, 1906, LII:1, 48.

73. "Mme. Gadski Is Dead After Motor Crash," *New York Times,* February 24, 1932, 21.

74. "Arrest Husband of Mme. Gadski on Conspiracy Charge," *New York Morning Telegraph,* March 31, 1916, 1–2; "2 More Arrests Made in Plot to Blow Up Canal," *New York Morning Telegraph,* April 1, 1916, 1–2.

75. "Blaze Under Electric Shoe Parlor," *New York Times,* February 17, 1908, 7; "Fire in Broadway Causes Excitement," *New York Evening Telegram,* February 17, 1908, 5; "Yesterday's Fires," *New York Herald,* February 17, 1908, 12.

76. New England Electric Music Company, Annual Report for 1908, April 30, 1908, filed at the Office of the Secretary of State, Trenton, N.J., May 12, 1908, 1, 3, 4.

77. New York Electric Music Company, Annual Report for 1908, April 30, 1908, filed at the Office of the Secretary of State, Trenton, N.J., May 8, 1908, 3, 4.

78. "A Glimpse Backward over the Rapidly Vanishing Season and Forward into Lent," *New York Times,* March 1, 1908, pt. 5, 5.

79. "The Plays That Won and the Public Taste," *New York Times,* June 7, 1908, pt. 5, 7.

80. "Budapest News-Telephone," *Electrical World,* February 18, 1909, LIII:8, 442; Elliot N. Sivowitch, "Musical Broadcasting in the Nineteenth Century," *Audio,* June 1967, 51:6, 22.

81. George F. Cahill, 8, 17; Edwin Hall Pierce, 331.

228 Magic Music from the Telharmonium

82. George F. Cahill, 8.

83. County Clerk, New York County, "1908 Judgments, Transcripts and Decrees: Incorporations," A.C.C., 215: "Business Troubles: Judgments," *New York Times,* May 23, 1908, 12; Letter from Warren C. Philbrook, Asst. Attorney-General of Maine, to Arthur I. Brown, Secretary of State of Maine, May 29, 1908, 1; "Telharmonic Co. in Trouble," *New York Times,* June 6, 1908, 3; "Business Troubles," *New York Sun,* June 6, 1908, 11; "N.Y. Electric Music Co. in Trouble," *Music Trade Review,* June 13, 1908, XLVI:24, S.C., 9; "Telharmonic Co. in Trouble," *Talking Machine World,* June 15, 1908, IV:6, 27.

CHAPTER VII

THE CENTRAL STATION
ON WEST 56TH STREET

STARTING OVER

In the early summer of 1908, the Cahill brothers retrieved the silenced Telharmonium; they slowly dismantled the central station and shipped it back to Holyoke.[1] It would, however, sound no more.

Although it was a bitter blow, Thaddeus Cahill did not falter. He resolved not to suffer the work of 14 years to be demolished.[2] During the last two years, he had been busy developing and testing new alternators. Their far ampler output had enabled switchboard complexities and expenses to be correspondingly attenuated. No more would he have to fabricate switchboards as cumbersome and costly as the one installed in Telharmonic Hall in 1907, at a net gain of only one voice. In addition to designs for new, simpler switchboards, he was ready with plans for improved, high-speed journals and gears.[3] He would build a totally new and better central station and make electric music sing as never before.

He shouldered even heavier exertions as well. Since investors and events had failed him, he undertook to establish electric music himself. He set about to free the licensed territory of New York from the New York Electric Music Co., to gain control of the New York Cahill Telharmonic Co., to push the latter's pending application with the Board of Estimate, and ultimately to secure that franchise to lay cables in the streets.[4]

If it would take several valuable years to build the third Telharmonium, it would consume that same precious time for tempers to cool and wounds to heal, so that the remaining agenda might be accomplished on hard practical terms. Cahill could afford to retrieve his license and secure ownership of the company at no greater cost than a distress-sale disbursal. His fortune, gained largely from license fees, would about cover the expense of the new central station and little else.

Several months later John C. Rowe, who had been euchred in as one of the main backers of the Telharmonic Securities Co., bailed out. It seems that the young New York lawyer had unfortunately agreed to be designated as the person upon whom legal process against the corporation could be served within the state of New York. With the enterprise in ruins, he had no use for this phase of the endeavor and revoked the designation.[5]

As 1908 ended, Nelson P. Lewis, chief engineer of the Board of Estimate, issued his annual report. It revealed no fewer than 17 franchise applications awaiting action of select committees going as far back as 1905. Among them was the application of the New York Cahill Telharmonic Co.[6]

With the new year New York was smiling once again. Stocks were up 50% over a year earlier, the time of greatest tension and retrenchment. New bond issues were being floated and businesses were reorganizing. Money was still tight, but not nearly so pinched as before. Optimism was back.[7]

In February the city proudly flaunted how well it had developed the careful conduct of its franchise business. No more would the store be given away. The extensive report on the New York Cahill Telharmonic Co. and the proposed contract were reproduced in detail as a public example in the latest issue of *Engineering News*.[8] Engineers could admire how far the wonderful new science of franchise-granting had evolved, now that investigations were in their hands instead of the lawyers' and politicians'. Their integrity and the way they protected the best interests of the citizenry reflected credit upon the new profession. The only problem seemed to be that public service enterprises were no longer being launched with the accustomed frequency, on account of the severity of proposed terms.[9]

The irrepressible Lee de Forest was back in front-page news with confident claims about the forthcoming unbounded success of wireless. Some not too distant day would see opera, news, and even advertising brought into every home. De Forest had developed a new low-noise tuning system requiring much less voltage. The perfection of wireless seemed practically at hand.[10] A few months later the inventor Nikola Tesla made an even more startling prediction: with an apparatus the size of a watch, speech or song would some day be heard anywhere in the world.[11]

Thaddeus Cahill plodded on in Holyoke. One day he met pianist Ossip Gabrilowitsch, who was concertizing in the vicinity. "Doctor!" said the great musician, "When I first heard your wonderful music in New York, I said to myself, 'That will displace all other music.' And now I cannot even find it."[12] Gabrilowitsch's interest in the Telharmonium was a family affair: he had recently married Clara Clemens, daughter of Telharmonium fan Mark Twain. And so Cahill persevered, determined that soon electric music would be found and heard once again.

Another year went by; Chief Engineer Lewis of the Board of Estimate issued another report. By now 28 unsettled franchise applications had accumulated, some as long as four years, still among them that of the New York Cahill Telharmonic Co. Meanwhile the election of 1909 had extensively altered the membership of the Board of Estimate. The franchise committees were staffed with new members hopelessly ignorant of the elaborate minutiae of franchise questions. Accordingly, in February 1910 the board withdrew all the pending applications from the separate select committees and returned them to the Division of Franchises for reconsideration and resubmission to the board. Once so returned, the applications would be referred to a single select committee familiar with franchise conditions and empowered to make recommendations consistent with general policy. Perhaps no few applications would prove dormant and thus be easily disposed of. The division duly contacted all applicants, including Oscar T. Crosby, to ascertain whether they still intended to prosecute for franchises.[13]

The president of the New York Cahill Telharmonic Co., at that time probably Frederick C. Todd, replied that negotiations for a shift in proprietorship of the company and its property were currently underway. Upon their completion a revised proposal would be submitted to pursue the application. In anticipation of a victorious accession, Thaddeus Cahill also began to correspond with the Division of Franchises. He stated that he expected the reorganization of the company to be completed about the middle of August, at which time he would make a proposition for a franchise to furnish music throughout the city by means of his vastly improved instrument.[14]

Meanwhile, the Cahill brothers commenced the promotional fund raising for their new machine. In a booklet published simply by "Arthur T. Cahill, Secretary"—with no company identity disclosed as that matter awaited settlement—they touted electrical music. It now responded "more perfectly" to the performer's touch than the violin, although its quality did differ from "the violin of fir-wood, catgut, and horsehair."[15] The Telharmonic Hall testimonials from Metropolitan Opera directors and performers were recalled.[16] And investors were reminded that a 100-piece orchestra, playing every day at the union rate of $500, would cost $182,500 per year. That same sum "would pay the interest, depreciation, and all operating expenses of a fine electric-music plant for New York City."[17]

EXHIBITING THE THIRD TELHARMONIUM

At last the work had progressed to the point where the new instrument could be demonstrated. It was an impromptu affair, the invitations having been circulated by telephone less than 24 hours prior to the event. As soon as the receiver diaphragms left a grinding shop in New York on Friday afternoon the calls went out. The following afternoon, on April 9, 1910, the Hotel Hamilton in Holyoke hosted about 200 music lovers from New York, Boston, Springfield, Amherst, and Northampton, as well as from the town. The site of the original demonstrations four years ago was outfitted once again, this time with two huge horn-loaded receivers. They were mounted near the ceiling of the ballroom on a longitudinal axis, like a gigantic hourglass. The performers, half a mile away at the Cabot Street Mill, were cheered and encored repeatedly as they trilled and fingered their way through 18 selections, among them *Nearer My God to Thee,* Handel's *Largo,* Schumann's *Träumerei,* Gounod's *Meditation, Palm Leaves,* Lehár's *Merry Widow Waltz, Kerry Mills Barn Dance,* and *Henry's Barn Dance.* Among the five musicians was Washington businessman Paul W. Fishbaugh, who had played Handel's *Largo* on the first Telharmonium in Washington eight long years ago to the incredulous investors at the Maryland Club in Baltimore. There was much wonder and astonishment that the performers, located as they were amid the distracting roar and pounding thunder of mill machinery, were able to perform convincingly. Reported allusions to this and other difficulties faced by the performers—insufficient rehearsal time, learning an unfamiliar and delicate fingering technique—attest to the unconquered imperfections tolerated by this friendliest of audiences.[18]

THE TECHNOLOGY OF THE THIRD TELHARMONIUM

The birth of the new instrument was announced in the faithful pages of *Electrical World,* which hailed the great progress of electric music in a front-page editorial. The biggest news was the abolishment of the complicated keyboard. The Telharmonium was now fitted with a standard keyboard enabling any trained musician to make better music in a few days than would have been possible after a lifetime of endeavor at Telharmonic Hall. Musicians could no longer consider the machine imperfect.[19]

The expense to Cahill had reached $200,000. Building a really complete machine, with eight switchboards and more alternators, would raise the cost to $300,000.[20]

The Alternators

The alternating current dynamos (Fig. 45) were again of the inductor type. However, the design of the alternators above 1000 Hz had undergone great improvement. Built to a larger scale, with smaller air gaps, improved windings, and newly shaped pole pieces, the alternators could be run at higher speeds to generate many times the power output of those on the Telharmonic Hall instrument.[21]

The alternators varied in power output from 10 to 20 hp; assuming an average power of 15 hp, the entire complement totaled 1.57 megawatts. With 50 or 60 alternators on the line at any one time, the instantaneous power output would normally have been about 671 kw.[22]

Fig. 45. Dynamos of the Third Telharmonium, Cabot Street Mill. (*Electrical World,* April 28, 1910, LV:17, 1060)

The Deployment of the Alternators

The ponderous alternators could not all be fitted onto one pitch-shaft per chromatic scale tone, so Cahill built two, a total of 24 pitch-shafts. This time he did not skip any notes. Each shaft was $8^{1}/2$ inches in diameter and mounted on a mainframe constructed of 20-inch steel beams. The mainframe was set upon a masonry base and measured 65 feet long and 13 feet wide. The strength of construction was so great that the shafts ran without any perceptible vibration. They were mounted on chrome-nickel steel ball bearings and locked together by encased gears run in lubricating grease.[23]

The alternator total was given as 140, with no tooth count or range divulged.[24] With a count of only 11 or 12 alternators per chromatic pitch, it is difficult to envision how the third Telharmonium could have eclipsed the second, either in pitch range or in flexibility of timbral synthesis.

The Keyboard

The three keyboard manuals had twelve keys to the octave, in traditional design (Fig. 46). Yet Cahill had tenaciously restored, without multiple key banks, the absolutely just intonation of both thirds and fifths of the Washington Telharmonium. It is not known if or how the instrument could play in just intonation in more than one key. Perhaps modulation within one piece of music being performed in just intonation was avoided and, between selections, throwing switches effected the transfer among equal temperament and several just-intonation keys. The sacrifice enabled reductions in cost, complexity, and performance difficulties. Touch control on each key, another feature of the first Telharmonium, had also been restored to the new instrument. This and other new expression devices increased the power of the machine.[25]

The Switchboards

The simplification of the circuitry allowed for much smaller switchboards (Fig. 47) for each of the three voices, in some cases containing

Fig. 46. Musicians at the Keyboard of the Third Telharmonium, Cabot Street Mill. (*Electrical World,* April 28, 1910, LV:17, 1061)

only one-sixth the number of switches and circuits found in the Telharmonic Hall machine. Full chords without "robbing" were possible on the new instrument.[26]

The Transformers

The tone-mixing transformers had also been reduced in number. Their design had been altered to resemble more closely those used in the first Telharmonium in Washington. These were open circuit Ruhmkorf or induction coils in which the current could be interrupted. The second Telharmonium had utilized the more common and cheaper closed circuit static transformers of electric lighting. The earlier type had proven to be more suitable for musical circuits.[27]

The Receivers

The ordinary telephone receivers had reproduced *fortissimo* close chords in the bass with a growling sound. Arthur T. Cahill had

Fig. 47. Switchboards in Process of Erection for the Third Telharmonium, Cabot Street Mill. (*Electrical World,* April 28, 1910, LV:17, 1061)

tackled this difficulty, designing a new receiver with a diaphragm ten times larger and three times as thick. The magnet was more powerful, the coils and electromagnetic field were of new design, and even the shapes of the horn and the air passages were reconfigured. The volume and purity of chords in any range were thus markedly improved.[28]

LISTENING TO THE THIRD TELHARMONIUM

Even with the ten manuals recommended by Thaddeus Cahill to produce orchestral effects, he now admitted his electric music could never authentically simulate a real orchestra. Here was a new realism to the claims for the powers of the instrument. In some ways the Telharmonium would be better; in others, not so good. For electric music still retained its markedly individual character while imitating, in a way, orchestral instruments. However, its loud-and-soft expressivity was now truly powerful, with the pitch-key touch control and other loudness controllers combining to rival the bow in instantaneous rendition of volume. The gear-locked pureness of intonation added much to the instrument's prowess.[29]

PRESS RESPONSE

Electric music was no longer a new story, and this time the magazines did not flock to report the tale. The story in *Electrical World* was synopsized in a few column inches by *Engineering News,* which was in turn lifted by the *Literary Digest.*[30] And that was all.

GETTING READY

Ever since he had begun to manufacture music machinery Cahill had operated as a sole proprietor. But now with the potential growth in Telharmonic demand so near at hand, it became advisable to incorporate. Accordingly, on April 21, 1910, the three Cahill brothers and attorney E. Hilton Jackson formed the Cahill Music Machinery Manufacturing Co. in New Jersey, with its principal office in Holyoke.[31] Now the business of fabricating central stations would be penetrable by astute investment capital. Furthermore, the new corporation would also quite separately and distinctly retain ownership of the Telharmonium—until, if ever, title to the instrument were accepted by the New York Cahill Telharmonic Co., whose assets were subject to seizure by the city in case of default on the franchise contract.

The Cahill Music Machinery Manufacturing Co. declared itself to be the successor licensee to John W. Crawford, Pickens Neagle, and Robert E. Logan—Oscar T. Crosby's legal counselors and the named recipients of Thaddeus Cahill's June 19, 1902, license to manufacture equipment under Cahill's granted and pending patents. In return for these exclusive rights, the new company issued Thaddeus Cahill its entire authorized capital stock—10,000 shares with a par value of $50 per share.[32] The company prohibited itself from purchasing, leasing, mortgaging, or selling land or buildings; issuing stocks or bonds; or acquiring or assigning patent rights—in short, assuming any obligation or undertaking except the normal business of manufacturing music machinery—without the written consent of either the majority of the board of directors or of the executive committee, plus that of a majority of the stockholders.[33]

To make sure all bases were covered, the Cahills took the precaution of stipulating that the new company was authorized to manufacture any type of machinery that would permit propagation of music to subscribers by any means whatever, "whether with or without wires."[34]

The Cahills then let it be known that they were about to vacate the Cabot Street Mill and erect their own new plant in Holyoke. That was fine economic news for the town: even though the size would be nowhere near that of the great paper mills, there would be many new well-paid jobs for the best skilled mechanics. The plan was to have the new facility in operation by year's end.[35]

As plans for music by wire rolled ahead, music by wireless was installed in many amusement parks across the United States for the summer. It was not true high frequency wireless, only a magnetic induction scheme that utilized 80 to 100 turns of wire strung around an entire room or building. Outside, a phonograph was played into a telephone that supplied audio signals into the huge coil. Inside, the magnetic field induced the music into small portable coils attached to receivers. It proved to be an immensely popular display, and aroused considerable conjecture and interest in the wireless of the future.[36]

Meanwhile, Cahill's system was practically in working order, reported a journalist in passing as he examined Edward Bellamy's prophecies in *Looking Backward.* Other manifestations the reporter cited of the trend to the new order were increased restaurant patronage, gigantic department stores, and paper plates.[37]

The Cahills then formed another corporation—the North River Telharmonic Co.—on August 22, 1910. This was a holding company intended specifically to acquire the New York Electric Music

Co., the New England Electric Music Co., the New England Cahill Telharmonic Co.,[38] and the New York Cahill Telharmonic Co.[39]

Early in October Cahill contacted the Board of Estimate, asking for a little more time in which to complete his company reorganization before inaugurating franchise negotiations. The board decided that there had been quite enough dawdling and gave Cahill until the middle of December to indicate his intentions and to present any objections he may have to the contract proposed in 1907.[40]

Chicago was the next locale to be proffered a Telharmonium. The Cahills announced a local company to establish a Chicago Telharmonic central station and supply music to all the restaurants, hotels, clubs, and theatres. The massive machine would be demonstrated for the first time at next year's Electrical Show. New Yorkers must have roared at the claim that the instrument "duplicates band, orchestral, or vocal music with the same volume, technique and finish that would be given by the best instrumental or vocal organizations of the world."[41]

The Cahill brothers managed to complete their purchase of the stock of the New York Cahill Telharmonic Co. a few days before the Board of Estimate's deadline. Thaddeus Cahill, now president of the company, informed the board of the new, improved Telharmonium, which had been built to incorporate far greater musical powers at a cost of $250,000. He also proposed various contract modifications and after several conferences, "practically without expenditure for lawyers or entertaining,"[42] won the agreement of Board Engineer Harry P. Nichols. Nichols presented the revisions to the board at its meeting just before Christmas.[43]

Cahill first withdrew the proposal to run a line to Coney Island. The central station in Manhattan was too distant to provide service, and a separate station would no doubt be built in Brooklyn if music were desired at the amusement park.[44]

Instead of having to build 4,000 music outlets within three years, the company would be required to establish only 2,500 connections over five years. Even this reduced requirement would be waived altogether if the company had spent in excess of $500,000 on its central station and its distribution apparatus. Since service was not a necessity in the same sense as telephone or gas utilities, the prompt installation of many receivers was not of material interest to the city.[45]

Free installation in schools was eliminated, and school service at one-third regular rates was raised: both would now be provided at one-half rates.[46]

Cahill complained that the initial payment was far too severe and had been impossible to remit when fixed in 1907. Furthermore, the minimum annual payments had greatly exceeded the percentage of gross receipts required. Since the estimated gross receipts were purely theoretical and unassured, and the board desired that the percentage of gross receipts coincide with minimum annual payments, the amounts were lowered considerably:

Within three months, initial payment installment	$5,000
Within twelve months, remainder of initial payment	5,000
During the first five years, 3% of the gross receipts, not less than $2,500 per year	12,500
During the second five years, 3% of the gross receipts, not less than $5,000 per year	25,000
During the third five years, 3% of the gross receipts, not less than $7,500 per year	37,500
During the fourth five years, 4% of the gross receipts, not less than $10,000 per year	50,000
During the remaining five years, 5% of the gross receipts, not less than $15,000 per year	75,000
Total minimum compensation over 25 years	210,000[47]

This was not quite a third of the amount stipulated in the 1907 proposal.

The initial security deposit was also reduced from $10,000 to $5,000. Since the company would be placing its wires only in existing conduits of the Empire City Subway Co., a New York Telephone Co. subsidiary, it would not be tearing up the streets. Without such privileges a large security deposit was unnecessary.[48]

The proposed contract was tentatively approved by the Board of Estimate and referred to the corporation counsel for approval of its form.[49]

As the new year of 1911 was welcomed, Cahill must have been grateful even for the small publicity afforded the Telharmonium in one of the annual news almanacs. Nestled between progress reports on a floating electric welding plant and a new system of transmitting halftone photographs by wire was a brief acknowledgment of the great improvements and simplifications in his telephonic music system.[50]

Nevertheless, there was much greater attention focused on a new advance in combining wire and wireless transmission technologies. George Owen Squier of the U.S. Signal Corps patented a system in which a number of audio signals could modulate a number of carrier waves of various frequencies broadcast along one power or telephone line. It was the advent of multiplexing, the system of transmitting several messages simultaneously over a single line, also called "wired wireless." Squier dedicated his invention to the public: anyone was free to use it without payment of royalties.[51]

Just before the new year Acting Corporation Counsel George L. Sterling[52] approved the contract without additions or changes. At the meeting of the Board of Estimate on January 5, the contract was ordered to be published in the *Minutes of the Board,* and a final public hearing was set for February 16, 1911, with due notice given as well as the text of the contract to be printed in the *Sun* and the *Herald.*

Several weeks before the hearing the Cahill brothers, through their North River Telharmonic Co., petitioned New Jersey's new governor, Woodrow Wilson, for reinstatement of their recently acquired subsidiary, the New York Electric Music Co. Its charter had just been revoked several weeks earlier, a result of the company's having paid no franchise taxes since 1907. The amount owed was now $2,611.82.[53]

Thaddeus Cahill deposed that the only remaining assets held by the latter company were the ten-year patent license (granted to the New England Electric Music Co. in 1902, transferred to the New York Electric Music Co. in 1904, and due to expire in $1\frac{1}{2}$ years) and an interest in the second Telharmonium, now in storage at Holyoke. However, the value of these assets was severely diminished because they were forbidden to be assigned by the New York Electric Music Co. without permission of the grantors (the three Cahill brothers and their attorneys E. Hilton Jackson and Ellis Spear). Furthermore, Cahill stated that the company was indebted to its grantors to the tune of $70,000 with no means of payment. Finally, as Cahill pointed out: the company had suspended business in 1908; the company had, at its last election, installed "a board of directors consisting of irresponsible persons,"[54] *viz.,* "clerks, mechanics and musicians";[55] all the former officers and directors of the company had assigned their stock to the North River Telharmonic Co.; and, the company sought now to "resume business with a reduced capitalization and with safety to the public."[56] The petition, having been accompanied by a certified check for $150, was clearly attractive; it was granted immediately.[57]

Next came the public hearing by the Board of Estimate. No one bothered to appear either in favor or in opposition, so the hearing was declared closed. By unanimous vote the board thereupon authorized the mayor to execute the franchise contract with the New York Cahill Telharmonic Co.[58]

Thaddeus Cahill signed the contract on March 2 and Mayor William J. Gaynor signed it on March 9. The Cahills were in business for themselves at last. They were free to begin putting their electric music cables into the streets of New York, and could continue to do so for the next 25 years, provided that the initial security deposit was now given to the city within the next three months. The city in turn agreed to make available all its present and future conduits for electrical wires to the company. The company was required to file an annual map showing all the cables in use. The city was given absolute power to regulate Telharmonic rates to subscribers and compelled the company each year to report its gross receipts, stock issued, debt, real estate holdings, number of subscribers, and operating expenses.[59]

With the Telharmonium headed for Manhattan it was time for two swan songs in Massachusetts. First the instrument was connected from Holyoke to the Springfield Board of Trade office, some ten miles to the south. There, on ladies' night, March 3, 1911, the transmissions of three musicians, among them the redoubtable Paul W. Fishbaugh, entertained more than 600 people of Springfield with Lehár's *Merry Widow Waltz, That Polka Rag,* the *Intermezzo* from Mascagni's *Cavalleria Rusticana,* Eilenberg's *The Return of the Troops* [*Die Wachtparade Kommt!*], *My Firefly Lady,* Rolfe's *Kiss of Spring Waltz,* Gillet's *Loin du Bal, Yip-I-Addy-I-Ay,* Hoschna's *Every Little Movement Has a Meaning All Its Own* from *Madame Sherry,* Handel's *Largo,* Renard's *Berceuse No. 2,* Schumann's *Träumerei, The Evening Star* from Wagner's *Tannhäuser, Old Black Joe,* and Mason's *Nearer My God to Thee.* The standing-room-only crowd was much taken with the sweetness of timbre and the absence of scraping and other noises of mechanization; however, the volume was but a quarter of what the

Telharmonium could produce. The use of a telephone line longer than a mile attenuated the full power of the transmission, yet the limpid tones were plainly audible even in the most distant corners of the room. George F. Cahill was present and explained the mysteries of the machine before the musical presentation. After the concert, which had been delayed by the telephone company's difficulties in making connections, Arthur T. Cahill complained that the long wait had rattled the musicians to the point that they had played with less skill than he had ever heard. Those in the know agreed that the performance did not meet previous standards. The players, Arthur added, were but students in the use of the new instrument. Yet most of the audience enjoyed the music immensely.[60]

Next the same trio of keyboardists supplied music to the banquet of the Holyoke Board of Trade, held at the Hotel Hamilton on March 6, 1911. The governor of Massachusetts joined some 200 in attendance. The three Cahill brothers were on hand to savor their triumph and to bid farewell to the Holyokers who had witnessed the mighty Telharmonic development of the past nine years. The crowd duly marveled that here at last was music placed within earshot of Everyman. Undoubtedly this latest version of the Telharmonium seemed fitted to all styles of music, as the performers offered ragtime, Handel's *Largo,* selections from *Madame Sherry, The Merry Widow Waltz,* and *The Return of the Troops.* Then Telharmonic accompaniment supported a male quartet and afterward singing by the entire assemblage. It was an occasion for all Holyokers to swell with pride—these beautiful sounds, about to conquer New York, would forever sing testimony to the manufacturing splendors of Holyoke.[61]

Meanwhile, George F. Cahill had earlier taken on the task of securing a new headquarters for the enterprise. For weeks he had walked along the streets of Manhattan, inspecting both vacant and occupied buildings. The structure had to possess a dry, well-ventilated basement and a ground floor of considerable strength. It should also be located near conduits running over to Broadway. A few days after the mayor signed the franchise contract, he settled on the building at 535–537 West 56th Street. The 50-by-100-foot, one-story structure had more machinery space than the old Telharmonic Hall, yet cost the Cahills slightly less per year than Oscar T. Crosby had paid on Broadway per month.[62] The lease ran from April 1, 1911, to June 30, 1916, for a flat fee of $3,500 plus an annual rent of $2,400.[63]

Meanwhile, Telharmony was not the only technology marching on to supplant the orchestra. Pipe organ builder Robert Hope-Jones captured the attention of the musical public, and particularly that of theatre owners, with his unconventional "Unit-Orchestra," introduced at the Hotel Statler in Buffalo on March 18. In this instrument, built by the Wurlitzer Co., the organ apparatus was completely regrouped into string, brass, woodwind, and percussion sections. Each had its own swell box so that all stops were now expressive. It was said to be just what the Telharmonium would be: "in effect an orchestra controlled by one player."[64] Wurlitzer priced the various models from $4,000 to $30,000.[65]

The Cahills lost no time vacating their space in the Cabot Street Mill in Holyoke. A large force of workmen began dismantling the Telharmonium the day after Mayor Gaynor signed the contract. All the newer fixtures and machinery were shipped to New York.[66] William Hogan, who as a boy delivered telegrams to Cahill, recalled later, "When his machine went out, most of the heavy castings went back to the foundry to be broken up for scrap."[67] Thus ended the second Telharmonium.

EXPERIMENTAL SERVICE

It took an agonizing five months to take down, ship, and put up the Telharmonium. When the completed instrument began to be tested in August 1911, the luckless Cahills discovered that the soil beneath their central station was wetter than George had discerned. The ensuing circuit difficulties necessitated alterations to the apparatus and the addition of a relay switchboard and two accessory switchboards, at a loss of several more months. Then the Cahills' cables suffered aberrant frequency response and amplitude losses as their music was transmitted through the wet soil. The grounding, shielding, and capacitance problems were novel and complicated. Many experimental cable configurations had to be tried. Despite its franchise, the company did not itself employ workers stringing cables beneath the streets of the city; the earliest connections were made with lines installed by and leased from the New York Telephone Co. The Cahills established a connection to the Chapter

Room, a small hall for chamber music on the fifth floor of Carnegie Hall, directly above Carnegie Recital Hall (now Weill Recital Hall). This was the room where Andrew Carnegie's Masonic Chapter met; it was not quite the size of the main stage. The first test music was at long last received there near the end of November 1911.[68]

The final New York debut of the Telharmonium was held at Carnegie Hall on February 23, 1912.[69] By now an old story, it was but little noticed in the press. The occasion was a meeting of the New York Electrical Society. There was no report on the quality of the music, but Thaddeus Cahill's remarks were documented in detail.[70]

He explained, as he had so often in the past, how the Telharmonium was not canned, how its music was generated and distributed "with delicacy not possible with any other instrument,"[71] how great were its powers of intonation, timbre, and volume, and on and on. He admitted, "In the variety of contrasted tone colors—of different instruments—it is not yet equal to an orchestra."[72] He foresaw great commercial possibilities in hotels, theatres, and motion picture houses. And he would not accept blame for having been at this endeavor so long now without great commercial development. He pointed out that a crude electric telegraph had been proposed in 1753, yet the device was not commercially ready until 1840. Electric lamps had been experimented with in the 1850s and did not become commercially feasible until 20 years later. Telephone experiment began in 1854 and again required more than 20 years of laboratory development before that invention was ready for practical use. Cahill concluded:

> The electrical music, after twenty-seven years of laboratory work, is now in a thoroughly practicable condition. And if we may judge from the analogy of other great electrical arts, we ought soon to see an immense commercial development.[73]

A month or two later, the grand Hotel Astor, which occupied the entire block on Broadway between 44th and 45th Streets, was the scene of a demonstration banquet of Cahill electric music. Paul W. Fishbaugh and H. Franklin Harris performed a concert of 16 selections:

Marche Militaire.	Schubert
The Shadows.	Finck
La Sarella.	Borel-Clerc

Valse Blue. . . . . Margis
Song d'Automne (Valse). . . . . Joyce
Make Me Love You Like I Never Loved Before. . . . . . . Fischer
The Liberty Bell March. . . . . Sousa
Pizzicati from the ballet *Sylvia; or,*
   The Nymph of Diana. . . . . Delibes
Excerpts from the musical comedy *The Pink Lady.* . . . Caryll
Edelweiss. . . . . ———
El Capitan March. . . . . Sousa
Chant sans Paroles. . . . . Tschaikowsky
Song of Spring. . . . . Mendelssohn
Waltz, Op. 64, No. 1. . . . . Chopin
Every Little Movement Has a Meaning All Its Own. . . . Hoschna
Selections from the musical comedy *The Red Widow.* . Gebest

To avert reminiscences of past defects and defeats, the Telharmonium was rechristened the "Electrophone" in the printed program.[74]

By midyear Telharmonic demonstrations were continuing at Carnegie Hall and were being transmitted by telephone to interested persons in Boston, Springfield, Baltimore, Washington, and elsewhere. Yet the anticipated flow of capital failed to materialize even as a trickle, and in June the Cahills approached the Board of Estimate to renegotiate their franchise contract. Thaddeus Cahill enumerated the manifold delays and torments he had suffered, and recounted the improvements installed in order to render the music thoroughly commercial in New York, "where the musical standards are much higher than in Holyoke."[75] He somewhat disingenuously asserted that he had expected all along to employ telephone circuits, "as had been successfully used in Holyoke," and now had to face installing his own cable system. (Then why obtain a franchise in the first place? Because New York Telephone was compelled to yield use of its conduits to all franchise holders. Even though the Cahills were thoroughly cognizant that their music currents were up to millions of times stronger than those of ordinary telephone transmission, as franchise holders they could expect some level of cooperation from New York Telephone in solving any cable difficulties.) Cahill reported on the transmission they had made to the Hotel Astor and on another to Healy's restaurant on Columbus Avenue and 66th Street. (The latter boasted eight dining rooms and was noted for Egyptian quail, French partridge, and English grouse; at its "dungeon dinners," popular with the Columbia University crowd, no knives or forks were permitted—the beefsteak was so tender that they were not needed.) The two transmissions had used New York Telephone lines and had demonstrated that improvements in the music were desirable. Finally, Cahill accounted to the Board of Estimate for his expenses to date: $200,000 for the instrument, $5,000 for the franchise security payment, and $40,000 to move, install, and operate the electric music plant. About 90% of these costs had been borne by the three embarrassed Cahills, who had by now invested nearly all the money they possessed, and who found themselves unable to enlist outside capital "by reason of the ill-success of an earlier attempt by another Company."[76]

Meanwhile, exciting reports of the advances of wireless continued to flow. The *Marseillaise* was plainly heard across the Mediterranean, from Fort de Leau, Algeria, to Toulon, France, a distance of 434 miles. The remarkable thing was the time: high noon, when reception was most difficult.[77]

The Cahills next helplessly watched the theatre and motion picture market disappear to Hope-Jones's Unit-Orchestra, the new electrically controlled pipe organ with its clattering array of drums, cymbals, and castanets, as well as percussion stops for celeste, harp, xylophone, and bells. The music press was not hesitant in its encomium: "It brings forth really orchestral effects and can be played like a solo instrument with the manifold colors and combinations of a symphony orchestra."[78] Heard behind a high oak screen at a series of concerts, 300,000 Philadelphians thought it was a real full orchestra. By mid-July the Wurlitzer Co. claimed to have had received orders totaling $2 million.[79]

Al Leech was a well-known comedian who had long played the vaudeville circuit, including the New York houses during the days of Telharmonic Hall. In late June he fell ill at the age of 43 and died a week later of cerebral meningitis. The comic had his last laugh posthumously over the Telharmonium. Out came an obituary claiming his death to have been

the result of overwork and nervousness over his invention, "The Telharmonium." The perfecting of this appliance, whereby persons in homes are placed in telephonic connection with what is going on in theatres, occupied his attention day and night. For the last month he was constantly at work on it, and his nerves eventually broke down.[80]

In fact, although he had done some inventive work with musical instruments, he had had no connection with the Telharmonium whatever.[81] The obituary was either someone's idea of a joke or an honest mistake by the newspaper.

In September the Board of Estimate authorized a new contract with the New York Cahill Telharmonic Co., which was then in debt to the tune of $69,261.02.[82] The Cahills had managed to negotiate the postponement of music distribution, which had been required to begin on December 9, 1911, to January 1, 1914. The company was still compelled to have 2,500 music outlets in operation, or $500,000 invested in its music plant, within five years of the inauguration date. Furthermore, the initial deposit of $5,000, to have been paid on June 9, 1911, and the final $5,000 deposit, due March 9, 1912, were postponed. An easier payment schedule was instituted: $1,000 by January 1, 1913; $3,000 by December 30, 1913; and the remaining $6,000 by December 30, 1914. Next, the first term of five years, during which annual franchise payments had to be 3% of gross receipts, and no less than $2,500, was lengthened and the payments reduced. The Cahills still had to part with $2,500 for the 1911 payment, but the five succeeding annual payments to 1916 were halved to $1,250; however, the percentage was increased to 4%. Payments over the next five-year period were similarly modified from $5,000 and 3% to $2,500 and 4%. Finally, the payments for 1911 and 1912 did not have to be remitted until 1914. Thaddeus Cahill signed the contract on October 3, 1912, and Mayor Gaynor signed it a week later.[83]

With the new year of 1913 came reports of the splendid progress of the Unit-Orchestra, now being installed in nine major New York theatres. The managers' woes with the musicians' union were ending at long last, for here was the instrument to replace the stubborn, unruly theatre orchestra for good.[84]

And what of the Telharmonium? The somber year passed all too quietly. In the required report to the Board of Estimate, filed November 1, Arthur T. Cahill disclosed that the New York Cahill Telharmonic Co. had accumulated $89,296.41 in debts, not including its as-yet-undetermined bill for the Telharmonium. The company had issued 16 shares of stock, for which $10 per share had been paid in. No dividends had been paid out. In the matter of income, Arthur stated that no receipts had been received and there were no regular subscribers, the company not yet having established commercial business. The company was "still engaged chiefly in installing, adjusting and perfecting the plant and in making necessary additions thereto."[85] He was careful to point out that the company had "not yet settled with the builders nor taken over the plant, the work of the builders not yet having been completed."[86] In a distinction more apparent than real, Arthur informed the board that the work on the Telharmonium was being performed partly by its builders and partly by the New York Cahill Telharmonic Co. He stated that the cash expenses to the company for that year had totaled $53,061.21, most of which had gone into installing and adusting Telharmonic apparatus.[87]

In his report Arthur T. Cahill mentioned that directors Orville Keeler, Thaddeus Cahill's chief electrician since Washington, and E. Hilton Jackson, one of the original 1902 patent license trustees, had both resigned. They had been replaced by prosperous Holyoke paper manufacturer Clifton A. Crocker,[88] owner of the Cabot Street Mill where the Cahills had labored for nine years, and Frank H. Page, a Springfield businessman.[89] Arthur further reported that, in order to test the Telharmonic equipment, noncommercial experimental service was still being furnished to the Chapter Room of Carnegie Hall and also to the Pabst Grand Circle Hotel on Columbus Circle, Eighth Avenue, and West 58th Street. (The exterior of the latter was brilliantly lit at night by three dozen flambeau torches on the cornice. Inside, red velour walls and large golden sunbursts on the ceiling gave a bright and roomy effect. When the electric music was off, live music was rendered by an eight-piece orchestra.)[90]

Finally, Arthur carefully described the new wire that the company had installed in the streets. It ran north across the block to West 57th Street, east to the end of the block at 10th Avenue, north one block to West 58th Street, east 2¹/2 blocks through Columbus Circle to Broadway, and then south on Broadway to its terminus at West 53rd Street:[91] "five pairs or ten wires of No. 5 stranded copper wire, that is, each of said wires is stranded out of nineteen [sic] smaller wires."[92] The route was shown on a map supplied to the Board of Estimate.[93]

The year 1913 had seen great developments and public interest in wireless telegraphy and telephony. Transmitting and receiving stations were going up all over the globe, and recognizable voice transmissions reached as far as 600 miles.[94]

BUSINESS TROUBLES

Yet the Telharmonium was soaking up the last of Thaddeus Cahill's fortune in a bid to become a ready and working system once again. The family investment had ballooned to over $300,000. All the expenses proliferated into a severe burden: the franchise taxes; the operation and demonstration of the new Telharmonium; the factory at which generating equipment, cables, and receivers were being constructed; the placing of lines in the streets; the salaries to musicians; everything took time to establish and cost a great deal of money. The Cahill brothers could draw no salary.[95] Still the Cahills managed to maintain their corporation tax payments for the New York Cahill Telharmonic Co., the Cahill Music Machinery Manufacturing Co., and the North River Telharmonic Co. However, the New York Electric Music Co., with its patent license expired and its title to the discarded second Telharmonium of no further worth, was allowed to go into tax default to the State of New Jersey. Accordingly, the charter of the New York Electric Music Co. was proclaimed null and void on March 11, 1914.[96]

About the only cheer for the Cahills during the bleak year of 1914 was the granting in August of Thaddeus Cahill's second Telharmonium patent.[97] The general business climate in 1913 had been hard enough to weather, with investors inclined only to mark time or sell while awaiting the unsure effects of new tariffs with reduced protectionism, of other recent legislation, and of numerous governmental trust investigations. However, the further economic erosions in 1914 became so alarming as to elicit comparison with the Panic of 1907. Sales were off 25% compared to 1913, which itself had posted a 30% decline against 1912. Bond sales had dropped 60% since 1911. Iron and steel plants were operating at only 40% of capacity. Even railroad earnings were in the throes of an unheard-of 12% decline. Incorporations had fallen by one-third, and business failures, both in numbers and in dollars, were now the highest in history. By September 1914 bank suspensions had doubled to 161, with nearly half occurring in the most recent three months.[98]

The severity of the situation was due to World War I. Hostilities had just broken out in August, decimating exports to most European markets and to South America as well. Imports from Europe had also dropped substantially, for which a slight increase from South America could not begin to compensate.[99]

Against these woeful obstacles the Cahills battled hopelessly:

> When the most successful merchants could not borrow a dollar from their banks on prime stocks that were worth twice par, it was simply impossible to raise money for any new undertaking. We strained every resource. We sold our property. Noble souls made sacrifices to keep the ship afloat. But all to no avail! Mars was sucking the money of the world into his maw. The thoughts of men were on war. And the prosperity that later flowed from the war did not come until too late.[100]

There were other miseries. The Cahills lacked a fresh product; the tired Telharmonium was by now very old hat. The limitations of the instrument from 1906 to 1908 and the failure of Telharmonic Hall were well remembered, and the fact that here was the same struggling venture still attempting to raise financing six years later made investors fearful and skeptical.

Furthermore, the anticipation of wireless, which could carry speech and song as well as all kinds of music, had captivated the public. Radio was undeniably the medium of the future.[101]

At the end of September the total debt of the New York Cahill Telharmonic Co. had risen to $122,654.14, not including whatever would be owed for the Telharmonium. Company expenditures for the previous twelve months totaled $29,857.73, mostly for work on the Telharmonium and musicians' salaries. There were still only 16 shares of stock issued. No more cables had been put into the streets. The company had still not taken legal title to the new instrument. As Thaddeus Cahill complained to the Patent Office when it requested an improved layout of a patent drawing, "The times are hard, applicant is poor, the expense is burdensome."[102]

By December it was all over. In spite of a new ease in the country's financial predicament, and a concomitant improvement in the musical instrument industry,[103] there was absolutely no money to be had for Telharmony. Directors Clifton A. Crocker and Frank H. Page brought a friendly equity suit against the company in Federal District Court, claiming $25,347 was owed them for money loaned and for unissued bonds. The total debt of the company had mush-roomed to $145,583. The complaint stated that a grand total of $700,000 had been spent to perfect the Telharmonium, the installation on West 56th Street had cost another $400,000, and that the company owed the city $8,050 for franchise payments, plus a further $6,000 coming due on December 14. Apparently the company had made only $2,200 in franchise payments, although it had claimed it had paid $6,000. The suit was filed on December 22 along with the company's answer admitting all allegations and asking for the appointment of a receiver. The New York Cahill Telharmonic Co. was bankrupt. The judge appointed George F. Cahill temporary receiver on the same date and permanent receiver the next week. George valiantly stated to the press that this did not mean the system was a failure, only that the cost of music production and laying cables was simply greater than had been anticipated.[104]

Within the year came news that Lee de Forest's audion was not only able to amplify signals 20,000 times their ordinary strength, but also could be harnessed to generate pleasant musical tones. It was immediately compared to the Telharmonium—all its possibilities were there, but the size and cost of audion circuitry would be but a fraction of the ponderous old contraption.[105] De Forest demonstrated his amplifier to the New York Electrical Society on December 10, 1915, and the dynamo music-generator became forever locked in the past.[106]

BUSONI AND VARÈSE

The last major composer known to have seen the Telharmonium was Edgard Varèse. It was after the bankruptcy, but the seed had been planted years ago by Busoni. In his 1907 classic, *Sketch of a New Aesthetic of Music,* the eminent composer-pianist Ferruccio Busoni had set down a miscellany of thoughts on the nature, spirit, and role of music. The lengthiest section of this monograph was a tirade against the tyranny of equal-tempered tuning. Nature, he claimed, had created an infinite gradation of tones. Yet music was locked into 24 keys which were really only two keys, major and minor, the rest being mere transpositions. Furthermore, since major and minor represented two faces of the same whole, there was left really but a single meager key for composers to work with. Busoni then began to tinker with the arrangement of seven tones in an octave, reporting that he had managed to construct 113 different seven-tone scales, using the twelve tones of equal temperament. The wealth of new melodic and harmonic possibilities was obvious.[107]

Busoni then proposed a one-sixth tone scale, which would allow the formation of a one-third tone scale within the framework of the familiar semitone scale. Enter the Telharmonium. The article "New Music for an Old World" by Ray Stannard Baker, in the July 1906 issue of *McClure's Magazine,* had reached Busoni while writing his essay. Thaddeus Cahill's invention solved the problem, wrote Busoni, of how such scale divisions were to be produced. The infinite gradation of the octave could obviously be produced on the Telharmonium by simply setting a lever. "Let us take thought," he exulted, "how music may be restored to its primitive, natural essence; . . . let it follow the line of the rainbow and vie with the clouds in breaking sunbeams."[108]

Edgard Varèse had read Busoni's little book in 1907, when he was 24. It made a great impression on the young composer. Varèse moved to Berlin the same year and soon became friends with Busoni. They avidly discussed the new electrical instruments, in which Busoni was very much interested. Varèse was surprised, in view of Busoni's interests in such unrestrainedly unconventional theories, "to find his musical tastes and his own music so orthodox."[109] This was evident in Busoni's American tours of 1910 and 1911. He played only the traditional repertory—to gloriously enthusiastic tributes—and apparently made no effort to see the Telharmonium while in the United States.[110]

Varèse arrived in America on December 29, 1915.[111] He was then greatly concerned with the need for new instruments and expressed these ideas in a newspaper interview several months later.[112] It must have been around this time that he learned that the Telharmonium was still in operation on West 56th Street, even though all thoughts of commercial service had been abandoned. He went to hear it.

> [Busoni] was very much interested in the electrical instruments we began to hear about and I remember particularly one he had read of in an American magazine, called the Dynamophone, invented by a Dr. Thaddeus Cahill, which I later saw demonstrated in New York and was disappointed.[113]

THE END OF THE TELHARMONIUM

That the Telharmonium lingered on until sometime in 1918 can only be inferred from Thaddeus Cahill's correspondence with the Patent Office. His letters up through May 7, 1918, show 535–537 West 56th Street, where the instrument was installed, as his office address. In his next letter, dated December 2, 1918, he announced, "Applicant's office has been moved." This and all subsequent correspondence show his residence at 316 West 84th Street to be the location of his office as well.

No report of the machine's fate has been uncovered; it seems probable, however, that when the premises on West 56th Street were vacated, the third Telharmonium was sold for salvage.

NOTES

1. "New York Cahill Telharmonic Company," *Minutes, Meeting of Board of Estimate and Apportionment,* December 22, 1910, 5575.

2. George F. Cahill, "Thaddeus Cahill (June 18, 1867-April 12, 1934): A Preliminary Paper," New York?, 1934?, typewritten, C.R.L.C. E-1488, Cat. C, L609.214, C115, 9.

3. "Electrical Transmission of Music," *Electrical World,* April 28, 1910, LV:17, 1060.

4. George F. Cahill, 9.

5. Telharmonic Securities Company, Revocation of the designation heretofore made to John C. Rowe, August 24, 1908, filed and recorded at the Office of the Secretary of State, Albany, N.Y., August 28, 1908, 1, 4.

6. Nelson P. Lewis, *Report of the Chief Engineer of the Board of Estimate and Apportionment of the City of New York for the Year 1908,* New York: The Board, 1909, 374.

7. "Once More New York Is 'The City of Happy Faces,' " *New York Times,* January 31, 1909, pt. 5, 11.

8. "Result of Investigation by the Division of Franchises of the Application of the New York Cahill Telharmonic Company for a Franchise to Lay Wires in the Streets of New York for the Purpose of Distributing Music Electrically, with Suggestions as to the Proposed Form of Contract," *Engineering News,* February 11, 1909, 61:6, 146–149.

9. "How New York City Submits Applications for Public-Service

Franchises to an Engineering Department," *Engineering News,* February 11, 1909, 61:6, 146.

10. "De Forest Tells of a New Wireless," *New York Times,* February 14, 1909, pt. 2, 1.

11. "Wireless of the Future," *New York Times,* May 23, 1909, pt. 5, 8.

12. George F. Cahill, 9.

13. Nelson P. Lewis, *Report of the Chief Engineer of the Board of Estimate and Apportionment of the City of New York for the Year 1909,* New York: The Board, 1910, 335, 369; "Status of Pending Petitions for Franchises and Revocable Privileges," *Minutes, Meeting of Board of Estimate and Apportionment,* January 21, 1910, 114; Nelson P. Lewis, *Report of the Chief Engineer of the Board of Estimate and Apportionment of the City of New York for the Year 1910,* New York: The Board, 1911, 191–192; "Status of Pending Petitions for Franchises and Revocable Privileges," *Minutes, Meeting of Board of Estimate and Apportionment,* February 4, 1910, 365–367.

14. "New York Cahill Telharmonic Company," *Minutes, Meeting of Board of Estimate and Apportionment,* December 22, 1910, 5574; "New York-Cahill Telharmonic Company," *Minutes, Meeting of Board of Estimate and Apportionment,* October 28, 1910, 4286–4287.

15. Arthur T. Cahill, *The Cahill Electrical Music,* Holyoke: Arthur T. Cahill, Secretary, 1910?, M.C.S., 5.

16. *Ibid.,* 10–12.

17. *Ibid.,* 20.

18. "Telharmonium Exhibition," *Holyoke Daily Transcript,* April 11, 1910, 2.

19. "The Electrical Production and Transmission of Music," *Electrical World,* April 28, 1910, LV:17, S.C., 1039–1040.

20. "Electrical Transmission of Music," 1062.

21. *Ibid.,* 1060, 1061.

22. "Electrically Made Music—Its High Possibilities Viewed Commercially," *Musical Age,* March 2, 1912, LXXVII:6, 92; 746 w times 15 hp times 140 alternators = 1,566,600 w; "Electrical Transmission of Music," 1059; 746 w times 15 hp times 60 alternators = 671,000 w.

23. "Electrical Transmission of Music," 1060.

24. *Ibid.*

25. *Ibid.;* Thaddeus Cahill?, "The Cahill Electrical Music," supplement, September 21, 1910, typewritten, M.C.S., 6; Arthur T. Cahill, 6.

26. "Electrical Transmission of Music," 1061, 1060, 1059.

27. *Ibid.,* 1060, 1061.

28. *Ibid.,* 1059, 1061.

29. *Ibid.,* 1061.

30. "A New 'Telharmonium,' " *Engineering News,* May 26, 1910, 63:21, S.C., 627–628; "Improved Electric Music," *Literary Digest,* June 18, 1910, XL:25, S.C., 1219.

31. Cahill Music Machinery Manufacturing Company, Certificate of Incorporation, April 21, 1910, received and recorded at the Office of the Hudson County Clerk, Jersey City, N.J., May 14, 1910, filed and recorded at the Office of the Secretary of State, Trenton, N.J., May 17, 1910, 1; "The Cahill Music Machinery Manufacturing Company," *Electrical World,* May 26, 1910, XV:21, S.C., 1416; "Cahill Music Machinery Co.," *Music Trade Review,* May 28, 1910, L:22, S.C., 11.

32. Cahill Music Machinery Manufacturing Company, Certificate of Incorporation, 2, 20–21.

33. *Ibid.,* 7–8.

34. *Ibid.,* 4.

35. "New Plant for Holyoke," *Boston Evening Transcript,* June 3, 1910, S.C., n.p.

36. "Music by 'Wireless,' " *Electrical World,* June 23, 1910, LV:25, 1645.

37. "A True Prophet," *Bridgeton* [N.J.] *Pioneer,* August 21, 1910, S.C., n.p.

38. Given as a Massachusetts corporation in the North River Telharmonic Company Certificate of Incorporation. No further mention of the company has been found in any document or press report. The Cahill brothers probably intended to form it at some future date. The Office of the Secretary of State of Massachusetts has no record of the company. Letter from K.J.Q., Clerk, Office of the Secretary of State, Commonwealth of Massachusetts, Boston, February 18, 1987, 1.

39. North River Telharmonic Company, Certificate of Incorporation, August 22, 1910, received and recorded at the Office of the Hudson County Clerk, Jersey City, N.J., August 26, 1910, filed and recorded at the Office of the Secretary of State, Trenton, N.J., September 7, 1910, 1.

40. "New York–Cahill Telharmonic Company," *Minutes, Meeting of Board of Estimate and Apportionment,* October 28, 1910, 4287.

41. "Chicago to See Flowers Blooming in Pictures," *Chicago Examiner,* October 30, 1910, S.C., n.p.

42. George F. Cahill, 9.

43. "New York Cahill Telharmonic Company," *Minutes, Meeting of Board of Estimate and Apportionment,* December 22, 1910, 5574–5575.

44. *Ibid.,* 5575–5576.

45. *Ibid.,* 5576.

46. *Ibid.,* 5577–5578.

47. *Ibid.,* 5578.

48. *Ibid.,* 5579.

49. *Ibid.,* 5586.

50. S. N. D. North, ed., "Miscellaneous," *The American Year Book, 1910,* New York: D. Appleton and Company, 1911, 697.

51. "Multiplex Telephone Makes One Wire Do Work of Four," *New*

York Herald, January 8, 1911, sec. 2, 6; Francis G. Wickware, ed., "Telegraphy," *The American Year Book, 1911,* New York: D. Appleton and Company, 1912, 701; E. T. Welch, *Muzak,* New York: Muzak Corporation, 1974?, 33–34.

52. "Sterling, George L.," *Who's Who in New York City and State,* third edition, New York: L. R. Hamersly and Company, 1907, 1228; "New York Cahill Telharmonic Company," *Minutes, Meeting of Board of Estimate and Apportionment,* January 5, 1911, 49–56; "Approval of Resolutions by the Mayor," *Minutes, Meeting of Board of Estimate and Apportionment,* January 19, 1911, 213.

53. North River Telharmonic Company, Petition for Re-Instatement of New York Electric Music Company, January 31, 1911, filed and recorded at the Office of the Secretary of State, Trenton, N.J., February 2, 1911, 1–3.

54. Affidavit of Thaddeus Cahill, sworn before Fred T. Partridge, Notary Public, January 31, 1911, filed and recorded at the Office of the Secretary of State, Trenton, N.J., February 2, 1911, 1.

55. *Ibid.*

56. *Ibid.,* 1–2.

57. Woodrow Wilson, Governor of New Jersey, Permit to Re-Instate the New York Electric Music Company, filed and recorded at the Office of the Secretary of State, Trenton, N.J., February 2, 1911, 1; S. D. Dickinson, Secretary of State of New Jersey, Certificate of Authorization to the New York Electric Music Company, February 2, 1911, filed and recorded at the Office of the Secretary of State, Trenton, N.J., February 2, 1911, 1.

58. "New York Cahill Telharmonic Company," *Minutes, Meeting of Board of Estimate and Apportionment,* February 16, 1911, 674, 675, 680.

59. City of New York and New York Cahill Telharmonic Company, Boroughs of Manhattan and the Bronx, West of Bronx River, Contract, March 9, 1911, B.E., 21–22, 19–20, 1–2, 4, 8, 9, 10, 12–13.

60. "Cahill Electrical Music Tonight," *Springfield Republican,* March 3, 1911, 4; "Telharmonic Demonstrations," *Holyoke Daily Transcript,* March 4, 1911, 7; "Telharmonium Concert at Board of Trade," *Springfield Evening Union,* March 4, 1911, 7; "Telharmonium Exhibited," *Springfield Republican,* March 4, 1911, 6.

61. "Telharmonic Development," *Holyoke Daily Transcript,* March 2, 1911, 6; "The Oracle," *Holyoke Daily Transcript,* March 7, 1911, 10.

62. George F. Cahill, 9; Thaddeus Cahill, letter to the Honorable the Chairman and Other Members of the Board of Estimate and Apportionment of the City of New York, June 10, 1912, in "New York Cahill Telharmonic Company," *City Record,* June 20, 1912, 5258; "New York Cahill Telharmonic Company," *City Record,* August 13, 1912, 6632.

63. Letter from Arthur T. Cahill, Assistant Treasurer, New York Cahill Telharmonic Company, to the Chairman and Members of the Board of

Estimate and Apportionment of the City of New York, November 1, 1913, B.E., 2.

64. "Now the 'Unit-Orchestra,' " *Music Trade Review,* March 25, 1911, LII:12, 48.

65. *Ibid.*

66. Thaddeus Cahill, 5258; "Another Mill," *Holyoke Daily Transcript,* April 8, 1911, 2; "According to the Holyoke Transcript: 'In April 1911 . . . ,' " Memorandum, n.n., n.d., typewritten, H.P.L., 1; Ruth Douglass, "Thaddaeus [*sic*] Cahill, a Holyoker, Is Mentioned in History of Electronic Music; Name Appears in Many References," *Holyoke Transcript-Telegram,* March 6, 1968, 24.

67. Letter from Wm. J. Hogan to Miss Ruth Douglass, March 7, 1968, R.W., 1.

68. Thaddeus Cahill, 5258; "New York Cahill Telharmonic Company," *City Record,* August 13, 1912, 6632–6633; "Carnegie Hall Opens Studio for Rehearsal and Recording," *New York Times,* April 4, 1985, C16.

69. "The Week in Town," *New York Evening Post,* February 23, 1912, 6.

70. "Electrically Made Music—Its High Possibilities Viewed Commercially," *Musical Age,* March 2, 1912, LXXVII:6, 92, 94.

71. *Ibid.,* 92.

72. *Ibid.*

73. *Ibid.,* 94.

74. George F. Cahill, *Program of Cahill Electrical Music,* New York: George F. Cahill, February 1912?, M.C.S., 2, 3.

75. Thaddeus Cahill, 5258.

76. "Thaddeus Cahill, Inventor, 66, Dies," *New York Times,* April 13, 1934, 19; Thaddeus Cahill, 5258; Arthur T. Cahill, *The Cahill Electric Music,* 13; Lewis, Scribner and Co., *Where and How to Dine in New York,* New York: The Company, 1903, 190–192; "New York Cahill Telharmonic Company," *City Record,* August 13, 1912, 6663.

77. "Wireless Music Heard Plainly 434 Miles Distant at Mid-Day," *Musical Age,* June 8, 1912, LXXVIII:7, 168.

78. "The Problem and the Solution," *Musical Age,* July 6, 1912, LXXVIII:11, 215.

79. "Unit Orchestra Amazes Striking Musicians with Its Perfection," *Musical Age,* July 13, 1912, LXXVIII:12, 232; "Wurlitzers Get $2,000,000 Order for Hope-Jones Unit Orchestras," *Musical Age,* July 13, 1912, LXXVIII:12, 242.

80. "Comedian Al Leech Dead," *New York Times,* July 6, 1912, 7; "Invented the 'Telharmonium,' " *Music Trade Review,* July 13, 1912, LV:2, 16.

81. "Mr. Albert Leech, Comedian, Is Dead," *New York Herald,* July 6, 1912, 7.

82. Letter From Engineer [n.n.], Chief of Bureau of Franchises, to John

Purroy Mitchel, Mayor, Chairman of the Board of Estimate and Apportionment, January 2, 1914, B.E., 1.

83. City of New York and New York Cahill Telharmonic Company, Amendment of Contract Dated March 9, 1911, Granting Said Company a Franchise, by Extending the Time for the Commencement of Construction and Modifying the Annual Compensation, October 10, 1912, B.E., 2–4, 6, 8.

84. "Unit Orchestra Featured in Science and Invention Column," *Musical Age,* January 11, 1913, LXXX:12, 194.

85. Letter from Arthur T. Cahill, 3.

86. *Ibid.*

87. *Ibid.,* 1–4.

88. "Clifton A. Crocker," *New York Times,* December 15, 1939, 25.

89. Letter from Arthur T. Cahill, 2.

90. *Ibid.,* 3; Lewis, Scribner and Co., 197–198.

91. New York Cahill Telharmonic Company, "Map Showing the Wires Used by the Company on September 30, 1913, and the Streets and Avenues on Which the Same Are Located," attached to letter from Arthur T. Cahill to the Chairman and Members of the Board of Estimate and Apportionment of the City of New York, hereafter Map Showing the Wires, November 1, 1913, B.E.

92. Letter from Arthur T. Cahill, 3–4.

93. Map Showing the Wires.

94. Thomas Commerford Martin, "Electrical Engineering," in Francis G. Wickware, ed., *The American Year Book, 1913,* New York: D. Appleton and Company, 1914, 583–584.

95. George F. Cahill, "Thaddeus Cahill (June 18, 1867-April 12, 1934): A Preliminary Paper," 9.

96. *Marvyn Scudder Manual of Extinct or Obsolete Companies,* vol. I, New York: Marvyn Scudder Manual of Extinct or Obsolete Companies, 1926, 859.

97. "To Distribute Music" *Music Trade Review,* August 29, 1914, LIX:9, 49.

98. S. S. Huebner, "Economic Conditions and the Conduct of Business," in Francis G. Wickware, ed., *The American Year Book, 1914,* New York: D. Appleton and Company, 1915, 318–319, 325.

99. *Ibid.,* 324.

100. George F. Cahill, "Thaddeus Cahill (June 18, 1867-April 12, 1934): A Preliminary Paper," 10.

101. *Ibid.,* 10, 17.

102. Letter from Arthur T. Cahill, Assistant Treasurer, New York Cahill Telharmonic Company, to the Chairman and Members of the Board of Estimate and Apportionment of the City of New York, November 13, 1914, B.E., 1–3; New York Cahill Telharmonic Company, "Map Showing

the Wires Used by the Company on Sept. 30, 1914 and the Streets and Avenues on Which the Same Are Located," attached to Letter from Arthur T. Cahill to the Chairman and Members of the Board of Estimate and Apportionment of the City of New York, November 13, 1914, B.E.; Thaddeus Cahill, Amendment K from Thaddeus Cahill to the Commissioner of Patents, October 16, 1914, filed October 19, 1914, N.A. 241, 1,213,803, 1.

103. "Financial Situation Easing Up, Says Ernest Urchs," *Music Trade Review,* December 5, 1914, LIX:23, 24.

104. "Cahill Telharmonic Co. Fails," *Music Trade Review,* December 26, 1914, LIX:26, 39; "Telharmonic Co. Finances Crippled," *New-York Daily Tribune,* December 23, 1914, 5; "Name Telharmonic Receiver," *New York Herald,* December 23, 1914, 4; "Business Troubles," *New York Herald,* December 23, 1914, 15; "Canned Music Co. Fails," *New York Sun,* December 23, 1914, 9; " 'Wired' Music Was Very Expensive," *New York Morning Telegraph,* December 23, 1914, 12; "Music by Telephone Fails," *New York Times,* December 23, 1914, 15; Letter from Engineer [n.n.], Chief of Bureau of Franchises, to John Purroy Mitchel, Mayor, Chairman of the Board of Estimate and Apportionment, January 15, 1915, B.E., 1, 2; "Business Troubles," *New York Times,* December 23, 1914, 14; Notice from George F. Cahill, Receiver, to the creditors of the New York Cahill Telharmonic Company, December 24, 1914, B.E., 1.

105. "Wireless Music from Light," *Music Trade Review,* October 9, 1915, LXI:15, 15.

106. "Farthest Reach of Electricity in the Musical Arts," *Music Trade Review,* December 18, 1915, LXI:25, 41.

107. Busoni, Ferruccio Benevenuto, *Entwurf einer neuen Aesthetik der Tonkunst,* Leipzig and Trieste, 1907, tr. Theodore Baker as *Sketch of a New Aesthetic of Music,* New York: G. Schirmer, 1911, reprinted, New York: Dover Publications, 1962, 89–92.

108. *Ibid.,* 93–95.

109. Edgard Varèse, "Ferruccio Busoni—A Reminiscence," *Columbia University Forum,* Spring 1966, IX:2, 20.

110. "Busoni and the Chickering," *Musical Age,* January 15, 1910, LXVIII:12, 214–215; "Busoni and the Chickering," *Music Trade Review,* January 28, 1911, LII:4, 53; "Touring the United States with Busoni and Garden," *Music Trade Review,* June 24, 1911, LII:25, 49.

111. Fernand Ouellette, *Edgard Varèse,* tr. from the French by Derek Coltman, New York: The Orion Press, 1968, 44.

112. *Ibid.,* 46–47.

113. Louise Varèse, *Varèse: A Looking-Glass Diary, Vol. I,* New York: W. W. Norton and Company, 1972, 50; cf. the publication of this text in *Columbia University Forum,* Spring 1966, IX:2, 20, in which the words "and was disappointed" were omitted.

CHAPTER VIII

EPILOGUE

THADDEUS CAHILL

And so the efforts and accomplishments of the inventor were stymied for the third time: twice with the Telharmonium as they had been once earlier with the electric typewriter. The fortune he had been paid for the patent license in 1902 was gone. Deeply wounded, he did not lament to others. Yet his faith in his inventive work seemed for the first time to vacillate. He commenced to read law and spoke of joining a law firm.[1]

His brothers and sisters would not hear of it. They decided that Eleanor and Mary, who was nicknamed "Majesty," would continue to keep the home, a dark, floor-through flat at 316 West 84th Street. George, Arthur, and Margaret would support the family. Thaddeus would then be free to pursue the Cahill obsession with electric music yet again so that it would not be lost to the world.[2]

With little enthusiasm his attentions turned toward reducing the expense and intricacy of a central plant for electric music. He realized that a small instrument would now do as well, since its faint-sounding output could be amplified to any strength desired with the aid of Lee de Forest's audion. And he continued to seek a practical solution to the problem of just intonation, in his view the greatest attainment of the Telharmonium. But how could he fashion a transposing just-intonation instrument with a standard keyboard?[3]

Faith and a few tax dollars kept the Cahill Music Machinery Manufacturing Co. and the North River Telharmonic Co. in hopeful existence for a few years, but their charters were finally forfeited in 1919. The Cahills would not, however, give up just yet their beloved New York Cahill Telharmonic Co.[4] It may have been in receivership, but it still had a 25-year franchise with the City of New York—admittedly in forfeit but perhaps not without some undiscovered future value.

Then came 1920 and the devastating reality of commercial radio. Here were voice and song added to music, broadcast into space, a vivid sorcery heard for nothing more than the onetime cost of a receiver. Compared to electric music it was a sonic feast—orchestras, choruses, bands, singers, chamber ensembles, and soloists of all kinds, any note that could be picked up with a microphone or played from a record—the whole of music was at hand. And with this came the sounds of human speech and action in all their glorious variety: drama, comedy, news, sports, religious services, instruction, political events, advertising, and on and on. It was a mirror of the entire culture, and it overcame isolation by providing events as they still occurred. There was truly everything for anyone. The central stations sprouting everywhere required no complex specialized mechanisms and not one foot of cable in the streets.

Many piano manufacturers, music dealers, and music teachers were put out of business along with Thaddeus Cahill. It was time to make a fresh start, and Cahill slowly began to tinker with some other inventions. He turned to typewriters and typesetting machines again and also experimented with heat engines.[5]

Meanwhile, the three income-generating Cahills were hard at work. Margaret continued to teach English and Latin at the Wadleigh Public High School in New York, as she had been doing since 1893.[6] George and Arthur were putting together an enterprise based on an idea George had begun working on in Holyoke many years ago.

THE NEW GIANT CAHILL GLARELESS DUPLEX FLOODLIGHT PROJECTOR

George F. Cahill was two years younger than Thaddeus. He had attended Oberlin College from 1889 to 1891 and had then studied law at George Washington University.[7] He had been a devoted baseball player in high school and college and continued to attend ball games when his school days were over.[8] In 1903, when Thaddeus was already the holder of 23 patents, George finally began inventing on his own. He applied for a patent covering his arrangement of lamps to illuminate baseball fields at night. He did not specify any particular design of reflector, merely the optimum placement of commonly available lighting instruments about the field. He drafted a design of carefully situated screens and shades in front of the lamps, calculated to block direct rays of light from falling into the eyes of the players while stationed at their regular positions. The patent was granted in a scant three months, record time for all 50 patents awarded to the three Cahill brothers.[9]

Nothing came of the invention in 1903. It was a busy time for the three, who were under great pressure to complete the second Telharmonium so it could begin to provide income to its investors.

In the spring of 1908, just as Telharmonic Hall was being abandoned, George introduced a pitching machine. It was operated by compressed air and could throw straight and curved pitches at various speeds.[10] Although the device was never patented, the Cahills had some sales success.[11]

The next year George applied for another lighting patent. He had improved the diffusion of the light, as well as the reflectors, and had contrived a system of double beams of light.[12] Once the application was in the Patent Office, George lost no time in promoting the invention. A night baseball exhibition game was given at Crosley Field in Cincinnati on June 19, 1909.[13] The results were praised, but neither the Cincinnati club nor any other ordered the equipment. The next year a newspaper report stated that Cahill lighting equipment had already been installed at National League ballparks in "Pittsburgh, Cincinnati, Philadelphia, and Chicago, and very soon it is expected that baseball games will be witnessed at night."[14] Perhaps it was another hopeful press release or just a ruse to scare some orders from the American League. The report did not prove true, and there were no orders. The lights performed well, but most people worked ten hours a day. There was no demand for night baseball.[15]

George was practical and reputed to be an even better businessman than Thaddeus;[16] he was not going to let go of a good idea just because it happened to be a few years too early. In the early 1920s he saw that increased leisure time would afford him his chance, so with Thaddeus and Arthur, the firm of Cahill Bros., floodlight manufacturers, was formed. George became the senior partner.[17]

The firm was located in a four-story building at 519 West 45th Street. By the mid-1920s the vogue for night sports was sweeping the country, and the company was shipping the "Cahill Giant Duplex Projector" to public and school sports fields of all kinds.[18] Several years later Yankee Stadium and the Polo Grounds in New York were illuminated, although major league baseball games were still not held at night. By the late 1920s skating rinks, swimming pools, dancing arenas, state fairs, amusement parks, gasoline stations, quarries, piers, and parking lots were all yielding their darkness to the glareless light of Cahill Giant Duplex Projectors. The U.S. Naval Academy at Annapolis had installed more than 100 of the huge devices, which measured better than a yard wide at the front opening. Each burned two 1,000-watt bulbs and diffused the beam over 90 degrees.[19] At last a Cahill invention was in the money.

THE FINAL YEARS

Arthur was the youngest in the family and the only one of the six siblings to marry. He was something of a dandy and a ladies' man. Physically he was in superb health, impressing doctors as being 20 years younger than his chronological age. Although he had declined the baseball scholarship to Harvard, he remained fond of sports. In New York he kept and rode a horse in Central Park. Years earlier, in 1909, he had met Margaret Louise Jamieson, a most fetching piano student at Oberlin Conservatory. She had been groomed for a concert career since the age of four. The two proceeded to keep company on and off for 17 years. Meanwhile, she debuted at Aeolian Hall in New York in 1917, gave several more New York concerts over the next couple of years, and received friendly but not outstanding reviews. At that her Uncle Archibald declined to fund her concert career any further. She went to teach at Wells College and then at the Eastman School of Music. In 1926, he was 54, she was 38. The Cahill family desperately desired an heir, a boy to carry on the name, another Thaddeus. The women were all well beyond childbearing age (Margaret, the youngest, was 62); the two older brothers were totally self-absorbed. But Arthur's fine physical condition and a family prosperity that seemed assured made him a good catch. Margaret

Jamieson dreamed of making a comeback; Arthur promised her that and a Steinway grand to boot. They were married that year. When Toscanini became a celebrity, she called her husband "Arturo," but they disagreed about the worth of electric music. The couple's only child, Margaret Eleanor, was born in 1928.[20]

Around 1930 the corporation tax payments were finally suspended to the state of New York by the New York Cahill Telharmonic Co. Its long-forfeited franchise with New York City had but a few years left to run; any exploitation was hopeless. The last surviving Telharmonic company charter expired in 1932.[21]

In 1932 and 1933 Thaddeus began to explore the idea of combining electric music with radio.[22] He experimented with wired-wireless means of transmission,[23] which was concurrently being developed energetically by Wired Radio, a predecessor of the Muzak Corporation, under George O. Squier's patent.[24] His brothers and sisters continued to encourage him, insisting that

> any Broadcasting Station that could send out music in that *just* intonation which had captivated even the leaders of the best string quartets, and the Conductors of the greatest Orchestras of the western world, would soon put all other Broadcasters out of Business.[25]

And for its loss, the Cahills nurtured an inexorable, implacable bitterness toward Oscar T. Crosby and Frederick C. Todd, whom they held completely accountable. Yet Thaddeus was serene and happy. He kept Hershey's chocolate kisses on his desk for his little niece, Margaret. He was unfailingly kind and sweet to her, often taking her on his knee.[26]

So Cahill continued to experiment, frequently saying that now he could build a central music station for a mere 5% to 10% of its former cost. He was much cheered by the progress of several new patent applications. One was a film and sound synchronization control, a precursor of television. He proposed to supply subscribers with low-cost film projectors. The soundtrack for the picture would be provided by radio broadcast, while the film prints would be distributed to subscribers in advance of the scheduled sound transmission. Synchronization was achieved by a separate control signal from the central station to the projector, governing its speed. Stripping the soundtrack from the film print meant that it could be projected at variable speed instead of a constant 24 frames per second. A single picture could be displayed for a few seconds, a minute, or more, vastly reducing the number of pictures needed for a motion picture entertainment. Consequently, the presentation would largely consist of changing pictures interposed with segments of motion pictures.[27] The other pending application was for a set of "soft-speakers," mounted near the ears in an easy chair, to afford semiprivate listening without enduring the discomfort of headphones or unduly bothering others who did not wish to hear the program.[28] These two inventions eventually received patent protection, but another application for wired-wireless did not.[29]

He met one of his former secretaries around the beginning of April 1934 and assured her that she would soon hear of his work again. He spoke of the longevity of his forebears, anticipating that he might well live at least another 20 years, even though early the previous year Mary had died suddenly of inflammation of the heart and congestive heart failure at 74.[30]

Less than two weeks later at his residence, on April 12, 1934, Thaddeus Cahill died without warning of a heart attack; his age was 66. He had been in good spirits and had mentioned nothing about feeling any pain or discomfort. His calm face betrayed no disturbance. The doctor who was immediately called in diagnosed the death as instantaneous. He detected some indication of pain—angina pectoris—probably caused by a blood clot in the heart. During the service at his home two days later, people remarked how small he seemed then, how he really did not appear to be the same person. The charismatic look that had held people's gazes had gone out of his face and with it his apparent size. After the home service there was a precremation ceremony at the funeral parlor. At its conclusion the casket, which was on an elevator platform, sank slowly beneath the floor as music was played. It was not hard for little six-year-old Margaret to imagine the flames licking at it already. But in fact the remains of Thaddeus Cahill were cremated in New Jersey on April 15. His ashes (which the crematorium employees persist in dubbing "cremains") were shipped via parcel post back to the funeral director in New York for return to the family, who kept them at home in a cardboard box for many years. His prayer book, hymnal, and the box of books which he had willed to his beloved Miss Mary C. Fairchild 36 years earlier were duly forwarded to her; she had married a man named Torsch and was living in Baltimore.[31]

The firm of Cahill Bros. continued to ship Projectors all over the United States and Europe. The major stadiums of the world were now lit by Cahill, and finally the resistance of the major leagues was broken. At Crosley Field in Cincinnati, the site of George F. Cahill's demonstration in 1909, 632 Giant Duplex Cahill Projectors burst into glareless light at precisely 8:30 P.M. on May 24, 1935. President Franklin D. Roosevelt had pressed a button in the White House to illuminate the ballpark. The Cincinnati Redlegs went on to defeat the Philadelphia Phillies by 2 to 1 before more than 20,000 fans. There was only praise from both spectators and players, and night baseball was established.[32]

George F. Cahill had but little time and no spirit to savor this triumph: he grieved mightily at the loss of Mary and Thaddeus. He died at home of congestive heart failure later that year, on October 13, 1935, also aged 66.[33] The business soon began to wither; initial demand had peaked and the Depression was widespread. Arthur vacated the Manhattan headquarters and for a year or two ran the remaining business himself with one assistant, building Projectors in the garage of a 13-room house he had purchased with Eleanor in Weehawken, N.J., in 1937. The two sisters moved in with Arthur and his family.[34]

Had Telharmonium recordings existed, they surely would have been preserved and played in that household, but none ever was. Mrs. Cahill practiced the piano daily, but never received her comeback or her Steinway grand. She had to labor on a Baldwin upright. Margaret and Eleanor were unhappy that there was a piano in the house at all. Mrs. Cahill continued not to share their opinion that electric music was superior to all other, and enjoyed filling the house with noncrackling acoustic music.[35]

By this time the Hammond Organ was sweeping the country. The surviving Cahills were outraged that in 1934 Laurens Hammond had been granted a patent on *their* electric music. But having been decimated by three deaths in less than three years, and now in their late sixties and seventies, they had no stamina for litigation. Yet Arthur made it his mission to continue the development of Thaddeus's inventions. A few months before George's death Arthur had applied for his first patent, an improvement in the soft-speakers. He pursued his brother's work in typewriters as well, with a 1938 mechanism that provided an extra keyboard of nine thumb keys located where the spacebar used to be. One of these keys could be struck simultaneously with a finger key. If a vowel finger key was depressed, a thumb key would produce a consonant; if the former key was a consonant, the same thumb key would produce a vowel. This duplex mechanism could even be elevated to triplex operation at the end of a word by striking the space key simultaneously with the other thumb. Embodying all of the Cahill propensity for overcomplication, this hellish keyboard attracted no licensees. The inventor asserted that learning the machine would be far simpler than learning chords on a piano.[36] Inexplicably, he claimed to have avoided the obstructing complexity of Thaddeus's dual-printing machines with their piano-style keyboards:

> those machines frequently required the use of two or more fingers for the production of a single letter, and involved high skill and a long period of special training for the operator.[37]

Later in 1938 Arthur applied for an electric music patent. The design was a combination electric organ and piano, featuring individual control of harmonics, touch control of loudness, touch control of attack by means of a piano hammer hitting a movable inductive or capacitive circuit, control of decay via movable circuits connected to dashpots, and reverse piano attack obtained by causing the piano hammer to hit a momentum piece connected to the movable circuit. The piano action and dashpots could be disconnected to facilitate a more organlike sound.[38]

Arthur paid homage to Thaddeus's movable circuit touch control as described in his 1897 patent, but criticized its shortcomings. The tones had the attack of a piano but were then held and dropped like an organ:

> Nor did the said Thaddeus Cahill have the power, with his action, to play from one instrument, real piano music, organ music, the music of the bowed instruments, the brasses and woodwinds, bells, percussion instruments, etc., as I have on my instruments, playing each with its own peculiar tone color, and with a very great degree of fidelity to its exact expression, etc.[39]

Early in 1943, just as the patent was about to be granted, Arthur went forward with another application for a further-improved electric music machine. This instrument generated sounds by means of 12 rotating tone wheels, multiplied into a six-octave range by means of 72 vacuum tubes and tuned circuits. Through tube circuitry all voltage leaks had been eliminated, thus forever wiping out the old problem of robbing. Low voltage levels and carefully controlled gradations of sudden loudness changes obliterated the switch transients that gave rise to that other ancient Telharmonic nemesis, diaphragm-crack.[40] Due to a new shape of condenser plate that controlled the envelope, Arthur boasted of "the most gorgeously smooth and velvety introduction, control, and ending of the tones."[41] There were new designs for the movable circuits and dashpots, here termed "tone-controlling cylinders."[42] The inventor concluded by pointing out specifically how the Hammond Organ could be improved by the adoption of his circuits.[43]

Arthur attempted to raise funds for these instruments, and on one such occasion he took his daughter along to the Skinner brothers' office in New York. Having lost money in the Telharmonium years ago, the silk magnates were not willing to invest further. There is no record that Arthur was ever able to sell or license his electric music patents, and he went on to pursue other inventions. In 1945 he applied for a patent on a water-cooled film projector for still or motion pictures. The film was supported by a glass gate so it could be held in perfect focus; the cooling apparatus enabled the use of a stronger projection lamp. His last patent, applied for in 1950, covered a parabolic projection lamp reflector that surpassed the efficiency of conventional lamp housings by at least 25 times.[44]

Arthur was vigorous into his early seventies, when his golf score matched his age. Then he contracted pernicious anemia, but cured himself with a diet of grapes. He would play golf until his early eighties. Neighbors recall that the inventor also played the part of a mad genius and was incessantly attempting to raise money to promote his inventions. His two elderly maiden sisters, particularly Eleanor, seemed to control most of the family finances. Arthur had no success with his inventions, yet his grandiose ideas were always about to make him a millionaire. He gave the impression that he had, or could have, invented the telephone before Bell and the phonograph before Edison. He did not discuss the music machine with his neighbors; his efforts were largely concerned with recruiting support for the film projector. The neighbors' lack of investment commitment eventually caused some strained relationships. Eventually film producer Mike Todd indicated some interest, but died soon thereafter.[45]

In 1951, at the age of 79, Arthur T. Cahill circulated a letter attempting to find a home for the first and only surviving Telharmonium. He recounted the dinner at the Maryland Club in Baltimore in 1902, at which investors had committed $150,000 for a license to distribute heavenly electric music in New England. In spite of the enthusiasm from all corners, "the promoters handled it dishonestly and ruined the enterprise."[46] Arthur said he had been keeping the historic 14,000-pound plant in storage at his expense, paying rent for almost 50 years (this was doubtful; it was probably in his garage), and now sought "a permanent and a public home for this priceless monument to man's genius."[47] Overreaching a little too extravagantly, Arthur asserted that Thaddeus's "great and immortal patents"[48] revealed all that could ever be accomplished in the field of electric music. Not even a great orchestra could begin to approach the Telharmonium. Except for amplification, everything found in the Hammond Organ and in all other electric musical instruments could be found first in Thaddeus's five patents.[49]

There were no takers, and the sad likelihood is that the only surviving Telharmonium was scrapped (along with the three cardboard boxes from the storage room on the third floor containing the ashes of Mary, Thaddeus, and George) around the time Mr. and Mrs. Arthur T. Cahill sold and vacated their 13-room Weehawken house for a three-room apartment in Cliffside Park, N.J., in 1958.[50] Margaret had died of a heart attack at 80 in 1944,[51] and Eleanor, aged 88, had finally succumbed to heart failure in 1951;[52] the elderly couple could no longer manage the house.

In 1959, then 87, Arthur wrote and offered to assist David Sarnoff at RCA in establishing Cahill electrical music as an improvement over Harry F. Olson's RCA Synthesizer. RCA Laboratories politely declined the opportunity to recreate Telharmonic rotating machinery and high-power outputs. Three years later, on January 24, 1962, Arthur T. Cahill died at his home of a heart attack, several weeks before attaining the age of 90. His widow survived him nearly two years, then died supposedly of liver failure, but really of grief, on November 7, 1963; she was 75. Their daughter had left home upon marrying in 1948 at age 20 and was living in England at the time of her parents' deaths. Evidence of intergenerational tension may seem to have been displayed in her Aunt Eleanor's will, in which any remaining principal of a bequest to Arthur had to be withheld until the niece reached the considerable age of 35. In fact the bequest was

totally meaningless. Eleanor could not have had any thought that
there would be any money left after Arthur had gotten to it.[53]

Thus ends the story of the Cahills and their central plant for
electric music. Of the others involved in the enterprise, some have
left little trace, while a few went on to mark achievements in other
endeavors.

OSCAR T. CROSBY

While the Cahill brothers were building the third Telharmonium in
Holyoke, Oscar T. Crosby was returning to the development of street
railways. Among other interests he became head of the Wilmington-
Philadelphia Traction Co. in 1910.[54] He also resumed writing, and
his book *Strikes: When to Strike, How to Strike*[55] was published that
same year. The manual presented various ethical and legal principles
that applied to labor problems and was praised for being "simply and
attractively written"[56] and for its judicious and balanced approach.
Crosby's interest in world affairs led him to be considered by
President Wilson for governor-general of the Philippines in 1913,[57]
but the appointment did not go to him. Later that year he published
a ringing defense of the legitimacy of children born out of wedlock,
maintaining "there are no illegitimate children; there are only
illegitimate parents."[58] That same year, at the age of 52, he retired
from his utilities businesses.[59] Crosby's expeditions resumed, to
Turkey in 1914[60] and to Borneo the following year.[61]

After World War I broke out Crosby headed Belgian relief under
Herbert Hoover in 1915. His daughter Juliette served as a Red Cross
nurse in France during the war. Two years later Crosby became
assistant secretary of the treasury and administered loans to the
Allied powers. He later became president of the Inter-Allied Council
of War Purchases and Finance, serving in that capacity until 1919.
That year he divested himself of another book, *International War: Its
Causes and Its Cure.*[62] In view of its advocacy of an international police
force, publication was delayed until the conclusion of the Paris Peace
Conference at the request of the Wilson administration. So ended his
public career. His wife died after a long illness in 1934. Oscar T.
Crosby died at his home, "View Tree," at Warrenton, Va., on

January 2, 1947, aged 85 years.[63] Living with him were two of his three surviving daughters; one had married a Milanese count. His other daughter, Juliette, had meanwhile achieved some renown as a Broadway actress in the 1920s and 1930s; she married and later divorced film producer Arthur Hornblow, Jr. Her appearances on Broadway included *Dodsworth, Home Fires,* and *Charley's Aunt.*[64]

EDWIN HALL PIERCE

The first major Telharmonist, after a brief stint as assistant editor of *The Etude* in 1917 and 1918, continued his musical career as a composer of religious anthems. About 30 were published. He eventually settled in Annapolis, where he served as organist and choirmaster of Old St. Anne's Church for nearly 20 years. In 1939 he bested 500 entries to win the Baltimore Community Fund campaign song contest. The prize was $100. He never spoke of the Telharmonium to friends or family, apparently considering it a closed chapter. Pierce died in 1954, aged 86, leaving 8 children by 2 wives, 32 grandchildren, and 31 great-grandchildren.[65]

CARL M. PIHL

The former manager of Telharmonic Hall was awarded a colonel's commission in World War I. After the war he became the largest utilities owner in New England. He retired to Jacksonville, Fla., in 1926, at the age of 52. After losing his fortune in the Depression he founded the Stucco Products Co. Pihl again became a millionaire and operated the business successfully until his death in 1933.[66]

CLARENCE REYNOLDS

Former Telharmonist Clarence Reynolds became one of the most listened-to musicians in America. Following his service at Telharmonic Hall, he served as organist at Ocean Grove, N.J.,[67] for eight seasons. There he was heard by hundreds of thousands at what was considered to be the largest organ in the country. When he became municipal organist of Denver in 1918, he had already given more than 2,000 organ recitals across the United States. He gave free daily noon recitals in Denver, about 100 per year, each heard by 1,500 to 1,800 people, until 1932. In 1936 he moved to Los Angeles where he died in 1949 at the age of 69.[68]

OTTO SCHEDA

After the first season closed at Telharmonic Hall, the violinist and occasional Telharmonist resumed his itinerant violin recitals as "Paganini's Ghost." During the 1910s he took a new act, a reincarnation of violin virtuoso Pietro Locatelli, to Canada and Europe. In spite of excellent reviews, he encountered increasing difficulties in securing bookings. He died poverty-stricken and neglected in Brooklyn in 1932 at the age of 68.[69]

ELLIOTT SCHENCK

The erstwhile music director of Telharmonic Hall went on to conduct operas and music festivals and gained considerable renown as a symphonic composer. His works were presented by orchestras in New York, Boston, Chicago, St. Louis, and Minneapolis. Schenck also wrote two grand operas that were never produced.[70]

Schenck became an enthusiastic writer of letters to the editor in the 1920s, participating in several epistolary debates on contradictions in the Bible.[71] He also lamented the fate of the American composer in print, asserting that second-rate European composers were accorded more programming opportunities. At the time, however, he was enjoying the considerable national success of his symphonic tone poem, *In a Withered Garden*.[72] Schenck died in 1939 at the age of 69.[73]

CHRISTIAN SCHIOTT

After his brief career at Telharmonic Hall, Schiott, who had studied with Busoni, concertized extensively in America and Europe. A native of Norway, he composed music for Norwegian lyrics, and his works became part of the concert repertory in the land of his birth. He adopted sculpture as a diversion while recuperating from a broken ankle, but his work soon displayed such accomplishment that he became recognized as a sculptor as well as a musician. After teaching at Steinway Hall in New York, he settled in Darien, Conn., where he taught voice and piano until his death in 1961, aged 78.[74]

FREDERICK C. TODD

The former partner of Oscar T. Crosby emerged from the last dark days of Telharmonic Hall a skilled and fire-tempered entrepreneur, but reluctant to tackle any more unconventional undertakings. With two partners he established an electric railway, a suburban real estate development, and an electric steam power plant, all in Charlottesville, Va. Upon his death in 1918 he was a 40% owner of these successful ventures, drawing salaries from the railway as well as from the General Electric Co. He died the day before Armistice Day at 54 years of age. His prominence in Charlottesville was indicated by a front page obituary above the fold, amid headlines reporting the surrender of Germany and the cessation of World War I. He had spent the final two years of his life as a "dollar-a-year man," serving in the Naval Intelligence Department, for which he traveled widely throughout the United States and Cuba.[75]

ISABELLE WINLOCKE

The mezzo-soprano who earned $400 to record her voice for transmission with the Telharmonium pursued a lengthy acting career; in later life she spelled her name "Isabel Winlock." She appeared in some eight or nine Broadway plays and in many touring productions. Winlocke garnered mixed notices, from "strongly impressed the audience"[76] to "plays listlessly and without a single flash of fun."[77] She later performed on radio and eventually became one of the first television actresses, on *Life Begins at Eighty* in the early 1950s. However, in 1953, when she herself became eligible to sample the delights of life at the age of 80, she died.[78]

NOTES

1. George F. Cahill, "Thaddeus Cahill (June 18, 1867-April 12, 1934): A Preliminary Paper," New York?, 1934?, typewritten, C.L.R.C. E-1488, Cat. C, L609.214, C115, 10–11.
2. *Ibid.,* 11; personal interview with Margaret Eleanor Cahill Schwartz, Rochester, Vt., August 29, 1990.
3. Cahill, 11.
4. *Marvyn Scudder Manual of Extinct or Obsolete Companies,* vol. IV, New York: Marvyn Scudder Manual of Extinct or Obsolete Companies, 1934, 414, 1766, 1728.
5. *Ibid.,* 13, 14.
6. "Miss Margaret J. Cahill," *New York Times,* February 24, 1944, 15.
7. "George F. Cahill," *Oberlin Alumni Magazine,* November 1935, O.C.A. 28/1, Box 38, n.p.
8. "Machine for Training Batters," *Cincinnati Enquirer,* March 2, 1908, N.B.H., n.p.
9. U.S. Patent 755,447, *System for Illuminating Fields So That Games May Be Played at Night,* George F. Cahill, Holyoke, Mass., Application December 26, 1903, Patented March 22, 1904, drawings sheets 1–5, 1–5.
10. "Machine for Training Batters," *Cincinnati Enquirer,* March 2, 1908, N.B.H., n.p.
11. Letter from Wm. J. Hogan to Miss Ruth Douglass, March 7, 1968, R.W., 1.
12. U.S. Patent 1,235,527, *Illuminating System for Base-Ball and Other Games,* George F. Cahill, New York, N.Y., Application June 1, 1909, Renewed December 21, 1916, Patented July 31, 1917, drawings sheets 1–3, 1–4.
13. "George F. Cahill," n.n., October 24, 1935, N.B.H., n.p.
14. "Baseball at Night for the Boston Fans," *New York Evening Journal,* September 5, 1910, S.C., n.p.

15. Letter from Wm. J. Hogan, 1.

16. Letter from Robert J. Cahill to Miss [Ruth] Douglass, June 25, 1968, R.W., 1.

17. "George F. Cahill," N.B.H.

18. Letter from Robert J. Cahill, 1–2.

19. Cahill Bros., *The New Giant Cahill Duplex Projector,* New York: The Firm, 1929?, N.B.H., 1–2, 4.

20. Personal interview with Margaret Eleanor Cahill Schwartz; "Two Piano Recitals," *New York Times,* February 10, 1917, 7; "Margaret Jamieson in Piano Recital," *New York Times,* January 31, 1918, 7; "About Margaret Jamieson's Career," *Musical Courier,* February 28, 1918, XXXVI:9, 26; "Margaret Jamieson, Pianist, Plays," *New York Times,* April 24, 1918, 13; "Margaret Jamieson, Pianist," *Musical Courier,* May 2, 1918, XXXVI:18, 16; "Walter Anderson to Manage Margaret Jamieson," *Musical Courier,* May 30, 1918, XXXVI:22, 48; "Oberlin Musical Club Meets," *Musical Courier,* May 1, 1919, XXXVIII:18, 31; "Miss Jamieson a Bride," *New York Times,* July 10, 1926, 16.

21. *Marvin Scudder Manual of Extinct or Obsolete Companies,* vol. IV, New York: Marvyn Scudder Manual of Extinct or Obsolete Companies, 1934, 1728.

22. George F. Cahill, 13.

23. "Dr. Cahill Dies at 66; Inventor of Telharmony," *New York Herald Tribune,* April 13, 1934, 19; George F. Cahill, 13.

24. E. T. Welch, *Muzak,* New York: Muzak Corporation, 1974?, 5, 8.

25. George F. Cahill, 13.

26. Personal interview with Margaret Eleanor Cahill Schwartz.

27. George F. Cahill, 13; U.S. Patent 2,103,766, *Synchronized Sound and Picture Control,* Thaddeus Cahill, New York, N.Y.: Arthur T. Cahill, Eleanor Cahill, and George Frederick Cahill, executors of the estate of said Thaddeus Cahill, deceased, Application November 24, 1930, Patented December 28, 1937, 1–2, 13–14, 33, 40–41.

28. U.S. Patent 2,009,138, *Electrical Speakers and Other Speakers,* Thaddeus Cahill, New York, N.Y.: Arthur T. Cahill, Weehawken, N.J., Eleanor Cahill and George Frederick Cahill, both of New York, N.Y., executors of Thaddeus Cahill, deceased, Applications July 3, 1931, March 14, 1933, Patented July 23, 1935, 1–2, 17, 35–36.

29. Application 534,150, filed May 1, 1931, cf. U.S. Patent 2,103,766, 43.

30. George F. Cahill, 13; John Randolph Graham, M.D., Certificate of Death of Mary Holland Cahill, January 12, 1933, filed at the Department of Health of the City of New York, Bureau of Records, January 12, 1933.

31. George F. Cahill, 1, 13; Henry Weinberg, Assistant Medical Examiner, Certificate of Death of Thaddeus Cahill, April 12, 1934, filed at the Department of Health of the City of New York, Bureau of Records, April 12,

278 Magic Music from the Telharmonium

1934, 1; "Deaths: Cahill," *New York Times*, April 13, 1934, 19; personal interview with Margaret Eleanor Cahill Schwartz; Letter from Garden State Crematory, North Bergen, N.J., n.n., n.d., postmarked January 13, 1989, 1; William Douglas Moore, Notice of Probate, In the Matter of Proving the Last Will and Testament of Thaddeus Cahill, September 7, 1934, filed at Surrogate's Court, New York County, New York, N.Y., 1.

32. "Redlegs Defeat Phils in Night Game," *Cincinnati Enquirer*, May 25, 1935, 1.

33. "George F. Cahill, 66, Inventor, Dies Here," *New York Times*, October 15, 1935, 23; John Randolph Graham, M.D., Certificate of Death of George Frederick Cahill, October 13, 1935, filed at the Department of Health of the City of New York, Bureau of Records, n.d., 1.

34. "Arthur Cahill: Was Inventor," *Union City Dispatch*, June 25, 1962, 16; personal interview with Margaret Eleanor Cahill Schwartz, August 31, 1990; Louise Margaret Jamieson Cahill, "Arthur Timothy Cahill," 1963?, typewritten, M.C.S., 3; County Clerk, Hudson County, N.J., "Liber 1900," April 7, 1937, R.O.H.C., 57.

35. Personal interviews with Margaret Eleanor Cahill Schwartz, August 29–30, 1990.

36. Personal interview with Margaret Eleanor Cahill Schwartz, August 29, 1990; U.S. Patent 2,161,995, *Speaker and Listening Device*, Arthur T. Cahill, Weehawken, N.J., Application July 22, 1935, Patented June 13, 1939, 1–3; U.S. Patent 2,354,196, *Typewriter Machine, Typesetting Machine, and Other Keyboard Instruments*, Arthur T. Cahill, Weehawken, N.J., Application February 3, 1938, Patented July 25, 1944, 2; Arthur T. Cahill, "The Cahill Duplex-Triplex Electrical Typewriter Patent," Weehawken, N.J., 1944?, typewritten, M.C.S., 1, 2.

37. U.S. Patent 2,354,196, 2.

38. U.S. Patent 2,308,051, *Means for Generating Music Electrically*, Arthur T. Cahill, Weehawken, N.J., Application December 5, 1938, Patented January 12, 1943, 2–5, 7.

39. *Ibid.*, 6.

40. U.S. Patent 2,463,597, *Art or Method and Means for Generating Music Electrically*, Arthur T. Cahill, Weehawken, N.J., Application January 9, 1943, Patented March 18, 1949, 1–4.

41. *Ibid.*, 31.

42. *Ibid.*, 3, 51, *et passim*.

43. *Ibid.*, 50–51.

44. Personal interview with Margaret Eleanor Cahill Schwartz; U.S. Patent 2,413,288, *Picture Projection Apparatus for Stills and for Motion Pictures*, Arthur T. Cahill, Weehawken, N.J., Application May 5, 1945, Patented December 31, 1946, 1, 3; U.S. Patent 2,413,288, *Picture Projection Apparatus for Stills and for Motion Pictures*, Arthur T. Cahill, Weehawken, N.J., Application May 5, 1945, Patented December 31, 1946, 1, 3.

45. Personal interview with Margaret Eleanor Cahill Schwartz; telephone interview with Mrs. Walter Koehler, Cranford, N.J., May 8, 1984; telephone interview with Dr. Fred Heimbuch, D.D.S., West Long Branch, N.J., May 11, 1984; telephone interview with Charles F. Krause III, Union City, N.J., July 27, 1990; telephone interview with George Gordon, Brooklyn, N.Y., October 1, 1990.

46. Arthur T. Cahill, "The Original and Scientifically Priceless Cahill Electric Music Instrument. The First Instrument That Created Music from the Electrical Waves of Alternating Current Generators," n.d. [rubber stamp: "AUG 31 1951"], mimeographed and typewritten, A.T.T.A. M-1, 1.

47. *Ibid.*

48. *Ibid.*

49. *Ibid.*; personal interview with Margaret Eleanor Cahill Schwartz.

50. Personal interview with Margaret Eleanor Cahill Schwartz; telephone interview with Sophie Struniewski, Cliffside Park, N.J., February 4, 1984; County Clerk, Hudson County, N.J., "Liber 2760," August 7, 1958, R.O.H.C., 48.

51. J. Fulton, Certificate of Death of Margaret Cahill, February 22, 1944, filed at the New Jersey Department of Health, Bureau of Vital Statistics, Trenton, N.J., February 24, 1944; "Miss Margaret J. Cahill," *New York Times,* February 24, 1944, 1.

52. Personal interview with Margaret Eleanor Cahill Schwartz; D. M. Gordon, M.D., Certificate of Death of Eleanor Cahill, December 12, 1951, filed at the Department of Health of the City of New York, Bureau of Records, December 12, 1951; County Clerk, Hudson County, N.J., "Liber 2619," January 21, 1955, R.O.H.C., 487.

53. Letter from C. D. Tuska, Staff Consultant, Patents, RCA Laboratories, to Arthur T. Cahill, February 17, 1959, M.C.S., 1; Stanley S. Berliner, O.D., Certificate of Death of Arthur Cahill, January 24, 1962, filed at the State Department of Health of New Jersey, Trenton, N.J., January 27, 1962; "Arthur T. Cahill Dies," *New York Times,* January 26, 1962, 31; "Arthur Cahill; Was Inventor," *Hudson Dispatch,* January 25, 1962, 16; "A. T. Cahill, Inventor, 89," *Newark Evening News,* January 26, 1962, 32; John J. Federer, M.D., Certificate of Death of Louise M. Cahill, November 7, 1963, filed at the New Jersey State Department of Health, Trenton, N.J., November 12, 1963; "Mrs. Louise Cahill," *Hudson Dispatch,* November 9, 1963, 14; "Mrs. Cahill Services," *Hudson Dispatch,* November 11, 1963, 10; Eleanor Cahill, Last Will and Testament, November 21, 1947, filed at Surrogate's Court, Hudson County, Jersey City, N.J., December 26, 1951, recorded in "Wills, Liber 306," 114; personal interview with Margaret Eleanor Cahill Schwartz, August 30, 1990.

54. "Crosby, Oscar Terry," *The National Cyclopaedia of American Biography,* vol. XXXV, New York: James T. White and Company, 1949, 84.

55. New York: G. P. Putnam's Sons, 1910.

56. "A Book on Strikes," *New York Times,* June 11, 1910, pt. 2, 334.

57. "Crosby for Philippines," *New York Times,* July 16, 1913, 9.

58. Oscar T. Crosby, "Illegitimate Parents," letter to the editor, *New York Times,* October 1, 1913, 8.

59. "Crosby, Oscar Terry," 84.

60. Oscar T. Crosby, "Turkey Building Roads," letter to the editor, *New York Times,* April 9, 1914, 10.

61. "Crosby, Oscar Terry," *Who Was Who in America,* vol. 2, Chicago: The A. N. Marquis Company, 1950, 136.

62. London: Macmillan and Co., 1919.

63. "Oscar Crosby Dies; Treasury Ex-Aide," *New York Times,* January 3, 1947, 21; "Mrs. Oscar T. Crosby," *New York Times,* January 16, 1934, 22; "Mrs. Hornblow, 73, a Former Actress," *New York Times,* May 3, 1969, 35.

64. "Mrs. Oscar T. Crosby," 22; "Mrs. Hornblow, 73, a Former Actress," 35.

65. Aldine R. Bird, "Wins Fund Song Test," *Baltimore News Post,* November 14, 1939, 17; "Noted Musician Dies; Father of Local Residents," *Smithfield* [Va.] *Times,* November 18, 1954, 1.

66. "Col. Pihl, Husband of Arline Maxwell, Dies at Jacksonville, Fla.," *Malden* [Mass.] *Evening News,* May 1, 1933, n.p.; "Jaxon Is Dead," *Jacksonville Journal,* May 1, 1933, 3; "Long Illness Takes Life of Colonel Pihl," *Florida Times-Union,* May 1, 1933, 9, 13; "Colonel Pihl to Be Buried at Malden," *Florida Times-Union,* May 2, 1933, 13; "Col. Carl M. Pihl," *New York Times,* May 2, 1933, 18; telephone interview with Murphy Thigpenn, Jacksonville, Fla., May 5, 1987.

67. "Big Organ for Ocean Grove," *New York Times,* January 4, 1908, 9.

68. "Denver's Mighty Municipal Organ," *Denver Municipal Facts,* March 1918, I:1, 4; "Reynolds, New Organist for City, Arrives Feb. 1," *Denver News,* January 6, 1918, 3; "Why Organ Recitals Are Popular in Denver," *Denver Municipal Facts,* July-August 1927, XI:7–8, 13–14; "Ex–City Organist, C. Reynolds, 69, Dies in California," *Denver Post,* September 19, 1949, 20.

69. Marion Knight, *A Comet Among the Stars,* New York: Pageant Press, 1953, 53–54, 71–75, 1–2.

70. "Elliott Schenck, Composer, Was 69," *New York Times,* March 6, 1939, 15.

71. Elliott Schenck, " 'Contradictions' in the Bible," letter to the editor, *New York Times,* July 30, 1923, 12; "Contradictions in the Bible," letters to the editor, *New York Times,* August 5, 1923, pt. 6, 6; Elliott Schenck, "The First Man," letter to the editor, *New York Times,* September 8, 1929, pt. 5, 5.

72. Elliott Schenck, "The Treatment of Americans," letter to the editor, *New York Times,* March 16, 1924, pt. 8, 6; *vide infra* Observer, "The Lot of

American Musicians," letter to the editor, *New York Times,* March 23, 1924, pt. 8, 6.

73. "Elliott Schenck, Composer, Was 69," 15.

74. "Norwegian Artist Succumbs," *Darien* [Conn.] *Review,* January 5, 1961, 3; Christian Schiott, *Christian Schiott: Klavier-Virtuose,* Berlin: The Author, 1912, J.S.

75. John K. Shaw and James Piper, Executors of the Estate of Frederick C. Todd, Petition, December 13, 1918, filed and recorded January 6, 1919, Baltimore County Orphans Court, Baltimore, Md., "Baltimore County Orphans Court: Proceedings, WJP #28," Maryland State Archives CR 255, 93–94; John K. Shaw and James Piper, Executors of the Estate of Frederick C. Todd, Assets of Estate, May 19, 1919, filed and recorded May 22, 1919, Baltimore County Orphans Court, Baltimore, Md., "Baltimore County: Inventories, WJP #43," Maryland State Archives CR 9107, 55; William M. Dabney, M.D., Certificate of Death of Frederick Charles Todd, November 10, 1918, filed at the Maryland Department of Health, Annapolis, Md., Certificate no. 42445, Maryland State Archives; "Death of F.C. Todd," *Charlottesville Daily Progress,* November 11, 1918, 1.

76. " 'Mary's Lamb' Well Liked at Olympic," *Newark Evening News,* August 3, 1916, N.Y.P.L.T., n.p.

77. " 'Bringing Up Father,' " *Variety,* December 29, 1916, 14.

78. "Isabelle Winlocke," list of plays, typewritten, n.n., n.d., N.Y.P.L.T.; "Isabel Winlock," *Variety,* October 14, 1953, 95; "Miss Isabel Winlock," *New York Times,* October 11, 1953, sec. 1, 89.

CHAPTER IX

LOOKING BACKWARD AT THE TELHARMONIUM

ASSESSMENTS BY OTHER INVENTORS

Although descriptions of Cahill's accomplishments almost routinely inaugurate even the briefest histories of electronic music synthesizers, it devolves finally upon his successors, persons of his own profession, to measure today Cahill's ultimate standing in the technical domain.

The first such inventor to assess Cahill's work was Benjamin F. Miessner (1890–1976), a distinguished radio pioneer. Having sold his basic radio patents, which eliminated hum from vacuum tubes, to RCA in 1930 for $750,000, Miessner opened up a laboratory that year and set out to build the stringless electric piano. His efforts were successful, and Miessner licensed nearly the entire electronic piano industry by the early 1940s. In the 1950s, he devised improvements that became the basis of the Wurlitzer electronic piano.[1]

Barely two years after Cahill's death, in a fundamental treatise on generating and controlling musical tones electronically, Miessner wrote:

> Probably the earliest and most important of all the early schemes for making music electrically were those proposed and used by the American, Thaddeus Cahill, in his Telharmonium.
>
> In Cahill's patents lie the broad foundation stones of all the rotating generator, synthetic timbre control instruments. He had a truly amazing and profound knowledge of the principles of this art that he was founding over thirty-five years ago. Nearly all that is fundamentally important today in instruments of this type, Cahill understood and utilized.[2]

Hugh Le Caine (1914–1977) was a Canadian inventor noted for his work in the 1940s on the first radar systems and in atomic physics. He also pursued an avid interest in electronic music, and from 1954 to 1974 worked full time on musical inventions at the National Research Council of Canada. A number of his instruments formed the basis for two early electronic music studios, at the University of Toronto (opened in 1959) and McGill University (opened in 1964). His designs were so advanced in their features of nuance and control, their "playability," that only in 1985 did they begin to be utilized in commercial designs.[3]

> In 1955, Le Caine acknowledged that Cahill . . . in 1895 drew up the first comprehensive scheme for a completely electrical instrument. . . . his auditors were amazed at the ease of control of loudness which this apparatus afforded the performer . . . Musicians were impressed by the stability of the tuning; in spite of the fact that . . . means for controlling the frequency of alternators were comparatively undeveloped.[4]

Harald Bode (1909–1987) began building electronic keyboard instruments in Germany in the late 1930s. His Melochord was employed at several major broadcast studios in West Germany in the late 1940s and early 1950s, including the Stockhausen studio in Cologne. From the 1960s to the 1980s, Bode designed ring modulators, frequency shifters, vocoders, and phasers that found wide acceptance among electronic musicians.[5]

Bode wrote, "Means for modifying electrically generated sound have been known since the late 19th century, when Thaddeus Cahill created his Telharmonium."[6] Regarding "instruments whose sound modification devices formed an integral part of the entire system,"[7] Bode observed, "A classic case is the Telharmonium, by Thaddeus Cahill . . . This instrument used the principle of additive tone synthesis for sound manipulation and modification."[8] Bode also pointed out, "The Hammond organ is of special interest, since it evolved from Cahill's work."[9]

Although Hammond organ inventor Laurens Hammond scrupulously acknowledged no debt to Cahill (Cahill's last patent was still in force at the time of Hammond's 1934 patent), others besides Bode have posited a strong link:

> The outstanding example [of rotating magnetic generators] is the Hammond generator, first produced in 1935 although anticipated as long ago as 1897 by Thaddeus Cahill.[10]

It was this configuration [tone wheels] that permitted
Laurens Hammond, with chief engineer John Hanert, to
update Thaddeus Cahill's patented 1897 system of large
rotating tone generators and turn from clock-maker to organ
builder in the 1930s.[11]

The aforementioned inventors were directly involved at one time
or another with additive synthesis, which originated with Cahill.
The analog synthesizers developed since the 1960s employ subtrac-
tive synthesis. A seminal figure in the advance of these instruments
is Robert A. Moog (b. 1934), who has commented on Thaddeus
Cahill and his work.

> Thaddeus Cahill, developer of the Telharmonium, was . . .
> endowed with the ability to think big. Although not strictly
> electronic (it predated the invention of the vacuum tube by
> about a decade), the Telharmonium embodied many basic
> principles that have been used in the electronic music medium:
> the generation of pitched tones from alternating electricity, the
> addition of harmonics to determine tone color (additive synthe-
> sis), and a touch sensitive keyboard to shape the sounds and
> control their strengths. This first polyphonic, touch sensitive
> music synthesizer remained in service in New York for only a
> few years . . . The basic idea was resurrected again in the 1930s
> in an instrument that was somewhat more of a commercial
> success: the Hammond Organ.[12]

Clearly, Cahill's station is one of acknowledged recognition and
esteem by his peers and successors. To this day they remember and
commend his work. Although additive synthesis has proved the road
less traveled in recent times, the promise of digitally controlled
resynthesizers may soon reopen the very trajectory charted first by
Thaddeus Cahill nearly a century ago.

THE SPIRIT OF THE AGE

The extraordinary diversity of American culture in the late nineteenth and early twentieth centuries spawned a robust eclecticism in
the arts. Uniting with the advance of entrepreneurial capitalism,

with the vision of creating a cornucopia of plenty, a new idea of commercial/art music became embodied in the Telharmonium. In a single distribution scheme, from only one source, here was art music to serve high culture, yet here was also entertainment music featuring show tunes, popular songs, and ragtime. Here also was sober religious music to usher in Lent. Here too were functional musics, assuming roles that could make money: sleep music, dinner music, music to keep factory laborers working and department store customers happy, music to divert hotel dwellers and theatregoers. Here was omnifarious music of every stripe and color except extended form: to accommodate variety, or opportunism, only short selections were played.

While in retrospect these conflicting characteristics and applications might suggest a confused excess of pragmatism, this multiplicity of uses was in fact a reflection of wide public interest and thus a sound business decision by the inventor and the backers of the Telharmonium. We do know that Cahill's own visions of the machine assumed the widest popular public usage. Although he had voiced bitter complaints about not getting a franchise before 1906 and about the expense of installing Telharmonic Hall in the heart of the theatre district, he had no objections to the economic and artistic management by others of his instrument. It was being exploited exactly as designed and intended. Restless energy and disorderly variety were the symptoms of the new vitality in American culture. The Telharmonium and its owners were a part of this optimistic spirit of diversity.

NERVOUS DISORDERS IN MODERN SOCIETY

The modern age brought new maladies along with its boring assembly-line factories, its sprawling and fragmented urban centers, and its complex technologies. Society was becoming more alienated and impersonal. Greater specialization brought with it increased social interdependence, yet the sense of community was being lost. Understanding and adjusting to this new life was a tall order. No wonder nervousness and insomnia became the new complaints heard everywhere.

The Telharmonium had a small healing role to play amid these anxieties. Individual isolation, sleeplessness, and nervous ills would succumb to soothing strains, thanks to Thaddeus Cahill's enlightened advocacy of electric sleep-music on tap in the home at any hour of the day or night. In addition, the service could be brought right to the workplace, providing bored and alienated employees with diversion to enhance their productivity and improve their morale.

Furthermore, it was natural for a device in the technological vanguard to be used at a revival service addressing spiritual crisis. Present-day evangelists are no slower than the Reverend Henry Marsh Warren in embracing newfangled contraptions. No doubt the Telharmonium's use at Lent helped to interest customers and publicize the instrument. Nevertheless, it was another use of new technology as a palliative for the deepening ills of society. What other instrument could have been employed as a glorified church organ in so many houses of nonworship simultaneously?

MIDDLE CULTURE

After the Civil War, the dissonances between coarse mass culture and refined high culture began to entangle as a new counterpoint. The stratum of a middle culture had formed to follow the modes of high culture, yet it lacked artistic quality. The result became veneer and cheap imitation. The purveyors were artists whose talent or training proved to be mediocre or who had succumbed to the financial rewards of the mercantilistic midcultural bazaar. The most glaring indications of middle culture were a dearth of aesthetic sense—good taste—and a tendency toward the overblown, the affected, and the grandiloquent. Money was its god, and the incorrigible venality of middle culture corroded its production.[13]

The Telharmonium at first emulated all the trappings of classical music (even to its installation across from the Metropolitan Opera House—which itself existed as much for finery and show as for music), but it could not evoke the substance. Built on an overly grand scale to make huge sums of money, it was introduced uncompleted at the behest of its backers. The Telharmonium presented but a limited number of classical selections, and these became fewer as time went on. All were brief, tuneful, and hence accessible or at least tolerable to the general public. Then, as public interest waned, the promoters tried to revive flagging attention by attaching wires or diaphragms to doorknobs, lily pads, and human bodies. As even the pretense of high culture finally wore off, it was no wonder that several newspapers switched their Telharmonium coverage from music columns to theatre or vaudeville columns. Nonetheless, such high jinks could not hope to compete with other developing technologies of mass diversion. Some of these were also hugely successful for a time and then faded into oblivion, notably the player piano and coin-operated mechanical music machines. Others, such as sound recordings and motion pictures, grew to become prominent features of our culture—high, middle, and low—then and now.

THE BOTTOM LINE

The massive economic development of America in the late nineteenth century led to the ascendancy of business competition as a dominant and omnipresent component of our culture. The country's breakneck growth, abundant natural resources, flowing supply of immigrant workers, expansion of production, new transportation networks, and restlessly mobile population—all fueled the headlong, motoric rush to market.

The ambitions for the Telharmonium were part of this development. The malleability of American culture under the dominance of a business ethic gave rise to distribution of live music as big business. Admittedly, the electric music corporations were never developed on the successful scale of the great trusts. No notable moguls or robber barons engineered the enterprise, only the minor capitalist Oscar T. Crosby, builder of electric street railways and power plants. Yet his and Cahill's ambition was to establish a utility matching the popularity and pervasiveness of the telephone, and the sums the two marshalled towards that end were not inconsiderable.

It is possible to estimate the total cost of all three Telharmoniums and their promotion. First, we know that the New York and New England Electric Music Cos. raised a total of $890,400 in capital.

The Cahill Music-Patents Trust probably sold at least $127,000 in shares to Crosby and Todd. These two entrepreneurs also apparently put around $38,150 into the Pacific Coast Telharmonic Co. and $198,000 into the Eastern Cahill Telharmonic Co. We may then estimate conservatively that the three Telharmonic corporations formed in 1906 and 1907 took in at least $100,000 apiece. That would represent a total investment by 1908 of well over $1 million—$1,554,150 to be exact. Finally, there were Thaddeus Cahill's expenditures to fuel the comeback of the instrument from 1908 to 1914. We know that by 1911 Cahill had completely expended his license-derived fortune of $200,000 to build the third Telharmonium. Its erection in New York and all subsequent cash expenditures were likely funded by the $145,583 debt reported at bankruptcy for the New York Cahill Telharmonic Co.

The total expenses from 1902 to 1914 thus amounted to some $1,899,733. The approximate value of this sum can be expressed in modern currency, based on consumer price indexes then and now. Although that measure was somewhat imperfect before 1935, it is the best information we have. In average 1991 dollars, the Telharmonic capital investment was worth $28,367,800.[14]

TECHNOLOGY AND SOCIETY

An idea advanced in the Introduction to this study was the persistence of the myth that technology is an autonomous and inevitable march to perfection. Its makers assert that technology is independent and value neutral, needing no outside justification. Yet, technology is a realized representation of human thought and an accomplishment of human purpose. An increasing body of belief holds that the tools of progress ought to be managed attentively and analyzed prudently in social terms. Technology not only causes social changes, it also arises from them, or from the desire for them, in the first place. Its developments do not just automatically and independently more or less appear in the common run of things. The inescapable implication is that technology must be assessed on two levels—its social validity as well as its intrinsic effectiveness. The means are judged for technical skill, and the ends are judged on a higher level of appropriateness to the values and needs of society.[15]

The view of technology as a variable that stems from and interacts with society suggests that comparative analysis would illuminate this intertwining relationship. The origin and development of the Telharmonium is a clear case in point. For centuries, the art of music was expressed using implements. The expressive power of such hand-held instruments as the violin grew directly from their extension of the human body and its capabilities. Other instruments, such as keyboards, were more elaborately mechanized, and produced a more attenuated range of expression. (A keyboard tone struck by a novice and a virtuoso sound the same; on a violin, the difference is readily apparent.) The only instrument not powered by the performer was the pipe organ, widely regarded as the least expressive of instruments. It was the "king of instruments" largely because of its magnificent sound pressure level, sufficient to fill 5,000-seat cathedrals. Expressive power, then, took a back seat in this specific sociocultural setting. Music used for one specific purpose, such as worship services for a large gathering, did not need to meet the same standards as music used for another purpose, such as art music in a small chamber hall.

Electrically transmitted music conveyed to loudspeakers was a technical innovation similarly bound to occur in a specific setting. That was the unprecedented growth of urban public gatherings for various specifically nonmusical purposes, at which music could be provided as a background entertainment. For the Telharmonium, these fell into three practical categories: (1) fancy restaurants, which already provided many hours daily of live music; (2) theatres, whose patrons gathered in the lobby before the show and during intermission, where music could serve as a lure and control; and, (3) smaller gathering places, such as doctors' and dentists' waiting rooms, barber shops, and the like, where patrons could be soothed by the charms of music or distracted by its novelty. Private "gatherings" created another venue that demanded mass music. The huge new Plaza Hotel, built in 1907, had every room wired for Telharmonic music, although none was ever supplied. Another proposed mass use, musical arc lighting of factories and department stores, never approached feasibility. The Telharmonium, then, was built specifically to supply these new assemblages of the metropolitan population. Its inherently limited expressive powers were sacrificed even further in order to produce gargantuan instruments for serving up widely disseminated music. The needs of society in this context radically influenced the scope and effectiveness of the technology, as well as defined its purpose and validity.

It was easily possible for the Telharmonium to have appeared in Europe. Comparative analysis may again shed light on why this did not happen, on why it appeared only in America at the end of the nineteenth century. The old European aristocracy was being replaced by a new elite, supported not by lineage but by wealth. Members of this new elite attained social legitimacy and retained social rank by behaving aristocratically. They carefully reproduced the behavior of their predecessors. With such concern for traditional form, there was little place for electrically generated music. After all, the Telefon-Hirmondó and the Electrohome delivered not electric music but the traditional sounds heard in the concert halls and theatres of Budapest and London. The masses of immigrants to America, however, fueled a new ruling class also based on property, but with no nobility to imitate. The rich were more free to express their social importance in new ways, such as being entertained by the great Telharmonium instead of ordinary live musicians. To many less-critical, undeveloped ears, the rather awkward musical expression sounded right good enough. It was simple, cheap, democratic, and up-to-date. And it could be sold to everyone—for only Americans believe that there is a universal market for new technologies, be they player pianos, phonographs, movies, automobiles, or computers. In short, to look at the development of American technology of music production and distribution is to look inescapably at American social development as well. The two are inextricably enmeshed.

It is difficult not to speculate how different this history would have been had Cahill decided to build and sell small Telharmoniums—the first electric organs. Recalling that the smaller first model had more responsive control and fewer sound problems, we can safely presume that such more perfectable instruments would have found favor with some musicians and composers. Music, perhaps even some great music, would have been written especially for the instrument, making use of its unique sound qualities. Varèse, after all, was ready for the Telharmonium in 1916. And a few machines would have survived to the present day.

In fact a road very much like this was traveled by the builders of another new instrument of the day, the Choralcelo. This early-1900s organlike hybrid mechanical-electrical instrument used vibrating strings and reeds, bars of wood, steel, aluminum, and glass, and buggy springs for the bass. Today two instruments survive, only one playable in part; neither has been reconstructed. The few known to have existed were used in private homes in Chicago, Cleveland, Denver, and Englewood, N.J., at a retreat house in Niagara Falls, and at a mountain lodge in New Paltz, N.Y.; another was installed on a yacht.[16] Such could well have been the fate of the Telharmonium.

Had such a scenario reflected the mission of Thaddeus Cahill, we would have gained some surviving instruments of real interest and no doubt some music. We would, however, have lost some fascinating reflections of the beginning of the modern age. The energetic commercial exploitation by Oscar T. Crosby, the establishment of Telharmonic Hall as a central station to transmit many varieties of electric music, the contract and falling-out with the New York Telephone Co., the radio broadcasts by Lee de Forest, the establishment of seven highly capitalized corporations, the pursuit and capture of the Pyrrhic franchise from New York City—none of these phenomena, groundbreaking in the history of musical instruments, would have occurred had Thaddeus Cahill been a solitary instrument builder. Yet the social settings and nascent demands for music as a background entertainment were seen and heeded by others besides Cahill, and one of those schemes would inevitably have arisen to transmit music by wire in America. And it probably would have been just as typically American as the Telharmonium—big, slightly crazy, and unable to work exactly as planned.

NOTES

1. Thomas LaMar Rhea, "The Evolution of Electronic Musical Instruments in the United States," Ph.D. dissertation, George Peabody College for Teachers, 1972, 107–109, 114, 117–119. The $750,000,000 cited in Rhea is a misprint. Telephone conversation with Thomas LaMar Rhea, July 21, 1988.

2. Benjamin F. Miessner, "Electronic Music and Instruments," *Proceedings of the Institute of Radio Engineers,* November 1936, 24:11, 1441–1442.

3. Gayle Young, "Hugh Le Caine: Pioneer in Electronic Music Instrument Design," liner notes, stereo 33⅓-rpm record No. JWD-02, JWD Music, 1985.

4. Hugh Le Caine, "Electronic Music," *Proceedings of the Institute of Radio Engineers,* April 1956, 44:4, 458.

5. Harald Bode, "History of Electronic Sound Modification," *Journal of the Audio Engineering Society,* October 1984, 32:10, 730, 732, 733, 735, 736, 739.

6. *Ibid.,* 730.

7. *Ibid.*

8. *Ibid.*

9. *Ibid.*

10. G. A. Briggs, *Musical Instruments and Audio,* Idle, England: Wharfedale Wireless Works, 1965, 172.

11. Edward Peterson, "The Rich History of the Electric Organ," *Keyboard,* November 1983, 9:11, 32.

12. Robert A. Moog, "Electronic Music," *Journal of the Audio Engineering Society,* October/November 1977, 25:10/11, 856.

13. A penetrating description of middle culture may be found in Stow Persons, *The Decline of American Gentility,* New York: Columbia University Press, 1973, 99–103.

14. Calculated by breaking down figures into annual expenditures and multiplying each by a multiplier obtained by dividing the annual average 1991 consumer price index by the cost of living index of the year of the expenditure. Gary A. Greene, "Understanding Past Currency in Modern Terms," *Sonneck Society Bulletin,* Summer 1987 XIII:2, 48; Standard & Poor's Statistical Service, "Cost of Living Indexes," *Basic Statistics: Price Indexes: Commodities, Producer, Cost of Living,* 1988, 54:4, sec. 2, 76; "Consumer Price Index for All Urban Consumers," *Monthly Labor Review,* January 1991, 114:1, 102, and March 1992, 115:3, 75.

15. These ideas are developed luminously by W. G. L. De Haas, "Technology as a Subject of Comparative Studies: The Case of Photography," *Comparative Studies of Society and History,* July 1979, 21:3, 362–371.

16. Edith Borroff, "An Early Electro-Magnetic Experiment," *College Music Symposium,* Spring 1979, 19:1, 54–59: Edith Boroff, "The Choralcelo: One Uniquely American Instrument," *College Music Symposium,* Spring 1982, 22:1, 46–54.

APPENDIX 1

THE FOUR LATER TELHARMONIUM PATENTS

THE SECOND TELHARMONIUM PATENT: 1,107,261

On February 10, 1902, Cahill filed a new patent application. This was a division, or extension, of his original 1895 application. As a result, he was not allowed to describe any new designs, only improvements that amounted to equivalents of the devices illustrated in the drawings of the original document.[1]

The primary improvement in this application was the use of ac dynamos, or alternators, in place of rheotomes to produce sound vibrations of far greater power. Again they were mounted on twelve belt-driven pitch-shafts, one for each note in the chromatic scale. The toothed alternator rotor was constructed of laminated plates of soft iron. The design was simple and cheap, with no moving wires or moving connections. These dynamos could not produce perfect sine waves, so their waveforms were to be purified, and weakened, by inductive transfer. The transformers employed to filter the notes below middle C could be of the economical iron-core type. The higher notes, and the tone-mixing circuits, however, required air-core transformers. The latter were costlier because a greater number of turns of expensive copper wire were needed to substitute for the iron cores. The receivers were specified as any of the well-known common telephone types, or as a wooden soundboard driven by an electromagnet. They did not, Cahill noted, have to produce vibrations as complex as those of speech, but they had to be able to deliver a loud volume.[2]

The response from examiner Charles H. Lane was to reject many of Cahill's claims as indefinite, particularly where the phrases "shafts corresponding to notes" and "alternators caused to sound notes" or "to produce notes" appeared. Lane felt that the descriptions linking Cahill's shafts to his alternators, then to his waveforms and finally to his notes, were technically vague. After all, notes could be produced only by vibration frequencies, not alternators. Occasionally the terminology could result in an interpretation that Cahill was claiming any group of ordinary ac power-station alternators as his device. Lane also rejected a few claims as having trespassed on Berliner or Van Rysselberghe.[3]

It was fully a year before Cahill replied to Lane's objections. He defended his wording of "alternators corresponding to notes" as analogous to the common designations of organ pipes and piano or violin strings. He also pointed out that the Berliner and Van Rysselberghe patents were for completely different inventions with no alternators or shafts of any sort.[4]

Too vague, responded examiner Henry Blandy to the use of the word "corresponding." It merely denoted a mental association and had no clear structural or functional meaning. Furthermore, some of Cahill's claims were so indefinite as to impinge on Berliner.[5] Cahill's amendments and the examiner's objections proceeded at the rate of one exchange per year. To prolong the life of a patent, it was customary for an inventor to postpone its issue by taking the full year allowed by statute to reply to a letter from the Patent Office. Finally, by 1909, all of the wording had been hammered out, with the exception of one insoluble problem: the use of the phrase "said alternators" to refer to alternators described in a previous clause. The relationship between the alternators in the two clauses, objected the examiners year after year, was not positive and specific.[6]

Cahill retorted pithily, "It is not fitting that the applicant should introduce into his claims unnecessary limitations or load them up with idle tautology."[7] He appealed to the commissioner.[8] After repeated postponements, an oral hearing before Commissioner Moore was held on October 10, 1911. Edward B. Moore was emphatic in his annoyance over the delays in prosecuting the case. Unvexed, Cahill reminded him that the Patent Office itself had delayed the hearing for a year. Furthermore, if he were not sustained, Cahill threatened to continue to prosecute the case, submitting amendments of his numerous claims as required, which would certainly delay the application further.[9] Commissioner Moore gave in to Cahill, remarking that the case had been pending for nearly ten years because Cahill was not represented by an attorney and was reluctant to comply with well-recognized requirements.[10] Furthermore, he conceded that "the position taken by applicant concerning formal matters will apparently keep the case pending indefinitely before the office."[11] While not in the best form, the claims would be properly construed by the courts, so there was no point in delaying issue of the patent.[12]

By 1912 Cahill was involved in establishing a second Telharmonium in New York. He delayed the issuance of the patent until he could supply a list of cross-references to copending applications to be included in the text. He did not manage to do this until August 1, 1914.[13] The patent was finally issued later that month.

THE THIRD TELHARMONIUM PATENT: 1,213,803

The scope of Cahill's improvements in Telharmonic design became so extensive that it grew necessary to rewrite and then finally divide the massive 140-claim patent application he had submitted on January 19, 1901. He reapplied on February 26, 1903, and then prepared seven divisional applications covering all of his claims a year later, on February 16, 1904.[14] Only four were eventually accepted after 13 years. The applications described and illustrated largely the same working apparatus; they differed primarily in the statements of claims.[15]

In this application Cahill cited four of the original features of his first patent, 580,035, and the improvements he had devised thereto: toothed gearing, direct production of virtual sine waves, a telephonic vibration-translating device (receiver), and independent wiring of the alternator electromagnets (see Chapter III above).

PROSECUTING THE THIRD PATENT

The Patent Office responded to the application with routine requests that the claims be related to those in the parent application, and that Cahill demarcate the various divisional applications.[16] The inventor replied in a year less one day.[17]

As in earlier cases, the Patent Office then objected to the use of the word "corresponding" and rejected some of the claims as having trespassed not only on various telephone patents, but this time also on Cahill's own first patent.[18] The inventor waited until a year had gone by, again less one day, and filed an amendment. He argued to retain "corresponding," since it was unambiguous to those who understood the Telharmonium.[19] Furthermore, "some liberality in the use of language is necessary in dealing with a radically new thing."[20] And finally, he asserted that no less than one former commissioner and two former assistant commissioners, now working as patent attorneys, had advised that the language was accurate and could suggest no improvement.[21]

The Patent Office waived some of its objections and insisted on others.[22] One day before a year had gone by, Cahill filed an amendment insisting on the use of "corresponding," since its use in the claim would be clear to those knowledgeable in the specifications of the invention. He also disputed the relevance of the telephone patents cited by the Patent Office—these, he asserted, were for a nonanalogous art, the transmission of the human voice and not of vibrations created by running machinery.[23]

The Patent Office held fast to its objections, maintaining that "corresponding" was indefinite and that, in the disputed claims, it was immaterial how the electrical vibrations had been produced, for they were being converted into audible sound by a device no different than a telephone.[24]

Exactly one year later Cahill's next amendment reached the Patent Office. He propounded the familiar argument that a shaft could "correspond" to a note of a scale just as could a string or organ pipe. As for the telephone patents, these were analogous to only one element of his invention, which had to be considered in its entirety.[25]

The Patent Office was not convinced and refused to budge from its side of the standoff.[26] Two days short of another year, Cahill submitted another amendment again requesting that the objection to "corresponding," which had already been waived in several claims, be further waived in the several remaining claims that he felt unable to reword. Cahill capitulated to the demands that the telephone claims be dropped, provided that other differences between him and the Patent Office could be eliminated.[27] Before an examiner could respond to this latest amendment, Cahill applied for an oral conference to resolve the impasse.[28] It did not. Shortly after the interview Cahill submitted an amendment with ten new claims.[29] The Patent Office refused again to accept most of the claims earlier rejected and turned down six of the new ones.[30] Cahill fought back again, filing an amendment two days shy of another year, defending his right not to accede to the examiner's demands in this case even though he had already done so in other cases. He pointed out that similar use of the word "corresponding" had been accepted in his own patent no. 580,035.[31] Cahill's citation, retorted the examiner, "shows how indefinite the word 'corresponding' is and that it was an inadvertence to allow such claims."[32] He suggested that Cahill petition the commissioner, as the examiner had no intention of allowing the claims.[33] Precisely another year went by, and Cahill filed another lengthy amendment, with rewritten claims and requests for reconsideration.[34] The response was to assail his entire application as "prolix and repetitious,"[35] and to stipulate many passages as needing to be condensed. The previously rejected claims were again refused, with a warning: "All the above requirements, objections and rejections are made *final;* complete and proper response to all of them must be made in the next action or within one year from this date to save the case from abandonment."[36]

Cahill again timed his reply to be filed exactly one year later, asserting that "it is obviously safer and better to err on the side of fullness than on that of brevity."[37] He offered some amendments to shorten the text and reserved the right to appeal the disputed claims, while amending 30 others and rewriting 11 more.[38]

The next month Cahill delivered himself of a furious rebuttal to the examiner's unwarranted exercise of power. He reminded his adversary that under the law Cahill was allowed one year to respond to an action of the Patent Office. In 1897 the Supreme Court had upheld the right of the American Bell Telephone Co. to keep a pending application in the Patent Office for many years, when it was already profiting lucratively from the invention. An applicant had every right to take the full time stipulated by statute. Cahill, however, angrily asserted that he was doing no such booming business, having by this time

> expended more than two hundred thousand dollars ($200,000) of his own money in developing his art, without having reached the stage of commercial operations nor the enjoyment of any income from it; but is, on the contrary, under the

constant necessity of putting money into it, in order to perfect it and make it thoroughly commercial.[39]

The life of a patent was 17 years from the date of its issue, preceded by whatever time the application had been pending in the Patent Office, preceded by a two-year limit in which to make the application. These were statutory provisions which the examiner could not abrogate. Furthermore, many of the formal requirements made in the examiner's last letter were made for the first time. Cahill tenaciously asserted his lawful entitlement to seek reconsideration from the examiner, and then to petition the commissioner, and finally to wait until all matters of new requirements and reconsiderations were settled before going to appeal.[40]

The chastened Patent Office made no further mention of final demands, but did not budge from its prior rejections.[41] Cahill waited the customary full year, then filed an amendment satisfactory to the office. The final arguments were reduced to very technical jousts over the wording of claims relating to subcombinations of the apparatus. Cahill reasserted the claims relating to telephone apparatus, but accepted their demise without appeal.[42] The patent was allowed two months later, on December 28, 1914.[43]

By this time the New York Cahill Telharmonic Co. had gone bankrupt. The impoverished Cahill allowed the approved application to expire by failing to pay the required fee, then resuscitated the patent by paying a $15 renewal fee in 1916.[44] A few days later he remitted the final fee of $20.[45] The patent was issued on January 23, 1917.[46]

THE FOURTH TELHARMONIUM PATENT: 1,213,804

One of the seven divisional applications Cahill filed in 1904, which were carved out of his 1901 application, was allowed by the Patent Office in 1914, and then forfeited by Cahill in 1915, several months after his company's bankruptcy.[47] Its resuscitation enabled the inventor to submit a partially rewritten application consisting of three parts, one old and two new. The first section was the text of the 1904 British patent[48] he had applied for in 1903.[49] They embodied two of the seven divisional applications of 1904. The second and third parts were new material, the results of twelve years of experience in building and operating his Telharmoniums. With his enterprise in ruins, public adulation a receding memory, and press coverage consequently nonexistent, this was his last remaining forum to disclose the techniques and improvements he had devised to eliminate or at least attenuate the defects and difficulties of his designs.[50]

Since the Patent Office does not preserve correspondence pertaining to applications that have been forfeited, there are no records of how Cahill prosecuted the original application from 1904 to its allowance in 1914. The rewritten application was initially refused as having already been passed upon by the Patent Office, then allowed after Cahill explained the situation to the commissioner in an interview in 1916.[51]

Part One

Cahill listed nine improvements over his first patent.[52] Some of these could also be found in the second and third patents, while others were quite new:

1) Toothed gearing to drive the alternator shafts.
2) Production of several harmonics from one single generator, *viz.*: from one upper fundamental generator, e.g., the second, fourth, eighth, and sixteenth harmonics of lower-octave fundamentals; similarly, from a third-partial generator, the third, sixth, and twelfth harmonics of various fundamentals; and, from a fifth-partial generator, the fifth and tenth harmonics.
3) Generation of waveforms very similar to the sine wave, so that almost no filtering was needed; the small amount required was provided by the mixing and expression circuits.
4) Use of a telephone receiver fitted with a horn.
5) A loudness control on the premises of the subscriber.
6) A separate switched circuit for each harmonic, so that each could be controlled independently.
7) Key switches controlled by a pneumatic power device instead of by direct action, enabling a light and rapid touch.
8) Independent circuits to the excitation windings of the alternators, with a rheostat on each circuit, allowing the alternators to be varied independently.

9) Instead of the pianolike expression control of the first patent, in which the loudness of each note was independently controllable, expression devices that more resembled a pipe organ, thus:

(*a*) A plurality of keyboards, all supplied from one set of vibration-generating devices.

(*b*) Means for the performer to alter the timbre at will.

(*c*) Loudness devices common to all the notes of a keyboard.

(*d*) Independent timbral and loudness alterations for each keyboard.

(*e*) Independently acting electrical swell devices.

(*f*) A dynamic manual consisting of a keyboard wherein each key corresponded to a different degree of loudness, so the performer could govern volume by accurate degrees and change instantly from one degree to another. This was a timely resurrection of Cahill's 1887 organ patent.

The great advantages of his new design, claimed Cahill, were its abilities: to produce more than one kind of timbre and expression simultaneously; to emphasize the melody while the accompaniment was subdued; to increase or decrease the note of a chord by playing it upon a different keyboard; and, to produce a great variety of other effects, many heretofore unknown.[53]

Cahill specified a series of resistive impedance coils instead of simple resistors in the circuits controlling the volume levels of the tone-partials, the electrical swell, the dynamic manual, and the receivers. He was careful to vary the inductance and resistance in equal proportions, thereby avoiding time-constant differences between coils, which would filter out some frequencies more than others.[54] One advantage of switching a resistive coil into a circuit was a slightly smoother, slower, more transient-free change in loudness. The coils were also useful in suppressing unwanted partials of supposedly pure harmonics and in reducing the upper products of harmonic distortion and intermodulation distortion. More importantly, the coils served to maintain current flow within narrower limits than equivalent resistance circuits so that large signal variations in one part of the system would not disrupt another signal somewhere else.[55] Unlike pure resistors, coils did not drain energy from the circuits.

In the mixing transformers, where the ten individual harmonic circuits were combined into one composite signal, Cahill built transformers in which ten primary coil circuits were wound around a single core, interspersed with multiple layers of the secondary winding, for maximum induction.[56]

The movable inductors of the first patent, controlling the loudness of each key, were no longer possible in such a large machine. In having to carry enormous currents, they would be far too heavy and cumbersome to respond to the performer's touch.[57] Of the numerous possible modifications to the basic design—different types of alternators, transformers, etc.—the only one for which he indicated a preference was the use of alternators with more teeth for the higher pitch-shafts. This enabled the angular velocities of these pitch-shafts to be reduced, providing a more stable rotation. Cahill recommended that the rotor teeth of the six upper pitch-shafts be increased by one-third to one-half, and the shafts be correspondingly geared to rotate more slowly, resulting in the production of the desired frequencies of the chromatic scale.[58]

Even though he was in fact building an instrument that could play in just intonation as well as equal temperament, he did not include this complication in his patent description. There was mention of just intonation as a separate design, using the seven diatonic tones only, for an instrument that could play in a single key. He disclaimed any perfect thirds and fifths in the equal-tempered version.[59]

Part Two

In this section of the patent, Cahill discussed the feasibility and desirability of using some features of the instrument and not others. He noted again that the harmonics in his system were not apt to be completely sinusoidal in actual practice.[60]

Part Three

"Good commercial music involves close attention to many things,"[61] wrote Thaddeus Cahill in this supplement to his patent description, and proceeded to give the benefit of his experience in operating a commercial system in New York.

First, the receivers left much to be desired. If the expense could be borne, Cahill suggested a multiple set of lines and receivers, one for each harmonic. It was a complicated matter, and further designs would be found in three patent applications of 1908 and 1909—none of which was granted.[62]

Second, it was important to locate the performer in an acoustically isolated room, away from the alternators, switchboards, and transformers.[63]

Third, the receivers exhibited the problem known as "shouting"—certain notes were reproduced with such excessive loudness as to ruin the musical effect. The pitches were not always consistent—at one time a particular note would shout, then later a different one. Cahill diagnosed the phenomenon as due to (1) diaphragm resonances, (2) changes in diaphragm resonant frequencies due to shifts in temperature, and (3) variations in the running speed of the driveshaft. To eliminate the defect Cahill recommended (1) regulating by rheostat the voltage provided to each alternator, (2) varying the numbers of coils on each armature for each harmonic circuit, so that the individual harmonics from one alternator could be separately voiced, (3) establishing a uniform design of receiver with a dependably set resonant frequency and discarding all others, (4) keeping the receivers at the same temperature, and (5) running the alternators at a constant speed, most importantly, the same speed at which they were voiced. To effect this last measure, Cahill installed the rheostat that regulated the driveshaft motor right at the console of the Telharmonium, within reach of the musicians.[64]

Fourth, a most vexing difficulty was "robbing," in which a note alone, at sufficient loudness, would become softer as other notes were sounded with it. This was due to current flowing into the other closed armature circuits instead of to the tone-combining transformer. To get the current to flow to the transformer, the armature circuits were given a higher impedance, with the unfortunate result that then the unison notes between two keyboards would weaken each other. In the commercial installation in New York, such unisons had to be avoided, and some chordal robbing was still present. Cahill recommended that the problem be solved by outfitting each alternator with a separate set of armature windings, to supply each harmonic separately to each keyboard. This would have been a considerable undertaking, with one alternator that supplied four keyboards with five harmonics requiring 20 such windings. Another expensive solution he proposed was to route the output of each alternator directly into its own transformer, which would possess up to 20 secondary coils, one to feed each harmonic to each keyboard. His major solution came too late for the commercial Telharmonium, being an isolation coil inserted in each branch circuit. This was described in detail in his unsuccessful 1908 and 1909 patent applications.[65] Cahill was fighting the lack of a true mixing circuit, which could not be achieved at the power levels he required without amplification.

Fifth, the system exhibited another woeful phenomenon called "diaphragm-crack," in which the beginning or ending of a note was accompanied by a brief roughness or harshness in the tone. For these transient bursts of noise, Cahill devised several cures. The first was an apparatus to apply the signal to the line with a gradual rise time, described in his 1908 and 1909 patent applications. The second palliative was simply for the player to employ a *legato* touch, so that two successive notes would overlap. This gave a much lesser degree of diaphragm-crack than when a separated or *staccato* touch was used. Cahill stated that the problem was much worse in New York, where the mainframe was grounded and set on cement foundations set in damp earth. In Holyoke, the machine had rested upon dry bricks set on dry sand or a pine floor. A further deterioration was noticed when underground lines were used instead of overhead telephone lines. The transients were also exacerbated by use of high voltages in small conductors; lower voltages in large conductors gave less difficulty. Finally, Cahill contrived a method to make and break the circuit in not one but three places: two very close to the alternator and one at the switchboard. This tended to smooth out the transients, since the greater parts of most of the circuits were now disconnected from ground at any one time. It reduced the system capacitance and with it the ringing of switch transients.[66]

Sixth, the independent switches used to regulate the strengths of the various timbres did not work so well as a draw-stop or rheostat type of control with a single handle.[67]

Seventh, the pneumatic power action to operate the switches was less practical than an ordinary electromagnetic power action.[68]

Eighth, better results could be obtained with a separate circuit, complete with a separate common ground, for each harmonic produced in the system. To combine the harmonics into one composite signal, it was advisable first to premix them into three small groups instead of blending them all together at once. A rheostat was inserted in the secondary coil of each premixing transformer, and the resultant signals were subsequently mixed into one complex signal in another transformer.[69]

Ninth, the revolving-disk type of alternator used in the bass did not work so well as the toothed inductor alternator.[70]

Tenth, the range of the instrument was not great enough. Instead of seven octaves, it should have spanned eight or possibly even nine. The original design did not provide for the use of the eighth harmonic in notes an octave above middle C. This harmonic proved to be indispensable for the production of "brilliant, cheerful"[71] tones and should have been available throughout more of the range of the instrument. With the bass tones, he had experimented with much higher harmonics—the 24th, 32nd, and 48th—and found them advantageous if used with little intensity.[72]

Eleventh, the fifth and tenth harmonics had proved to be of no great importance and could be omitted.[73]

Twelfth, it was vital that the third, sixth, and twelfth harmonics be tuned absolutely true. An alternate design for drawing them from another pitch-shaft, in equal temperament, was a useless economy. Even though the error was very slight, they were greatly inferior to true harmonics.[74]

Corrections and amendments of a formal nature kept the fourth patent from issue for eight months; it was finally released on January 23, 1917.

THE FIFTH TELHARMONIUM PATENT: 1,295,691

The descriptive text and drawings of this patent are virtually identical to those of the previous patent, no. 1,213,804. The application for this patent was a continuation of two more of the seven divisional applications filed in 1904.[75] These seven divisions varied only in their claims for the device, which ranged from very simple combinations to more complex ones.

As with the previous patent, Cahill permitted the original applications, which had been allowed in 1914 and 1915, to be forfeited. Reexamination was initially refused and then allowed. The application was shortly thereafter accepted, in May 1916.[76]

In an amendment Cahill attempted to clarify the divisions of claims in the last three patents as follows:

1,213,803

This was the simplest form of apparatus, with only one keyboard or switchboard, no expression devices, only one timbral register, and a tone of comparative simplicity.[77]

1,213,804

This was an apparatus of intermediate complexity similar to the first, but with one or more loudness expression devices, production of harmonics using multiple alternators, multiple timbral registers of circuits corresponding to the various harmonics, and controlling devices for the timbral registers.[78]

1,295,691

This was an apparatus of great complexity, similar to the second, but with multiple keyboards and switchboards and with different timbres and loudnesses available at each keyboard.[79] It was also an apparatus similar to any of the foregoing, but with unison sets of alternators, differing in waveform and timbre.[80]

Formal corrections kept the final Telharmonium patent from issue until February 25, 1919. Hence, Cahill managed to extend his patent protection, which had begun in 1895 with his first application, to 1936, 17 years from the date of issue of the fifth patent.

NOTES

1. Application of Thaddeus Cahill for letters patent to the Commissioner of Patents, February 10, 1902, filed February 10, 1902, N.A. 241, 1,107,261, H29–H30, H34.

2. *Ibid.*, H2–H3, H5, H9, H11–H12, H14–H15, H17, H19–H20, H29.

3. Letter from C. H. Lane, Head Examiner, U.S. Patent Office, to Thaddeus Cahill, March 27, 1902, N.A. 241, 1,107,261, 1–3.

4. Amendment A from Thaddeus Cahill to the Commissioner of Patents, March 25, 1903, N.A. 241, 1,107,261, 2–5.

5. Letter from Henry Blandy, Examiner, Division 5, U.S. Patent Office, to Thaddeus Cahill, April 16, 1903, N.A. 241, 1,107,261, 1–4.

6. Letter from C. H. Lane, Examiner, Division 5, U.S. Patent Office, to Thaddeus Cahill, June 19, 1906, N.A. 241, 1,107,261, 1; Letter from J. F. MacNab, Examiner, Division 5, U.S. Patent Office, to Thaddeus Cahill, October 16, 1909, N.A. 241, 1,107,261, 1.

7. Amendment G from Thaddeus Cahill to the Commissioner of Patents, October 12, 1910, filed October 13, 1910, N.A. 271, 1,107,261, 2.

8. *Ibid.*, 5.

9. Brief for the Applicant, Thaddeus Cahill, On Petition to the Commissioner, October 21, 1911, filed October 21, 1911, N.A. 241, 1,107,261, 6–7.

10. Ruling by E. B. Moore, Commissioner, U.S. Patent Office, January 5, 1912, N.A. 241, 1,107,261, 2.

11. *Ibid.*, 2–3.

12. *Ibid.*, 2.

13. Letter from Thaddeus Cahill to the Commissioner of Patents, July 9, 1912, N.A. 241, 1,107,261, 1; Amendment H from Thaddeus Cahill to the Commissioner of Patents, August 1, 1914, filed August 3, 1914, N.A. 241, 1,107,261.

14. Amendment [no ordinal letter] from Thaddeus Cahill to the Commissioner of Patents, filed March 16, 1905, N.A. 241, 1,213,803, 1, 2, 4; Application of Thaddeus Cahill for letters patent to the Commissioner of Patents, February 16, 1904, filed February 17, 1904, N.A. 241, 1,213,803, F1–F2.

15. Amendment A from Thaddeus Cahill to the Commissioner of Patents, December 8, 1916, filed December 9, 1916, N.A. 241, 1,213,804, 7.

16. Letter from C. H. Lane, Examiner, Division 5, U.S. Patent Office, to Thaddeus Cahill, March 17, 1904, N.A. 241, 1,213,803, 1.

17. Amendment [no ordinal letter] from Thaddeus Cahill to the Commisssioner of Patents, filed March 16, 1905, N.A. 241, 1,213,803, 1–4.

18. Letter from C. H. Lane, Examiner, Division 5, U.S. Patent Office, to Thaddeus Cahill, April 11, 1905, N.A. 241, 1,213,803, 2–3.

19. Amendment A from Thaddeus Cahill to the Commissioner of Patents, February 9, 1906, filed April 10, 1906, N.A. 241, 1,213,803, 1, 4–6.

20. *Ibid.*, 6.

21. *Ibid.,* 7.

22. Letter from C. H. Lane, Examiner, Division 5, U.S. Patent Office, to Thaddeus Cahill, June 7, 1906, 1–2.

23. Amendment B from Thaddeus Cahill to the Commissioner of Patents, June 4, 1907, filed June 6, 1907, N.A. 241, 1,213,803, 1–2, 7–15.

24. Letter from C. H. Lane, Examiner, Division 5, U.S. Patent Office, to Thaddeus Cahill, June 29, 1907, N.A. 241, 1,213,803, 1–3.

25. Amendment C from Thaddeus Cahill to the Commissioner of Patents, June 27, 1908, filed June 30, 1908, N.A. 241, 1,213,803, 2–4, 10–12.

26. Letter from C. H. Lane, Examiner, Division 5, U.S. Patent Office, to Thaddeus Cahill, July 14, 1908, N.A. 241, 1,213,803, 1–2.

27. Amendment D from Thaddeus Cahill to the Commissioner of Patents, July 10, 1909, filed July 12, 1909, N.A. 241, 1,213,803, 4–5, 7.

28. Letter from Thaddeus Cahill to the Commissioner of Patents, July 31, 1909, N.A. 241, 1,213,803, 1–2.

29. Amendment E from Thaddeus Cahill to the Commissioner of Patents, September 27, 1909, filed September 30, 1909, N.A. 241, 1,213,803, 1–6.

30. Letter from J. F. MacNab, Examiner, Division 5, U.S. Patent Office, to Thaddeus Cahill, October 20, 1909, N.A. 241, 1,213,803, 1–2.

31. Amendment F from Thaddeus Cahill to the Commissioner of Patents, October 15, 1910, filed October 18, 1910, N.A. 241, 1,213,803, 5–6.

32. Letter from C. K. Wead, Acting Examiner, Division 5, U.S. Patent Office, to Thaddeus Cahill, December 20, 1910, N.A. 241, 1,213,803, 1.

33. *Ibid.,* 1.

34. Amendment G from Thaddeus Cahill to the Commissioner of Patents, December 20, 1911, filed December 20, 1911, N.A. 241, 1,213,803, 1–18.

35. Letter from J. F. MacNab, Examiner, Division 5, U.S. Patent Office, to Thaddeus Cahill, May 25, 1912, N.A. 241, 1,213,803, 1.

36. *Ibid.,* 3.

37. Amendment H from Thaddeus Cahill to the Commissioner of Patents, May 23, 1913, filed May 24, 1913, N.A. 241, 1,213,803, 4.

38. *Ibid.,* 10–16.

39. Letter from Thaddeus Cahill to the Commissioner of Patents, June 1, 1913, N.A. 241, 1,213,803, 2. Cahill conveniently ignored the period 1906–1908, when the invention was in full commercial operation in New York.

40. *Ibid.,* 3–4.

41. Letter from J. F. MacNab, Examiner, Division 5, U.S. Patent Office, to Thaddeus Cahill, October 17, 1913, N.A. 241, 1,213,803, 1–2.

42. Amendment K from Thaddeus Cahill to the Commissioner of Patents, October 16, 1914, filed October 19, 1914, N.A. 241, 1,213,803, 3–5.

43. Petition for renewal from Thaddeus Cahill to the Commissioner of Patents, December 15, 1916, filed December 27, 1916, N.A. 241, 1,213,803, 1.

44. *Ibid.*, 1.

45. Memorandum of fee paid at U.S. Patent Office from Thaddeus Cahill, December 30, 1916, filed December 30, 1916, N.A. 241, 1,213,803, 1.

46. U.S. Patent 1,213,803, *Art of and Apparatus for Generating and Distributing Music Electrically,* Thaddeus Cahill, Holyoke, Mass., Assignor to Ellis Spear, E. Hilton Jackson, George F. Cahill, Arthur T. Cahill, and Thaddeus Cahill, Trustees: Applications January 19, 1901, February 26, 1903, February 17, 1904, November 6, 1913, December 14, 1916, Patented January 23, 1917.

47. Affidavit of Thaddeus Cahill, sworn before A. H. Dirkas, Notary Public, April 26, 1915, N.A. 241, 1,213,804, 1; Letter from Thomas Ewing, Commissioner of Patents, U.S. Patent Office, to Thaddeus Cahill, May 20, 1915, N.A. 241, 1,213,804, 1.

48. 3666, 3666A, 3666B, 3666C.

49. Affidavit of Thaddeus Cahill, 1.

50. Application of Thaddeus Cahill for letters patent to the Commissioner of Patents, April 26, 1915, filed April 27, 1915, N.A. 241, 1,213,804, B80; Amendment A from Thaddeus Cahill to the Commissioner of Patents, December 8, 1916, filed December 9, 1916, N.A. 241, 1,213,804, 3–5.

51. Letter from Thomas Ewing, Commissioner of Patents, U.S. Patent Office, to Thaddeus Cahill, May 20, 1915, N.A. 241, 1,213,804, 1–3; Letter from Thaddeus Cahill to Thomas Ewing, Commissioner of Patents, April 1, 1916, N.A. 241, 1,213,804, 1; Letter from J. F. MacNab, Examiner, Division 5, U.S. Patent Office, to Thaddeus Cahill, April 26, 1916, 1.

52. Application of Thaddeus Cahill for letters patent to the Commissioner of Patents, April 26, 1915, filed April 27, 1915, N.A. 241, 1,213,804, B3–B6, B11.

53. *Ibid.*, B6.

54. *Ibid.*, B29–B31.

55. *Ibid.*, B42.

56. *Ibid.*, B29–B30.

57. *Ibid.*, B49.

58. *Ibid.*, B51–B52.

59. *Ibid.*, B71–B72.

60. *Ibid.*, B78.

61. *Ibid.*, B81.

62. *Ibid.*, B78.

63. *Ibid.*, B82.

64. *Ibid.*, B83–B87.

65. *Ibid.*, B87–B89.

66. *Ibid.*, B89–B92; U.S. Patent 1,213,804, drawings sheet 9.

67. *Ibid.*, B96.

68. *Ibid.*

69. *Ibid.*, B96–B99.

70. *Ibid.*, B100.

71. *Ibid.*

72. *Ibid.*, B100–B101.

73. *Ibid.*, B101.

74. *Ibid.*, B101–B102.

75. Application from Thaddeus Cahill for letters patent to the Commissioner of Patents, June 26, 1915, filed June 26, 1915, N.A. 241, 1,295,691, H81; Affidavit of Thaddeus Cahill, sworn before Gaddison Hicks, Notary Public, June 26, 1915, N.A. 241, 1,295,691, 1.

76. Letter from the Commissioner of Patents [n.n.], U.S. Patent Office, to Thaddeus Cahill, November 13, 1915, N.A. 241, 1,295,691, 1–2; Letter from Thaddeus Cahill to Thomas Ewing, Commissioner of Patents, April 1, 1915 [*sic:* actually 1916], filed April 1, 1916, N.A. 241, 1,295,691, 1; Letter from J. F. MacNab, Examiner, Division 5, U.S. Patent Office, to Thaddeus Cahill, May 9, 1916, N.A. 241, 1,295,691, 1.

77. Amendment [no ordinal letter] from Thaddeus Cahill to the Commissioner of Patents, January 30, 1919, filed February 6, 1919, N.A. 241, 1,295,691, 12, 15.

78. *Ibid.*, 12–15.

79. *Ibid.*, 14–15.

80. *Ibid.* There is no evidence that Cahill built such a machine or advocated such a design.

APPENDIX 2

SOURCES OF DATA

ARCHIVES OF THE COUNTY CLERK OF NEW YORK COUNTY

The 1908 judgment against the New York Electric Music Co. has been preserved at the Archives of the County Clerk of New York County.

A.T.&T. ARCHIVES

A treasure trove of correspondence from Oscar T. Crosby, Frederick P. Fish, and Hammond V. Hayes has been preserved at the A.T.&T. Archives in New York. Business dealings and the falling-out between the New York Electric Music Co. and the New York Telephone Co. are clearly and completely described. Also held here is Arthur T. Cahill's poignant if hyperbolic 1951 letter soliciting a final home for the Telharmonium he had been storing through the years.

Copies of some of these letters, along with valuable technical reports and a Telharmonic Hall program, are held at the A.T.&T. Bell Laboratories Archives in Warren, N.J.

BOARD OF ESTIMATE, BUREAU OF FRANCHISES, CITY OF NEW YORK

Without the records of this agency, the story of Cahill's attempt at a Telharmonium comeback in 1911 would be maddeningly sketchy. Fortunately, the board printed and published its voluminous *Minutes,* which feature full reports on the New York Cahill Telharmonic Co. The board also printed copies of the contract and the revised contract between New York City and the company. In addition, the company was required to file very detailed annual reports, with maps. Most of these, by Assistant Treasurer Arthur T. Cahill, are still held at the Bureau of Franchises of the board. Finally, some court documents relating to the 1914 bankruptcy of the company may be found on file at this agency; no such records could be located by the Federal Court.

CENTER FOR RESEARCH LIBRARIES, CHICAGO

Upon Thaddeus Cahill's death in 1934, his brother George undertook to write a memorial tribute to the man and his work. The ensuing 18-page paper took ten days to write and is inscribed "to be read when alone and unhurried." This typescript contains a remarkable range of data on Thaddeus's childhood, his education, his character, his physical characteristics, his conception of the Telharmonium, the responses to the instrument, the mistakes by the New York Electric Music Co., and the ultimate inability to finance the third machine. As may be expected, the paper is written with compelling feeling. Despite a strong urge to lionize and enshrine his departed brother—and despite convenient omissions, errors in chronology, and a tendency to gild the lily—this unpublished typescript held by the Center for Research Libraries, Chicago, offers a unique and close perspective on the Telharmonium.

RAMONA CLARK

Ramona [Mrs. Eugene M.] Clark, a genealogist living in Stockport, Iowa, kindly furnished information on the tombstone of Thaddeus Cahill's mother, Ellen Harrington Cahill.

ELLA MERKEL DICARLO

Formerly assistant to the publisher of the *Holyoke Daily Transcript-Telegram,* historian Ella Merkel DiCarlo of Conway, Mass., generously provided much knowledge and background material on Holyoke history and located many important newspaper accounts.

RUTH DOUGLASS

Emerita Professor of Music Ruth Douglass, of Mount Holyoke College, very kindly gave the author her notes for two 1968 articles on Telharmonium reminiscences published in the *Holyoke Daily Transcript-Telegram.* Included were several valuable letters by persons who recalled Thaddeus Cahill and his work in Holyoke.

FOOTHILL ELECTRONICS MUSEUM; YALE UNIVERSITY

The notes and manuscripts for Lee de Forest's autobiography, *Father of Radio,* are held at the Foothill Electronics Museum, Foothill College, Los Altos Hills, Calif., and at Yale University. The material provides a few items and remarks about de Forest's Telharmonium broadcasts not found in the published version.

HALL OF HISTORY FOUNDATION

Reminiscences of Oscar T. Crosby by Frank J. Sprague are included in the publicity file compiled by John Hammond of the General Electric Co. The materials are housed in this museum-archive located on company premises, Schenectady, N.Y.

HOLYOKE DAILY TRANSCRIPT-TELEGRAM

The newspaper office has early maps and city directories of Holyoke as well as microfilm copies of the *Holyoke Daily Transcript* beginning with 1906.

HOLYOKE PUBLIC LIBRARY

The library has early maps and photographs of Holyoke. There is also a clipping file of items on the Telharmonium, including a few of the articles published in the *Holyoke Daily Transcript.* The library has microfilm copies of the newspaper beginning with 1906.

STODDARD LINCOLN

The author received a wealth of documents from harpsichordist and baroque specialist Stoddard Lincoln, professor of music at Brooklyn College. His father, the late Edwin Stoddard Lincoln, was a pioneer in electricity who worked with such inventors as Thomas Edison, Charles Steinmetz, and Frank Sprague. The elder Lincoln received the documents from William J. Hammer, an assistant of Edison. Hammer was present at demonstrations of the Telharmonium and kept some printed materials as part of his "William J. Hammer Scientific Collection." The items are: the 1906 stock prospectus of the New York Electric Music Co., a 1906 broadside adapted from Ray Stannard Baker's article in *McClure's Magazine,* the 1906 brochure *Telharmony,* an invitation to Hammer to attend the opening in January 1907, and a Telharmonic Hall program from late 1907.

NATIONAL ARCHIVES

Thaddeus Cahill prosecuted his patent applications with prolix and disputatious vigor. His correspondence with the Patent Office on his five successful Telharmonic patents amounts to about 1,000 pages and has been preserved as part of the patent files held by the National Archives in Washington, D.C. Much of the material deals with tedious minutiae, but a significant segment sheds interesting light on the early development of Telharmonic design.

NATIONAL ARCHIVES TRUST FUND BOARD

This agency maintains veterans' records, among them the military and pension files of Dr. Timothy Cahill. There are letters describing his medical condition from doctors and his 14-year-old daughter Mary, the army discharge certificate, and several pension documents.

NEW YORK PUBLIC LIBRARY

The Performing Arts Branch at Lincoln Center has a file containing the 1906 brochure *Telharmony*, the first Telharmonic Hall program, the 1907 brochure *Telharmony: A New Art*, and several clippings.

NEWSPAPERS AND PERIODICALS

New York was fortunate to have been served by a plethora of daily newspapers in the early part of the century. Some dozen or so have been preserved on microfilm at the New York Public Library and the New-York Historical Society. They contain hundreds of contemporary reports on the Telharmonium. Some periodicals, notably the *Talking Machine World* and the *Music Trade Review*, took a special interest in covering the instrument.

OBERLIN COLLEGE ARCHIVES

The archives contain a letter from Thaddeus Cahill, one semester of his academic records, and some interesting clippings with reminiscences of the Cahill brothers by a boyhood companion.

PERSONAL COMMUNICATIONS

In 1984 the author mailed queries to every residence located within a block of Arthur T. Cahill's house on Hudson Place in Weehawken, N.J., some 135 letters. This yielded responses from Dr. Fred Heimbuch, D.D.S., of West Long Branch, N.J., and Mrs. Walter Koehler of

Cranford, N.J. Both knew Arthur T. Cahill in the 1940s and 1950s. Regrettably, they could not furnish any information on the storage or disposition of the Telharmonium that Arthur T. Cahill had preserved into the 1950s. The present occupant of the house, Mr. Manuel Perez, had discarded "two small boxes" that included the remains of a Cahill typewriter with piano-style keys and "some other apparatus" in 1982. Mr. Perez knew nothing of the musical instrument.

JAMES EDWARD PIERCE

Through the kind assistance of Cynthia Adams Hoover of the Smithsonian Institution, the author was able to contact and speak with the son of Telharmonium performer Edwin Hall Pierce. Still physically well and mentally keen at 87, Mr. Pierce granted an extended tape-recorded interview to the author in 1983 at his farm near Smithfield, Va. He also generously provided brochures published by his father, photographs, a copy of his mother's diary from 1898 to 1908, and written accounts of the Telharmonium by himself and his late brother, the Reverend Roderic Pierce.

MARGARET ELEANOR CAHILL SCHWARTZ

The daughter of Arthur T. and Louise M. Cahill was unfailingly patient and helpful during a series of tape-recorded interviews in August 1990 which lasted three days. Mrs. Schwartz allowed the author to photograph her collection of correspondence, typewriter and Telharmonium brochures, newspaper clippings, family photographs, written accounts by her parents, and Thaddeus Cahill's unpublished treatise on just intonation. She is living in seclusion in a small town in Vermont.

SECRETARIES OF STATE OF MAINE, NEW JERSEY, AND NEW YORK

The offices of corporate records have all faithfully preserved the certificates of incorporation of the Telharmonic companies that were

formed from 1902 to 1910. New Jersey deserves special appreciation
for continuing to hold the annual reports and certificates of capital
increase of the New England Electric Music Co. and the New York
Electric Music Co. These documents have revealed the only solid
evidence we are likely to receive on the amounts of funds invested in
the enterprise. The reports are very brief and reveal little else but the
names of officers and directors.

SMITHSONIAN INSTITUTION

Francis Arthur Hart was an early radio enthusiast who logged
broadcast transmissions in the New York area from 1906 to 1909.
Thanks to Mr. Elliot N. Sivowitch of the Smithsonian Institution,
the author obtained copies of several pages from Hart's logbook
describing Lee de Forest's Telharmonium broadcasts in 1907. The
Smithsonian also has copies of some of the items written by James
Edward Pierce, some clippings, and a copy of the 1906 brochure
Telharmony.

THE STRUNIEWSKI COLLECTION

One of the few surviving records of the Telharmonium preserved by
the Cahills themselves is a collection of 82 newspaper and magazine
clippings. These were supplied by clipping services, generally Henry
Romeike, from 1906 to 1910. They were mailed to Thaddeus Cahill
at his office at the Water Power Building on Cabot Street in
Holyoke. The collection was given by Arthur T. Cahill to his
landlord, whose widow, Sophie Struniewski of Cliffside Park, N.J.,
gave it to the author in 1983. Many of the clippings are from
newspapers that have not been preserved in libraries and represent a
valuable resource of unique information.

BIBLIOGRAPHY

MANUSCRIPTS

"According to the Holyoke Transcript: 'In April 1911 . . . ,' " Memorandum, n.n., n.d., typewritten, H.P.L.

Assistant Engineer [n.n.], Letter and Drawing from Assistant Engineer [n.n.], American Telephone and Telegraph Co., to E. S. Warren, American Telephone and Telegraph Co., January 3, 1907, A.T.T.B.L.A., Boston File 500, 20.03.01.02.

Bell, John, M.D., Affidavit of John Bell, M.D., sworn before M. D. Snyder, Clerk of the District Court, September 30, 1872, N.A.T.F.B., SC-127-969.

Berliner, Stanley S., O.D., Certificate of Death of Arthur Cahill, January 24, 1962, filed at the State Department of Health of New Jersey, Trenton, N.J., January 27, 1962.

Blandy, Henry, Letter from Henry Blandy, Examiner, Division 5, U.S. Patent Office, to Thaddeus Cahill, April 16, 1903, N.A. 241, 1,107,261.

Cahill, Arthur Timothy, "The Cahill Duplex-Triplex Electrical Typewriter Patent," Weehawken, N.J., 1944?, typewritten, M.C.S.

————, Last Will and Testament, May 18, 1955 [not filed or recorded], M.C.S.

————, Letter from Arthur T. Cahill, Assistant Treasurer, New York Cahill Telharmonic Company, to the Chairman and Members of the Board of Estimate and Apportionment of the City of New York, November 1, 1913, B.E.

————, Letter from Arthur T. Cahill, Assistant Treasurer, New York Cahill Telharmonic Company, to the Chairman and Members of the
317

Board of Estimate and Apportionment of the City of New York, November 13, 1914, B.E.

———, "The Original and Scientifically Priceless Cahill Electric Music Instrument. The First Instrument That Created Music from the Electrical Waves of Alternating Current Generators," n.d. [rubber stamp: "AUG 31, 1951"], mimeographed and typewritten, A.T.T.A, M-1.

———, "Who Was Thaddeus Cahill?" Central Commercial Company, 1947, typewritten, M.C.S.

———, and Lawrence Victor Merrill, Oath, Power of Attorney and Petition of Arthur T. Cahill and Lawrence Victor Merrill, sworn before Meyer Cohen, Notary Public, July 22, 1950, N.A., 2,584,546, Federal Records Center, Suitland, Md.

Cahill, Eleanor, Last Will and Testament, November 21, 1947, filed at Surrogate's Court, Hudson County, Jersey City, N.J., December 26, 1951, recorded in "Wills, Liber 306," 113–115.

Cahill, George Frederick, Affidavit of George F. Cahill, in the Matter of Proving the Last Will and Testament of Thaddeus Cahill, December 17, 1934, filed at Surrogate's Court, New York County, New York, N.Y.

———, Notice from George F. Cahill, Receiver, to the Creditors of the New York Cahill Telharmonic Company, December 24, 1914, B.E.

———, "Thaddeus Cahill (June 18, 1867-April 12, 1934): A Preliminary Paper," New York?, 1934?, typewritten, C.R.L.C. E-1488, Cat. C, L609.214, C115.

Cahill, Louise Margaret Jamieson, "Arthur T. Cahill," 1950?, typewritten, M.C.S.

———, "Arthur Timothy Cahill," 1963?, typewritten, M.C.S.

Cahill, Margaret, Last Will and Testament, June 1, 1936, filed at Surrogate's Court, Hudson County, Jersey City, N.J., March 24, 1944, recorded in "Wills, Liber 250," 218–220.

Cahill, Mary Holland, Affidavit of Mary Cahill, sworn before Joshua S. Sloan, Clerk of the District Court, October 9, 1872, N.A.T.F.B., SC-127-969.

————, Last Will and Testament, January 10, 1933, filed at Surrogate's Court, New York County, New York, N.Y., November 16, 1935, recorded in "Record of Wills, Liber 1583," 227–228.

Cahill Music Machinery Manufacturing Company, Certificate of Incorporation, April 21, 1910, received and recorded at the Office of the Hudson County Clerk, Jersey City, N.J., May 14, 1910, filed and recorded at the Office of the Secretary of State, Trenton, N.J., May 17, 1910.

Cahill, Robert J., Letter from Robert J. Cahill to Miss [Ruth] Douglass, June 25, 1968, R.W.

Cahill, Thaddeus, Affidavit of Thaddeus Cahill, sworn before A. H. Dirkas, Notary Public, April 26, 1915, N.A. 241, 1,213,804.

————, Affidavit of Thaddeus Cahill, sworn before Fred T. Partridge, Notary Public, January 31, 1911, filed and recorded at the Office of the Secretary of State, Trenton, N.J., February 2, 1911.

————, Affidavit of Thaddeus Cahill, sworn before Gaddison Hicks, Notary Public, June 26, 1915, N.A. 241, 1,295,691.

————, Amendment A from Thaddeus Cahill to the Commissioner of Patents, March 25, 1903, N.A. 241, 1,107,261.

————, Amendment A from Thaddeus Cahill to the Commissioner of Patents, February 9, 1906, filed April 10, 1906, N.A. 241, 1,213,803.

————, Amendment A from Thaddeus Cahill to the Commissioner of Patents, December 8, 1916, filed December 9, 1916, N.A. 241, 1,213,804.

————, Amendment A from Thaddeus Cahill to the Commissioner of Patents, January 31, 1919, filed January 31, 1919, N.A. 241, 1,295,691.

————, Amendment B from Thaddeus Cahill to the Commissioner of Patents, April 5, 1904, N.A. 241, 1,107,261.

————, Amendment B from Thaddeus Cahill to the Commissioner of Patents, June 4, 1907, filed June 6, 1907, N.A. 241, 1,213,803.

————, Amendment C from Thaddeus Cahill to the Commissioner of Patents, May 14, 1906, filed May 15, 1906, N.A. 241, 1,107,261.

————, Amendment C from Thaddeus Cahill to the Commissioner of Patents, June 27, 1908, filed June 30, 1908, N.A. 241, 1,213,803.

————, Amendment C from Thaddeus Cahill to the Commissioner of Patents, December 30, 1916, filed January 2, 1917, N.A. 241, 1,213,804.

————, Amendment C from Thaddeus Cahill to the Commissioner of Patents, January 2, 1917, filed January 2, 1917, N.A. 241, 1,213,804.

————, Amendment D from Thaddeus Cahill to the Commissioner of Patents, January 27, 1897, N.A. 241, 580,035.

————, Amendment D from Thaddeus Cahill to the Commissioner of Patents, June 15, 1907, filed June 17, 1907, N.A. 241, 1,107,261.

————, Amendment D from Thaddeus Cahill to the Commissioner of Patents, July 10, 1909, filed July 12, 1909, N.A. 241, 1,213,803.

————, Amendment E from Thaddeus Cahill to the Commissioner of Patents, August 7, 1908, filed August 8, 1908, N.A. 241, 1,107,261.

————, Amendment E from Thaddeus Cahill to the Commissioner of Patents, September 27, 1909, filed September 29, 1909, N.A. 241, 1,213,803.

————, Amendment F from Thaddeus Cahill to the Commissioner of Patents, February 13, 1897, filed March 13, 1897, N.A. 241, 580,035.

————, Amendment F from Thaddeus Cahill to the Commissioner of Patents, September 15, 1909, filed September 17, 1909, N.A. 241, 1,107,261.

————, Amendment F from Thaddeus Cahill to the Commissioner of Patents, October 15, 1910, filed October 18, 1910, N.A. 241, 1,213,803.

————, Amendment G from Thaddeus Cahill to the Commissioner of Patents, February 2, 1897, filed March 2, 1897, N.A. 241, 580,035.

————, Amendment G from Thaddeus Cahill to the Commissioner of Patents, October 12, 1910, filed October 13, 1910, N.A. 241, 1,107,261.

————, Amendment G from Thaddeus Cahill to the Commissioner of Patents, December 20, 1911, filed December 20, 1911, N.A. 241, 1,213,803.

————, Amendment H from Thaddeus Cahill to the Commissioner of Patents, May 23, 1913, filed May 24, 1913, N.A. 241, 1,213,803.

————, Amendment H from Thaddeus Cahill to the Commissioner of Patents, August 1, 1914, filed August 3, 1914, N.A. 241, 1,107,261.

————, Amendment I from Thaddeus Cahill to the Commissioner of Patents, May 23, 1913, filed May 26, 1913, N.A. 241, 1,213,803.

————, Amendment K from Thaddeus Cahill to the Commissioner of Patents, October 16, 1914, filed October 19, 1914, N.A. 241, 1,213,803.

————, Amendment L from Thaddeus Cahill to the Commissioner of Patents, December 29, 1916, filed December 29, 1916, N.A. 241, 1,213,803.

————, Amendment M from Thaddeus Cahill to the Commissioner of Patents, January 5, 1917, filed January 6, 1917, N.A. 241, 1,213,803.

————, Amendment [no ordinal letter] from Thaddeus Cahill to the Commissioner of Patents, March 15, 1905, filed March 16, 1905, N.A. 241, 1,213,803.

————, Amendment [no ordinal letter] from Thaddeus Cahill to the Commissioner of Patents, April 24, 1905, filed April 25, 1905, N.A. 241, 1,107,261.

————, Amendment [no ordinal letter] from Thaddeus Cahill to the Commissioner of Patents, January 30, 1919, filed February 6, 1919, N.A. 241, 1,295,691.

————, Application from Thaddeus Cahill for letters patent to the Commissioner of Patents, February 10, 1902, filed February 10, 1902, N.A. 241, 1,107,261.

————, Application from Thaddeus Cahill for letters patent to the Commissioner of Patents, February 16, 1904, filed February 17, 1904, N.A. 241, 1,213,803.

————, Application from Thaddeus Cahill for letters patent to the Commissioner of Patents, April 26, 1915, filed April 27, 1915, N.A. 241, 1,213,804.

————, Application from Thaddeus Cahill for letters patent to the Commissioner of Patents, June 26, 1915, filed June 26, 1915, N.A. 241, 1,295,691.

————, Brief for the Applicant, Thaddeus Cahill, on Petition to the Commissioner, October 20, 1911, filed October 21, 1911, N.A. 241, 1,107,261.

————? "The Cahill Electrical Music," 1906?, with supplement, September 21, 1910, typewritten, M.C.S.

————, Last Will and Testament, October 13, 1898, filed at Surrogate's Court, New York County, New York, N.Y., January 3, 1935, recorded in "Record of Wills, Liber 1563," 40–45.

————, Letter from Thaddeus Cahill to George M. Jones, Secretary, Oberlin College, June 10, 1908, O.C.A. 28/1, Box 38.

————, Letter from Thaddeus Cahill to J. T. Newton, Commissioner of Patents, February 9, 1919, N.A. 241, 1,295,691.

————, Letter from Thaddeus Cahill to the Commissioner of Patents, February 10, 1902, N.A. 241, 1,107,261.

————, Letter from Thaddeus Cahill to the Commissioner of Patents, April 14, 1904, N.A. 241, 1,107,261.

————, Letter from Thaddeus Cahill to the Commissioner of Patents, July 31, 1909, N.A. 241, 1,213,803.

————, Letter from Thaddeus Cahill to the Commissioner of Patents, January 18, 1912, N.A. 241, 1,213,803.

————, Letter from Thaddeus Cahill to the Commissioner of Patents, July 9, 1912, N.A. 241, 1,107,261.

————, Letter from Thaddeus Cahill to the Commissioner of Patents, June 17, 1913, N.A. 241, 1,213,803.

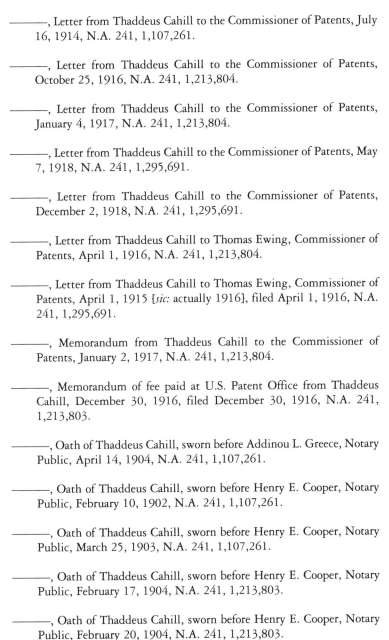

————, Letter from Thaddeus Cahill to the Commissioner of Patents, July 16, 1914, N.A. 241, 1,107,261.

————, Letter from Thaddeus Cahill to the Commissioner of Patents, October 25, 1916, N.A. 241, 1,213,804.

————, Letter from Thaddeus Cahill to the Commissioner of Patents, January 4, 1917, N.A. 241, 1,213,804.

————, Letter from Thaddeus Cahill to the Commissioner of Patents, May 7, 1918, N.A. 241, 1,295,691.

————, Letter from Thaddeus Cahill to the Commissioner of Patents, December 2, 1918, N.A. 241, 1,295,691.

————, Letter from Thaddeus Cahill to Thomas Ewing, Commissioner of Patents, April 1, 1916, N.A. 241, 1,213,804.

————, Letter from Thaddeus Cahill to Thomas Ewing, Commissioner of Patents, April 1, 1915 [*sic:* actually 1916], filed April 1, 1916, N.A. 241, 1,295,691.

————, Memorandum from Thaddeus Cahill to the Commissioner of Patents, January 2, 1917, N.A. 241, 1,213,804.

————, Memorandum of fee paid at U.S. Patent Office from Thaddeus Cahill, December 30, 1916, filed December 30, 1916, N.A. 241, 1,213,803.

————, Oath of Thaddeus Cahill, sworn before Addinou L. Greece, Notary Public, April 14, 1904, N.A. 241, 1,107,261.

————, Oath of Thaddeus Cahill, sworn before Henry E. Cooper, Notary Public, February 10, 1902, N.A. 241, 1,107,261.

————, Oath of Thaddeus Cahill, sworn before Henry E. Cooper, Notary Public, March 25, 1903, N.A. 241, 1,107,261.

————, Oath of Thaddeus Cahill, sworn before Henry E. Cooper, Notary Public, February 17, 1904, N.A. 241, 1,213,803.

————, Oath of Thaddeus Cahill, sworn before Henry E. Cooper, Notary Public, February 20, 1904, N.A. 241, 1,213,803.

————, Petition for Renewal from Thaddeus Cahill to the Commissioner of Patents, January 8, 1914, filed January 10, 1914, N.A. 241, 1,107,261.

————, Petition for Renewal from Thaddeus Cahill to the Commissioner of Patents, December 15, 1916, filed December 27, 1916, N.A. 241, 1,107,261.

————, Petition from Thaddeus Cahill to the Commissioner of Patents, February 13, 1919, filed February 13, 1919, N.A. 241, 1,295,691.

————, Telegram from Thaddeus Cahill to J. T. Newton, Commissioner of Patents, February 10, 1919, N.A. 241, 1,295,691.

————, and Ellis Spear, Amendment A from Thaddeus Cahill and Ellis Spear, Counsel, to the Commissioner of Patents, April 7, 1896, N.A. 241, 580,035.

————, and Ellis Spear, Letter from Thaddeus Cahill and Ellis Spear, Counsel, to the Commissioner of Patents, April 7, 1896, N.A. 241, 580,035.

————, Ellis Spear, E. Hilton Jackson, George F. Cahill, and Arthur T. Cahill, Indenture, April 29, 1902, recorded in "Records of Transfers of Patents, Liber D65," P.T.O., 165.

Cahill, Timothy, M.D., Declaration of Timothy Cahill for Original Pension of an Invalid, sworn before Joshua S. Sloan, Clerk of the District Court, October 11, 1872, N.A.F.T.B., SC-127-969.

————, Declaration of Timothy Cahill for the Increase of an Invalid Pension, sworn before Robert Hunter, Clerk of the District Court, September 26, 1879, N.A.F.T.B., SC-127-969.

Cahill Writing-Machine Manufacturing Company, Certificate of Change of Name, November 21, 1900, filed and recorded at the Office of the Secretary of State, Trenton, N.J., November 22, 1900.

————, Certificate of Decrease of Capital Stock, July 30, 1897, filed and recorded at the Office of the Secretary of State, Trenton, N.J., July 31, 1897.

————, Certificate of Incorporation, December 5, 1896, and June 17, 1897, received and recorded at the Office of the Hudson County Clerk,

Jersey City, N.J., June 18, 1897, filed and recorded at the Office of the Secretary of State, Trenton, N.J., June 18, 1897.

——, Certificate of Increase of Capital Stock, November 10, 1900, filed and recorded at the Office of the Secretary of State, Trenton, N.J., November 10, 1900.

Chetwood, Robert E., Jr., Letter from Robert E. Chetwood, Jr., American Telephone and Telegraph Co., to G. M. Yorke, Assistant Engineer, American Telephone and Telegraph Co., January 2, 1907, A.T.T.B.L.A., Boston File 500, 603822.

Chief Clerk, Letter from the Chief Clerk [name indecipherable], U.S. Patent Office, to Thaddeus Cahill, February 14, 1919, N.A. 241, 1,295,691.

——, Letter from the Chief Clerk [n.n.] U.S. Patent Office, to Thaddeus Cahill, December 15, 1916, N.A. 241, 1,213,804.

——, Letter from the Chief Clerk [n.n.] U.S. Patent Office, to Thaddeus Cahill, January 6, 1917, N.A. 241, 1,213,803.

——, Letter from the Chief Clerk [n.n.] U.S. Patent Office, to Thaddeus Cahill, December 3, 1918, N.A. 241, 1,295,691.

Chief Engineer, Letter from the Chief Engineer [n.n.], to C. H. Wilson, General Superintendent, American Telephone and Telegraph Co., January 2, 1907, A.T.T.B.L.A., Boston File 500, 603822.

Collector of the 1st Collection District, State of Rhode Island, Internal Revenue License no. 7552, granted to Timothy Cahill, May 1, 1865, M.C.S.

Commissioner of Patents, Letter from the Commissioner of Patents [n.n.], U.S. Patent Office, to Thaddeus Cahill, November 13, 1915, N.A. 241, 1,295,691.

Cooper, C. N., M.D., Affidavit of C. N. Cooper, M.D., sworn before Joshua S. Sloan, Clerk of the District Court, October 4, 1872, N.A.F.T.B., SC-127- 969.

County Clerk, New York County, "1908 Judgments, Transcripts and Decrees: Incorporations," A.C.C., 215.

Crady, William, M.D., Affidavit of William Crady, M.D. [not sworn], October 2, 1872, N.A.T.F.B., SC-127-969.

Crawford, John W., Pickens Neagle, Robert E. Logan, Ellis Spear, E. Hilton Jackson, George F. Cahill, Arthur T. Cahill, and Thaddeus Cahill, Indenture, June 19, 1902, recorded in "Records of Transfers of Patents, Liber S65," P.T.O., June 20, 1902, 40–71.

Crosby, Oscar Terry, Letter from Oscar T. Crosby, President, New York Electric Music Company, to Charles F. Cutler, President, New York Telephone Company, January 27, 1907, A.T.T.A., 16878, L.B. 46/427.

————, Letter from O. T. Crosby, President, New York Electric Music Company, to F. P. Fish, President, American Telephone and Telegraph Co., December 16, 1904, A.T.T.A., 520155.

————, Letter from Oscar T. Crosby, President, New York Electric Music Company, to F. P. Fish, President, American Telephone and Telegraph Co., January 25, 1907, A.T.T.A., 16878, L.B. 46/427.

————, Letter from O. T. Crosby, President, New York Electric Music Company, to F. P. Fish, President, American Telephone and Telegraph Co., January 28, 1907, A.T.T.A., 16878.

————, Letter from Oscar T. Crosby, New York Electric Music Company, to Frederick P. Fish, President, American Telephone and Telegraph Co., January 29, 1907, A.T.T.A., 16878.

————, Letter from O. T. Crosby to F. P. Fish, President, American Telephone and Telegraph Co., March 8, 1907, A.T.T.A., 604519.

Dabney, William M., M.D., Certificate of Death of Frederick Charles Todd, November 10, 1918, filed at the Maryland Department of Health, Annapolis, Md., Certificate no. 42445, Maryland State Archives.

de Forest, Lee, "Autobiographical Notes, vol. IV (1905–1911)," F.E.M., 435.

————, "Diary," typewritten, Y.U., Lee de Forest Papers, CTYV84-A1065, Box 2, Folder 9–11, 328–331.

Dickinson, S. D., Secretary of State of New Jersey, Certificate of Authorization to the New York Electric Music Company, February 2, 1911, filed and recorded at the Office of the Secretary of State, Trenton, N.J., February 2, 1911.

Donohoe, Michael, Certificate of Disability for Discharge, Army of the United States, Timothy Cahill, Hospital Steward, November 10, 1862, N.A.F.T.B., Timothy Cahill, 10th N.H. Inf.

Douglass, Ruth, "Hogan Brothers Knew Thaddaeus [*sic*] Cahill," Worksheet for article published in *Holyoke Daily Transcript-Telegram,* May 8, 1968, R.W.

―――, "Holyoke's Place in the Evolution of Electronic Music," Worksheet for article published in *Holyoke Daily Transcript-Telegram,* March 6, 1968, R.W.

Downie, Kate Whitmore [Mrs. Merrill A.], Letter from Kate Whitmore Downie to Ruth [Douglass], June 16, 1968, R.W.

Eastern Cahill Telharmonic Company, Certificate of Change, August 6, 1906, received and filed at the Office of the Secretary of State, recorded in vol. 5, p. 351, Augusta, Me., August 7, 1906.

―――, Certificate of Organization of a Corporation, August 2, 1906, received and filed at the Office of the Secretary of State, recorded in vol. 56, p. 357, Augusta, Me., August 3, 1906.

Engineer, Letter from Engineer [n.n.], Chief of Bureau of Franchises, to John Purroy Mitchel, Mayor, Chairman of the Board of Estimate and Apportionment, January 2, 1914, B.E.

―――, Letter from Engineer [n.n.], Chief of Bureau of Franchises, to John Purroy Mitchel, Mayor, Chairman of the Board of Estimate and Apportionment, January 15, 1915, B.E.

Espenschied, Lloyd, "Early Experiments in the Electrical Transmission of Music," October 12, 1944, typewritten, A.T.T.B.L.A., Espenschied 60.10.01.03.

Ewing, Thomas, Letter from Thomas Ewing, Commissioner of Patents, U.S. Patent Office, to Thaddeus Cahill, January 21, 1914, N.A. 241, 1,107,261.

―――, Letter from Thomas Ewing, Commissioner of Patents, U.S. Patent Office, to Thaddeus Cahill, December 28, 1914, N.A. 241, 1,213,803.

————, Letter from Thomas Ewing, Commissioner of Patents, U.S. Patent Office, to Thaddeus Cahill, May 20, 1915, N.A. 241, 1,213,804.

————, Letter from Thomas Ewing, Commissioner of Patents, U.S. Patent Office, to Thaddeus Cahill, April 27, 1916, N.A. 241, 1,213,804.

————, Letter from Thomas Ewing, Commissioner of Patents, U.S. Patent Office, to Thaddeus Cahill, May 16, 1916, N.A. 241, 1,295,691.

————, Letter from Thomas Ewing, Commissioner of Patents, U.S. Patent Office, to Thaddeus Cahill, October 28, 1916, N.A. 241, 1,213,804.

————, Letter from Thomas Ewing, Commissioner of Patents, U.S. Patent Office, to Thaddeus Cahill, December 30, 1916, N.A. 241, 1,213,803.

————, Letter from Thomas Ewing, Commissioner of Patents, U.S. Patent Office, to Thaddeus Cahill, June 8, 1918, N.A. 241, 1,295,691.

Fauth, George, and James S. Whedbee, appraisers, Frederick Charles Todd: Inventory: Personal Estate, December 10, 1918, filed and recorded at Baltimore County Orphans Court, Baltimore, Md., "Baltimore County: Inventories, WJP #42," Maryland State Arhives CR 9107, 537–539.

Federer, John J., M.D., Certificate of Death of Louise M. Cahill, November 7, 1963, filed at the New Jersey State Department of Health, Trenton, N.J., November 12, 1963.

Fish, Frederick Perry, Letter from F. P. Fish, President, American Telephone and Telegraph Co., to O. T. Crosby, Esq., December 24, 1904, A.T.T.A., 520156, Pres. L.B. 37/86.

————, Letter from F. P. Fish, President, American Telephone and Telegraph Co., to O. T. Crosby, Esq., January 28, 1907, A.T.T.A., 16878, L.B. 46/463.

————, Letter from F. P. Fish, President, American Telephone and Telegraph Co., to O. T. Crosby, Esq., January 30, 1907, A.T.T.A., 16878, 427.

————, Letter from F. P. Fish, President, American Telephone and Telegraph Co., to O. T. Crosby, Esq., New York Electric Music Company, March 30, 1907, A.T.T.A., 604507, LB 47/410.

————, Letter from F. P. Fish to Chas. F. Cutler, President, New York Telephone Co., January 28, 1907, A.T.T.A., 402/454.

Fulton, J., Certificate of Death of Margaret Cahill, February 22, 1944, filed at the New Jersey Department of Health, Bureau of Vital Statistics, Trenton, N.J., February 24, 1944.

Gordon, D. M., M.D., Certificate of Death of Eleanor Cahill, December 12, 1951, filed at the Department of Health of the City of New York, Bureau of Records, December 12, 1951.

Graham, John Randolph, M.D., Certificate of Death of George Frederick Cahill, October 13, 1935, filed at the Department of Health of the City of New York, Bureau of Records, n.d.

————, Certificate of Death of Mary Holland Cahill, January 12, 1933, filed at the Department of Health of the City of New York, Bureau of Records, January 16, 1933.

Hammond, Evan B., M.D., Affidavit of Evan B. Hammond, M.D., sworn before Bernard B. Whittemore, Notary Public, September 16, 1872, N.A.T.F.B., SC- 127–969.

Hammond, John, "Reminiscences of Frank J. Sprague," n.d., typewritten, H.H.F., John Hammond File, H-73.

Hart, Francis Arthur, "Call Letters and Log Book of Francis Arthur Hart," 1906–1909, holograph, S.I., 23, 34.

Harvard University, "Cahill, Timothy," Record of attendance, Harvard University Archives.

Hayes, Hammond Vinton, Letter from Hammond V. Hayes, Chief Engineer, American Telephone and Telegraph Company, to F. P. Fish, President, American Telephone and Telegraph Company, April 12, 1907, A.T.T.A., 604507.

Hogan, William J., Letter from Wm. J. Hogan to Miss Ruth Douglass, March 7, 1968, R.W.

————, Letter from Wm. J. Hogan to Miss [Ruth] Douglass, April 12, 1968, R.W.

————, Letter from Wm. J. Hogan to Miss [Ruth] Douglass, April 22, 1968, R.W.

"Isabelle Winlocke," list of plays, typewritten, n.n., n.d., N.Y.P.L.T.

Lane, Charles, H., Letter from C. H. Lane, Examiner, Division 5, U.S. Patent Office, to Thaddeus Cahill, March 17, 1904, N.A. 241, 1,213,803.

————, Letter from C. H. Lane, Examiner, Division 5, U.S. Patent Office, to Thaddeus Cahill, April 26, 1904, N.A. 241, 1,107,261.

————, Letter from C. H. Lane, Examiner, Division 5, U.S. Patent Office, to Thaddeus Cahill, April 11, 1905, N.A. 241, 1,213,803.

————, Letter from C. H. Lane, Examiner, Division 5, U.S. Patent Office, to Thaddeus Cahill, May 16, 1905, N.A. 241, 1,107,261.

————, Letter from C. H. Lane, Examiner, Division 5, U.S. Patent Office, to Thaddeus Cahill, June 7, 1906, N.A. 241, 1,213,803.

————, Letter from C. H. Lane, Examiner, Division 5, U.S. Patent Office, to Thaddeus Cahill, June 19, 1906, N.A. 241, 1,107,261.

————, Letter from C. H. Lane, Examiner, Division 5, U.S. Patent Office, to Thaddeus Cahill, June 29, 1906, N.A. 241, 1,213,803.

————, Letter from C. H. Lane, Examiner, Division 5, U.S. Patent Office, to Thaddeus Cahill, July 14, 1908, N.A. 241, 1,213,803.

————, Letter from C. H. Lane, Examiner, Division 5, U.S. Patent Office, to Thaddeus Cahill, September 18, 1908, N.A. 241, 1,107,261.

————, Letter from C. H. Lane, Head Examiner, U.S. Patent Office, to Thaddeus Cahill, May 12, 1896, N.A. 241, 580,035.

————, Letter from C. H. Lane, Head Examiner, U.S. Patent Office, to Thaddeus Cahill, August 4, 1896, N.A. 241, 580,035.

————, Letter from C. H. Lane, Head Examiner, U.S. Patent Office, to Thaddeus Cahill, March 27, 1902, N.A. 241, 1,107,261.

Lincoln, Stoddard, Memorandum on [William J.] Hammer, n.d., S.L.

————, "The Rise and Fall of the New York Electric Music Company: A Study in Early Musak [*sic*], of the Wonderful Telharmonium," presented as "The Rise and Fall of the New York Electric Music

Company: A Study of the Telharmonium," at the Thirty-eighth Annual Meeting of the American Musicological Society, November 4, 1972, Dallas, Tex., and as "The Telharmonium—A Study in Early Muzak," at the American Musical Instrument Society National Meeting, April 5, 1975, New York, n.d., typewritten, S.L.

Lockwood, Thomas D., Letter from Thomas D. Lockwood to F. P. Fish, President, April 17, 1907, A.T.T.A.

McLean, Harry C., Letter from Harry C. McLean, Chief Clerk and Deputy Health Officer, Commissioners of the District of Columbia, Health Department, to Dr. W. W. Foster, May 22, 1911, H.U.

MacNab, J. F., Amendment B by J. F. MacNab, Examiner, Division 5, U.S. Patent Office, December 22, 1916, N.A. 241, 1,213,804.

————, Amendment D by J. F. MacNab, Examiner, Division 5, U.S. Patent Office, January 15, 1917, N.A. 241, 1,213,804.

————, Examiner's Statement from J. F. MacNab, Examiner, Division 5, U.S. Patent Office, to the Commissioner of Patents, December 13, 1916, N.A. 241, 1,213,804.

————, Examiner's Statement from J. F. MacNab, Examiner, Division 5, U.S. Patent Office, to the Commissioner of Patents, February 6, 1919, filed February 6, 1919, N.A. 241, 1,295,691.

————, Examiner's Statement from J. F. MacNab, Examiner, Division 5, U.S. Patent Office, to the Commissioner of Patents, February 14, 1919, filed February 14, 1919, N.A. 241, 1,295,691.

————, Letter from J. F. MacNab, Examiner, Division 5, U.S. Patent Office, to Thaddeus Cahill, August 5, 1909, N.A. 241, 1,213,803.

————, Letter from J. F. MacNab, Examiner, Division 5, U.S. Patent Office, to Thaddeus Cahill, October 16, 1909, N.A. 241, 1,107,261.

————, Letter from J. F. MacNab, Examiner, Division 5, U.S. Patent Office, to Thaddeus Cahill, October 20, 1909, N.A. 241, 1,213,803.

————, Letter from J. F. MacNab, Examiner, Division 5, U.S. Patent Office, to Thaddeus Cahill, May 25, 1912, N.A. 241, 1,213,803.

———, Letter from J. F. MacNab, Examiner, Division 5, U.S. Patent Office, to Thaddeus Cahill, October 17, 1913, N.A. 241, 1,213,803.

———, Letter from J. F. MacNab, Examiner, Division 5, U.S. Patent Office, to Thaddeus Cahill, April 26, 1916, N.A. 241, 1,213,804.

———, Letter from J. F. MacNab, Examiner, Division 5, U.S. Patent Office, to Thaddeus Cahill, May 9, 1916, N.A. 241, 1,295,691.

———, Letter from J. F. MacNab, Examiner, Division 5, U.S. Patent Office, to Commissioner of Patents, January 2, 1917, N.A. 241, 1,213,804.

———, Letter from J. F. MacNab, Examiner, Division 5, U.S. Patent Office, to Thaddeus Cahill, January 15, 1917, N.A. 241, 1,213,803.

———, Letter from J. F. MacNab, Examiner, Division 5, U.S. Patent Office, to Thaddeus Cahill, June 3, 1918, N.A. 241, 1,295,691.

Mitchell, H. E., Letter from H. E. Mitchell to Wm. J. Hammer, January 13, 1907, S.L.

Moore, Edward B., Letter from E. B. Moore, Commissioner of Patents, U.S. Patent Office, to Thaddeus Cahill, January 13, 1912, N.A. 241, 1,107,261.

———, Notice of hearing from E. B. Moore, Commissioner of Patents, U.S. Patent Office, to Thaddeus Cahill, December 17, 1910, N.A. 241, 1,107,261.

———, Notice of postponement from E. B. Moore, Commissioner of Patents, U.S. Patent Office, to Thaddeus Cahill, December 23, 1910, N.A. 241, 1,107,261.

———, Notice of postponement from E. B. Moore, Commissioner of Patents, U.S. Patent Office, to Thaddeus Cahill, March 20, 1911, N.A. 241, 1,107,261.

———, Notice of postponement from E. B. Moore, Commissioner of Patents, U.S. Patent Office, to Thaddeus Cahill, April 3, 1911, N.A. 241, 1,107,261.

———, Notice of postponement from E. B. Moore, Commissioner of Patents, U.S. Patent Office, to Thaddeus Cahill, April 29, 1911, N.A. 241, 1,107,261.

————, Notice of postponement from E. B. Moore, Commissioner of Patents, U.S. Patent Office, to Thaddeus Cahill, July 1, 1911, N.A. 241, 1,107,261.

————, Petition from E. B. Moore, Commissioner of Patents, U.S. Patent Office, to Examiner in charge of Division 5, December 17, 1910, N.A. 241, 1,107,261.

————, Ruling by E. B. Moore, Commissioner, U.S. Patent Office, January 5, 1912, N.A. 241, 1,107,261.

Moore, Robert, Ass't. Marshal, "Schedule 1.—Free Inhabitants in Ward 5, City of Nashua, in the County of Hillsborough, State of New Hampshire, enumerated by me, on the 15th day of June, 1860," in *Population Schedules of the Eighth Census of the United States, 1860,* Roll 673, New Hampshire, vol. 5, Washington: National Archives Microfilm Publications, National Archives and Records Service, General Services Administration, 1967, 113.

Moore, William Douglas, Notice of Probate, in the Matter of Proving the Last Will and Testament of Thaddeus Cahill, September 7, 1934, filed at Surrogate's Court, New York County, New York, N.Y., February 4, 1935.

New England Electric Music Company, Annual Report for 1902, July 24, 1902, filed at the Office of the Secretary of State, Trenton, N.J., July 31, 1902.

————, Annual Report for 1903, April 17, 1903, filed at the Office of the Secretary of State, Trenton, N.J., n.d.

————, Annual Report for 1904, April 21, 1904, filed at the Office of the Secretary of State, Trenton, N.J., April 27, 1904.

————, Annual Report for 1905, April 27, 1905, filed at the Office of the Secretary of State, Trenton, N.J., n.d.

————, Annual Report for 1906, April 20, 1906, filed at the Office of the Secretary of State, Trenton, N.J., n.d.

————, Annual Report for 1907, April 24, 1907, filed at the Office of the Secretary of State, Trenton, N.J., May 1, 1907.

————, Annual Report for 1908, April 30, 1908, filed at the Office of the Secretary of State, Trenton, N.J., May 12, 1908.

————, Certificate of Incorporation, June 28, 1902, received and recorded at the Office of the Hudson County Clerk, Jersey City, N.J., June 30, 1902, filed and recorded at the Office of the Secretary of State, Trenton, N.J., July 1, 1902.

————, Certificate of Increase of Capital Stock, May 23, 1904, filed and recorded at the Office of the Secretary of State, Trenton, N.J., May 24, 1904.

————, Certificate of Increase of Capital Stock, September 11, 1907, filed and recorded at the Office of the Secretary of State, Trenton, N.J., September 16, 1907.

New York Cahill Telharmonic Company, Certificate of Incorporation, May 7, 1907, filed and recorded at the Office of the Secretary of State, Albany, N.Y., May 8, 1907, also filed and recorded at the Office of the New York County Clerk, New York, N.Y., May 9, 1907, A.C.C. 2757–1907.

————, "Map Showing the Wires Used by the Company on September 30, 1913, and the Streets and Avenues on Which the Same Are Located," attached to Letter from Arthur T. Cahill to the Chairman and Members of the Board of Estimate and Apportionment of the City of New York, November 1, 1913, B.E.

————, "Map Showing the Wires Used by the Company on September 30, 1914, and the Streets and Avenues on Which the Same Are Located," attached to Letter from Arthur T. Cahill to the Chairman and Members of the Board of Estimate and Apportionment of the City of New York, November 13, 1914, B.E.

New York Electric Music Company, Annual Report for 1904, August 12, 1904, filed at the Office of the Secretary of State, Trenton, N.J., August 12, 1904.

————, Annual Report for 1905, April 25, 1905, filed at the Office of the Secretary of State, Trenton, N.J., n.d.

————, Annual Report for 1906, May 8, 1906, filed at the Office of the Secretary of State, Trenton, N.J., n.d.

————, Annual Report for 1907, April 24, 1907, filed at the Office of the Secretary of State, Trenton, N.J., May 1, 1907.

————, Annual Report for 1908, April 30, 1908, filed at the Office of the Secretary of State, Trenton, N.J., May 8, 1908.

————, Certificate of Incorporation, August 10, 1904, received and recorded at the Office of the Hudson County Clerk, Jersey City, N.J., August 10, 1904, filed and recorded at the Office of the Secretary of State, Trenton, N.J., August 10, 1904.

————, Certificate of Increase of Capital Stock, April 25, 1905, filed and recorded at the Office of the Secretary of State, Trenton, N.J., May 2, 1905.

————, Certificate of Increase of Capital Stock, May 7, 1906, filed and recorded at the Office of the Secretary of State, Trenton, N.J., May 18, 1906.

————, Invitation from the Company to Mr. W. J. Hammer, January 1907, S.L., Copy S.I.

North River Telharmonic Company, Certificate of Incorporation, August 22, 1910, received and recorded at the Office of the Hudson County Clerk, Jersey City, N.J., August 26, 1910, filed and recorded at the Office of the Secretary of State, Trenton, N.J., September 7, 1910.

————, Petition for Re-Instatement of New York Electric Music Company, January 31, 1911, filed and recorded at the Office of the Secretary of State, Trenton, N.J., February 2, 1911.

Pacific Coast Telharmonic Company, Articles of Incorporation, September 3, 1904, filed and recorded at the Office of the Secretary of State, Olympia, Wash., September 12, 1904, 1–4.

Philbrook, Warren C., Letter from Warren C. Philbrook, Asst. Attorney-General of Maine, to Arthur I. Brown, Secretary of State of Maine, May 29, 1908.

Pierce, Edna Leaf Woodruff, Diary, Auburn, N.Y., February 4, 1898, to March 6, 1908, J.E.P.

Pierce, James Edward, "Item Regarding Pioneer Inventor of Electric Music and His Association with the Pierce Family," August 1970, typewritten, J.E.P., S.I.

————, "James E. Pierce and Frances Hall Married July 11, 1866, in Auburn, N.Y.," List of family birthdates, April 23, 1983, R.W.

————, Letter from James E. Pierce to Cynthia Hoover, Smithsonian Institution, May 25, 1974, S.I.

————, Letter from James E. Pierce to Cynthia Hoover, Smithsonian Institution, June 7, 1974, S.I.

————, Letter from James E. Pierce to Cynthia Hoover, Curator, Smithsonian Institution, June 23, 1974, S.I.

Pierce, Roderic, Letter from Rod[eric Pierce] to Jim [James Edward Pierce], June 12, 1974, J.E.P.

Seymour, John S., Letter from John S. Seymour, Commissioner of Patents, to Thaddeus Cahill, April 6, 1897, N.A. 241, 580,035.

Shaw, John K., and James Piper, Executors of the Estate of Frederick C. Todd, Assets of Estate, May 19, 1919, filed and recorded May 22, 1919, Baltimore County Orphans Court, Baltimore, Md., "Baltimore County: Inventories, WJP #43," Maryland State Archives CR 9107, 53–56.

————, Executors of the Estate of Frederick C. Todd, Petition, December 30, 1918, filed and recorded January 6, 1919, Baltimore County Orphans Court, Baltimore, Md., "Baltimore County Orphans Court: Proceedings, WJP #28," Maryland State Archives CR 255, 92–101.

Telharmonic Securities Company, Application for a certificate to do business in the State of New York, November 19, 1907, and sworn Copy of Certificate of Incorporation, filed and recorded at the Office of the Secretary of State, Albany, N.Y., November 21, 1907.

————, Certificate of Incorporation, August 19, 1907, received and recorded at the Office of the Hudson County Clerk, Jersey City, N.J., August 19, 1907.

————, Revocation of the designation heretofore made to John C. Rowe, August 24, 1908, filed and recorded at the Office of the Secretary of State, Albany, N.Y., August 28, 1908.

Treasurer's Office, State of New York, Receipt from New York Cahill Telharmonic Company, Albany, N.Y., May 8, 1907, A.C.C.

Tuska, Clarence D., Letter from C. D. Tuska, Staff Consultant, Patents, RCA Laboratories, to Arthur T. Cahill, February 17, 1959, M.C.S.

U.S. Patent Office, Insert 80H, Memorandum attached to printed application, handwritten, n.d., N.A. 241, 1,213,804.

————, Memorandum of receipt, January 31, 1919, N.A. 241, 1,295,691.

————, Wrapper for Patent 580,035, *Electric Pianoforte &c.*, n.d., N.A. 241, 580,035.

————, Wrapper for Patent 1,107,261, *Music Generating and Music Distributing Apparatus,* February 10, 1902, *et al.* to August 7, 1914, N.A. 241, 1,107,261.

————, Wrapper for Patent 1,213,803, *Art of and Apparatus for Generating and Distributing Music Electrically,* February 17, 1904, *et al.* to January 23, 1917, N.A. 241, 1,213,803.

————, Wrapper for Patent 1,213,804, *Art of and Apparatus for Generating and Distributing Music Electrically,* April 27, 1916, *et al.* to January 23, 1916 [*sic:* actually 1917], N.A. 241, 1,213,804.

————, Wrapper for Patent 1,295,691, *Art of and Apparatus for Generating and Distributing Music Electrically,* June 26, 1915, *et al.* to February 25, 1919, N.A. 241, 1,295,691.

————, Wrapper for Patent 2,584,546, *Light-Beam Projecting Means for Projecting Pictures, Floodlighting, Spotlighting, Etc.,* August 2, 1950, *et al.* to February 5, 1952, N.A., Federal Records Center, Suitland, Md.

Wead, C. K., Examiner's Statement, C. K. Wead, Acting Examiner, Division 5, on Petition to the Commissioner, December 20, 1910, N.A. 241, 1,107,261.

————, Letter from C. K. Wead, Acting Examiner, Division 5, U.S. Patent Office, to Thaddeus Cahill, August 9, 1907, N.A. 241, 1,107,261.

————, Letter from C. K. Wead, Acting Examiner, Division 5, U.S. Patent Office, to Thaddeus Cahill, December 20, 1910, N.A. 241, 1,213,803.

Weinberg, Henry, M.D., Assistant Medical Examiner, Certificate of Death of Thaddeus Cahill, April 12, 1934, filed at the Department of Health of the City of New York, Bureau of Records, April 12, 1934.

Wilson, S. S., Certificate of Pension Dropped, October 12, 1899, N.A.F.T.B., Timothy Cahill, 10th N.H. Inf.

Wilson, Woodrow, Governor of New Jersey, Permit to Re-Instate the New York Electric Music Company, filed and recorded at the Office of the Secretary of State, Trenton, N.J., February 2, 1911.

Woolard, W. F., Letter from W. F. Woolard, Chief Clerk, U.S. Patent Office, to Thaddeus Cahill, August 6, 1914, N.A. 241, 1,107,261.

Yorke, George M., Letter from George M. Yorke, Assistant Engineer, American Telephone and Telegraph Co., to Hammond V. Hayes, Chief Engineer, American Telephone and Telegraph Co., April 5, 1907, A.T.T.B.L.A., Boston File 500, 20.03.01.02.

LETTERS TO THE AUTHOR

Bigglestone, W. E., Archivist, Oberlin College Archives, Oberlin, Ohio, June 29, 1982.

Clark, Ramona [Mrs. Eugene M.], Stockport, Iowa, September 13, 1983.

DiCarlo, Ella Merkel, Assistant to the Publisher, *Holyoke Transcript-Telegram,* Holyoke, Mass., April 23, 1984; n.d., postmarked June 8, 1984.

————, Conway, Mass., July 27, 1984.

Douglass, Ruth, Professor Emerita, Mount Holyoke College, Granville, N.Y., May 8, 1984.

Garden State Crematory, North Bergen, N.J., n.n., n.d., postmarked January 13, 1989.

Heilakka, Edwin E., Curator, Stokowski Collection, Curtis Institute of Music, Philadelphia, Pa., September 28, 1992.

K. J. Q., Clerk, Office of the Secretary of State, Commonwealth of Massachusetts, Boston, February 18, 1987.

Pierce, James Edward, Smithfield, Va., n.d., postmarked March 30, 1983; May 11, 1983; August 25, 1983.

Pound, Mary E., Special Collections Division, Gelman Library, George Washington University, Washington, D.C., August 4, 1982; August 1, 1984.

Trampler, Allen, Necker-Sharpe Funeral Home, Union City, N.J., July 11, 1983.

PERSONAL COMMUNICATIONS

Personal interview with James Edward Pierce, Echo Lake Farm, Great Spring Road, Smithfield, Va., April 23, 1983.

Personal interviews with Margaret Eleanor Cahill Schwartz, Rochester, N.Y., August 28–31, 1990.

Telephone interview with Bill Massa, Manuscripts and Archives Department, Sterling Memorial Library, Yale University, New Haven, Conn., September 25, 1989.

Telephone interview with Dr. Fred Heimbuch, D.D.S., West Long Branch, N.J., May 11, 1984.

Telephone interviews with Dr. John T. Hornblow, M.D., West Hartford, Conn., October 4, 1989, March 26, 1990.

Telephone interview with George Gordon, Brooklyn, N.Y., October 1, 1990.

Telephone interview with Manuel Perez, Weehawken, N.J., February 14, 1984.

Telephone interview with Mrs. Walter Koehler, Cranford, N.J., May 8, 1984.

Telephone interview with Mrs. Mieczyslaw Horszowski, Philadelphia, Pa., May 13, 1986.

Telephone interview with Murphey Thigpenn, Jacksonville, Fla., May 5, 1987.

Telephone interview with Otto Luening, New York, N.Y., September 21, 1992.

Telephone interview with Sophie Struniewski, Cliffside Park, N.J., February 4, 1984.

THE CAHILL BROTHERS' U.S. PATENTS

345,028. *Organ.* Thaddeus Cahill, Oberlin, Ohio, Assignor of Two Thirds to Timothy Cahill, Oberlin, Ohio. Application August 14, 1885. Patented July 6, 1886.

359,557. *Piano-Action.* Thaddeus Cahill, Oberlin, Ohio, Assignor of Two Thirds to Timothy Cahill, Oberlin, Ohio. Application November 16, 1886. Patented March 15, 1887.

359,842. *Organ.* Thaddeus Cahill, Oberlin, Ohio, Assignor of Two Thirds to Timothy Cahill, Oberlin, Ohio. Application June 5, 1886. Patented March 22, 1887.

458,219. *Piano-Forte Action.* Thaddeus Cahill, Oberlin, Ohio. Application March 1, 1888. Divided, application March 17, 1891. Patented August 25, 1891.

502,700. *Type-Writing Machine.* Thaddeus Cahill, Washington, D.C. Application May 5, 1892. Patented August 8, 1893.

520,667. *Pianoforte-Action.* Thaddeus Cahill, New York, N.Y. ["residing temporarily at Washington"]. Application March 21, 1893. Patented May 29, 1894.

531,904. *Type-Writing Machine.* Thaddeus Cahill, Washington, D.C. Application September 24, 1892. Patented January 1, 1895.

541,222. *Type-Writing Machine.* Thaddeus Cahill, New York, N.Y. ["temporarily residing at Washington"]. Application July 30, 1894. Patented June 18, 1895.

554,108. *Pianoforte-Action.* Thaddeus Cahill, New York, N.Y. ["residing temporarily at Washington"]. Application March 21, 1893. Patented February 4, 1896.

554,109. *Pianoforte-Action.* Thaddeus Cahill, New York, N.Y. ["residing temporarily at Washington"]. Application March 21, 1893. Patented February 4, 1896.

566,442. *Type-Writing Machine.* Thaddeus Cahill, New York, N.Y. ["residing temporarily at Washington"]. Application January 4, 1896. Patented August 25, 1896.

580,035. *Art of and Apparatus for Generating and Distributing Music Electrically.* Thaddeus Cahill, New York, N.Y. ["residing temporarily at Washington,"]. Applications August 10, 1895, February 4, 1896. Patented April 6, 1897.

582,898. *Type-Writing Machine.* Thaddeus Cahill, New York, N.Y. ["temporarily residing at Washington"]. Application July 30, 1894. Patented May 18, 1897.

600,119. *Type-Writing Machine.* Thaddeus Cahill, New York, N.Y. ["residing temporarily at Washington"]. Assignor to Himself, Amos J. Cummings, George F. Cahill, Arthur T. Cahill, and E. Hilton Jackson, Trustees. Application December 14, 1895. Patented March 1, 1898.

600,120. *Type-Writing Machine.* Thaddeus Cahill, New York, N.Y. ["residing temporarily at Washington"]. Assignor to Himself, Amos J. Cummings, George F. Cahill, Arthur T. Cahill, and E. Hilton Jackson, Trustees. Application December 14, 1895. Patented March 1, 1898.

604,001. *Type-Writing Machine, &c.* Thaddeus Cahill, New York, N.Y. ["temporarily residing at Washington"], Assignor to James B. Lambie, E. Hilton Jackson, George Frederick Cahill, and Arthur T. Cahill, Trustees. Application June 19, 1897. Patented May 10, 1898.

605,777. *Linotype-Machine, Line-Casting Machine, and Machine for Making Type-Bars, Linotypes, and Matrices.* Thaddeus Cahill, New York, N.Y.

["temporarily residing at Washington"]. Application October 21, 1896. Divided, application August 11, 1897. Patented June 14, 1898.

654,133. *Type-Writing Machine.* Thaddeus Cahill, Washington, D.C. ["of New York, temporarily residing at Washington"], Assignor to James B. Lambie, E. Hilton Jackson, George Frederick Cahill, and Arthur T. Cahill, Trustees. Application February 1, 1898. Patented July 24, 1900.

656,576. *Type-Writing Machine.* Thaddeus Cahill, New York, N.Y. ["temporarily residing at Washington"], Assignor to Himself, Amos J. Cummings, George F. Cahill, Arthur T. Cahill, and E. Hilton Jackson, Trustees. Application January 4, 1896. Divided, application August 3, 1896. Patented August 21, 1900.

657,477. *Piano-Action or Other Keyboard Instrument.* Thaddeus Cahill, New York, N.Y. ["temporarily residing at Washington"], Assignor to James B. Lambie, E. Hilton Jackson, George Frederick Cahill, and Arthur T. Cahill, Trustees. Application September 8, 1894. Patented September 4, 1900.

657,478. *Type-Writing Machine, Linotype-Machine, Type-Setting Machine, or Other Keyboard Printing Instrumentality.* Thaddeus Cahill, Washington, D.C., Assignor to James B. Lambie, E. Hilton Jackson, George Frederick Cahill, and Arthur T. Cahill, Trustees. Application June 30, 1898. Patented September 4, 1900.

657,479. *Type-Writing Machine, or Other Keyboard Printing Instrumentality.* Thaddeus Cahill, New York, N.Y. ["temporarily residing at Washington"], Assignor to James B. Lambie, E. Hilton Jackson, George Frederick Cahill, and Arthur T. Cahill, Trustees. Application June 30, 1898. Patented December 24, 1900.

705,559. *Type-Writing Machine.* Thaddeus Cahill, New York, N.Y. ["residing temporarily at Washington"], Assignor to James B. Lambie, E. Hilton Jackson, George Frederick Cahill, and Arthur T. Cahill, Trustees. Application October 26, 1899. Patented July 29, 1902.

755,447. *System for Illuminating Fields So That Games May Be Played at Night.* George F. Cahill, Holyoke, Mass., Application December 26, 1903. Patented March 22, 1904.

770,260. *Approach to Movable Walks, Stairways, &c.* George F. Cahill, Holyoke, Mass. Application December 18, 1903. Patented September 20, 1904.

777,651. *Type-Writing Machine or Other Similar Instrument.* Thaddeus Cahill, New York, N.Y. ["residing temporarily at Washington"], Assignor to Ellis Spear, John T. Schaaff, E. Hilton Jackson, and Joseph J. Darlington, Trustees. Application February 28, 1901. Renewed April 18, 1904. Patented December 13, 1904.

777,652. *Type-Writing Machine or Other Similar Instrument.* Thaddeus Cahill, New York, N.Y. ["residing temporarily at Washington"]. Application February 28, 1901. Patented December 13, 1904.

897,959. *Type-Writing Machine.* Thaddeus Cahill, New York, N.Y. ["temporarily residing at Washington"], Assignor to Ellis Spear, John T. Schaaff, E. Hilton Jackson, and Joseph J. Darlington, Trustees. Application February 28, 1901. Patented September 8, 1908.

1,097,789. *Type-Writing Machine.* Thaddeus Cahill, New York, N.Y. ["temporarily residing at Washington"]. Application October 17, 1900. Renewed December 4, 1905. Patented May 26, 1914.

1,107,261. *Music-Generating and Music-Distributing Apparatus.* Thaddeus Cahill, Washington D.C. ["residing temporarily at Washington"], Assignor to Ellis Spear, E. Hilton Jackson, George F. Cahill, Arthur T. Cahill, and Thaddeus Cahill, Trustees. Applications August 10, 1895, February 10, 1902. Renewed January 10, 1914. Patented August 18, 1914.

1,197,103. *Type-Writing Machine.* Thaddeus Cahill, New York, N.Y. ["residing temporarily at Washington"], Assignor to James B. Lambie, E. Hilton Jackson, George Frederick Cahill, and Arthur T. Cahill, Trustees. Application November 4, 1899. Renewed February 5, 1916. Patented September 5, 1916.

1,213,803. *Art of and Apparatus for Generating and Distributing Music Electrically.* Thaddeus Cahill, Holyoke, Mass., Assignor to Ellis Spear, E. Hilton Jackson, George F. Cahill, Arthur T. Cahill, and Thaddeus Cahill, Trustees. Applications January 19, 1901, February 26, 1903, February 17, 1904. Renewed November 6, 1913, December 14, 1916. Patented January 23, 1917.

1,213,804. *Art of and Apparatus for Generating and Distributing Music Electrically.* Thaddeus Cahill, New York, N.Y. Assignor to Ellis Spear, E. Hilton Jackson, George F. Cahill, Arthur T. Cahill, and Thaddeus Cahill, Trustees. Applications January 19, 1901, February 26, 1903, February 17, 1904, April 27, 1915. Patented January 23, 1917.

1,235,527. *Illuminating System for Base-Ball and Other Games.* George F. Cahill, New York, N.Y. Application June 1, 1909. Renewed December 21, 1916. Patented July 31, 1917.

1,295,691. *Art of and Apparatus for Generating and Distributing Music Electrically.* Thaddeus Cahill, New York, N.Y. Applications January 19, 1901, February 26, 1903, February 17, 1904, June 26, 1915. Renewed May 8, 1918. Patented February 25, 1919.

1,569,260. *Bowling Alley and Bowling Apparatus.* George F. Cahill, New York, N.Y. Application January 29, 1919. Renewed June 6, 1925. Patented January 12, 1936.

1,775,222. *Type-Composing Machine and Other Similar Instrument.* Thaddeus Cahill, New York, N.Y. Application December 8, 1927. Patented September 9, 1930.

1,983,734. *Race Track Illumination.* George F. Cahill, New York, N.Y. Applications January 17, 1934, May 4, 1934. Patented December 11, 1934.

1,987,000. *Bowling Alley.* George F. Cahill, New York, N.Y., Application February 11, 1933. Patented January 8, 1935.

2,000,123. *Game and Game Apparatus.* George F. Cahill, New York, N.Y. Application November 28, 1932. Patented May 7, 1935.

2,004,888. *Sports Arena and the Accessories Thereto.* George F. Cahill, New York, N.Y. Application September 6, 1934. Patented June 11, 1935.

2,009,138. *Electrical Speakers and Other Speakers.* Thaddeus Cahill, New York, N.Y.; Arthur T. Cahill, Weehawken, N.J., Eleanor Cahill and George Frederick Cahill, both of New York, N.Y., executors of Thaddeus Cahill, deceased. Applications July 3, 1931, March 14, 1933. Patented July 23, 1935.

2,018,833. *Game and Game Apparatus.* George F. Cahill, New York, N.Y. Application September 12, 1931. Patented October 29, 1935.

2,103,766. *Synchronized Sound and Picture Control.* Thaddeus Cahill, New York, N.Y.; Arthur T. Cahill, Eleanor Cahill, and George Frederick Cahill, executors of the estate of said Thaddeus Cahill, deceased. Application November 24, 1930. Patented December 28, 1937.

2,161,995. *Speaker and Listening Device.* Arthur T. Cahill, Weehawken, N.J. Application July 22, 1935. Patented June 13, 1939.

2,308,051. *Means for Generating Music Electrically.* Arthur T. Cahill, Weehawken, N.J. Application December 5, 1938. Patented January 12, 1943.

2,354,196. *Typewriting Machine, Typesetting Machine, and Other Keyboard Instruments.* Arthur T. Cahill, Weehawken, N.J. Application February 3, 1938. Patented July 25, 1944.

2,413,288. *Picture Projection Apparatus for Stills and for Moving Pictures.* Arthur T. Cahill, Weehawken, N.J. Application May 5, 1945. Patented December 31, 1946.

2,463,597. *Art or Method and Means for Generating Music Electrically.* Arthur T. Cahill, Weehawken, N.J. Application January 9, 1943. Patented March 8, 1949.

2,584,546. *Light-Beam Projecting Means for Projecting Pictures, Floodlighting, Spotlighting, Etc.* Arthur T. Cahill, Weehawken, N.J., and Lawrence Victor Merrill, Brooklyn, N.Y. Application August 2, 1950. Patented February 5, 1952.

THADDEUS CAHILL'S FOREIGN PATENTS

Brevet d'Invention 265721. *Procédé et appareil pour engendrer et distribuer de la musique électriquement.* Thaddeus Cahill. Application April 6, 1897. Patented July 16, 1897.

Brevet d'Invention 338982. *Procédé et appareil pour produire et distribuer de la musique électriquement.* Thaddeus Cahill. Application April 23, 1903. Patented August 13, 1904. Published October 18, 1904.

Brevet d'Invention 343221. *Procédé et appareil pour produire et distribuer de la musique électriquement.* Thaddeus Cahill. Application May 17, 1904. Patented July 30, 1904. Published September 28, 1904.

British Patent 8725. *Art of and Apparatus for Generating and Distributing Music Electrically.* Thaddeus Cahill, New York City. Robert Alexander

Sloan, Patent Agent, Liverpool. Application April 6, 1897. Patented August 21, 1897.

British Specification of Invention 3666. *Improvements in the Art of and Apparatus for Generating and Distributing Music.* Thaddeus Cahill. William Bottomley, Patent Agent, Glasgow. Provisional Specification Application February 17, 1903. Complete Specification December 17, 1903. Accepted May 17, 1904.

British Specification of Invention 3666A. *Improvements in the Art of and Apparatus for Generating and Distributing Music.* Thaddeus Cahill. William Bottomley, Patent Agent, Glasgow. Provisional Specification Application February 17, 1903. Complete Specification May 10, 1904. Accepted May 17, 1904.

British Specification of Invention 3666B. *Improvements in the Art of and Apparatus for Generating and Distributing Music.* Thaddeus Cahill. William Bottomley, Patent Agent, Glasgow. Provisional Specification Application February 17, 1903. Complete Specification May 10, 1904. Accepted May 17, 1904.

British Specification of Invention 3666C. *Improvements in the Art of and Apparatus for Generating and Distributing Music.* Thaddeus Cahill. William Bottomley, Patent Agent, Glasgow. Provisional Specification Application February 17, 1903. Complete Specification May 10, 1904. Accepted May 17, 1904.

Kaiserliches Patentamt Patentschrift 115631. *Verfahren und Vorrichtung zur Erzeugung und übertragung von Musik auf elektrischem Wege.* Thaddeus Cahill in New-York. Application April 7, 1897. Patented January 3, 1901.

Kaiserliches Patentamt Patentschrift 118151. *Schwingungsregler an Vorrichtungen zur Erzeugung und übertragung von Musik auf elektrischem Wege.* Thaddeus Cahill in Washington. Application March 29, 1903. Patented March 7, 1907.

Kaiserliches Patentamt Patentschrift 183948. *Regelungsvorrichtung für die Lautstärke der Töne bei Anlagen zur Erzeugung und übertragung von Musik auf elektrischem Wege.* Thaddeus Cahill in Washington. Application March 29, 1903. Patented April 26, 1907.

Kaiserliches Patentamt Patentschrift 184101. *Schaltvorrichtung an Apparaten zur Erzeugung und übertragung von Musik auf elektrischem Wege.* Thaddeus

Cahill in Washington. Application March 29, 1903. Patented April 24, 1907.

Kaiserliches Patentamt Patentschrift 190001. *Vorrichtung zur Erzeugung und übertragung von Musik auf elektrischem Wege, bei welcher die einen musikalischen Klang zusammensetzenden Partialtöne in besonderen Stromkreisen erzeugt und alsdann in der Fernleitung vereinigt werden.* Thaddeus Cahill in Washington. Application March 29, 1903. Patented October 18, 1907.

GENERAL REFERENCE

De Vries, Louis. *German-English Science Dictionary.* Third edition. New York: McGraw-Hill Book Company, 1959.

Godman, A., and E. M. F. Payne. *Longman Dictionary of Scientific Usage.* Harlow and London: Longman Group, 1979.

Gottschalk, Louis. *Understanding History: A Primer of Historical Method.* New York: Alfred A. Knopf, 1951.

Winks, Robin W., ed. *The Historian as Detective: Essays on Evidence.* New York: Harper and Row, 1969.

PUBLICATIONS

"A Beszelő Ujságról," *Magyar Salon,* October 1897, M.R., 185–186.

"A Fővárosi Lapok hangversenye a Telefon Hirmondóban," *Fővárosi Lapok,* January 18, 1896, M.R., 6.

"A. L. Whipple with Telharmonic Co.," *Musical Age,* November 23, 1907, LX:4, 57.

"A. T. Cahill, Inventor, 89," *Newark Evening News,* January 26, 1962, 32.

"About Margaret Jamieson's Career," *Musical Courier,* February 28, 1918, XXXVI:9, 26.

"Addams S. M'Allister," *New York Times,* November 27, 1946, 25.

"Admiral Sigsbee of the *Maine* Dies," *New York Times,* July 20, 1923, 13.

"Agnes Brown Scores in 'Rose of Alhambra,' " *New York Evening Journal,* February 5, 1907, 6.

"Al Leech Seriously Ill," *Billboard,* May 5, 1906, XVIII:18, 17.

"All Can Now Be Musical," *Music Trade Review,* November 30, 1907, XLV:22, 47.

"Always Eat to Slow Music," *Music Trade Review,* May 4, 1907, XLIV:18, 40.

"American Explorer Visits Central Asia," *New York Times,* January 31, 1904, pt. 1, 4.

"Among the features of the performances . . .," *New York American,* February 17, 1907, S.C., n.p.

"Among the new features . . .," *New York American,* February 10, 1907, S.C.. n.p.

"Andreas Dippel Outlines His Plans for 'Musical America,' " *Musical America,* March 7, 1908, VII:17, 1, 4.

Andrews, Wayne, "Mackay, Clarence Hungerford," *Dictionary of American Biography,* vol. XI, supp. 2. New York: Charles Scribner's Sons, 1958, 415–416.

"Anna F. de Koven, Author and Poet," *New York Times,* January 13, 1953, 27.

"The Annual Awakening of the Only Coney Island," *New York Times,* May 6, 1906, pt. 4, 8.

"Another Mill," *Holyoke Daily Transcript,* April 8, 1911, 2.

"Approval of Resolutions by the Mayor," *Minutes, Meeting of Board of Estimate and Apportionment,* January 19, 1911, 213.

"Arc Lights Shed Electrical Music," *New York World,* November 10, 1906, 6.

"Arrest Husband of Mme. Gadski on Conspiracy Charge," *New York Morning Telegraph,* March 31, 1916, 1–2.

"The Art of Telharmony," *Electrical World,* March 10, 1906, XLVII:10, 509–510.

"Arthur Cahill; Was Inventor," *Hudson Dispatch,* January 25, 1962, 16.

"Arthur T. Cahill Dies," *New York Times,* January 26, 1962, 31.

"Arthur T. Cahill, Inventor, at 89," *Jersey Journal,* January 25, 1962, 11.

Askew, Antony, "The Amazing Clement Ader," pt. 1, *Studio Sound,* September 1981, 23:9, 44–46, 48.

————, "The Amazing Clement Ader," pt. 2, *Studio Sound,* October 1981, 23:10, 66–68.

————, "The Amazing Clement Ader," pt. 3, *Studio Sound,* November 1981, 23:11, 100–102.

"At Telharmonic Hall the novelties . . .," *New York World,* February 12, 1907, S.C., n.p. [not found].

"At Telharmonic Hall, Thirty-ninth . . . ," *New York Dramatic Mirror,* February 23, 1907, LVII:1470, S.C., 16.

"At Telharmonic Hall to-morrow . . . ," *New York Evening World,* February 16, 1907, S.C., n.p. [not found].

"At the City Churches," *New York Evening Sun,* February 16, 1907, 6.

"Attractions at New York Theatres for the Coming Week," *New York Evening Journal,* January 25, 1908, 11.

"Attractions at the Theatres," *New York Evening Sun,* February 9, 1907, 11.

"Attractions at the Theatres," *New York Evening Sun,* February 16, 1907, 2.

"Attractions at the Theatres," *New York Evening Sun,* February 19, 1907, 10.

"Attractions at the Theatres," *New York Evening Sun,* March 2, 1907, 5.

"Attractions at the Theatres," *New York Evening Sun,* March 5, 1907, 10.

"Attractions at the Theatres," *New York Evening Sun,* March 9, 1907, 8.

"Attractions at the Theatres," *New York Evening Sun,* March 12, 1907, 10.

"Attractions at the Theatres," *New York Evening Sun,* March 23, 1907, 11.

"Attractions at the Theatres," *New York Evening Sun,* March 26, 1907, 10.

"Attractions at the Theatres," *New York Evening Sun,* November 2, 1907, 6.

"Attractions at the Theatres," *New York Evening Sun,* November 5, 1907, 8.

"Attractions at the Theatres," *New York Evening Sun,* November 9, 1907, 5.

"Attractions at the Theatres," *New York Evening Sun,* November 12, 1907, 10.

"Attractions at the Theatres," *New York Evening Sun,* November 23, 1907, 4.

"Attractions at the Theatres," *New York Evening Sun,* November 26, 1907, 8.

"Attractions at the Theatres," *New York Evening Sun,* November 30, 1907, 9.

"Attractions at the Theatres," *New York Evening Sun,* December 3, 1907, 12.

"Attractions at the Theatres this Week," *New York Evening Journal,* January 14, 1908, 9.

"Attractions for the Coming Week," *New York Evening Journal,* January 4, 1908, 9.

"Attractions for the Coming Week," *New York Evening Journal,* January 11, 1908, 7.

"Attractions for the Coming Week at New York Theatres," *New York Evening Journal,* January 18, 1908, 11.

"Audience 600 Miles Away," *New York Times,* April 8, 1906, pt. 2, 6.

"The Audion Described," *New York Times,* October 27, 1906, 9.

"Auto Club at Dinner," *New-York Daily Tribune,* December 9, 1906, 7.

Baker, Ray Stannard. *American Chronicle.* New York: Charles Scribner's Sons, 1945.

————, "New Music for an Old World," *McClure's Magazine,* July 1906, XXVII:3, 291–301.

————, *The Wonderful Telharmonic System,* broadside, edited text of Ray Stannard Baker's "New Music for an Old World," *McClure's Magazine,* July 1906, XXVII:3, 291–301. New York: New York Electric Music Co., late December 1906?, S.L.

Bannister, Robert C., Jr., "Baker, Ray Stannard," *Dictionary of American Biography,* supp. 4, 1946–1950. New York: Charles Scribner's Sons, 1974, 46–48.

Barbour, J. Murray, "Music and Electricity," *Papers, American Musicological Society,* December 29–30, 1937, 3–10.

————. *Tuning and Temperament: A Historical Survey.* East Lansing: Michigan State College Press, 1951.

Barclay, Dolores, "Muzak Has 50th Year of Mellifluence," *Philadelphia Inquirer,* July 8, 1984, 14-H.

Barnard, Charles, "Music Made by Electricity," *Saint Nicholas Magazine,* May 1907, 34, 636–638.

Barnouw, Erik. *A History of Broadcasting in the United States.* 3 volumes. New York: Oxford University Press, 1966–1970.

Barr, E. Scott, "Kelvin," *The McGraw-Hill Encyclopedia of World Biography,* vol. 6. New York: McGraw-Hill Book Company, 1973, 161–162.

"Baseball at Night for the Boston Fans," *New York Evening Journal,* September 5, 1910, S.C., n.p.

Beaver, Donald deB., "Lee De Forest," in John A. Garraty, ed., *Dictionary of American Biography,* supp. 7. New York: Charles Scribner's Sons, 1981, 174–177.

Beeching, Wilfred A. *Century of the Typewriter.* New York: St. Martin's Press, 1974.

"Before the Footlights," *New-York Daily Tribune,* March 10, 1907, pt. IV, 6.

"Behind the Scenes in a 'Smart' New York Restaurant," *New York Times,* July 15, 1906, pt. 3, 2.

"A Bellamy Dream Realized," *Springfield Republican,* April 3, 1904, 17.

Bellamy, Edward. *Equality.* D. Appleton and Co., 1897. Reprinted. New York: Greenwood Press, Publishers, 1969.

————. *Looking Backward: 2000–1887.* With an introduction by Heywood Broun. Boston: Houghton Mifflin Company, The Riverside Press, 1887, 1926.

"Bellamy Was a Prophet," *Music Trade Review,* November 16, 1907, XLV:20, 40.

"Ben Greet Actors to Present ye Olden Plays at the Garden," *New York Evening Journal,* March 2, 1907, 4.

"Bethlehem Steel Reports Deficit," *New York Times,* October 26, 1934, 31.

"Big Drawing Card," *New York Globe and Commercial Advertiser,* February 28, 1907, S.C., 14.

"Big Organ for Ocean Grove," *New York Times,* January 4, 1908, 9.

"Bill for Telharmonic Co. Failed to Pass," *Musical Age,* April 20, 1907, LVII:12, 315.

"Bill to Transport Music," *Music Trade Review,* February 2, 1907, XLIV:5, 31.

"Bills Presented at Theatres," *New York Evening Journal,* November 12, 1907, 9.

Bird, Aldine R., "Wins Fund Song Test," *Baltimore News-Post,* November 14, 1939, 17.

Blanchard, Carroll Henry, Jr. *Word Processing: Keyboards, Kinesthesis and Women.* Lake George, N.Y.: Educators—Project IV, 1981, K12–K13.

"Blaze Under Electric Shoe Parlor," *New York Times,* February 17, 1908, 7.

"Board of Estimate and Apportionment," *City Record,* May 28, 1907, 5700; May 29, 1907, 5787–5788; May 31, 1907, 5820; June 1, 1907, 5856–5857; June 3, 1907, 5880–5881; June 4, 1907, 5912–5913; June 5, 1907, 5977; June 6, 1907, 6041; June 7, 1907, 6097.

"A Book on Strikes," *New York Times,* June 11, 1910, pt. 2, 334.

Borroff, Edith, "An Early Electro-Magnetic Experiment," *College Music Symposium,* Spring 1979, 19:1, 54–59.

———, "The Choralcelo: One Uniquely American Instrument," *College Music Symposium,* Spring 1982, 22:1, 46–54.

"Bostonians May Soon Have Music 'Delivered by Wire' at Their Homes," *Boston Post,* March 31, 1904, 12.

"Bringing Up Father," *Variety,* December 29, 1916, 14.

Browne, William Hand, Jr., "Orchestral Music from a Dynamo," *Harper's Weekly,* April 7, 1906, 50:14, 477–478, 493, 495.

———, "The Year in Electricity," *New York Times Annual Financial Review,* January 5, 1908, 52.

"Budapest News-Telephone," *Electrical World,* February 18, 1909, LIII:8, 442.

"Business Troubles," *New York Sun,* June 6, 1908, 11.

"Business Troubles," *New York Herald,* December 23, 1914, 15.

"Business Troubles," *New York Times,* May 23, 1908, 12.

"Business Troubles," *New York Times,* December 23, 1908, 14.

"Busoni and the Chickering," *Music Trade Review,* January 28, 1911, LII:4, 53.

"Busoni and the Chickering," *Musical Age,* January 15, 1910, LXVIII:12, 214, 215.

Busoni, Ferruccio Benevenuto. *Entwurf einer neuen Aesthetik der Tonkunst.* Leipzig and Trieste, 1907. Translated by Theodore Baker as *Sketch of a New Aesthetic of Music.* New York: G. Schirmer, 1911. Reprinted. New York: Dover Publications, 1962.

"Busy Week of Rival Grand Operas, Concerts and Recitals," *New York World,* February 17, 1907, S.C., Metropolitan Section, 4.

"Buy Music by Meter Like Gas or Water," *Chicago Examiner,* February 3, 1907, S.C., n.p.

"Buying Music by Meter Now—Just Like Gas or Water," *New York World,* January 27, 1907, Magazine Section, 7.

Byron, "Everyday scene . . . ," photograph, November 1906, P.C.M.M.A., G. NEW YC Broa.

Cadman, John W., Jr. *The Corporation in New Jersey.* Cambridge: Harvard University Press, 1949.

"Cafe Martin," display advertisement, *New-York Daily Tribune,* December 10, 1906, 8, and December 14, 1906, 10.

Cahill, Arthur T., *The Cahill Electric Music,* Holyoke: Arthur T. Cahill, Secretary, 1910?, M.C.S.

Cahill Bros., *The New Giant Cahill Duplex Projector,* New York: The Firm, 1929?, N.B.H.

Cahill Brothers, *The Cahill Famous Flood-Light Projectors,* New York: The Firm, 1932?, M.C.S.

"Cahill Company Gives Concert," *Springfield Republican,* March 21, 1906, 8.

"Cahill Electrical Music Tonight," *Springfield Republican,* March 3, 1911, 4.

Cahill, George Frederick, *Program of Cahill Electrical Music,* New York: George F. Cahill, February 1912?, M.C.S.

"Cahill Music by Wireless," *Holyoke Daily Transcript,* March 7, 1907, 2.

"Cahill Music Machinery Co.," *Music Trade Review,* May 28, 1910, L:22, S.C., 11.

"The Cahill Music Machinery Manufacturing Company," *Electrical World,* May 26, 1910, XV:21, S.C., 1416.

"Cahill Telharmonic Co. Fails," *Music Trade Review,* December 26, 1914, LIX:26, 39.

"Cahill, Thaddeus, Am. Inventor," Allen G. Debus, ed., *World Who's Who in Science,* first edition. Chicago: Marquis–Who's Who, 1968, 288.

Cahill, Thaddeus, "The Electrical Music as a Vehicle of Expression," *Papers and Proceedings of the Music Teachers' National Association at Its Twenty-ninth Annual Meeting, Columbia University, New York City, December 27–31, 1907,* 1908, 206–222.

————, Letter to the Honorable the Chairman and Other Members of the Board of Estimate and Apportionment of the City of New York, June 10, 1912, in "New York Cahill Telharmonic Company," *City Record,* June 20, 1912, 5257–5258.

————, Petition to the Honorable the Chairman and Other Members of the Board of Estimate and Apportionment of the City of New York, June 10, 1912, in "New York Cahill Telharmonic Company," *City Record,* June 20, 1912, 5258.

The Cahill Writing-Machine Manufacturing Company, *The Cahill Electric Typewriter,* Washington, D.C.: The Company, 1900?, M.C.S.

Caldwell, Orestes H., "Westinghouse, George," *Dictionary of American Biography,* vol. X. New York: Charles Scribner's Sons, 1936, 16–18.

"Canned Music Co. Fails," *New York Sun,* December 23, 1914, 9.

"Carl M. Pihl Spoke," *Holyoke Daily Transcript,* January 30, 1907, 3.

Carneal, Georgette. *A Conqueror of Space.* New York: Horace Liveright, 1930.

"Carnegie Hall Opens Studio for Rehearsal and Recording," *New York Times,* April 4, 1985, C16.

"Casino," display advertisement, *New York Times,* February 3, 1907, pt. 4, 3.

"Central Plant Sends Music over Wires," *New York Herald,* November 10, 1906, 5.

"Century's Musical Wonder," *Holyoke Daily Transcript,* March 21, 1906, 8.

"Chap. 310," *Laws of the State of New York Passed at the One Hundred and Thirtieth Session of the Legislature,* vol. I. Albany: J. B. Lyon Company, State Printer, 1907, 563.

"Charles F. Cutler's Death," *New York Times,* May 20, 1907, 9.

"Chas. M'H. Howard, Baltimore Lawyer," *New York Times,* May 20, 1942, 20.

Cheney, Margaret. *Tesla: Man Out of Time.* Englewood Cliffs, N.J.: Prentice-Hall, 1982.

"Chicago to See Flowers Blooming in Pictures," *Chicago Examiner,* October 30, 1910, S.C., n.p.

Chilton, Carroll Brent, "Music by Wire," *Independent,* April 25, 1907, 62:4, 948–949.

"Christian Schiott Dies," *New York Times,* December 30, 1960, 20.

"Cincinnati's May Music Festival," *Musical Courier,* April 11, 1906, LII:15, 34a.

City of New York and New York Cahill Telharmonic Company, "Amendment of Contract Dated March 9, 1911, Granting Said Company a Franchise, by Extending the Time for the Commencement of Construction and Modifying the Annual Compensation," Contract, October 10, 1912, B.E.

City of New York and New York Cahill Telharmonic Company, "Boroughs of Manhattan and the Bronx, West of Bronx River," Contract, March 9, 1911, B.E.

"Clarence H. Mackay Has Electric Buck," *New York Times,* April 16, 1905, pt. 1, 9.

"Clarence Reynolds," *Denver News,* September 19, 1949, 35.

"Clifton A. Crocker," *New York Times,* December 15, 1939, 25.

"Clowry, Robert C.," *Who's Who in New York City and State,* third edition. New York: L. R. Hamersly and Company, 1907, 229.

"Clowry, Robert Charles," *The National Cyclopaedia of American Biography,* vol. XIII. New York: James T. White and Company, 1906, 119–120.

"Clyde Fitch Again," *New-York Daily Tribune,* January 6, 1907, pt. IV, 6.

"Clyde Fitch Dead After an Operation," *New York Times,* September 5, 1909, pt. 2, 1.

"Col. Carl M. Pihl," *New York Times,* May 2, 1933, 18.

"Col. Pihl, Husband of Arline Maxwell, Dies at Jacksonville, Fla.," *Malden* [Mass.] *Evening News,* May 1, 1933, n.p.

"Colonel Pihl to Be Buried at Malden," *Florida Times-Union,* May 2, 1933, 13.

"Comedian Al Leech Dead," *New York Times,* July 6, 1912, 7.

"The Commissioner of Patents," *New York Times,* January 18, 1877, 1.

"The Commissioner of Patents," *New York Times,* March 24, 1878, 7.

"Concert Music By Wire," *New York Evening Mail,* November 12, 1906, 7.

"A Concert Through Nine Hundred Miles of Wire," *Phonogram,* January 1893, 3:1, 307.

"Concerts at Telharmonic Hall," *New-York Daily Tribune,* April 7, 1907, pt. IV, 7.

"Concerts at Telharmonic Hall," *New York World,* February 3, 1907, Metropolitan Section, M7.

"Contradictions in the Bible," letters to the editor, *New York Times,* August 5, 1923, pt.6, 6.

"Converting Music into Electricity," *British Deaf Times,* September 1907, IV:45, 206.

Cooke, James Francis, "Das Telharmonium: Ein neues Wunder in der Musikwelt," *Musikalisches Wochenblatt,* December 13, 1906, 37:50, 933–935, tr. Martin Wulfhorst.

"Costs More to Incorporate in Maine," *Music Trade Review,* June 8, 1907, XLIV:23, 9.

" 'Covers for Two': A Gastronomic Study," *New York Times,* September 2, 1906, pt. 4, 2.

Cronk, H. Taylor, M.D., "The Deadly Pocket," letter to the editor, *New York Times,* January 8, 1929, 30.

"Crosby for the Philippines," *New York Times,* July 16, 1913, 9.

Crosby, Oscar Terry. *Adam and Eve: A Probable Origin of the Garden of Eden Tradition.* Boston: The Stratford Company, Publishers, 1926.

————, "Illegitimate Parents," letter to the editor, *New York Times,* October 1, 1913, 8.

————. *International War: Its Causes and Its Cure.* London: Macmillan and Co., 1919.

————, Letter to the Honorable Board of Estimate and Apportionment of New York, January 29, 1907, in "New York Electric Music Company," *City Record,* February 5, 1907, 1202.

————, *New York Electric Music Company* [Stock Prospectus], New York: April 1906? [penciled on cover: "W. J. Hammer, Aug. 17-'06"], S.L.

————. *Strikes: When to Strike, How to Strike.* New York: G. P. Putnam's Sons, 1910.

————, *Tibet and Turkestan.* New York: G. P. Putnam's Sons, The Knickerbocker Press, 1905.

————, "Turkey Building Roads," letter to the editor, *New York Times,* April 9, 1914, 10.

————, and Louis Bell. *The Electric Railway in Theory and Practice.* New York: W. J. Johnston Co., 1892.

"Crosby, Oscar Terry," *The National Cyclopedia of American Biography,* vol. XXXV. New York: James T. White and Company, 1949, 83–84.

"Crosby, Oscar Terry," *Who Was Who in America,* vol. 2. Chicago: The A. N. Marquis Company, 1950, 136.

Crutchfield, Will, "Music by Musak: [*sic*] Orchestrating the Workday," *New York Times,* September 1, 1984, 9.

"Current Literature," *Bridgeport* [Conn.] *Journal,* June 30, 1906, n.p., L.C.M.D., Ray Stannard Baker Papers.

"Current News and Notes: The Telharmonium," *Electrical World,* July 7, 1906, XLVIII:1, 8.

"Cutler, Charles Frederic," *Who's Who in New York City and State,* third edition. New York: L. R. Hamersly and Company, 1907, 369.

"Damrosch, Walter (Johannes)," *The National Cyclopaedia of American Biography,* vol. XLIII. New York: James T. White and Company, 1961, 8–9.

"Damrosch, Walter Johannes," *Who's Who in New York City and State,* third edition. New York: L. R. Hamersly and Company, 1907, 374.

"Das Haus-Orchester der Zukunst," *Morgen Journal,* February 11, 1907, S.C., n.p., tr. Martin Wulfhorst.

"David A. Munro Dead," *New York Times,* March 10, 1910, 9.

Davies, Hugh. *Répertoire International des Musiques Electroacoustiques/ International Electronic Music Catalog.* Paris: Le Groupe de Recherches Musicales de l'O.R.T.F., and Trumansburg, New York: The Independent Electronic Music Center, 1968. Distributed by M.I.T. Press, Cambridge. Also published as *Electronic Music Review,* nos. 2/3.

"The Day of 'Canned' Music," *New York Times,* August 24, 1906.

de Forest, Lee. *Father of Radio.* Chicago: Wilcox-Follett, 1950.

"De Forest, Lee," *Who's Who in New York City and State,* third edition. New York: L. R. Hamersly and Company, 1907, 392–393.

"De Forest Tells of a New Wireless," *New York Times,* February 14, 1909, pt. 2, 1.

De Haas, W. G. L., "Technology as a Subject of Comparative Studies: The Case of Photography," *Comparative Studies of Society and History,* July 1979, 21:3, 362–371.

"De Koven, Anna Farwell," *The National Cyclopaedia of American Biography,* vol. XVI. New York: James T. White and Company, 1918, 290.

"De Koven, Anna Farwell," *Who Was Who in America,* vol. 3. Chicago: Marquis–Who's Who, 1960, 218–219.

"De Koven, Henry Louis Reginald," *Who's Who in New York City and State,* third edition. New York: L. R. Hamersly and Company, 1907, 395.

De Koven, Mrs. Reginald [Anna Farwell], "A Fictitious Paul Jones Masquerading as the Real," *New York Times,* June 10, 1906, pt. 3, 1–3.

"Death of F.C. Todd," *Charlottesville Daily Progress,* November 11, 1918, 1.

"Death of Inventor Recalls Odd Machine," *Springfield Republican,* April 14, 1934, 4.

"Deaths: Cahill—Arthur T.," *New York Times,* January 26, 1962, 31.

"Deaths: Cahill—Margaret," *New York Times,* February 24, 1944, 15.

"Deaths: Cahill—Suddenly," *New York Times,* April 24, 1934, 19.

"Deaths: Crosby—Oscar Terry," *New York Times,* January 3, 1947, 21.

"Demonstrates Range of Electrical Organ," *New York Times,* June 13, 1931, 17.

"Demonstration of Wireless Telephone," *New York Evening Mail,* March 7, 1907, 5.

"Denver's Mighty Municipal Organ," *Denver Municipal Facts,* March 1918, I:1, 3- 4, 17.

DiCarlo, Ella Merkel. *Holyoke—Chicopee: A Perspective.* Holyoke: Transcript-Telegram, 1982.

"Died: Ryan," *New York Times,* December 17, 1913, 11.

"Dippel, Tenor, Dies in Want on Coast," *New York Times,* May 14, 1932, 15.

"Disease Due to the Phone," *New York Times,* October 13, 1889, 11.

"Dismissing the Duma," *New York Times,* July 23, 1906, 6.

"Distributing Music," *Electrical World,* November 17, 1906, XLVIII:20, 949.

Douglass, Ruth, "Thaddaeus [sic] Cahill, a Holyoker, Is Mentioned in History of Electronic Music; Name Appears in Many References," *Holyoke Daily Transcript-Telegram,* March 6, 1968, 24.

———, "Hogan Brothers Knew Thaddaeus [sic] Cahill," *Holyoke Daily Transcript-Telegram,* May 8, 1968, 12.

"Dozen Grand Operas and Many Concerts," *New York World,* January 27, 1907, Metropolitan Section, 4.

"Dr. Cahill Built His Electrical Music Machine in Holyoke," *Holyoke Daily Transcript and Telegram,* April 14, 1934, 1.

"Dr. Cahill Dies at 66; Inventor of Telharmony," *New York Herald Tribune,* April 13, 1934, 19.

"Dr. Cahill Dies; Widely Known for Inventions," *Washington Post,* April 16?, 1934, n.p.

"Dr. Cahill's Great Work," *Holyoke Daily Transcript,* January 26, 1907, 6.

"Dr. Cahill's Interesting Talk," *Music Trade Review,* January 4, 1908, XLVI:1, 15.

"Dr. Cahill's Invention," *Holyoke Daily Transcript,* November 10, 1906, 2.

"Dr. Cahill's Telharmonic System of Developing Music," *Music Trade Review,* December 22, 1906, XLIII:25, 18–19.

"Dr. Cahill's Telharmonium," *Talking Machine World,* April 15, 1906, II: 4, 42.

"Dr. Cahill's Telharmonium a Remarkable Invention," *Musical America,* August 25, 1906, 17.

"Dr. Clarence Reynolds," *New York Times,* September 19, 1949, 23.

"Dr. Cronk Discharged from Custody," *New York Times,* June 20, 1902, 3.

"Dr. H. M. Warren, Baptist Minister," *New York Times,* December 23, 1940, 19.

"Dr. Thaddeus Cahill," *Electrical World,* March 31, 1906, XLVII:13, 656.

"Dr. Thaddeus Cahill," *Holyoke Daily Transcript,* April 14, 1934, 4.

"Dr. Thaddeus Cahill, 66, Once Local Inventor, Dies," *Holyoke Daily Transcript and Telegram,* April 13, 1934, 1.

Dreiser, Theodore. *Sister Carrie.* [Doubleday, Page and Company, 1900.] Afterword by Willard Thorp. New York: The New American Library, 1961.

"Duma," *Encyclopaedia Britannica,* vol. 7. Chicago: Encyclopaedia Britannica, 1968, 746–747.

"Duma Dissolved; Army in Capital," *New York Times,* July 22, 1906, pt. 2, 1–2.

"Dynamophone Music Heard," *New-York Daily Tribune,* September 27, 1906, 13.

"E. G. Baetjer Dies; Lawyer 54 Years," *New York Times,* July 22, 1945, 38.

Easterbrook, A. B., "The Wonderful Telharmonium," *Gunter's Magazine,* June 1907, 3:5, S.C., 560–568.

Eastern Cahill Telharmonic Company, *Telharmony: The New Art of Electric Music,* New York: The Company, June? 1907, M.C.S.

"Edward Bellamy Dead," *New York Times,* May 23, 1898, 7.

"Electric Music," *Electrician and Mechanic,* November 1907, S.C., n.v., n.i., n.p.

"Electric Music," *New York Evening Post,* January 15, 1907, 9.

"Electric Music Boom," *Holyoke Daily Transcript,* April 30, 1907, 7.

"Electric Music Boom," *Music Trade Review,* May 4, 1907, XLIV:18, 13.

"Electric Music Demonstration," *Musical Age,* September 29, 1906, LV:9, 231.

"Electric Music Factory to Open Soon," *Musical Age,* June 23, 1906, LIV:8, 389.

"Electric Music for Diners," *Musical America,* December 15, 1906, V:5, 6.

"Electric Music for Theatre Patrons," *Musical Age,* January 12, 1907, LVI:11, 330.

"Electric Music Generating System," *Talking Machine World,* July 15, 1906, II:7, 34–35.

"Electric Music in the Street," *New-York Daily Tribune,* January 22, 1907, 14.

"Electric Music Report," *Baltimore News,* June 28, 1907, S.C., n.p.

"The electric organ, or 'telharmonium' . . . ," *Cleveland Leader,* April 7, 1907, S.C., n.p.

"Electrical Music," *Holyoke Daily Transcript,* March 13, 1906, 4.

"Electrical Music," *Scientific American,* March 31, 1906, XCIV:13, 268–269.

"The Electrical Production and Transmission of Music," editorial, *Electrical World,* April 28, 1910, LV:17, S.C., 1039–1040.

"Electrical Transmission of Music: Developments in the Cahill Telharmonic System," *Electrical World,* April 28, 1910, LV:17, 1059–1062.

"Electrically Made Music—Its High Possibilities Viewed Commercially," *Musical Age,* March 2, 1912, LXXVII:6, 92, 94.

"Electro-Music Ready on August First," *Musical Age,* July 14, 1906, LIV:11, 486.

"Elektrische Musik nach dem System von Dr. Cahill," *Zeitschrift für Instrumentenbau,* November 1906, 26:21, 651, 653.

"Elliott Schenck, Composer, Was 69," *New York Times,* March 6, 1939, 15.

"Elliott Schenck's Latest Successes," *Musical Courier,* January 9, 1907, LIV:2, 31.

"The Enchanted House and Its Electrical Wonders," *New York Times,* March 10, 1907, pt. 3, 11.

"The Erring Sister Again," *New York Sun,* November 10, 1907, sec. 3, 6.

"Ex-City Organist, C. Reynolds, 69, Dies in California," *Denver Post,* September 19, 1949, 20.

"Excitement at Climax," *Holyoke Daily Transcript,* March 1, 1911, 2.

"Expert Electric Typewriter," *Holyoke Daily Transcript,* n.d., 1901, n.p., H.P.L.

"F. W. Lord, Leader of Electric Firm," *New York Times,* January 1, 1952, 25.

"Farthest Reach of Electricity in the Musical Arts," *Music Trade Review,* December 18, 1915, LXI:25, 41.

Fawcett, Walden, "The New Banking System and the Music Trade," *Music Trade Review,* November 21, 1914, LIX:21, 15, 17.

Figaro, Charles, "The Telharmonium—An Apparatus for the Electrical Generation and Transmission of Music," cover illustration, *Scientific American,* March 9, 1907, XCVI:10, 205.

"The Financial Situation," *New York Times,* September 9, 1907, 8.

"Financial Situation Easing Up, Says Ernest Urchs," *Music Trade Review,* December 5, 1914, LIX:23, 24.

"Fire in Broadway Causes Excitement," *New York Evening Telegram,* February 17, 1908, 5.

"First Annual Report of Tel-Harmonic Co.," *Musical Age,* July 20, 1907, LVIII:12, S.C., 366.

"The First Public Telharmonic Concert," *Electrical World,* October 6, 1906, XLVIII: 14, 637.

"Fish, Frederick Perry," *The National Cyclopaedia of American Biography,* vol. XXVI. New York: James T. White and Company, 1937, 202.

Fitch, Clyde, "The Truth," in John Gassner and Mollie Gassner, eds., *Best Plays of the Early American Theatre,* New York: Crown Publishers, 1967, 458–510.

"Fitch, Clyde," *The National Cyclopaedia of American Biography,* vol. XIII. New York: James T. White and Company, 1906, 452.

"Fitch, (William) Clyde," *The National Cyclopaedia of American Biography,* vol. XV. New York: James T. White and Company, 1916, 192–193.

"Fitch, (William) Clyde," *Who's Who in New York City and State,* third edition. New York: L. R. Hamersly and Company, 1907, 499.

"40 Years Ago," *Holyoke Daily Transcript,* March 13, 1946, 8.

"Fragrant Hit for 'Orchid' at Herald Square," *New York Evening Journal,* April 9, 1907, 8.

"Franchise Matters," *City Record,* February 11, 1910, 1803.

"Franchise Matters," *City Record,* January 23, 1911, 600–601; January 24, 1911, 625–626; January 25, 1911, 649–650; January 26, 1911, 673–674; January 27, 1911, 694–695; January 28, 1911, 718–719; February 1, 1911, 878–879; February 4, 1911, 997–998.

"Franchise Matters," *City Record,* September 19, 1912, 7454–7455.

"Franchise Matters," *City Record,* October 23, 1912, 8452.

"Franchise to Distribute Music," *Music Trade Review,* June 29, 1907, XLIV:26, 9.

"Free Music on Meriden Trolleys," *Meriden* [Conn.] *Record,* December 16, 1907, S.C., n.p.

"Futurist School of Music," *Music Trade Review,* March 23, 1912, LIV:12, 26.

"G.F. Peabody Dead; Philanthropist, 85," *New York Times,* March 5, 1938, 17.

"G. Schirmer," *Etude,* September 1907, XXV:9, 618.

"Gadski's Recommendation," *Musical Courier,* January 3, 1906, LII:1, 48.

Galpin, Francis W., "The Music of Electricity: A Sketch of Its Origins and Development," *Proceedings of the Royal Musical Association,* 1937–1938, 64, 71–83.

Geissler, Ludwig W. *Looking Beyond.* London: William Reeves, 1891. Reprinted. New York: Arno Press and The New York Times, 1971.

"Gen. Ellis Spear Dies in Florida," *New York Times,* April 6, 1917, 13.

"The Generating and Distributing of Music by Means of Alternators," *Electrical World,* March 10, 1906, XLVII:10, 519–521.

"The Generation and Distribution of Music by Means of Alternators," *Musical Age,* March 17, 1906, LIII:7, 596–597.

"George F. Cahill," n.n., October 24, 1935, N.B.H., n.p.

"George F. Cahill," *Oberlin Alumni Magazine,* November 1935, O.C.A. 28/1, Box 38, n.p.

"George F. Cahill, 66, Inventor, Dies Here," *New York Times,* October 15, 1935, 23.

"George F. Peabody Retires," *New York Times,* May 1, 1906, 1.

Gerson, Virginia, "Fitch, William Clyde," *Dictionary of American Biography,* vol. III, pt. 2. New York: Charles Scribner's Sons, 1959, 428–431.

"Get Music by Telephone," *New York Sun,* November 10, 1906, 4.

"Get Music by Telephone," *Talking Machine World,* November 15, 1906, II:11, 43.

"A Glimpse Backward over the Rapidly Vanishing Season and Forward into Lent," *New York Times,* March 1, 1908, pt. 5, 5.

Government Printing Office. *List of Pensioners on the Roll, January 1, 1883,* vol. III. Washington: The Office, 1883, 195.

"Grand Opera by Wire," *New York Evening Sun,* November 10, 1906, 3.

"Grand Opera by Wireless," *New York Herald,* March 1, 1907, 8.

Grant, John, "Experiments and Results in Wireless Telephony," *American Telephone Journal,* January 26, 1907, XV:4, 49–51.

————, "The Electrical Generation of Music," *American Telephone Journal,* October 27, 1906, XIV:17, 268–271.

"Greatest Single Shipment," *Music Trade Review,* April 27, 1907, XLIV:17, 42.

Green, Constance McLaughlin. *Holyoke, Massachusetts: A Case History of the Industrial Revolution in America*. New Haven: Yale University Press, 1939.

Green, Gary A., "Understanding Past Currency in Modern Terms," *Sonneck Society Bulletin,* Summer 1987, XIII:2, 48.

Griffin, L. A., ed., *Marvyn Scudder Manual of Extinct or Obsolete Companies,* vol. II. New York: Marvyn Scudder Manual of Extinct and Obsolete Companies, 1928, 423.

"H. H. Westinghouse Dead at Age of 80," *New York Times,* November 19, 1933, pt. l, 34.

"Hammond V. Hayes," *New York Times,* March 23, 1947, 60.

Harris, G. W., "Music Transmitted by Wires Suggested by Inventor in 1906," *New York Sun,* March 7, 1931, 32, 37.

Harrison, Richard C., "Corporations and Franchises," in Francis G. Wickware, ed., *The American Year Book, 1911.* New York: D. Appleton and Company, 1912, 445–446.

"Harry Frey Stevenson," *New York Times,* November 10, 1939, 23.

"Hayes, Hammond Vinton," *Who Was Who in America,* vol. 2. Chicago: The A. N. Marquis Company, 1950, 243.

"Hear Electrical Music," *Musical America,* November 17, 1906, V:1, 13.

"Hearing Before the Assembly Committee on General Laws on a Bill Introduced by Mr. Krulewitch, Entitled 'An Act to Regulate the Toll Charges for Local Telephone Communications,' " in *The Telephone System and Service Charges in New York City,* Report of the Committee on City Affairs of the Republican Club. New York: The Committee, 1906, 1–7, 12–13, 20–21.

Helmholtz, Hermann Ludwig Ferdinand. *On the Sensations of Tone.* Second English edition, translated and conformed to the fourth German edition of 1877 with notes by Alexander J. Ellis, 1885. Reprinted with an introduction by Henry Margenau. New York: Dover Publications, 1954.

"Henrietta Crosman Sustains 'All-of-a-Sudden Peggy,' " *New York Evening Mail,* February 12, 1907, S.C., 5.

"Herbert, Victor," *Who's Who in New York City and State,* third edition. New York: L. R. Hamersly and Company, 1907, 659.

"Hewitt, Peter Cooper," *American Biography: A New Cyclopedia,* vol. XIII. New York: The American Historical Society, 1923, 253–255.

"Hewitt, Peter Cooper," *Dictionary of American Biography,* vol. IV. New York: Charles Scribner's Sons, 1960, 607–608.

"Hewitt, Peter Cooper," *The Cyclopaedia of American Biography,* vol. VIII. New York: The Press Association Compilers, 1918, 169–171.

"Hewitt, Peter Cooper," *The National Cyclopaedia of American Biography,* vol. XIV. New York: James T. White and Company, 1917, 470–471.

"Hewitt, Peter Cooper," *Who Was Who in America,* vol. I. Chicago: Marquis–Who's Who, 1966, 558.

"Hewitt, Peter Cooper," *Who's Who in New York City and State,* third edition. New York: L. R. Hamersly and Company, 1907, 664.

"Hewitt's Patent Granted," *New York Times,* April 20, 1910, 6.

Hidy, Ralph W., and Muriel E. Hidy. *Pioneering in Big Business, 1882–1911: History of Standard Oil Company (New Jersey).* New York: Harper and Brothers, 1955, 308–309.

Higgins, E. E., "A Wonderful Musical Instrument," *Success,* May 1906, 9:114, N.Y.P.L., *MKY Box, n.p.

Higham, John, "The Reorientation of American Culture in the 1890's," in *Writing American History: Essays on Modern Scholarship,* Bloomington: Indiana University Press, 1970, 73–102.

Hirst, Francis W., "The American Crisis—A Diagnosis and a Prescription," *New York Times Annual Financial Review,* January 5, 1908, 3.

Hofstadter, Richard, and Beatrice Kevitt, "Industrialism and Social Reform: Introduction," in *Great Issues in American History: From Reconstruction to the Present Day, 1864–1981,* New York: Vintage Books, 1982, 58–62.

"Holyoke: 40 Years Ago: March 7, 1907," *Holyoke Daily Transcript and Telegram,* March 7, 1947, 13.

"Holyoke's Log for 1906," *Holyoke Daily Transcript,* December 31, 1906, 7.

Hoover, Cynthia Adams. *Music Machines—American Style.* Washington, D.C.: Smithsonian Institution Press, 1971.

Hope-Jones, Robert, "The Future of the Church Organ," *New Music Review,* February 1908, 7:75, S.C., 175–176.

"The House of 100 Years from Now," *New York World,* October 20, 1907, Magazine Section, 2.

Houston, Edwin J. *Electricity In Every-Day Life,* vol. 3. New York: P. F. Collier and Son, 1905.

"How New York City Submits Applications for Public-Service Franchises to an Engineering Department," *Engineering News,* February 11, 1909, 61:6, 145–146.

"How the Duma Is to Be Constituted," *American Monthly Review Of Reviews,* April 1906, XXXIII:4, 405.

Huebner, S. S., "Economic Conditions and the Conduct of Business," in Francis G. Wickware, ed., *The American Year Book, 1914,* New York: D. Appleton and Company, 1915, 318–327.

"Hughes's Busy Day with Bills," *Albany Evening Journal,* May 7, 1907, 2.

"Hungarian Telephonic News Service," *Phonogram,* March and April 1893, 3:3–4, 387.

"Hymns by Electricity," *New York Herald,* February 18, 1907, S.C., 7.

"Improved Electric Music," *Literary Digest,* June 18, 1910, XL:25, S.C., 1219.

"In Memory of Gustave Schirmer," *New Music Review,* February 1908, 7:75, 162.

"In the Five Forks Woods," *New York Times,* May 28, 1880, 3.

"In the Musical World," *Music Trade Review,* December 15, 1906, XLIII:24, 13.

"Incorporated," *Music Trade Review,* May 11, 1907, XLIV:19, 29.

"Incorporation Filed in Maine," *Music Trade Review,* August 18, 1906, XLIII:7, 11.

"Incorporations Fell Off Heavily in 1907," *New York Times,* January 5, 1908, pt. 2, 12–13.

"Incorporations 1905," *Presto,* January 4, 1906, 47.

"Influence of Music on Dining," *Music Trade Review,* November 3, 1906, XLIII:18, 3.

"Invented the 'Telharmonium,' " *Music Trade Review,* July 13, 1912, LV:2, 16.

"Isabel Winlock," *Variety,* October 14, 1953, 95.

"It's Magical Music," *New York Globe and Commercial Advertiser,* January 12, 1907, 9.

"Jackson, E(rnest) Hilton," *Who Was Who in America,* vol. 3. Chicago: Marquis–Who's Who, 1960, 441.

"James G. White, 80, Engineer, Is Dead," *New York Times,* June 3, 1942, 23.

"James, Nathaniel Willis," *National Cyclopedia of American Biography,* vol. XXVI. New York: James T. White and Company, 1937, 371–372.

James, Richard Schmidt, "Expansion of Sound Resources in France, 1913–1940, and Its Relationship to Electronic Music," Ph.D. dissertation, University of Michigan, 1981.

"Jaxon Is Dead," *Jacksonville Journal,* May 1, 1933, 3.

"John C. Rowe", *New York Times,* December 16, 1946, 23.

"John R. Turner," *New York Times,* November 15, 1958, 23.

Johnson, William A., Charles R. McHugh, Howard Rice, and Thomas L. Rhea, "History of Electronic Music, Part One," *Synthesis,* 1971, I:2, 15–38.

"Joker in Electric Music Bill," *Music Trades,* March 30, 1907, XXXIII:13, 33.

Journal of the Assembly of the State of New York, vol. I, Albany: J. B. Lyon Company, State Printers, 1907, 233, 612, 613, 643, 665, 834, 909; vol. II, 1083, 1162, 1199–1200; vol. III, 2472, 2475.

Journal of the Senate of the State of New York, vol. I, Albany: J. B. Lyon Company, State Printers, 1907, 579, 581, 843–844, 1018–1019, 1022, 1113–1114.

"Judgments," *New York Herald,* May 23, 1908, 12.

Jullien, Lt. Col., "Applications du Courant Electrique, des Oscillations Radioélectriques et des Phénomènes Photoélectriques à la Réalisation d'Instruments de Musique," in *Conférences d'Actualités Scientifiques et Industrielles.* Paris: Conservatoire des Arts et Métiers, 1929.

" 'Kiss Me' Proves Keith Headliner," *Toledo Times,* December 16, 1919, N.Y.P.L.T., n.p.

Knight, Marion. *A Comet Among the Stars.* New York: Pageant Press, 1953.

Kouwenhoven, John A. *Made in America.* New York: Doubleday, 1948. (Paperback edition: *The Arts in Modern American Civilization.* New York: Norton, 1967.)

"Largest Instrument Ever Built," *Poughkeepsie News Press,* February 19, 1907, S.C., n.p.

"Le Téléharmonique," *Le Monde artiste,* June 23, 1907, S.C., n.p.

Leroy-Beaulieu, Paul, "An Analysis of the American Crisis," *New York Times Annual Financial Review,* January 5, 1908, 5.

Lessing, Lawrence. *Man of High Fidelity: Edwin Howard Armstrong.* Philadelphia: J. B. Lippincott Co., 1956.

Leupp, Francis E. *George Westinghouse: His Life and Achievements.* Boston: Little, Brown and Company, 1919.

Lewis, Nelson P. *Report of the Chief Engineer of the Board of Estimate and Apportionment of the City of New York for the Years 1906 and 1907.* New York: The Board, 1908.

————. *Report of the Chief Engineer of the Board of Estimate and Apportionment of the City of New York for the Year 1908.* New York: The Board, 1909.

————. *Report of the Chief Engineer of the Board of Estimate and Apportionment of the City of New York for the Year 1909.* New York: The Board, 1910.

————. *Report of the Chief Engineer of the Board of Estimate and Apportionment of the City of New York for the Year 1910.* New York: The Board, 1911.

"Life of Lord Kelvin," *New York Times Book Review,* April 2, 1910, 177.

"Living by Electricity," *New-York Daily Tribune,* January 19, 1908, pt. V, 3.

"Long Illness Takes Life of Colonel Pihl," *Florida Times-Union,* May 1, 1933, 9, 13.

"Lord Kelvin," *New York Times,* December 19, 1907, 8.

"Lord Kelvin Dead, Years a Sufferer," *New York Times,* December 18, 1907, 4.

Lubell, Samuel, "Magnificent Failure," *Saturday Evening Post,* January 24, 1942, 214:30, 20.

Luening, Otto, "Origins," in Jon H. Appleton and Ronald C. Perera, eds., *The Development and Practice of Electronic Music,* Englewood Cliffs, N.J.: Prentice-Hall, 1975, 1–21.

————, "Some Random Remarks About Electronic Music," *Journal of Music Theory,* Spring 1964, 8:1, 89–98.

————, "An Unfinished History of Electronic Music," *Music Educators Journal,* November 1968, LV:3, 42–49, 135–142, 145.

"Luxuries Not in Demand Just at Present," *New York Times,* January 12, 1908, pt. 5, 3.

McAllister, Addams Stratton, "Some Electrical Features of the Cahill Telharmonic System," *Electrical World,* January 5, 1907, XLIX:1, 22–24.

"McAllister, Addams Stratton," *The National Cyclopaedia of American Biography,* vol. XV. New York: James T. White and Company, 1916.

"McAllister, Addams Stratton," *Who Was Who in America,* vol. 2. Chicago: The A. N. Marquis Company, 1950, 354.

McCardell, Roy L., "What the Casino's Twenty-fifth Birthday To-Morrow Means to Broadway's History Explained by McCardell," *New York World,* June 30, 1907, Metropolitan Section, 2.

McFarland, Asa, George Edwin Jenks, and Henry McFarland. *The Statesman: Political Manual for the State of New Hampshire.* Concord: McFarland and Jenks, 1864, M.C.S.

"Machine for Training Batters," *Cincinnati Enquirer,* March 2, 1908, N.B.H., n.p.

"Machine Goes to New York," *Holyoke Daily Transcript,* June 9, 1906, 4.

"Mackay, Clarence H.," *Who's Who in New York City and State,* third edition. New York: L. R. Hamersly and Company, 1907, 883.

"Mackay, Clarence Hungerford," *American Biography: A New Cyclopedia,* vol. VI. New York: The American Historical Society, 1919, 7–9.

"Mackay, Clarence Hungerford," *The National Cyclopaedia of American Biography,* vol. XIV. New York: James T. White and Company, 1917, 85.

"Mackay, Clarence Hungerford," *The National Cyclopaedia of American Biography,* vol. XXXI. New York: James T. White and Company, 1944, 24–25.

"Mackay, Clarence Hungerford," *Webster's American Biographies.* Springfield: G. and C. Merriam Company, Publishers, 1974, 672.

"Magic Music from the Telharmonium," *New York Times,* December 16, 1906, pt. 3, 3.

"Maine the Birthplace of Freak Corporations," *New York Times,* June 23, 1907, pt. 5, 9.

"Make Way for the Blue and Gold," *New York Times,* July 9, 1989, Real Estate Section, 6R.

"Makes Electric Music," *Springfield Evening Union,* March 13, 1906, 4.

"A Manhole Spouts Music in Broadway," *New York World,* October 22, 1907, 1.

"Many Fine Bills at Theatres This Week," *New York Evening Journal,*
    January 7, 1908, 17.

"Many New Plays in Easter Week," *New York Evening Mail,* March 30,
    1907, Supplement Section, 2.

"Many New Plays to Vary Theatrical Bills Next Week," *New York Evening
    Journal,* April 6, 1907, 9.

"Many Triumphs for Vigna," *Musical Courier,* January 24, 1906, LII:4, 45.

"Margaret Jamieson in Piano Recital," *New York Times,* January 31,
    1918, 7.

"Margaret Jamieson, Pianist," *Musical Courier,* May 2, 1918, XXXVI:18, 16.

"Margaret Jamieson, Pianist, Plays," *New York Times,* April 24, 1918, 13.

"Mark Twain," display advertisement, *New York Times,* February 2, 1908,
    pt. 6, 3.

"Market News by Marconi System to Ships at Sea," display advertisement,
    New York Times Annual Financial Review, January 5, 1908, 26.

Martin, Thomas Commerford, "Electrical Arts Output $210,000,000,"
    New York Herald, January 2, 1907, S.C., 48.

———, "Electrical Engineering," in Francis G. Wickware, ed., *The
    American Year Book, 1913,* New York: D. Appleton and Company,
    1914, 583–584.

———, "The Telharmonium: Electricity's Alliance with Music," *American
    Monthly Review of Reviews,* April 1906, XXXIII:4, 420–423.

Marvyn Scudder Manual of Extinct or Obsolete Companies, vol. I. New York:
    Marvyn Scudder Manual of Extinct or Obsolete Companies, 1926,
    371, 859.

Marvyn Scudder Manual of Extinct or Obsolete Companies, vol. IV. New York:
    Marvyn Scudder Manual of Extinct or Obsolete Companies, 1934,
    414, 761, 1728, 1730, 1766.

" 'Mary's Lamb' Well Liked at Olympic," *Newark Evening News,* August 3,
    1916, N.Y.P.L.T., n.p.

Mason, Daniel Gregory, "Electrically Generated Music," *New Music Review,* March 1907, 6:64, 238–241.

——, "The Telharmonium: Its Musical Basis," *Outlook,* February 9, 1907, LXXXV:6, 296–298.

Maxwell, Mary Mortimer, "Once More New York Is 'The City of Happy Faces,' " *New York Times,* January 31, 1909, pt. 5, 11.

"May Send Music by Electricity," *New-York Daily Tribune,* December 28, 1907, S.C., 4.

Mayer, Alfred M., "Researches in Acoustics," *Philosophy Magazine,* 1876, 2:500–507, in Earl D. Schubert, ed., *Psychological Acoustics,* Stroudsburg, Pa.: Dowden, Hutchinson, and Ross, 1979.

Melius, Marion, "Music by Electricity," *World's Work,* June 1906, XII:2, 7660–7663.

"Metropolitan Opera Near Its Close, but New York's Music Feast Continues," *New York World,* March 17, 1907, Metropolitan Section, 6.

Miessner, Benjamin F., "Electronic Music and Instruments," *Proceedings of the Institute of Radio Engineers,* November 1936, 24:11, 1441–1444.

" 'Mills of the Gods' Proves Startling Play," *New York Evening Journal,* March 5, 1907, 9.

"Minister Tells of Saving Many from Suicide," *New York World,* December 9, 1906, pt. II, 15.

"Minutes of the Annual Meeting, 1907," *Papers and Proceedings of the Music Teachers' National Association at Its Twenty-ninth Annual Meeting, Columbia University, New York City, December 27–31, 1907,* Hartford, Conn.: Music Teachers' National Association, 1908, 261–264.

"Miss Crossman to Introduce 'Sudden Peggy,' " *New York Evening Journal,* February 9, 1907, 9.

"Miss Isabel Winlock," *New York Times,* October 11, 1953, sec. 1, 89.

"Miss Isabelle Winlocke," *New York Morning Telegraph,* February 5, 1907, S.C., n.p.

"Miss Jamieson a Bride," "Cahill-Jamieson," *New York Times,* July 10, 1926, 16.

"Miss Margaret J. Cahill," *New York Times,* February 24, 1944, 15.

"Miss Robson's New Play," *New-York Daily Tribune,* January 13, 1907, pt. IV, 6.

"Miss Terry Here Again," *New-York Daily Tribune,* January 27, 1907, pt. IV, 6.

"Mme. Gadski Is Dead After Motor Crash," *New York Times,* February 24, 1932, 21.

"Mme. Johanna Gadski," display advertisement, *New-York Daily Tribune,* February 9, 1908, pt. IV, 3.

"Mme. Johanna Gadski," display advertisement, *New York Times,* February 9, 1908, pt. 6, 3.

Monaco, Cynthia, "The Difficult Birth of the Typewriter," *American Heritage of Invention and Technology,* Spring/Summer 1988, 4:1, 12–13.

Moore, Edward B., "Great Increase in Patents," *New York Times,* January 12, 1908, pt. 5, 8–9.

Morris, Lloyd. *Incredible New York.* New York: Random House, 1951, 111, 182, 183, 189, 204, 227, 246, 260.

"Mr. Albert Leech, Comedian, Is Dead," *New York Herald,* July 6, 1912, 7.

"Mr. George Westinghouse," *New York Times,* November 30, 1902, pt. 2, 17.

"Mr. Trask Notable in Varied Fields," *New York Times,* January 1, 1910, 2.

"Mrs. Cahill Services," *Hudson Dispatch,* November 11, 1963, 10.

"Mrs. Ellen C. Howard," *New York Times,* May 14, 1928, 21.

"Mrs. Hornblow, 73, a Former Actress," *New York Times,* May 3, 1969, 35.

"Mrs. Louise Cahill," *Hudson Dispatch,* November 9, 1963, 14.

"Mrs. Oscar T. Crosby," *New York Times,* January 16, 1934, 22.

"Mrs. R. C. Ogden, of Pneumonia," *New York Times,* December 4, 1909, 11.

" 'Mrs. Warren's Profession' Opens Tonight," *New York Evening Journal,* March 9, 1907, 9.

"Multiplex Telephone Makes One Wire Do Work of Four," *New York Herald,* January 8, 1911, sec. 2, 6.

"Munro, David Alexander," *Who Was Who in America,* vol. I. Chicago: Marquis–Who's Who, 1966, 879.

"Music," *New York Times,* June 7, 1886, 10.

"Music Across the Hudson," *Musical Courier,* March 27, 1907, LIV:13, 26C.

"Music and Musicians," *New York Evening Sun,* January 12, 1907, 5.

"Music and Musicians," *New York Evening Sun,* November 12, 1907, 8.

"Music as an Aid to Digestion," *Musical America,* May 11, 1907, V:25, 12.

"Music at Meals and What It Costs," *New York Times,* August 30, 1908, pt. 5, 7.

"Music by Telegraph," *New York Times,* July 10, 1874, 2.

"Music by Telegraph," *New York Times,* April 3, 1877, 5.

"Music by Telephone," *New York World,* November 3, 1907, Editorial Section, 6E.

"Music by Telephone Fails," *New York Times,* December 23, 1914, 15.

"Music by Transmittograph," *Inventive Age,* February 1907, XIX:2, 3.

"Music by Wire," *Boston Evening Transcript,* March 30, 1904, 7.

"Music by Wire," *Musical Age,* March 23, 1907, LVII: 8, 186.

"Music by Wireless," *Clinton* [Iowa] *Herald,* June 10, 1907, S.C., n.p.

"Music by Wireless," *New York Globe and Commercial Advertiser,* March 7, 1907, 5.

"Music by Wireless Now," *Holyoke Daily Transcript,* March 1, 1907, 10.

"Music by Wireless Telephone," *New-York Daily Tribune,* March 7, 1907, 4.

"Music by Wireless to the Times Tower," *New York Times,* March 8, 1907, 16.

"Music Excites Broadway," *Music Trade Review,* October 26, 1907, XLV:17, 25.

"Music First Transmitted by Wires in Holyoke," *Holyoke Daily Transcript and Telegram,* April 11, 1931, 4.

"Music for the Million," *Holyoke Daily Transcript,* April 4, 1904, n.p., H.P.L. Biography.

"Music from Electricity," *Music Trade Review,* August 3, 1907, XLV:5, 37.

"Music from Electricity," *Talking Machine World,* July 15, 1907, III:7, 3.

"Music from the Ground," *Talking Machine World,* November 15, 1907, III:11, 6.

"Music Heard by Wire," *New-York Daily Tribune,* January 12, 1907, 7.

"Music: Horszowski and Orchestra of St. Luke's," *New York Times,* February 2, 1986, pt. 2, 51.

"Music in America," *The American History and Encyclopedia of Music: History of American Music.* Toledo: Irving Squire, 1908, 338–339.

"Music in Restaurants," *New York Times,* August 20, 1908, 6.

"Music in the Cars," *Talking Machine World,* February 15, 1908, 4:1, 8.

"Music Is on Tap Now over New York 'Phones," *New York Times,* November 10, 1906, 6.

"Music Menu for Hotel Diners," *New York Press,* March 21, 1907, S.C., n.p.

"Music Now by Wireless," *Music Trade Review,* March 9, 1907, XLIV:10, 34.

" 'The Music of the Future,' " *Brooklyn Eagle,* February 16, 1907, S.C., n.p.

" 'The Music of the Future,' " *New York Press,* February 17, 1907, S.C., n.p.

"Music on Tap over 'Phone," *Music Trade Review,* November 17, 1906, XLIII:20, 3.

"Music on Wires," *New York Globe and Commercial Advertiser,* January 31, 1907, 4.

"Music over the Telephone," *Musical Age,* March 16, 1907, LVII: 7, 160.

"Music over the Wire," *New York Evening Mail,* December 11, 1906, 4.

"Music over the Wires," *Talking Machine World,* February 15, 1908, IV:2, 3.

"Music Teachers National Association," *New Music Review,* November 1907, 6:72, 785.

"Music to Distant Hearers," *Music Trade Review,* March 30, 1907, XLIV:13, 43.

"Musical Comedy Week," *New-York Daily Tribune,* February 3, 1907, pt. IV, 6.

"Musical Items," *Etude,* February 1907, XXV:2, 135.

"Musical Items," *Etude,* June 1907, XXV:6, 416.

"Musical News and Gossip," *New York Evening Post,* February 2, 1907, S.C., Saturday Supplement, 5.

"Musical News and Gossip," *New York Evening Post,* February 9, 1907, S.C., Saturday Supplement, 5.

"Musical News and Gossip," *New York Evening Post,* February 16, 1907, Saturday Supplement, S.C., 5.

"Musical News and Gossip," *New York Evening Post,* February 23, 1907, Saturday Supplement, 5.

"Musical News and Gossip," *New York Evening Post,* March 2, 1907, Saturday Supplement, 5.

"Musical News and Gossip," *New York Evening Post,* March 9, 1907, Saturday Supplement, 5.

"Musical News and Gossip," *New York Evening Post,* March 16, 1907, Saturday Supplement, 5.

"Musical News and Gossip," *New York Evening Post,* March 23, 1907, Saturday Supplement, 5.

"Musical News and Gossip," *New York Evening Post,* March 30, 1907, Saturday Supplement, 5.

"Musical News and Gossip," *New York Evening Post,* April 6, 1907, Saturday Supplement, 5.

"Musical News and Gossip," *New York Evening Post,* April 13, 1907, Saturday Supplement, 5.

"Muzak, at 40, Develops Plan to Play a New Tune," *New York Times,* August 17, 1974, 17.

"Name Telharmonic Receiver," *New York Herald,* December 23, 1914, 4.

Nash, Nathaniel C., "Muzak's Global Music," *New York Times,* March 16, 1975, pt. 3, 1.

"Nathaniel W. James," *New York Times,* July 25, 1911, 7.

"The Nation's Story in Five Great Periods," *New York Times,* February 28, 1909, pt. 5, 7.

"Neagle for Navy Law Post," *New York Times,* August 31, 1921, 15.

"Neagle, Pickens," *Who Was Who in America,* vol. 2. Chicago: The A. N. Marquis Company, 1950, 393.

"The New Directors of the Metropolitian Opera House," *Musical America,* March 7, 1908, VII:17, 1, 4.

"The New Electric Music," *Literary Digest,* March 23, 1907, XXXIV:12, 460–461.

"New Manager Here," *Holyoke Daily Transcript,* October 11, 1906, 7.

"A new mechanical appliance . . . ," *Musical Courier,* January 16, 1907, LIV:3, 20.

"New Musical Instument," *Denison* [Tex.] *Herald,* November 10, 1906, S.C., n.p.

"A New Musical Instrument," *Peoria* [Ill.] *Journal,* July 8, 1906, L.C.M.D., Ray Stannard Baker Papers, n.p.

"A New Opera by Elliot [*sic*] Schenck," *Musical Courier,* August 8, 1906, LIII:6, 33.

"New Plant for Holyoke," *Boston Evening Transcript,* June 3, 1910, S.C., n.p.

"New Play by Austin Strong," *New York Sun,* November 24, 1907, sec. 3, 6.

"A New Play by Miss Crothers," *New York Sun,* November 3, 1907, sec. 3, 8.

"The New Plays," *New York Evening Mail,* February 2, 1907, S.C., 7.

"New Plays This Week," *New-York Daily Tribune,* March 31, 1907, pt. IV, 6.

"A New Position for Schenck," *Musical Courier,* October 24, 1906, LIII:17, 24.

"A New 'Telharmonium,' " *Engineering News,* May 26, 1910, 63:21, 627–628.

"New Wireless Music," *Talking Machine World,* April 15, 1907, III:4, 9.

"New York Cahill Telharmonic Company," *City Record,* May 28, 1907, 5664–5665, June 5, 1907, 5926–5927.

"New York Cahill Telharmonic Company," *City Record,* June 11, 1907, 6209–6212.

"New York-Cahill Telharmonic Company," *City Record,* November 5, 1910, 10324–10325.

"New York Cahill Telharmonic Company," *City Record,* December 29, 1910, 11791–11794.

"New York Cahill Telharmonic Company," *City Record,* January 10, 1911, 141–143.

"New York Cahill Telharmonic Company," *City Record,* March 2, 1911, 1690.

"New York Cahill Telharmonic Company," *City Record,* March 23, 1911, 2479.

"New York Cahill Telharmonic Company," *City Record,* June 20, 1912, 5257–5258.

"New York Cahill Telharmonic Company," *City Record,* August 13, 1912, 6632–6634.

"New York Cahill-Telharmonic Company," *City Record,* October 10, 1912, 7910.

"New York Cahill Telharmonic Company," *Minutes, Meeting of Board of Estimate and Apportionment,* May 24, 1907, 1627–1629.

"New York Cahill Telharmonic Company," *Minutes, Meeting of Board of Estimate and Apportionment,* June 7, 1907, 1802–1819.

"New York-Cahill Telharmonic Company," *Minutes, Meeting of Board of Estimate and Apportionment,* October 25, 1910, 4286–4287.

"New York Cahill Telharmonic Company," *Minutes, Meeting of Board of Estimate and Apportionment,* December 22, 1910, 5574–5586.

"New York Cahill Telharmonic Company," *Minutes, Meeting of Board of Estimate and Apportionment,* January 5, 1911, 49–56.

"New York Cahill Telharmonic Company," *Minutes, Meeting of Board of Estimate and Apportionment,* February 16, 1911, 674–680.

"New York Cahill Telharmonic Company," *Minutes, Meeting of Board of Estimate and Apportionment,* June 13, 1912, 2635–2637.

"New York Cahill-Telharmonic Company," *Minutes, Meeting of Board of Estimate and Apportionment,* September 19, 1912, 3917–3919.

"New York Cahill Telharmonic Company (Cal. No. 53)," *City Record,* February 3, 1915, 876.

"New York Cahill Telharmonic Company (Cal. No. 86)," *City Record,* January 19, 1915, 395.

"New York City and the Ironclad Sunday Law," *New York Times,* December 8, 1907, pt. 5, 3.

"New York Electric Music Company," *City Record,* February 5, 1907, 1202, February 14, 1907, 1474.

New York Electric Music Company, *Program and Announcement: Telharmonic Hall, No. 1,* New York: The Company, January 27, 1907? [penciled on cover: "Gift of New York Electric Music Company, February 16th, 1907"], N.Y.P.L. *MKY Box.

————, *Program and Announcement, Telharmonic Hall, No. 1,* New York: The Company, mid-February? 1907 [revised musical program], M.C.S.

————, *Program and Announcement: Telharmonic Hall, No. 4,* New York: The Company, late March? 1907, A.T.T.B.L.A., Boston File 500.

————, *Telharmony,* New York: The Company, late December? 1906, N.Y.P.L. *MKY Box, S.L.

————, *Telharmony: A New Art,* New York: The Company, early January? 1907, N.Y.P.L. *MKY Box.

"The News This Morning," *New-York Daily Tribune,* October 22, 1907, 6.

Nichols, Harry P., *Result of Investigation by the Division of Franchises of the Application of the New York Cahill Telharmonic Company,* New York: Board of Estimate and Apportionment, Office of Chief Engineer, May 31, 1907, B.E.

"1905—A Retrospect of the Year," *New York Times Annual Financial Review,* January 7, 1906, 2.

"1906, Incorporations Reached into Billions," *New York Times,* January 6, 1907, 15, 20.

"1906–1907," *New York Times Annual Financial Review,* January 6, 1907, 2.

"1907–1908," *New York Times Annual Financial Review,* January 5, 1908, 2.

"1908–1909," *New York Times Annual Financial Review,* January 10, 1909, 2.

"No Telephone Monopoly," *New York Sun,* June 8, 1907, 8.

"Noble Edifices and Their Exhibits," *Phonogram,* March and April 1893, 3:3–4, 356–360.

North, S. N. D., ed., "Miscellaneous," *The American Year Book, 1910,* New York: D. Appleton and Company, 1911, 697.

————, ed., "Telegraphs and Telephones," *The American Year Book, 1910,* New York: D. Appleton and Company, 1911, 534–535.

"Noted Musician Dies; Father of Local Residents," *Smithfield* [Va.] *Times,* November 18, 1954, 1.

"Notes of Coming Events," *New-York Daily Tribune,* November 24, 1907, pt. V, 4.

"A Novel Phone," *Phonogram,* February, 1892, 2:2, 49.

"Novel Telharmonic Concerts," *New York World,* January 20, 1907, Metropolitan Section, 4.

"Novelli in 'Othello' Heads Week's Plays," *New York Evening Journal,* March 26, 1907, 11.

"Novelli, Noted Italian Actor, Opens at Lyric," *New York Evening Journal,* March 16, 1907, 9.

"Novelli Wins Laurels in His Opening Play," *New York Evening Journal,* March 19, 1907, 13.

"Novelties at Telharmonic Hall," *New York Morning Telegraph,* February 12, 1907, S.C., n.p.

"Now the 'Unit-Orchestra,' " *Music Trade Review,* March 25, 1911, LII:12, 48.

Noyes, Alexander D., "Finance: The Fall in the World's Markets," *Forum,* October 1907, XXXIX:2, 186–207.

————, "Finance: The Recovery from the Recent Panic," *Forum,* April 1908, XXXIX:4, 479–502.

————, "Finance: The Recent Depression and the Crop Situation," *Forum,* July 1907, XXXIX:1, 38–59.

————, "Finance: The Financial Panic in the United States," *Forum,* January 1908, XXXIX:3, 293–313.

"N.Y. Electric Music Co. in Trouble," *Music Trade Review,* June 13, 1908, XLVI:24, S.C., 9.

"Oberlin Musical Club Meets," *Musical Courier,* May 1, 1919, XXXVIII:18, 31.

"Obituary Notes: Martin A. Ryan," *New York Times,* December 17, 1913, 11.

"Obituary: Dr. Thaddeus Cahill," *Musical Courier,* April 21, 1934, 108:16, 18.

"Oboe and Flute at Telharmonic Hall," *New York American,* March 21, 1907, S.C., n.p.

Observer, "The Lot of American Musicans," letter to the editor, *New York Times,* March 23, 1924, pt. 8, 6.

O'Connell, Robert L., "Post Haste," *American Heritage,* September/October 1989, 40:6, 82.

"Of Music and Musicians," *Springfield Republican,* December 22, 1907, S.C., 22.

"Ogden, Robert Curtis," *The National Cyclopaedia of American Biography,* vol. XIV. New York: James T. White and Company, 1917, 415.

"Ogden, Robert Curtis," *Who's Who in New York City and State,* third edition. New York: L. R. Hamersly and Company, 1907, 995.

" 'Ye Olden Time' Feats Are Hits of the Circus," *New York Evening Journal,* March 30, 1907, 9.

"Oliver C. Reynolds, Founded Law Firm," *New York Times,* May 29, 1970, 29.

Olson, Harry F. *Music, Physics, and Engineering,* second edition. New York: Dover Publications, 1967.

" 'On Parole,' at Majestic, Play of Civil War," *New York Evening Journal,* February 23, 1907, S.C., 9.

" 'On Parole' Is Best War Play of the Decade," *New York Evening Journal,* February 26, 1907, S.C., 7.

"On the Pacific Coast," *Music Trade Review,* July 6, 1907, XLV:1, 27.

"One More Schenck Criticism," *Musical Courier,* June 12, 1907, LIV:24, 22.

"Only One New Play in the Week's Limelight, but Many Near at Hand," *New York World,* March 10, 1907, Metropolitan Section, 4.

"The Opera and the Play," *New York Herald,* January 13, 1907, sec. 3, 3.

"Opera over the Phone," *Baltimore Sun,* January 22, 1908, S.C., n.p.

"The Oracle," *Holyoke Daily Transcript,* October 23, 1906, 10.

"The Oracle," *Holyoke Daily Transcript,* March 7, 1911, 10.

"The Oracle," *Holyoke Daily Transcript-Telegram,* April 12, 1971, 24.

"Oracle," *Holyoke Daily Transcript-Telegram,* April 7, 1983, 18.

"The Oracle: The present dog restraining . . . ," *Holyoke Daily Transcript,* April 11, 1907, 10.

"Orchestras Divide Spoils," *New York Evening Mail,* November 19, 1906, 6.

"Oscar Crosby Dies; Treasury Ex-Aide," *New York Times,* January 3, 1947, 21.

Ouellette, Fernand. *Edgard Varèse.* Tr. from the French by Derek Coltman. New York: The Orion Press, 1968.

"Our Musical Millionaires," *Music Trade Review,* November 30, 1907, XLV:22, 50.

"P. Cooper Hewitt Dead in Paris," *New York Times,* August 26, 1921, 13.

"Peabody, George Foster," *The National Cyclopaedia of American Biography,* vol. XV. New York: James T. White and Company, 1916, 140–141.

"Peabody, George Foster," *The National Cyclopaedia of American Biography,* vol. XXVII. New York: James T. White and Company, 1939, 64–65.

"Peabody, George Foster," *Who's Who in New York City and State,* third edition. New York: L. R. Hamersly and Company 1907, 1025.

"Personal Briefs," *Music Trade Review,* January 5, 1907, XLIV: 1, 49.

Persons, Stow. *The Decline of American Gentility.* New York: Columbia University Press, 1973.

"Phonograph Concert," *Phonogram,* February, 1892, 2:21, 51.

"Phonograph Music While You Eat," *Musical Age,* May 4, 1907, LVIII:1, 18.

"Physician Shoots a Man," *New York Times,* June 5, 1902, 6.

"Piano-Radio Device Drops Microphone," *New York Times,* November 28, 1926, sec. II, 1.

Picard, George H., "Music for the Million," *Amsterdam* [N.Y.] *Recorder,* July 13, 1907, S.C., 9.

———, "Music for the Million," *Deseret Evening News,* July 13, 1907, S.C., 21.

Pierce, Edwin Hall, "A Colossal Experiment in 'Just Intonation,' " *Musical Quarterly,* July 1924, X:3, 326–332.

———, *Edwin H. Pierce, Teacher of Piano, Violin, Harmony and Composition; Also Sight-Reading for Singers,* Auburn, N.Y.: The Author, 1898?, J.E.P.

———, *Violin Lessons; Also Instruction in Harmony, Counterpoint and Composition,* Auburn, N.Y.: The Author, 1893?, J.E.P.

"Pierce, Edwin Hall," *The Macmillan Encyclopedia of Music and Musicians.* New York: The Macmillan Company, 1938, 1429.

"Pipeless Organ Heard in Debut on Radio," *New York Times,* June 15, 1931, 22.

"Plan Legislation for 'Phone Evils," *New York Herald,* January 14, 1907, 7.

"Plan to Distribute Music Around Town," *Brooklyn Times,* June 15, 1907, S.C., n.p.

"Plays That Are Good at the Theatres," *New York Evening Journal,* November 19, 1907, 8.

"Plays That Stay, Bills That Change," *New York World,* March 24, 1907, Metropolitan Section, 4.

"The Plays That Won and the Public Taste," *New York Times,* June 7, 1908, pt. 5, 7.

"Pope, Ralph Wainwright," *The National Cyclopaedia of American Biography,* vol. XXVII. New York: James T. White and Company, 1939, 469–470.

"Pope, Ralph Wainwright," *Who Was Who in America,* vol. I. Chicago: Marquis–Who's Who, 1966, 982.

"President Sets up Peace Objectives and Bides His Time," *New York Times,* January 10, 1940, 1, 6.

Price, Charles W., "Remarkable Progress in Electrical Development," *New York Times Annual Financial Review,* January 8, 1905, 22.

"The Problem and the Solution," *Musical Age,* July 6, 1912, LXXVIII:11, 215.

"Prof. Albert F. Ganz Dead," *New York Times,* July 29, 1917, 15.

"Prof. Gray's Life of Lord Kelvin," *New York Times Book Review,* August 15, 1908, 446.

"A Puzzle for the Board of Estimate," *New York Sun,* June 22, 1907, S.C., 6.

"R. C. Ogden Dies at Maine Home," *New York Times,* August 7, 1913, 7.

"Ralph W. Pope Dies, a Noted Engineer," *New York Times,* November 2, 1929, 17.

Ralston, Chester F., "Noted Inventor Who Dies Boy Here 50 Years Ago," *Oberlin News-Tribune,* November 5, 1935, O.C.A. 28/1, Box 38, n.p.

"Ray S. Baker Dead; Noted Biographer," *New York Times,* July 13, 1946, 15.

"Redlegs Defeat Phils in Night Game," *Cincinnati Enquirer,* May 25, 1935, 1.

"Reginald De Koven Dies at a Dance," *New York Times,* January 17, 1920, 11.

"Religious Music by Wire," *New York Herald,* February 16, 1907, S.C., 12.

"Remodeling Telharmonic Hall," *Musical Age,* April 13, 1907, LVII: 11, 285.

"Reports Progress Made," *Music Trade Review,* July 13, 1907, XLV:2, 7.

"Result of Investigation by the Division of Franchises of the Application of the New York Cahill Telharmonic Company for a Franchise to Lay Wires in the Streets of New York for the Purpose of Distributing Music Electrically, with Suggestions as to the Proposed Form of Contract," *Engineering News,* February 11, 1909, 61:6, S.C., 146–149.

"Reynolds, Clarence," *Who Was Who in America,* vol. VI. Chicago: Marquis–Who's Who, 1976, 342.

"Reynolds, New Organist for City, Arrives Feburary 1," *Denver News,* January 6, 1918, 3.

"Reynolds, Oliver C.," *New York Times,* May 29, 1970, 29.

"Reynolds, Oliver Charlick," *Who Was Who in America,* vol. VI. Chicago: Marquis–Who's Who, 1976, 342.

Rhea, Thomas LaMar, "The Evolution of Electronic Musical Instruments in the United States," Ph.D. dissertation, George Peabody College for Teachers, 1972.

"Rites Today," *Hudson Dispatch,* January 27, 1962, 12.

"Rivalry on Operatic Stages," *New York World,* February 24, 1907, Metropolitan Section, 4.

Rodet, Julien. *Notions d'Acoustique: Instruments de Musique: Le Télharmonium.* Paris: Gauthier-Villars et Cie, Editeurs, 1917.

" 'Rose of Alhambra' Will Bloom at the Majestic Theatre," *New York Evening Journal,* February 2, 1907, 9.

Rules of the Senate and House of Representatives of the State of New Hampshire. Concord: Amos Hadley, State Printer, June, 1864, M.C.S.

Russcol, Herbert. *The Liberation of Sound: An Introduction to Electronic Music.* Englewood Cliffs, N.J.: Prentice-Hall, 1972, 33.

"Salome Comes to Town," *New-York Daily Tribune,* January 20, 1907, pt. IV, 6.

"Samuel M. Green," *New York Times,* March 23, 1934, 23.

"Schenck Aids the 'Children's Crusade,' " *Musical Courier,* December 12, 1906, LIII:24, 29.

"Schenck and the Telharmonium," *Musical Courier,* March 6, 1907, LIV:10, 26.

"Schenck Conducts School Orchestra," *Musical Courier,* February 27, 1907, LIV:9, 37.

Schenck, Elliott, "Contradictions in the Bible," letter to the editor, *New York Times,* July 30, 1923, 12.

———, "The First Man," letter to the editor, *New York Times,* September 8, 1929, pt. 5, 5.

———, "The Treatment of Americans," letter to the editor, *New York Times,* March 16, 1924, pt. VIII, 6.

"Schenck for New Orleans," *Musical Courier,* July 18, 1906, LIII:3, 19.

"Schenck Not for New Orleans," *Musical Courier,* August 1, 1906, LIII:5, 31.

"Schenck Orchestra," *Musical Courier,* May 15, 1907, LIV:20, 25.

"Schenck 'Pop Concerts,' " *Musical Courier,* March 13, 1907, LIV:11, 29.

"Schenck Symphony Concert," *Musical Courier,* May 8, 1907, LIV: 19, 34.

"Schenck to Conduct Schubert Glee Club," *Musical Courier,* March 20, 1907, LIV:12, 19.

"Schenck to Lecture," *Musical Courier,* October 3, 1906, LIII:14, 41.

"Schenck's Success," *Musical Courier,* January 24, 1906, LII:4, 41.

Schiott, Christian, *Christian Schiott: Klavier-Virtuose,* Berlin: The Author, 1912?, J.S.

Schonberg, Harold C., "When Music Was Broadcast by Telephone," *New York Times,* May 11, 1975, D17.

"Science and Invention: Electrical Music," *Literary Digest,* April 14, 1906, XXXII:15, 566–567.

Secretary of State, New Jersey. *Corporations of New Jersey: List of Certificates Filed in the Department of State During the Year 1907.* Trenton: MacCrellish and Quigley, State Printers, 1908, 261.

———. *Corporations of New Jersey: List of Certificates to December 31, 1911.* Trenton: MacCrellish and Quigley, State Printers, 1914.

"A select committee of the Board . . . ," *New York Irish-American,* June 29, 1907, S.C., n.p.

" 'Send for Dippel!' Is the Cry When Caruso Sprains His Voice," *New York World,* February 2, 1908, Metropolitan Section, M3.

"Sending Music Through the Air," *Talking Machine World,* May 15, 1907, III:5, 12, 13.

"The Seventh Week of Telharmony," *New York Star,* February 26, 1907, S.C., n.p.

Severo, Richard, "Marconi Hailed on 80th Anniversary of Radio Message," *New York Times,* December 19, 1982, pt. 1, 56.

Shaw, William Bristol, "Ogden, Robert Curtis," *Dictionary of American Biography,* vol. VII. New York: Charles Scribner's Sons, 1962, 641–642.

Shiers, George. *Bibliography of the History of Electronics.* Metuchen, N.J.: The Scarecrow Press, 1972.

———. *The Telephone: An Historical Anthology.* New York: Arno Press, 1977.

"Signed by the Governor," *New-York Daily Tribune,* May 8, 1907, 2.

Sivowitch, Elliot N., "Musical Broadcasting in the Nineteenth Century," *Audio,* June 1967, 51:6, 19–23.

————, "A Technological Survey of Broadcasting's 'Pre-History,' 1876–1920," in George Shiers, ed., *The Development of Wireless to 1920.* New York: Arno Press, 1977, unpaginated. Reprinted from *Journal of Broadcasting,* Winter 1970–71, XV:1, 1–20.

"Skinner, Joseph Allen," *The National Cyclopaedia of American Biography,* XXXIV. New York: James T. White and Company, 1948, 555.

"Skinner, Joseph Allen," *Who Was Who in America,* vol. 2. Chicago: The A. N. Marquis Company, 1950, 490.

"Skinner, William," *The National Cyclopaedia of American Biography,* vol. XXXVII. New York: James T. White and Company, 1951, 109.

"Skinner, William," *Who Was Who in America,* vol. 2. Chicago: The A. N. Marquis Company, 1950, 491.

"Skinner, William," *Who's Who in New York City and State,* third edition. New York: L. R. Hamersly and Company, 1907, 1192.

Smith, William Ander. *The Mystery of Leopold Stokowski.* Rutherford, N.J.: Fairleigh Dickinson University Press, 1990, 198–199.

"Sold by Clarence Mackay," *New York Times,* July 20, 1903, 1.

"Sothern and Marlowe in 'The Merchant,' " *New York Evening Journal,* February 19, 1907, S.C., 7.

Sousa, John Philip, "The Menace of Mechanical Music," *Appleton's,* September 1906, VIII:3, 278–284.

"Sousa Severely Roasted by Editors," *Musical Age,* September 15, 1906, LV:7, 168.

"Spear, Ellis," *Appleton's Cyclopaedia of American Biography,* vol. V. New York: D. Appleton and Company, 1898, 625.

"Spear, Ellis," *The National Cyclopaedia of American Biography,* vol. XIII. New York: James T. White and Company, 1906, 364.

"Spear, Ellis," *Who Was Who in America,* vol. I. Chicago: Marquis–Who's Who, 1966, 1160.

"Special Article on Cahill Electrical Music," display advertisement, *Holyoke Daily Transcript,* March 19, 1906, 3.

"Stage Affairs," *New-York Daily Tribune,* December 15, 1907, pt. IV, 2.

"Status of Pending Petitions for Franchises and Revocable Privileges," *Minutes, Meeting of Board of Estimate and Apportionment,* January 21, 1910, 114.

"Status of Pending Petitions for Franchises and Revocable Privileges," *Minutes, Meeting of Board of Estimate and Apportionment,* February 4, 1910, 365.

"Sterling, George L.," *Who's Who in New York City and State,* third edition. New York: L. R. Hamersly and Company, 1907, 1228.

"Stevens, Frederick C.," *Who's Who in New York City and State,* third edition. New York, L. R. Hamersly and Company, 1907, 1230.

"Still Drawing Crowds," New York *Globe and Commercial Advertiser,* February 22, 1907, S.C., 2.

"Strings, Wood Winds, and Brasses," *New York Evening Telegram,* February 2, 1907, S.C., 11.

"Strings, Wood Winds, and Brasses," *New York Evening Telegram,* February 16, 1907, S.C., 11.

"Strong Bills at Theatres This Week," *New York Evening Journal,* March 12, 1907, 8.

"Successful Musical Comedies," *Music Trade Review,* January 5, 1907, XLIV:1, 48.

"Sunday Amusements Barred," *New York Dramatic Mirror,* December 14, 1907, LVIII:1512, 2.

"Sunday Ordinance Passed," *New York Dramatic Mirror,* December 28, 1907, LVIII:1514, 5.

"Sunday Services in Greater New York," *New York World,* February 16, 1907, 8.

"Synthetic Music," *New York Times,* June 12, 1931, 20.

Szabó, Miklós, "A Telefon Hírmondó jelentősége" *Jel-Kép,* 1983, no. 2, M.R., 132–135.

"Talker Music by Telephone," *Music Trade Review,* January 8, 1916, LCII:2, 50.

Telefon-Hirmondó, *Előfizetési feltételek,* subscription order card, Budapest: Telefon-Hirmondó, 1896, M.R.

————, *Telefon-Hirmondó: Kerepesi-ut 22. szám.,* advertising leaflet, Budapest: Telefon-Hirmondó, 1895, M.R.

Telefon-Hirmondó Értesítője, September 1895, I:1, M.R., 1.

"Telegraph Strike Is Now Threatened," *New York Times,* May 20, 1907, 1, 6.

"The Telephone: A Remarkable Experiment in Phonographic and Telephonic Transmission Between New York and Philadelpia," *Phonogram,* February, 1891, 1:2, 48–49.

"Telephone Companies Bid for a Monopoly," *New York Times,* July 18, 1906, 14.

"Telephone Concerts," *Steinway Hall Programme,* April 2, 1877, I:94, B.M.I.A.

"The Telephone Fight Will Be Reopened," *New York Times,* July 15, 1906, pt. 2, 18.

"Telephone Improvements," *Holyoke Daily Transcript,* April 3, 1906, 3.

"The Telephone Newspaper," *Scientific American,* October 26, 1895, LXXIII:17, 267.

"Telephone Newspaper, Two Cents," *New York World,* June 30, 1907, E3.

"Telephone Rate Readjustment," *New York Evening Post,* March 22, 1907, 8.

"The Telephone: The Long-Distance Telephone Concert in Philadelphia, *Phonogram,* February 1892, 2:21, 50.

"Telephony Without Wires," *Talking Machine World,* August 15, 1907, III:8, 4, 6.

"Telharmonic Bill Defeated," *Music Trade Review,* April 20, 1907, XLIV:16, 25.

"Telharmonic Co. Finances Crippled," *New-York Daily Tribune,* December 23, 1914, 5.

"Telharmonic Co. in Trouble," *New York Times,* June 6, 1908, 3.

"Telharmonic Co. in Trouble," *Talking Machine World,* June 15, 1908, IV:6, 27.

"Telharmonic Co. Wants a Franchise," *New York Times,* June 26, 1907, S.C., 7.

"Telharmonic Concerts," *New York Evening Mail,* November 11, 1907, 7.

"Telharmonic Demonstrations," *Holyoke Daily Transcript,* March 4, 1911, 7.

"Telharmonic Demonstration," *Music Trade Review,* January 19, 1907, XLIV:3, 11.

"Telharmonic Development," *Holyoke Daily Transcript,* March 2, 1911, 6.

"Telharmonic Franchises," *Electrical World,* June 29, 1907, XLIX:26, 1298.

"Telharmonic Hall," display advertisement, *New-York Daily Tribune,* January 20, 1907, pt. IV, 7.

"Telharmonic Hall," display advertisement, *New-York Daily Tribune,* January 27, 1907, pt. IV, 7.

"Telharmonic Hall," display advertisement, *New-York Daily Tribune,* February 10, 1907, pt. IV, 7.

"Telharmonic Hall," display advertisement, *New-York Daily Tribune,* February 17, 1907, pt. IV, 7.

"Telharmonic Hall," display advertisement, *New-York Daily Tribune,* February 24, 1907, pt. IV, 7.

"Telharmonic Hall," display advertisement, *New-York Daily Tribune,* March 3, 1907, pt. IV, 7.

"Telharmonic Hall," display advertisement, *New-York Daily Tribune,* March 10, 1907, pt. IV, 7.

"Telharmonic Hall," display advertisement, *New-York Daily Tribune,* March 24, 1907, pt. IV, 7.

"Telharmonic Hall," display advertisement, *New-York Daily Tribune,* March 31, 1907, pt. IV, 7.

"Telharmonic Hall," display advertisement, *New-York Daily Tribune,* April 13, 1907, 8.

"Telharmonic Hall," display advertisement, *New York Evening Journal,* March 30, 1907, 2.

"Telharmonic Hall," display advertisement, *New York Evening Post,* January 14, 1907, 9.

"Telharmonic Hall," display advertisement, *New York Evening Post,* January 15, 1907, 9.

"Telharmonic Hall," display advertisement, *New York Evening Telegram,* November 14, 1907, 4.

"Telharmonic Hall," display advertisement, *New York Evening Telegram,* November 16, 1907, 7.

"Telharmonic Hall," display advertisement, *New York Herald,* January 6, 1907, sec. 3, 15.

"Telharmonic Hall," display advertisement, *New York Herald,* January 20, 1907, sec. 3, 15.

"Telharmonic Hall," display advertisement, *New York Herald,* January 27, 1907, sec. 3, 14.

"Telharmonic Hall," display advertisement, *New York Herald,* February 3, 1907, sec. 3, 15.

"Telharmonic Hall," display advertisement, *New York Herald,* February 10, 1907, sec. 3, 14.

"Telharmonic Hall," display advertisement, *New York Herald,* "February 15, 1907, 17.

"Telharmonic Hall," display advertisement, *New York Sun,* January 6, 1907, sec. 3, 6.

"Telharmonic Hall," display advertisement, *New York Times,* January 6, 1907, pt. 4, 5.

"Telharmonic Hall," display advertisement, *New York Times,* January 13, 1907, pt. 4, 3.

"Telharmonic Hall," display advertisement, *New York Times,* January 20, 1907, pt. 4, 3.

"Telharmonic Hall," display advertisement, *New York Times,* January 27, 1907, pt. 4, 3.

"Telharmonic Hall," display advertisement, *New York Times,* February 10, 1907, pt. 4, 4.

"Telharmonic Hall," display advertisement, *New York Times,* February 17, 1907, pt. 4, 4.

"Telharmonic Hall," display advertisement, *New York Times,* March 3, 1907, pt. 4, 4.

"Telharmonic Hall," display advertisement, *New York Times,* March 10, 1907, pt. 4, 4.

"Telharmonic Hall," display advertisement, *New York Times,* March 17, 1907, pt. 4, 4.

"Telharmonic Hall," display advertisement, *New York Times,* March 24, 1907, pt. 4, 3.

"Telharmonic Hall," display advertisement, *New York Times,* March 31, 1907, pt. 4, 3.

"Telharmonic Hall," display advertisement, *New York Times,* April 7, 1907, pt. 4, 4.

"Telharmonic Hall," display advertisement, *New York Times,* November 15, 1907, 16.

"Telharmonic Hall," display advertisement, *New York Times*, November 16, 1907, 16.

"Telharmonic Hall," display advertisement, *New York Times*, November 17, 1907, pt. 6, 3.

"Telharmonic Hall," display advertisement, *New York Times*, November 18, 1907, 16.

"Telharmonic Hall," display advertisement, *New York Times*, November 19, 1907, 16.

"Telharmonic Hall," display advertisement, *New York Times*, November 24, 1907, pt. 6, 3.

"Telharmonic Hall," display advertisement, *New York Times*, November 27, 1907, 16.

"Telharmonic Hall," display advertisement, *New York Times*, December 1, 1907, pt. 6, 3.

"Telharmonic Hall," display advertisement, *New York Times*, December 8, 1907, pt. 6, 3.

"Telharmonic Hall," display advertisement, *New York Times*, December 15, 1907, pt. 7, 3.

"Telharmonic Hall," display advertisement, *New York Times*, December 22, 1907, pt. 6, 3.

"Telharmonic Hall," display advertisement, *New York Times*, December 29, 1907, pt. 6, 3.

"Telharmonic Hall," display advertisement, *New York Times*, January 5, 1908, pt. 6, 3.

"Telharmonic Hall," display advertisement, *New York Times*, January 12, 1908, pt. 6, 3.

"Telharmonic Hall," display advertisement, *New York Times*, January 19, 1908, pt. 6, 3.

"Telharmonic Hall," display advertisement, *New York Times*, January 26, 1908, pt. 6, 3.

"Telharmonic Hall," display advertisement, *New York World,* January 6, 1907, Metropolitan Section, 5.

"Telharmonic Hall," display advertisement, *New York World,* January 13, 1907, Metropolitan Section, 5.

"Telharmonic Hall," *New York Press,* February 5, 1907, S.C., n.p.

"Telharmonic Hall," *New York Press,* February 11, 1907, S.C., n.p.

"Telharmonic Hall, Broadway and . . . ," *New York American,* February 3, 1907, S.C., n.p.

"Telharmonic Hall Opens Tonight," *New-York Daily Tribune,* November 16, 1907, 7.

"Telharmonic Hall Plans," *Music Trade Review,* November 9, 1907, XLV:19, 17.

"Telharmonic Hall Plans," *New York Times,* November 3, 1907, pt. 6, l.

"Telharmonic Hall to Open," *New York Dramatic Mirror,* January 12, 1907, LVII:1464, S.C., 11.

"Telharmonic Improvements," *Music Trade Review,* November 23, 1907, XLV:21, 3.

"Telharmonic Incorporates in Maine," *Musical Age,* August 11, 1906, LV:2, 33.

"Telharmonic Music at a Public Function," *New York Globe and Commercial Advertiser,* December 10, 1906, 5.

"Telharmonic Novelties," *New York Evening Mail,* February 5, 1907, S.C., 12.

Telharmonic Securities Company, *Telharmonic Hall: Program, Week of December 30th,* New York: The Company, 1907, S.L.

"The Telharmonic System Installed," *Music Trade Review,* January 12, 1907, XLIV:2, 33.

"The Telharmonic System of Producing Music Electrically," *Engineering News,* February 28, 1907, 57:9, 234–235.

"Telharmonie als musikalische Kunst," *New York Morgen Journal,* February 3, 1907, S.C., n.p.

"Telharmonium," in Albert E. Wier, ed., *The Macmillan Encyclopedia of Music and Musicians.* New York: The Macmillan Company, 1938, 1843.

"The Telharmonium," *Outlook,* May 5, 1906, 83:18, 10–11.

"Telharmonium-America," in *The American History and Encyclopedia of Music: Musical Instruments.* Toledo: Irving Squire, 1908, 220–222.

"The Telharmonium—An Apparatus for the Electrical Generation and Transmission of Music," *Scientific American,* March 9, 1907, XCVI:10, 210–211.

"Telharmonium Concert at Board of Trade," *Springfield Evening Union,* March 4, 1911, 7.

"Telharmonium Concerts," *Electrical World,* January 19, 1907, XLIX:3, 136.

"The Telharmonium Concerts," *Music Trade Review,* April 3, 1907, XLIV:15, 43.

"Telharmonium Demonstration," *Electrical World,* January 5, 1907, XLIX:1, 8.

"Telharmonium Exhibited," *Springfield Republican,* March 4, 1911, 6.

"Telharmonium Exhibition," *Holyoke Daily Transcript,* April 11, 1910, 2.

"Telharmonium Makes Hit at Automobile Show," *Musical Age,* November 9, 1907, LX:2, 26.

"The Telharmonium of Dr. Cahill . . . ," *St. John* [N.B.] *Globe,* July 13, 1907, S.C., n.p.

"A Telharmonium Visit," *Electrical World,* January 25, 1908, LI:4, S.C., 173.

"Telharmonium Will Play," *New York Globe and Commercial Advertiser,* January 5, 1907, 9.

" 'Telharmonium' Works Well," *New-York Daily Tribune,* November 10, 1906, 16.

"Telharmony," *Musical Age,* February 16, 1907, LVII:3, S.C., 54.

"Telharmony: Sending Electric Music to Every Home," *Illustrated London News,* February 23, 1907, CXXX:3540, 291.

"Tenor to Help Inventor," *Musical America,* February 2, 1907, V:12, 7.

"Thaddeus Cahill, Inventor, Dies," *Washington Star,* April 16, 1934, A-9.

"Thaddeus Cahill, Inventor, 66, Dies," *New York Times,* April 13, 1934, 19.

" . . . That Are New at Theatres," *New York Evening Journal,* November 26, 1907, 9.

"That Dreadful New York Appetite," *New York World,* January 20, 1907, Magazine Section, 6.

"Theatrical Notes," *New York Times,* November 19, 1907, 9.

"There Are About a Quarter of a Million People Trying to Get Work in New York," *New York Times,* January 5, 1908, pt. 5, 11.

"They are doing a very large business . . . ," *New York Dramatic News,* February 23, 1907, S.C., n.p.

"Thousands of Actors Left Out of Work," *New York Times,* November 16, 1907, 4.

"The Three Conductors of the Metropolitan Opera," *Musical America,* December 16, 1905, III:5, 1.

"304th Organ Recital," *Holyoke Daily Transcript,* April 25, 1901, 3.

"Time and Car Fare Saved," *New York Times,* February 28, 1893, 5, 1.

"To Aid Wireless Telegraphy," *New York Times,* February 20, 1903, 5.

"To Distribute Music," *Music Trade Review,* August 29, 1914, LIX:9, 49.

"To Distribute Music by Electric Corporations," *Albany* [N.Y.] *Argus,* February 6, 1907, S.C., n.p.

"To Exhibit New Telephone," *New York Evening Post,* January 15, 1907, 4.

"To Manufacture Music by Electrical Device," *New York Times,* March 11, 1906, 4.

"To Preserve Miss Winlocke's Voice," *New York Morning Telegraph,* February 5, 1907, S.C., n.p.

"To Transport Music," *Electrical World,* February 9, 1907, XLIX:6, S.C., 296.

" 'Tone building' will be . . . ," *New York Evening World,* February 2, 1907, S.C., n.p. [not found].

"Topics of the Drama: Mr. Fitch and His Shortcomings," *New York Times,* January 18, 1903, 34.

"Touring the United States with Busoni and Garden," *Music Trade Review,* June 24, 1911, LII:25, 49.

The Tracies Co., *Map of Holyoke, Mass.,* Holyoke: The Company, 1913.

"The Trade in England," *Talking Machine World,* August 15, 1906, II:8, 17.

Transcript Publishing Company. *Holyoke City Directory, 1901.* Holyoke: Price and Lee Company, Publishers, 1901.

————. *Holyoke City Directory, 1902.* Holyoke: Price and Lee Company, Publishers, 1902.

————. *Holyoke City Directory, 1903.* Holyoke: Price and Lee Company, Publishers, 1903.

————. *Holyoke City Directory, 1904.* Holyoke: Price and Lee Company, Publishers, 1904.

————. *Holyoke City Directory, 1905.* Holyoke: Price and Lee Company, Publishers, 1905.

————. *Holyoke City Directory, 1906.* Holyoke: Price and Lee Company, Publishers, 1906.

————. *Holyoke City Directory, 1907.* Holyoke: Price and Lee Company, Publishers, 1907.

————. *Holyoke City Directory, 1909.* Holyoke: Price and Lee Company, Publishers, 1909.

————. *Holyoke City Directory, 1910.* Holyoke: Price and Lee Company, Publishers, 1910.

————. *Holyoke City Directory, 1911.* Holyoke: Price and Lee Company, Publishers, 1911.

————. *Holyoke City Directory, 1912.* Holyoke: Price and Lee Company, Publishers, 1912.

————. *Holyoke City Directory, 1913.* Holyoke: Price and Lee Company, Publishers, 1913.

"Trask, Spencer," *Who Was Who in America,* vol. I. Chicago: Marquis–Who's Who, 1966, 1251.

"Trask, Spencer," *Who's Who in New York City and State,* third edition. New York: L. R. Hamersly and Company, 1907, 1285.

"Tristan Hears Telharmonist," *Musical Age,* February 16, 1907, LVII:3, 54.

"Tristan Talks of Coming Season," *Musical Age,* May 4, 1907, LVIII:1, 8.

Trow Directory, Printing and Bookbinding Co. *The Trow Copartnership and Corporation Directory of the Borough of Manhattan and the Bronx, City of New York.* New York: The Company, March 1907, 561–562.

————. *The Trow Copartnership and Corporation Directory of the Borough of Manhattan and the Bronx, City of New York.* New York: The Company, March 1908, 586, 803.

————. *The Trow Copartnership and Corporation Directory of the Borough of Manhattan and the Bronx, City of New York.* New York: The Company, March 1909, 558, 560, 767.

"The True Paul Jones," *New York Times,* June 11, 1906, 6.

"A True Prophet," *Bridgeton* [N.J.] *Pioneer,* August 21, 1910, S.C., n.p.

"Turns Electricity into Music on Radio," *New York Times,* June 11, 1931, 1, 4.

"Twain and the Telephone," *New York Times,* December 23, 1906, pt. 2, 2.

"Twain and the Telharmonium," *Music Trade Review,* December 29, 1906, XLIII:26, 14.

"Twain at the Telharmonium," *Electrical World,* December 29, 1906, XLVIII:26, 1233.

"Two More Arrests Made in Plot to Blow Up Canal," *New York Morning Telegraph,* April 1, 1916, 1–2.

"Two Piano Recitals," *New York Times,* February 10, 1917, 7.

"Two Shaw Comedies, New Native Play and Other Dramatic Events," *New York World,* March 3, 1907, Metropolitan Section, 4.

Tyrrell, Henry, "Music and Mechanism," *New York World,* May 10, 1908, Music Section, 1–2.

"Unit Orchestra Amazes Striking Musicians with Its Perfection," *Musical Age,* July 13, 1912, LXXVIII:12, 232–233.

" 'Unit Orchestra' Featured in Science and Invention Column," *Musical Age,* January 11, 1913, LXXX:12, 194.

"The Unpopular Machine," *New York Evening Post,* February 16, 1907, sec. 1, 4.

"Unveil Busts of Noted Scientists," *New York Herald,* December 30, 1906, sec. 2, 5.

"Uperfected [*sic*] Invention," *Holyoke Daily Transcript,* May 25, 1905, 3.

"Value of Telharmony," *Hoboken* [N.J.] *Observer,* December 6, 1907, S.C., n.p.

Varèse, Edgard, "Ferrucio Busoni—A Reminiscence," *Columbia University Forum,* Spring 1966, IX:2, 20.

Varèse, Louise. *Varèse: A Looking-Glass Diary, Vol. I.* New York: W. W. Norton and Company, 1972, 48–50.

"Variety Theatres," *New-York Daily Tribune,* December 22, 1907, pt. IV, 3.

"Vaudeville," *New York Times,* November 24, 1907, pt. 6, 1.

"Vaudeville Notes," *New York Evening Mail,* April 20, 1907, 9.

"Victor Herbert," *New York Times,* May 28, 1927, 22.

"Victor Herbert Dies on Way to Physician," *New York Times,* May 27, 1924, 1, 3.

"Victor Herbert's Life as Shown in Anecdotes," *New York Times,* June 1, 1924, pt. 8, 12.

"Victor Herbert's Orchestra," display advertisement, *New York Times,* April 23, 1905, pt. 1, 11.

"Victor Herbert's 'Red Mill,' " *Music Trade Review,* December 29, 1906, XLIII:26, 50.

Viereck, George Sylvester, "The Democracy of Music Achieved by Invention," *Current Literature,* June 1907, 42:6, 670–673.

"Wall Street and the Drama", *New York Times,* October 6, 1907, pt. 6, 1.

"Walter Anderson to Manage Margaret Jamieson," *Musical Courier,* May 30, 1918, XXXVI:22, 48.

"Walter Damrosch Dies at Age of 88," *New York Times,* December 23, 1950, 1, 16.

Ware, Louise, "Peabody, George Foster," *Dictionary of American Biography,* vol. XI, 2. New York: Charles Scribner's Sons, 1958, 520–521.

"The Week in Town," *New York Evening Post,* February 23, 1912, 6.

Welch, E. T., *Muzak,* New York: Muzak Corporation, 1974?

"Westinghouse, George," *American Biography: A New Cyclopedia,* vol. II. New York: The American Historical Society, 1918, 348–354.

"Westinghouse, George," *Who Was Who in America,* vol. I. Chicago: Marquis–Who's Who, 1966, 1324.

"Westinghouse, Henry Herman," *Who Was Who in America,* vol. I. Chicago: Marquis–Who's Who, 1966, 1324.

"Westinghouse—Inventor and Human Dynamo," *New York Times,* November 3, 1907, pt. 5. 3.

"What 1907 Has Meant to Science," *New York World,* December 29, 1907, Magazine Section, 9.

"Where Music Soothes While Lobsters Broil," *New York Times,* April 24, 1910, pt. 5, 7.

" 'The White Hen' Lays for All at the Casino," *New York Evening Journal,* February 16, 1907, S.C., 9.

"White, James Gilbert," *National Cyclopedia of American Biography,* vol. XV. New York: James T. White and Company, 1916, f. 157, 157–158.

"White, James Gilbert," *Who Was Who in America,* vol. 2. Chicago: The A. N. Marquis Company, 1950, 572.

White, William Braid. *Piano Tuning and Allied Arts,* fifth edition. Boston: Tuners Supply Co., 1953.

————, "The Review's Technical Department," *Music Trade Review,* May 4, 1907, XLIV:18, 18.

————, "The Review's Technical Department: Telharmony," *Music Trade Review,* August 10, 1907, XLV:6, 10–11.

"Why Organ Recitals Are Popular in Denver," *Denver Municipal Facts,* July–August 1927, XI:7–8, 13–14.

Wickware, Francis G., ed., "Telegraphy," in *American Year Book, 1911.* New York: D. Appleton and Company, 1912, 700–701.

"Will Baffle Despair with Aid of Prayer," *New York Globe and Commercial Advertiser,* January 10, 1907, 6.

"Will Explain Invention," *New York Morning Telegraph,* December 27, 1907, S.C., n.p.

"Will Wire Music to Hotels," *New York Herald,* February 9, 1907, S.C., 8.

"William Skinner," *Holyoke Daily Transcript,* March 7, 1907, 8.

"William Skinner, a Silk Official, 90," *New York Times,* October 18, 1947, 15.

Williamson, Charles, "The Frequency Ratios of the Tempered Scale," *Journal of the Acoustical Society of America,* October 1938, 10:10, 135–136.

"'Wired Music' Was Very Expensive," *New York Morning Telegraph,* December 23, 1914, 12.

"Wireless Music from Light," *Music Trade Review,* October 9, 1915, LXI: 15, 15.

"Wireless Music Heard Plainly 434 Miles Distant at Mid-Day," *Musical Age,* June 8, 1912, LXXVIII:7, 168.

"Wireless of the Future," *New York Times,* May 23, 1909, pt. 5, 8.

"Wireless 'Phone Transmits Music," *New York Herald,* March 7, 1907, 8.

"Wireless Telegraph Music," *Musical America,* March 23, 1907, V:19, 13.

"Wireless Telephony," *New-York Daily Tribune,* March 10, 1907, pt. I, 8.

"Within a month in various . . . ," *San Francisco Argonaut,* June 15, 1907, S.C., n.p.

"Wonder Musical Machine Invented by Holyoke Men," *Boston Post,* March 18, 1906, 29.

"The Wonder of the Age," *New York Irish-American,* March 23, 1907, 1.

Woodland, William C., "A Musical Problem Solved by the Telharmonium," letter to the editor, *Scientific American,* March 30, 1907, XCVI:13, 271.

Woods, David L., "Semantics Versus the 'First' Broadcasting Station," *Journal of Broadcasting,* Summer 1967, XI:3, 199–207.

"Worcester Polytechnic Dinner," *Electrical World,* February 9, 1907, XLIX: 6, S.C., 295.

"Wurlitzers Get $2,000,000 Order for Hope-Jones Unit Orchestras," *Musical Age,* July 13, 1912, LXXVIII:12, 242.

Yarrow, Andrew L., "Other Business: Cable TV Moves to the Music," *New York Times,* July 4, 1982, pt. 3, 17.

"Yesterday's Fires," *New York Herald,* February 17, 1908, 12.

Zonano, Victor F., "Play It Again, Penny: Telephone Jukeboxes Have Personal Touch," *Wall Street Journal,* July 22, 1974.

INDEX

ABOUT THE AUTHOR

REYNOLD WEIDENAAR, born in 1945, is a composer and video artist. He interrupted his college studies in 1965 upon taking a seminar on the Moog synthesizer. He stayed in Trumansburg, N.Y., to found the Independent Electronic Music Center with Robert Moog and to become Editor of *Electronic Music Review*. He later worked in Cleveland as a recording engineer and recorded the weekly concerts of the Cleveland Orchestra under George Szell for broadcast syndication. He received a B. Mus. degree from the Cleveland Institute of Music in 1973, where he was valedictorian. After several years of working with electronic music and images on film, he moved to New York to pursue this interest. His second film, *Wavelines II,* received 15 awards. After receiving an M.A. from New York University in 1980, he began to work with video. His first concert video, *Love of Line, of Light and Shadow: The Brooklyn Bridge,* for clarinet, color video, and electronic sound, received the Grand Prize at the Tokyo Video Festival and numerous other awards. Since then he has produced four more concert videos; these works have received over 300 live performances and over 2,000 screenings and broadcasts in their tape versions. He received a Ph.D. from N.Y.U. in 1989 and has been awarded an NEA Composer Fellowship, a Fulbright Fellowship, and a Guggenheim Fellowship. He has taught at the Cleveland Institute of Music and the New School. From 1981 through 1993 he taught in the Film and TV Department at N.Y.U.'s Tisch School of the Arts. He is presently an assistant professor of Communication at William Paterson College, Wayne, New Jersey.

In addition to this book, Dr. Weidenaar is producing a concert video and a CD-ROM on the Telharmonium.